D1134336

MEDICINE AT THE COURTS OF EUROPE, 1500–1837

THE WELLCOME INSTITUTE SERIES IN THE HISTORY OF MEDICINE

Edited by W. F. Bynum and Roy Porter

The Wellcome Institute

MEDICINE AT THE COURTS OF EUROPE, 1500–1837

Edited by

VIVIAN NUTTON

ROUTLEDGE
LONDON AND NEW YORK

First published 1990
by Routledge
11 New Fetter Lane, London EC4P 4EE

Simultaneously published in the USA and Canada
by Routledge
a division of Routledge, Chapman and Hall, Inc.
29 West 35th Street, New York, NY 10001

Typeset directly from the publisher's word-processor disks by
NWL Editorial Services, Langport, Somerset, England

Printed in Great Britain

British Library Cataloguing in Publication Data

Medicine at the courts of Europe, 1500–1837.
1. Europe. Medicine, History
I. Nutton, Vivian II. Series
610'. 94

Library of Congress Cataloging-in-Publication Data

Medicine at the courts of Europe, 1500–1837 / edited by
Vivian Nutton.
p.   cm. – (The Wellcome Institute series in the
history of medicine)
Includes index.
1. Physicians–Europe–History–16th century. 2. Physicians–
Europe–History–17th century. 3. Physicians–Europe–
History–18th century. 4. Physicians–Europe–History–19th
century. 5. Courts and courtiers–Europe–History. 6. Power
(Social sciences)–History. I. Nutton, Vivian. II. Series.
R484.M434   1989
610'.94'0903–dc20   89–10484
                                                        CIP

ISBN 0-415-02264-9

Contents

Contents

Tables

Contributors

J. T. Alexander: University of Kansas
Laurence Brockliss: Magdalen College, University of Oxford
W. F. Bynum: The Wellcome Institute, London
Johanna Geyer-Kordesch: University of Cambridge
Colin Jones: University of Exeter
Werner Friedrich Kümmel: University of Mainz
Bruce T. Moran: University of Nevada at Reno
Vivian Nutton: The Wellcome Institute, London
Richard Palmer: The Wellcome Institute, London
Hugh Trevor-Roper: Peterhouse, University of Cambridge

Acknowledgements

This collection of essays is the fruit of a conference on the theme 'Hofmedizin in Europa bis zur Aufklärung' held at the Herzog August Bibliothek, Wolfenbüttel in September 1986. This conference, in which over twenty scholars participated, endeavoured to do for court medicine what an earlier Wolfenbüttel colloquium had done for the town and state physician.[1] In the impressive setting of the Bibelsaal, discussion was appropriately learned and polite. Four of the papers given there are not reprinted here. Professor Dietrich von Engelhardt's survey of court medicine and literature forms part of his forthcoming book on the interrelationships between medicine and literature, while Dr Roy Porter's study of the Chevalier Taylor will appear in his book on quackery. Dr Gül Russell's survey of the doctors at the Ottoman Court and Dr David Richards's investigations into Queen Victoria's dentists are scheduled for publication elsewhere. Illness prevented Professor Lopez-Piñero from attending and giving his paper on the Spanish court, the influence of whose doctors extended beyond the sea to the Americas. Their absence is to some extent balanced by the essays of Professor Bruce Moran, who has expanded his closing remarks on the prince-practitioner, and of Professor J. T. Alexander, whose survey of medicine at the court of Catherine the Great has been especially written for this volume.

Grateful acknowledgements must first be made to Dr Paul Raabe for allowing the meeting to take place in the incomparable and appropriate surroundings of a royal library, and to Dr Sabine Solf and her staff, whose advice and encouragement are beyond praise. Funding for the conference was provided by the Wellcome Trust, the Herzog August Bibliothek, and the Deutsche Forschungsgemeinschaft, to all of whom we express our thanks. Mention should also be made of Robin Price, who acted as the British link with Germany; Christine Nutton, who translated Professor Kümmel's paper into English; and Frieda Houser, who typed some of the manuscript. The publication of these conference proceedings was smoothed by Richard Stoneman, of Croom Helm, as it

Acknowledgements

then was, and by Gill Davies, his successor at Routledge.

Vivian Nutton
The Wellcome Institute, London

Note

1. Andrew W. Russell (ed.), *The Town and State Physician in Europe, from the Middle Ages to the Enlightenment* (Wolfenbütteler Forschungen, Band 17, 1981).

Introduction

Vivian Nutton

Thus says Washmuarea Shatepnarea, the Great King, King of the Land of Egypt, Child of the Sun, Rameses Mai-Amana, the Great King, the King of the Land of Egypt:

To Hattushilish, the great King, King of the Land of Hatti, my brother, says:

Lo, I, your brother, the King of the Land of Egypt, am well. May it be so with you, Hattushilish, my brother. Say to my brother: My brother wrote to me for his sister Matanazi: may my brother be pleased to send me a man to prepare a drug that will cause her to give birth. So has my brother written.

Thus say to my brother: Behold, Matanazi, the sister of my brother; O king, does she know your brother? Is she 50 years old? No, she is 60. Can she be a 50 year old? No, she is 60. No drug can be prepared that will cause her to give birth.

But, in truth, the god of the sun and the god of the weather may give the command, and the arrangement that they will make will be enforced for the sister of my brother. And I will send a priest skilled in incantations, and a skilled physician, and they will prepare a remedy by which she will give birth.

I send other gifts in greeting to my brother with my envoy: draperies of sea-cotton, tunics of sea-cotton.

This letter of Rameses II to Hattushilish, King of the Hittites, about 1270 BC is one of our earliest pieces of information about the activities of a court physician. It forms part of a whole dossier of cuneiform tablets from Boghazkoy in Turkey which re-

1

port in detail the diplomatic relations between Egypt and the kingdom of the Hittites. In its collocation of medicine and great-power politics, this letter is not unique in the collection There are other tablets recording requests from the Hittite court for medical assistance, and even a lament that the 'incantation-priest' is now dead and that the physician–envoy may now be wishing to return home to Egypt. Medicine and the court physician are already in this early document taking on a more than local significance.[1]

This is, in part, the very reason for this volume, which attempts to consider the court physician, or, to be more precise, *Hofmedizin*, medicine at the royal court, from the point of view of the medical historian and of the social historian, if this distinction can be properly made. For the truth is that, despite appearances, medicine within the setting of the royal courts of Europe has been very largely neglected. This is a surprising claim, and one which requires justification, albeit brief. To take the two most obvious recent discussions of the early modern courts, Norbert Elias's *Die hofische Gesellschaft*, which first appeared in 1969, and the three volumes of the proceedings of the splendid Wolfenbüttel conference of 1979, *Europäische Hofkultur im 16. u. 17. Jahrhundert*, neither devotes much attention to medicine.[2] The reason for the disappearance of the *Leibarzt* or *Hofarzt* from *Die hofische Gesellschaft* is instructive. That brilliantly perverse book, with its explanations and elucidations of court ritual, ceremonial, and space, disregards court physicians precisely because they are not easily slotted into the noble culture of the court. They are, as many papers here hint, rarely, if ever, of noble origin; rarely members of families attached to the court. They are outsiders, whose own talents, however they might be described, brought them into princely or royal favour. Socially they stand outside the court families; they are more akin in their professional skills to the court musician or the court librarian; yet their relation to the ruler is at the same time more intimate, perhaps even more necessary, than that of many of the courtiers. To locate the court physician within the court society is one of the prime objectives of this book.

The *Hofarzt*'s limited appearance in the Wolfenbüttel volumes, which was one of the stimuli to the planning of the conference from which this volume developed, is equally instructive. One paper was there devoted to a medical theme, an elegant account by Rolf Winau of medicine and science at the Brandenburg court of the Great Elector in the seventeenth century, and there were glances at the activities of court physicians in Sweden and, more tantalizingly, in Transylvania.[3] In all these discussions, however, the court physician's medical activities disappear from view until all that remains is a paragraph on Johann Sigismund Elsholtz and his introduction of Harvey's ideas into North Germany, and another on Christian Mentzel and his use of 'Chinese pulse diagnosis'.[4] The contrast provided here by Dr Geyer-Kordesch in her study of the Prussian court during the reigns of the successors of the Great Elector is eloquent. In Winau's paper we find the *Hofarzt* as botanist, as chemist, as traveller, as almost anything other than physician. The emphasis is on biographical details about an individual rather than an attempt to understand the place of the court physician in relation to the medical society of his time and to the constraints on his activities as a physician brought about by the need to serve a monarch and his court. The question of an heir (or too many heirs) was always pressing, and the role of the court physician in this was often crucial. He had the duty, too, of preserving the monarch's health amid the varying hazards of court life. It is here that Professor Kümmel's paper (Chapter 1) enlightens us, by focusing on the illnesses that the court physicians claimed to be treating, and wherein they boasted of special expertise. John Caius, writing in England in the 1540s, rejoiced that at last the English gentry and court were beginning to make proper use of doctors, to use them as personal physicians in a true Galenic manner; not just as emergency help, but allowing them to stay for long periods and observe the natural habits and conditions of their royal or noble patrons, whose diseases could only rightly be understood against a knowledge of their normal health and habits.[5] A similar claim was made a generation or more earlier by Paolo Cortesi in his *De Cardinalatu*, a book mentioned by Dr Palmer (Chapter 2), which incorporates a long section of medical advice to the Pope and his cardinals, advocating not least the playing of tennis.[6]

A dimension of health and sickness, of what it was like to fall ill and be treated in one of the frequently dirty and insalubrious palaces of a prince or ruler, is thus lacking in standard books on court life. However, while historians of high culture may perhaps be forgiven for their reluctance to pry into the bowels of a royal patient or to sniff the odour of the palace drains, medical historians have been equally culpable in their neglect of the courts and court medicine. In this they lag far behind the compilers of dictionaries and encyclopaedias in the sixteenth century, like Ravisius Textor and Theodor Zwinger, whose entries from classical literature bring forward a whole phalanx of royal physicians, beginning with Democedes of Croton, an Italian Greek who served both Athens, the tyrant ruler of Samos, and the King of Persia, and Hippocrates, who rejected on patriotic grounds a summons to attend the King of Persia.[7] Zwinger's lists of notable physicians, of physicians as miraclemen, adulterers, political fixers, and murderers, are filled with royal physicians, and their exploits, for good, or, more often, for ill, were retold at length by subsequent authors. The resulting literary image of the court physician is, on the whole, unfavourable, as Dr Brockliss (Chapter 5) reminds us, and it is merely one of the backgrounds against which the court doctor must be set. One may go on from this to enquire in what ways the doctor's career or his social standing conform to the literary image; and, if it does not, what this can tell us as historians of the use of such literary evidence in creating a picture of the doctor within his society.

Yet it would be wrong to neglect entirely the biographical approach, for it points to two important features that explain the lack of interest on the part of medical historians. The first is the court physician's broad range of non-therapeutic activities – a point to which I shall return – and, second, his general mediocrity as a medical scientist. In the standard historiography of medicine, and in such works as the *Biographisches Lexikon der hervorragenden Ärzte*, court physicians are far less well represented than professors. Yet it is perhaps only a modern academic perspective that sees a regius professorship of physic as somehow superior to a post as personal physician to a ruler, however small his territory. The aim of many young physicians must surely have been to impress, perhaps by a few lectures or a single cure, a wealthy or a noble patron, and become the latter's attendant – and thereby make far more money than their colleagues who remained behind in the university.[8] Once outside academia, the impulse to write, to publish, and to argue may have diminished, or been stifled by court duties; and hence, as at the end of the reign of Queen Elizabeth I, the royal physicians may have apparently sunk into inactivity and sloth. This is, however, to impose modern criteria, and to exalt the evidence of literary production over the demands of practical therapy, which rarely leaves its trace. We cannot tell, on the whole, how good were an individual's capabilities as a bedside physician, and it may have been this, far more than any book-learning, that impressed a monarch, or kept a physician in royal employment. However, to discover this from among the documentation is by no means easy, still less to differentiate between quacks and therapeutic geniuses.

Yet even if it is accepted that few of the court physicians made a great or a lasting name for themselves as writers or investigators, they may still deserve examination for their other activities, as propagandists, diplomats, and medical politicians. Here, above all, this volume breaks new ground by considering a wide range of themes and sub-themes. The most obvious, which is most clearly articulated by Dr Geyer-Kordesch (Chapter 6), is the relationship between the court physicians and general medical practitioners within the community. How far do the court physicians become almost the government ministers of health, setting norms for others to follow?; and, if they are able to exercise such authority, does their power rest with their relationship with an individual ruler or does it rather depend on the strength of an institutionalized and centralized monarchy? To take the example of England, the foundation of the London College of Physicians and its subsequent history turn on these questions. Without the political centralization of Henry VII and Henry VIII, it is likely that the plans of Linacre and his fellow royal physicians for a College of Physicians would have suffered the same fate as Keymer's college a century earlier.[9] The College's great activity (and, to a certain extent, success) under John Caius in the reign of Mary Tudor depended in part on the close relation, going back many years, between the leading members of the College and of the court, most notably Cardinal Pole. Its subsequent failures to enforce its writ even in London, to say nothing of the provinces, owed not a little to the opposition of courtiers to the College's wish to punish physicians in whom they themselves trusted. A similar argument for the importance of the relationship between court and College in the seventeenth century has recently been put forward by Harold Cook and by William Birken, although with different emphases.[10]

The importance of the court physician can also be seen in the spread of Paracelsianism. As Professor Trevor-Roper (Chapter

3) shows, it was through a network of court physicians rather than through medical colleges or the universities that Paracelsianism first spread round Europe in the mid-sixteenth century. His chapter prompts questions about the influence of the leading physicians at the court on the various territorial universities. Oxford and Cambridge, or Ingolstadt, which were some distance away from the ruler's residence, may have been more immune to what was going on at court than Heidelberg, where university and palace were in close proximity. Just as Adam von Bodenstein propagated Paracelsianism in both, so, only a few years earlier, the elector's physician, Johannes Lang, had played a major role in the creation of new Galenic statutes and a new syllabus for the medical faculty.[11] However, whether the immunity of the English universities from court fashions in medicine or the dependence of Heidelberg was more typical remains open to question.

The story of the introduction of Paracelsianism also raises a further problem in the history of court medicine – on the interactions between what one might loosely term orthodox and non-orthodox medicine. Even today in Great Britain, the royal family's support for alternative medicine contrasts strongly with the official attitudes of the medical profession as voiced by the British Medical Association. In this the court may be closer to the 'folk-perceptions' of the layperson, and may, for this reason, have been open in the past to the seductive claims of a Chevalier Taylor, who visited most of the courts of Europe in the mid-eighteenth century as an eye specialist. Yet some of Taylor's techniques in his eye operations may not have been too far removed from those of contemporary surgeons. Where he differed from them was in the pomp and panoply of his journeys, which were calculated to impress and to attract wealthy, royal patrons. It was precisely the existence of an abundance of courts throughout Europe that enabled Taylor to flourish through the practice of a limited speciality. In this way the medicine of the court helped to speed up and legitimize the process of medical specialization. In a paper presented at Wolfenbüttel but not included in this volume, Dr David Richards tentatively argued for a similar importance of the court in the increasing acceptability of dentistry as an independent speciality. His caveat about the possible manual dexterity of both of Queen Victoria's dentists at the end of their long careers is also a reminder that this process of gaining acceptability may have been both long and painful.

The influence of *Hofmedizin* must, to a large extent, depend on the influence of the *Hof* itself. It is perhaps here that differences between states are most marked. At one extreme, there is the court of eighteenth-century Prussia, whose physicians were trying also to control through centralization the various medical organizations throughout the kingdom; and at the other, as Dr Bynum (Chapter 9) shows, there is the almost middle-class life of the English court under the Georges, in which king and court were treated no differently from other well-paying clients. Unlike Istanbul, where the royal physician had his quarters in the palace, or at Versailles, where the chief physician had to be in constant attendance, the English royal physicians rarely lived in the palace, and when needed, came out from their comfortable homes in London to visit their royal patients at Windsor, returning the same day. The fact that this excursion also added to their charges may by itself explain why they disliked residence at court, but there is still a marked contrast between the relative informality of the Hanoverian court and its French or Russian equivalent.

It is unfortunate that there is no contribution in this volume that considers Spain, where the role of the chief physician, the *Protomedico*, within the court and within the realm as a whole, was very strong. The *Protomedico* was in theory the head of the examining body that regulated practice throughout Spain, and the chain of authority ran directly from the court to the provinces.[12] In France, by contrast, the elaborate organization of the court physicians, described in detail by Dr Jones (Chapter 8), was relatively impotent against the numerous local and educational bodies that governed medical practice. It was very different again in the Russia of Catherine the Great, in which, according to Professor Alexander (Chapter 7), there was a deliberate attempt by the empress to modernize the medical services of both court and country through the introduction of foreign experts and foreign expertise.

A study of the court physicians and their milieu also involves the personality of the ruler as both patient and patron. Physicians at court might see their role as crucial in the maintenance of good order throughout the kingdom through their oversight of the ruler's health, and, if Professor Kümmel (Chapter 1) is right, became increasingly free in their recommendations during the Enlightenment. However, their advice might be disregarded by a stubborn ruler, and, at times, it was the very interests of the monarch that determined the medical development of his or her physician. Professor Moran shows how Maurice of Hesse in the seventeenth century actively intervened in the medical activities of his court physicians. His love of chemistry and chemical experiment was mirrored in the practices of his physicians, and it was his money that enabled them to purchase materials and to construct apparatus. In return, the pharmaceutical preparations of the court pharmacist were sold for the pharmacist's and the prince's benefit. Smaller courts also joined in this alliance of medicine and chemistry. It was the facilities provided by Casimir zu Sayn-Wittgenstein at his residence in Berleburg that allowed Johann Conrad Dippel and the more famous Johann Christian Senckenberg to carry out their chemical experiments on drugs in the 1730s.[13] Likewise, the Brandenburg physician Mentzel's introduction of rare plants into the pharmacopoeia was made possible through the money made available to him for the purchase of such exotica and any necessary equipment.[14]

This involvement of the medical men of the court in pharmacology and botany goes back a long way, beyond even the Paracelsian International described by Professor Trevor-Roper (Chapter 3). Niccolò Leoniceno, Professor of Medicine at Ferrara and physician to the Dukes of Ferrara for over half a century until his death in 1524, had a passionate interest in botany as well as in classical pharmacological texts. His pupil, and later successor, Giovanni Manardi, made use of his contacts as physician to ruler of Hungary to send to his old teacher what he thought was conclusive identification of the rhubarb mentioned by the Roman author Pliny in his *Natural History*. Manardi had accompanied the King of Hungary in 1515 to an international conference with the rulers of Poland and Muscovy, and thanks to his Moscow contacts, had managed to have a specimen of genuine Pontic rhubarb sent all the way from the Black Sea through Russia and Northern Europe to Hungary. What the condition of the plant was in when it reached Manardi or when, as he promised, he delivered it to Leoniceno, cannot be imagined.[15] What is significant here is that its acquisition depended on Manardi's position as court doctor. A slightly later example is the dominance exercised in botany and pharmacology in the mid-sixteenth century by Giovanni Matthioli, a dominance gained largely at court by remaining at home while others roamed the hills and woods of Europe and beyond in search of plants known earlier to the classical pharmacologist Dioscorides. Matthioli's post at the Habsburg court, whether at Innsbruck, Trento, Prague, or Vienna, also gave him the funds to employ a whole staff of illustrators for the successive editions of his commentary on Dioscorides, as well as a range of impressive contacts across Europe. The translation of his herbal, first into Czech and later into German, was sponsored by the Emperor Ferdinand, his employer, for reasons of both practicality and prestige.[16]

Matthioli, like Vesalius, was one of the luminaries of the medical and scientific Renaissance. Both were taken into court service, and both continued to revise their major works while in royal employ, but Vesalius's fame rests largely on what he had done before his royal appointment.[17] The pressure of court duties may in part explain why there is a common falling off in the scientific activity of such doctors, once appointed, and why, in turn, historians of medicine and science have said so little about court physicians as scientists. Their image has, on the whole, been negative, as corrupt and ineffective placemen, wheeler-dealers on the fringes of power, fully part neither of the court nor of the intellectual world of the universities. Yet this intermediate position has its positive side. It was precisely because of his role as a middleman that the <i>Hofarzt</i> or the <i>Hofapothekar</i> could develop his links with the wider world, and promote and spread new ideas generated by others, be they in botany, medicine, or religion.

An excellent example of this in the sixteenth century is furnished by the career of Johannes Crato (Johann Krafft) von Crafftheim (1519–85) at the Imperial court in Vienna. Crato is not a familiar figure to historians of medicine, except perhaps to devotees of the University of Padua, where he studied in the mid-1540s. His printed works remain largely unread; or, if any are cited, they are more likely to be his versions of the lectures of his Paduan master, Giovanni Battista da Monte, than anything he wrote himself. One may look in vain for his name in standard histories of Renaissance science, and he merits only a brief entry in reference books. From the point of view of the traditional medical historian he is a second- or third-rate figure, at best a mere name from the past, deservedly neglected. It may thus come as something of a shock to discover that he is alone among Renaissance physicians in being the subject of a two-volume biography that is an excellent example of nineteenth-century German historical scholarship in the thoroughness of its documentation. J. F. A. Gillet's *Crato von Crafftheim und seine Freunde*, which appeared at Frankfurt-am-Main in 1860-1, was the work of an ecclesiastical historian interested in the religious developments among the Lutherans of Central Europe and, in particular, in Breslau, where Crato was born.[18] It traces his life, from his birth into a wealthy bourgeois family in a town that was beginning to pride itself on its cultural interests, to his studies with Luther and Melanchthon at Wittenberg – where he was advised by Melanchthon to forget a career in the Church and become a physician, since his health was not up to the strain of the religious life(!) – to his Italian stay at Padua, and finally back to imperial service with Ferdinand, Maximilian, and Rudolf II. Gillet's emphasis is largely on Crato's role as a guide and helper in the religious Reformation in Silesia and Bohemia. He documents clearly how Crato's role at court as personal physician to the emperor enabled him to gain the confidence of the Habsburg monarchs, and thereby to use his influence to secure a broad degree of toleration for all believers within the empire. We are shown his relations with the Lutherans and with the Jesuits; and with the motley crowd of Italian religious exiles, many of them physicians, who went on to spread their ideas of Socinianism and Unitarianism to the courts of Poland and Transylvania. As more than one Italian scholar has remarked, the spread of radical religious ideas out of Italy after the Council of Trent owed not a little to the ability of free-thinking doctors to find lucrative employment at these distant courts.[19] Gillet also describes Crato's relationship with his home city of Breslau; and how his frequent contacts with its leading families enabled him to gain the emperor's support for them in their policies. Crato was assisted in this by two things; his close proximity to the emperor, which took him on travels even as far as Spain, and his access to the imperial postal system.

Crato was an indefatigable letter writer. There is scarcely a major library in Europe that does not possess at least one of his epistles, and only a minute fraction of his output has ever been published. He knew and wrote to almost everyone of importance. Indeed, from a reading of his correspondence, it seems at times as if all lines lead through Crato, or at least through Vienna, Prague, or Breslau.[20] Gillet was interested in Crato's religious ideas, particularly as they were applied in Silesia, but he did not neglect his medicine. Here one can find Crato supporting and encouraging young aspiring physicians as well as more unusual characters like the Hungarian Catholic bishop turned Lutheran-cum-Unitarian, Andreas Dudith, in their medical and scientific pursuits.[21] He informs correspondents of news relayed to him from Padua; he engages in criticism of a Paduan professor, Girolamo Mercuriale, over some, Crato hoped unintended, theories on plague put out in his lectures; and he discusses botany and plants with friends throughout Europe, from the Netherlands and Basle to Italy.[22] Not only Matthioli but also Clusius and Dodoens received letters from him; and their botanical concerns, even if far removed spatially from Prague or Breslau, were furthered by him, and by other imperial agents. In his correspondence one can trace the workings of patronage, as well as the rising tide of Paracelsianism, the theories of Fracastoro as well as those of Sozzini. In short, the *Epistolarium* of Crato reveals the multiplicity of powers and opportunities open to a court physician, precisely because of his location at the centre of a network of other, not necessarily medical, contacts.

It might be objected here that this emphasis on Crato neglects the fact that similarly huge collections of correspondence survive from the Camerarius family in Nuremberg, from the Zwingers in Basel, and from Jacques Dalechamps in Lyons, none of whom were court physicians. However, these examples, in fact help to substantiate the case, for all three cities were major communication centres, for the exchange of ideas as well as of goods. A court like that of the Habsburgs functioned as a similar magnet for news and information from elsewhere; and the facilities it offered for communication outwards rivalled those of the major commercial centres. However, even if Crato von Crafftheim is a special case in his remarkably varied range of interests and correspondents, one can see a similar collocation of interests and contacts in other court physicians, such as Turquet de Mayerne or Peter Monau, Crato's friend and successor as physician to Rudolf II. To view the court medical men in this light is to gain a better understanding of their role within the medical community at large than if one were simply to rely on their brief biographical notices.

This volume of papers, then, although not comprehensive in its geography, is intended to offer a broad view of medicine at court, its practitioners and its problems. Even if we cannot be entirely sure of the etiquette needed to approach the royal person, we can gain a better understanding of the diseases from which rulers and their courts suffered, and the men whom they summoned to attend them. They are a varied group, including quacks as well as geniuses, charlatans as well as scholars. They are both of the court and outside it, capable of independent criticism as well as of tactful flattery. To indulge in generalizations about their role at court and within medicine is to forget the very diversity that is obvious from the various contributions in this volume. Whatever their posthumous reputations among historians, the court physicians and their associates enjoyed positions of power and influence that they could employ for ends both good and bad. Access to the monarch in some of his most intimate moments gave the court physician power to harm or benefit the State. It may not have been family piety alone that led Robert Southey, the brother of a physician-in-ordinary to George IV, to propose in 1837 the creation of a State Physician to the King, to watch over the royal health as connected with the discharge of the royal functions. Southey went even further. Convinced of the medical and political advantages to be gained from this medical supervision, he devised a whole phalanx of physicians for every political leader and grouping, from the Cabinet downwards.[23] For Southey's doctor, the role of the court physician was crucial to the well-being, not only of the monarch and his or her court, but also of the nation. Whatever the physician's qualifications or competence, his bedside manner, or his book-learning, the destiny of the State might ultimately depend on his therapies. In the eyes of contemporaries, medicine at court was no idle bagatelle.

Notes

1. E. Edel, *Ägyptische Ärzte und ägyptische Medizin am hethitischen Königshof* (Westdeutscher Verlag, Opladen, 1976), pp. 68–70. See also C. Burde, *Hethitische medizinische Texte* (Harrassowitz, Wiesbaden, 1974), pp. 5–7.

2. N. Elias, *Die höfische Gesellschaft* (Luchterhand, Neuwied and Berlin, 1969), English trans., *The Court Society* (Blackwell, Oxford, 1983); A. Buck (ed.), *Europäische Hofkultur im 16. und 17. Jahrhundert* (3 vols, Hauswedell, Hamburg, 1981).

3. Rolf Winau, 'Der Hof des Grossen Kurfürsten und die Wissenschaften', in Buck, *Hofkultur*, vol. 3, pp. 447–58; Christian

Introduction

Callmer, 'Königin Christina, ihre Bibliothekäre, und ihre Bibliotheken, ibid., pp. 659–66, esp. pp. 661–2; Horst Fassel, 'Der Fürstenhof von Weissenburg (Alba Iulia) und seine Bedeutung für Wissenschaft und Kunst in Siebenbürgen zur Zeit Gabriel Bethlens', ibid., pp. 637–46, esp. pp. 643–4.

4. Winau, 'Der Hof', pp. 655, 654.

5. J. Caius, *De medendi methodo* (A. M. Bergagne, Louvain, 1556), p. 39.

6. Martin Dolch, 'Paulo Corteses Bemerkungen über das Ballspiel der geistlichen Würdenträger (1510)', *Stadion*, vol. 8–9 (1982–3), pp. 85–97.

7. The story of Democedes is first told by Herodotus, *Historiae* 3.131–4. He is the archetypal doctor in the lists prepared by Ravisius Textor, *Officiana* (J. A. Julianus, Venice, 1617), pp. 332–5, and by Theodor Zwinger, *Theatrum humanae vitae* (E. Episcopius, Basle, 1586), vol. 30, cols 1232–46.

8. Details on fees and salaries are hard to find; for one example, cf. Carole Rawcliffe, 'The profits of practice: the wealth and status of medical men in later mediaeval England', *Social History of Medicine*, vol. 1 (1988), pp. 61–78.

9. Charles Webster, 'Thomas Linacre and the foundation of the College of Physicians', in F. Maddison, M. Pelling, and C. Webster (eds), *Essays on the Life and Work of Thomas Linacre* (Clarendon Press, Oxford, 1977), pp. 202–5).

10. H. J. Cook, *The Decline of the Old Medical Regime in Stuart London* (Cornell University Press, Ithaca, 1986); William J. Birken, 'The Royal College of Physicians of London and its support of the parliamentary cause in the English Civil War', *Journal of British Studies*, vol. 23 (1983), p. 50.

11. Vivian Nutton, 'John Caius and Johannes Lange', *NTM*, vol. 21 (1984), pp. 81–7.

12. J. T. Lanning, *The Royal Protomedico: The Regulation of the Medical Profession in the Spanish Empire* (Duke University Press, Durham, 1985).

13. Christa Habrich, 'Mediziner und Medizinisches am Hofe des Grafen Casimir zu Sayn-Wittgenstein (1687–1741)', *Beiträge zur Geschichte der Pharmazie*, vol. 31 (1983), pp. 138–44.

14. Winau, 'Der Hof', pp. 650–2.

15. J. Manardus, *Epistulae medicinales* (S. Gryphius, Lyons, 1549), V.5.

16. Richard Palmer, 'Medical botany in Northern Italy in the Renaissance', *Journal of the Royal Society of Medicine*, vol. 78 (1985), pp. 149–57. For the translations, see R. J. W. Evans, *Rudolf II and His World* (Clarendon Press, Oxford, 1975), p. 118.

17. C. D. O'Malley, *Andreas Vesalius of Brussels* (University of California Press, Berkeley, 1964), pp. 255–68; note also p. 296, for Vesalius's complaints of the stultifying effect of life at court.

18. J. F. A. Gillet, *Crato von Crafftheim und seine Freunde* (H. L. Bröner, Frankfurt, 1860–1), 2 vols.

19. D. Caccamo, *Eretici Italiani in Moravia, Polonia, Transilvania*

(1558–1611) (Sansoni, Florence, 1970); A. Rotondo, *Studi e Ricerche di Storia Ereticale Italiana del Cinquecento* (Giappichelli, Turin, 1974).

20. Cf. Gillet, *Crato*; Evans, *Rudolf II*, pp. 98–100.

21. Viktor Fossel, 'Die epistulae medicinales des Humanisten Andreas Dudith', *Sudhoffs Archiv*, vol. 6 (1913), pp. 34–51; P. Costil, *André Dudith, Humaniste Hongrois* (Les belles lettres, Paris, 1935); Lech Szczucki, 'L'epistolario di Andrea Dudith', *Rinascimento*, vol. 25 (1985), pp. 297–308.

22. J. Crato, *Epistulae*, vol. II (Wechel, Frankfurt, 1592), pp. 235–45; vol. V (Wechel, Hanover, 1619), p. 350; Evans, *Rudolf II*, pp. 118–24. Cf. also H. Gerstinger, *Die Briefe des Johannes Sambucus* (Hermann Bohlaus Nachf., Vienna, 1968).

23. R. Southey, *The Doctor* (London), vol. 7 (1847), pp. 426–9, a reference I owe to Roy Porter.

1

De Morbis Aulicis: On Diseases Found at Court

Werner Friedrich Kümmel

The treatise *On the Health of Princes*, which Bernardino Ramazzini, Professor of Medicine at Padua, published in 1710 has nowadays fallen into almost complete oblivion.[1] It was not always so. Although he had to bear the costs of publication himself because the publisher was not convinced that the book was likely to sell well, despite the author's reputation and standing, Ramazzini's book in fact aroused great interest amongst royal body-physicians and court physicians generally,[2] and was reprinted twice within two years. In 1724 there followed a French, and in 1753 even a Portuguese, translation, and its inclusion, from 1714 onwards, in the frequent reprintings of Ramazzini's *Complete Works* brought it to a still wider readership.

The first contributions to the corpus of writings about illness attributed to life at court had appeared in the sixteenth century, and more had followed towards the end of the seventeenth. However, Ramazzini was the first to embark on a broad discussion entailing an exploration of the related theme of the health of princes. Thus, the rapidly subdividing science of health and disease acquired a new speciality, which the present chapter will analyse and explain in relation to its context. There exist no earlier studies of this corpus, nor, indeed, has the whole process of differentiation to which I have referred yet been investigated.

Ramazzini's *De principum valetudine tuenda* was based on the same fundamental idea as, ten years previously, had inspired the book on the diseases of workers and craftsmen that had made his name and given him a place in history as the founder of occupational medicine;[3] namely, that 'not only diseases arising from the constitution of the body, but also disorders brought on by one's life-style or the practice of an art or job should be taken into consideration and the appropriate treatment set in hand'.[4] Underlying this challenge to the medical profession may already be discerned the thesis he was to formulate in 1710, of the connection between diseases and the conditions of the patient's life. 'Just as particular diseases are typical of different ages, temperaments, seasons, and places, so, equally, the conditions under which an individual lives, whether through chance or through choice, bring special diseases in their wake'.[5] Ramazzini did not claim to have made an entirely new discovery. Hippocratic medicine had already arrived at the basic conclusion that health and sickness were greatly influenced by individual living conditions – which were by no means confined to such externals as seasons, locality, and climate. The author of *On Regimen*, writing around 400 BC, put forward as his own discovery the idea that health depends not simply on nourishment, but on the quantitative balance between the intake of nourishment and physical activity; and that it was further affected by such factors as the age and constitution of the individual, the seasons, changes in wind direction, place of residence, the weather in a particular year, and the rising and setting of the planets.[6] Since most people have to earn their living, and, in the process, usually eat and drink whatever comes to hand, put themselves to great exertion, expose themselves to harmful extremes of heat and cold, and in general are forced to live an unplanned life, the author sketches out guidelines for healthy living mainly for this group, and only secondarily for the minority whose wealth allows them to arrange their lives entirely with a view to maintaining health, without concern for the means of sustaining life.[7]

This emphasis, which still reflects without qualification the high esteem in which riches were held in early Greek culture,[8] might have led to the emergence of an embryo 'occupational medicine', but this was not to be. Indeed, the doctors of Antiquity were remarkably uninterested in the connection between work and disease. This lack of interest, which has often been noted, but without any explanation being advanced, can perhaps be attributed to the fact that this conception of wealth as the best prerequisite for health was overshadowed by the opposite thesis, that, in reality, wealth was more likely than poverty to produce ill-health. In the Hippocratic treatise *Airs, Waters and Places*, we hear that, among the Scythians, the

16

noblest and most powerful suffer from rheumatic complaints, because they are constantly using their legs to hang on to their horses, which also causes sores and ulcers on their thighs; the 'poor', i.e. the working population, are not thus afflicted because they do not ride.[9]

Philosophers and poets went further, and linked wealth and leisure in general with sickness, and, conversely, the simple life with good health.[10] Some authors even described the individual threats to health of certain professions.[11] In Galen's view, too, the rich suffer more from disease than the working masses, and specifically from those arising from a superfluity of blood, because they eat and drink too much, take too little exercise, and thus allow an excess of blood and harmful fluids to accumulate in their bodies.[12]

Even though connections between work and disease in general scarcely concerned doctors in Antiquity, one particular life-style did, certainly from the first century onwards, come into their purview – that of the intellectual worker, which was their own in so far as they were also engaged in study or writing. The health risks to which this group was exposed were discussed by Aretaeus of Cappadocia, Plutarch, Galen, and Rufus of Ephesus. Celsus even put forward the ingenious suggestion that the science of medicine had actually originated in the unhealthy life-style of intellectuals![13]

These early outlines of a theory of health incorporating the influence of people's occupations remained virtually unknown in the Middle Ages. The most that happened was that ancient ideas led Arabic physicians to extend the specialization of medicine with particular modes of treatment for individual target-groups – for women in pregnancy or labour, for unweaned infants and wet-nurses, for children and young people, for the old, for convalescents, and for travellers. However, they did not take particular occupations into account, not even that of the scholar. This theme was first taken up from the fourteenth century onwards in Latin-speaking western Europe, when a growing orientation towards outward reality tended to sharpen perceptions of the varying conditions of life.[14] In 1489, there appeared in Book I of Marsilio Ficino's extraordinarily influential *De vita* the first comprehensive set of medical recommendations for the scholar, the earliest example of a regimen tailored to a specific occupational group.[15] At the same period, individual doctors also began to take an interest in diseases re-

lated to manual labour. In 1473 Ulrich Ellenbog composed for
the goldsmiths of Augsburg his short treatise *On the Poisonous
and Evil Fumes and Vapours of Metal*, which, although not published until 1524, was frequently reprinted thereafter.[16] Then,
around 1520, Paracelsus is thought to have written the first part
of *On the Diseases of Miners*.[17] A lost work of Burkhard von Horneck (c. 1440–1522), *Regimen principum*, written for the Emperor Maximilian II, would appear to have applied a similar
approach to life at court.[18] That doctors should become more
aware of the special life-style at court and its associated diseases,
at a period when they were paying increasing attention to the
life-styles of people in general, is hardly surprising when one
remembers that, outside the realm of medicine, life at court had
long been a conventional subject for criticism. The morally
based critique of life at court, begun in the twelfth century, had
by the sixteenth century hardened into an established commonplace of European moralists. Such critiques 'developed into a
focus for the exposure of every moral evil'.[19] There had even
appeared a full-scale anthology of passages critical of court life,
published in its second edition by Henricus Petreus Herdesia-
nus (1578) under the title *Aulica vita* (Life at court). Although
such criticism of court life had a moral thrust, and its authors
were not doctors, they had begun to touch on certain individual
health-related aspects of life at court, such as irregular mealtimes and frequently interrupted sleep, as early as the fifteenth
century, well before physicians had made diseases at court into
a separate subject for discussion.[20] Thus, it can be seen that by
1500 the ground was prepared in various ways for the emergence of this theme.

Towards the concept of 'court disease'

As an examination of the lexicons confirms, Antiquity and the
Middle Ages had no specific terms for diseases regarded as particularly widespread at court, and designated accordingly. Constantinus Africanus merely remarks in one of his reworkings
and translations of Arabic texts on gout that it afflicts mainly
princes and those who live in luxury without physical exertion,
and who eat and drink a lot.[21]

The term 'court disease' was coined in Spain, towards the
end of the fifteenth century, as one of the numerous names for

the apparently new disease, syphilis. The Valencian physician, Gaspar Torrella (1452–1520), doctor at the courts of Pope Alexander VI and Cesare Borgia, noted in 1497 in his book on syphilis that, in southern Spain, the disease was known as '*morbus curialis*', because it was always to be found in the vicinity of a court.[22] This connection, enshrined in the name '*Mal de Cour*', survived up to the nineteenth century.[23] However, shortly after the first appearance of the concept of 'court disease', it was already ceasing to be limited to just one individual illness, and was being used as a collective term. The Spaniard Luis Lobera de Avila, one of Emperor Charles V's personal physicians, published in 1544 a book dealing with *The Four Diseases of Courtiers*.[24] Later authors, who took up the subject again in monographs only after a long gap, at the end of the seventeenth century, never refer to Lobera de Avila's work, and hold divergent and only partially overlapping conceptions of what constitute the 'diseases of the court'. The body of literature which revived the subject, under the name of '*morbi aulici*' or some similar term, appeared over more than a century, from Johann Jakob Waldschmiedt (1686) to Franz Anton Mai (1799). However, the concept 'court disease' is nowhere to be found in the standard medical dictionaries of the time, any more than in the disease classifications of the later eighteenth century. However, by the end of the century, it does begin to appear in medical bibliographies.[25]

By the later stages of the Enlightenment, horizons were widening, especially, as might be expected, in the works of those who were municipal rather than court physicians, to include not just the households of noblemen, but also the prosperous urban bourgeoisie, whose illnesses were recognized as comparable to those of courtiers, and were therefore described together with them (Langhans and Tissot, 1770). After 1800, the nobility vanishes completely from title pages. Books are now addressed to wider groupings, embracing also the higher reaches of the bourgeoisie, such as 'elegant society' (Kitchiner, 1825), 'the rich' (Fleckles, 1834), or the 'upper ranks and classes' (Rohatzsch, 1840). It is no coincidence that this last work marks the end of this body of literature just at the moment when the long Hippocratic-Galenic tradition was coming to an end, at least in academic medicine.[26]

Sources

The richest sources are naturally the works already mentioned which deal with the theme of 'Diseases of the court', either under this or a similar title, as well as treatises on the health of princes. Books of advice to princes, usually not composed by doctors, often include hints for healthy living, but scarcely ever mention the diseases associated with life at court.[27] The medical writings dedicated to individual princes, or written expressly for them, are usually equally uninformative.[28] Apart from Ramazzini's tract, which deals particularly with the health of princes, they mostly do not go beyond the framework of general dietary advice, despite the status of their dedicatee. Nor do the numerous prescriptions for noble invalids discuss in detail the diseases of court life. They confine themselves to the particular case in hand, but as we see from the example of Friedrich Hoffmann, they could include occasional references to the unhealthy habits of highly placed patients.[29] If one reads these prescriptions in the light of the treatises on diseases of the court, it is clear that they cover precisely the types of disorder most prevalent there.

With the exception of Avila, Ramazzini, and Tissot, the literature on court diseases and the health of princes is concentrated in the German-speaking countries. It is remarkable that no French or English court doctor contributed to it. With the exception of Ramazzini, Juncker, Langhans, and Tissot, the authors all practised as body-physicians or court doctors. As the formulation of the various titles shows, they were addressed to the members of princely families, and the court nobility, whereas there is seldom any mention of servants as patients.[30]

'Vita aulica'

Although in theory princes had every opportunity to provide themselves with everything necessary for a long and healthy life,[31] their health is impaired to an extent unknown among any other section of the population. 'One must ask in amazement why they do not fall ill more seriously and more frequently, since their way of life deviates so drastically from the normal.'[32] The arguments which lead Ramazzini and other authors to conclusions such as this derive from their assessment of court life according to the criteria of Hippocratic-Galenic medicine.[33] The following survey of critical factors of regimen observes the division into the six 'non-naturals', a classification which goes back to Galen in the second century, and which remained in force down to the beginning of the nineteenth.

The air

According to traditional ideas, cold, damp, wind, or night air were all detrimental to health, especially when there was a sudden transition from warm to cold air. This fostered feverish diseases and digestive disorders, especially when, as was often the case at court, the change was preceded by a heavy meal.[34] Rulers themselves were in particular danger, as they were more inclined than ordinary mortals to head and chest colds, since the head was put under added strain by brainwork and frequent changes of residence.[35] Hunting and travel hold hidden dangers.[36] On journeys, however, the servants suffer the effects of bad weather almost more than rulers themselves.[37] To remain in damp, foggy air is most unhealthy. It is particularly those who have been pampered and coddled by upbringing and life at court who must take this factor into account when choosing a place to live. The ruler usually has the advantage of being able to select from a number of differently sited palaces the one which offers the best air.[38] The most healthy building material for a princely residence would be wood, 'were it not at odds with majesty'.[39] To ensure proper monitoring of atmospheric conditions, barometers, hygrometers and wind-gauges are recommended for the prince's study.[40] Stables in the vicinity of the palace are, from a medical point of view, highly suspect, since unless removed daily, the horses' dung poisons the air.[41]

Food and drink

Traditionally, nourishment took up most space within the framework of the six non-naturals: in the context of court life, this chapter receives greater weight still, for royal eating-habits and healthy living are fundamentally almost irreconcilable.[42] Wealth tempts people to gluttony; this is the chief vice of courtiers.[43] Plain bread, the healthy food of the people, serves the prince only for wiping his greasy hands.[44] Health may be undermined, serious diseases triggered, and in the end, the mental faculties impaired simply by too much to eat and drink, and also by odd and irregular mealtimes,[45] constant changes of diet, the extreme variety of dishes offered, the preference for indigestible, highly seasoned, or over-sweetened dishes[46] and for iced or alcoholic drinks,[47] and, finally, over-indulgence in stimulants such as tea, coffee, chocolate, and tobacco.[48] A *Fürstenspiegel* (Mirror of Princes) of 1537 warns readers against ruining their minds with too much rich food:[49] and, two hundred years later, the conviction still reigned that the faculties indispensable for the office of ruler were diminished by excessive eating and drinking.[50]

Physical exercise and rest

There is a close interaction between nourishment and physical activity. Exercise or daily work can counteract an excess in the diet. For this reason poorer people, engaged in physical work, can tolerate heavier, fattier, and cheaper foodstuffs better than the upper classes, who find that, in the absence of sufficient exercise, food of the choicest quality will disagree with them: for 'meals are overcome by work' (*cibos a laboribus superari*).[51]

Thus, no other group of people was in more urgent need of a proper physical balance than princes, whose eating habits were in striking contradiction to the demands of doctors.[52] When lengthy conferences on state business are immediately followed by lavish banquets or when, as one sarcastic observer put it, the court life-style invariably leads from bed to table, from table to cards, and back again to the table, damage to health is unavoidable.[53]

However, it is only with great difficulty that the upper classes, like the learned, with whom they share a sedentary life-style, are to be persuaded of the value and importance of physical exercise – when they do not overdo things in that direction too, and ride, hunt, or dance to excess.[54] '*Vita sedentaria*', lack of exercise combined with an over-rich diet, is responsible for most diseases at court, and even results in the premature death of many courtiers.[55] For women, the effects of this lack of exercise are even more prejudicial than for men. This is because they exercise even less than men, from childhood onwards, and thus, despite the fact that, in general, their offences against the rules of health are less extreme, they are often less healthy than men.[56] Similarly, they are less healthy than women 'who have of necessity to undertake work of any kind'.[57]

Suitable physical activities include walks (especially if they lead to 'healthy' spots), riding, hunting, or travelling by carriage or ship, games of bowls or archery, billiards, exercises on gymnastic apparatus, dancing, and also sexual intercourse – but all in proper moderation.[58]

Sleep and waking

The tasks of rulers are difficult, intellectually taxing, and fraught with repeated excitement. Sufficient sleep is thus for them especially important. However, a court is precisely where people sleep too long, or too little, or at the wrong time.[59] Affairs of state, but unfortunately also the frequent revels, are the excuse for turning night into day, thus seriously defying the order of nature.[60] Since, of course, the bodily functions are designed to be at their most active in the morning, sleep at that time of day is disturbed: one is not refreshed by it, and soon begins to suffer from digestive problems, because the natural and necessary early-morning excretions cannot be performed. In the longer term, pathological conditions, similar to melancholic and manic afflictions, develop. Life at court, however, makes it almost impossible to break deep-rooted habits. Thus, those who 'for the sake of the court' must go without sleep for several nights, are allowed a siesta, normally strictly forbidden, in order to balance out the effects of the unnatural division of time.[61]

Evacuation and repletion

The bad habits of the court as far as food and exercise are concerned often lead to diarrhoea or constipation, with all their concomitant unpleasantnesses.[62] Franz Anton Mai, who does not mince words in his antipathy to court life, even maintains that every court doctor knows that the excretions of princes give off an unbearable stink, since a body constantly overfilled with food is bound to accumulate a lot of evil-smelling oil. The use of scented toilet waters is thus indispensable. In this connection, Mai gives a very graphic description of a post-mortem he personally carried out.[63]

The constraints of court etiquette did great harm, in particular the custom of ignoring the call of nature out of modest consideration for highly placed people, and postponing the right moment to go to the lavatory. From a medical viewpoint, this resulted in pains in the gut (colics), persistent constipation, and disturbances of bladder function. This code of conduct obviously caused particular suffering to women.[64]

Emotions

The last element in the traditional system, normally only given a brief formal mention, is here of unusual importance since, as all authors agreed, the members of the court are exposed to much stronger and much more frequent emotions than other people.[65] Life at court is dominated by excitement, intrigues, spite, envy, anger, ambition, love affairs, and mistrust of others to the point of phobia. This last state of mind had been identified by Philippe de Commynes as early as the end of the fifteenth century as a 'sickness of princes', brought on by the insincere flattery of their courtiers.[66] A great part of court illness must be ascribed to an excess of all these various emotions. The prince himself is again most at risk, because the emotions of the great are more violent.[67] To this must be added the fact that life at court is 'a life of leisure for the body without leisure for the mind', and thus the emotions lack any compensating activity to dampen them down.[68]

The harmful effects of the individual emotions are to some extent differentiated by doctors. Thus, for example, envy gnaws like poison, anger drives bile into the stomach and gut, but can also lead to apoplexy through the dilation of the blood vessels in the brain.[69] Medicine could do very little against emotionally caused illnesses. Reason was recommended as the best means of controlling the passions, but, from the perspective of humoral theory, a suitable diet might also help, and even sexual intercourse, provided it was undertaken in moderation.[70]

'Sensibilis principum natura':
the susceptible constitution of princes

The multifarious risks to health at court led Alberti to observe that not even a man of metal or marble could tolerate such a life. But princes are, on the contrary, particularly 'delicate' and 'sensitive'.[71] Carl refers to the observations of the old court doctors, confirmed by experience and reason, that with court-bred patients one must always adopt first the gentlest mode of treatment, rather than allow oneself to be driven to heroic measures. Such patients are by heredity and temperament more sensitive, highly strung, and delicate.[72] This heightened susceptibility is evident not just in regard to therapeutic interventions, but also in respect of atmosphere, environment, climate, and external influences of all kinds, to which courtiers are, in any case, excessively exposed.[73] Carl goes so far as to speak of an ongoing 'sickliness without actual illness', while Fleckles, a hundred years later, talks of the 'delicate balance of health' of the rich and educated, which is in constant danger of breaking down.[74]

The 'pampering and mollycoddling' so distressingly prevalent at court begins in earliest childhood.[75] According to Carl, the children of the Royal Household ('*Staatskinder*') are 'very delicate, small, thin, with wretched limbs and bodies, suited only for a sheltered and prosperous life-style'. Since they are wrongly nourished, eating too much 'heating' food, but no bread, in order to avoid a 'peasant ruddiness of the face', they often fall ill and are more prone than other children to the 'English disease' (rickets). Only one in ten children reared at court reach adulthood. They are 'like wax dolls, so delicate and pretty, or like skeletons risen from the grave. Their life and strength consists of one continual sickening.'[76]

According to Alberti, this is particularly true of those 'sensitive princesses' who, through a one-sided concentration on mental exertions and lack of exercise, bring on themselves an excessive 'sensibility', which in turn develops into serious ailments and diseases and leads to an early death.[77]

As an antidote, Carl suggests, among other things, a vegetarian diet, since the decaying residues of meat, together with an indolent life-style and emotional agitation, provoke and intensify a constant disturbance in the economy of the body. Bread, water, and vegetable foods are thus to be recommended for

delicate and sensitive natures. Tissot advises, in particular, cold
baths, milk drinks, plenty of exercise, and fresh air, and also
gives detailed instruction on how to avoid the children of the
court becoming 'delicate' from the outset.[78]

'Morbi aulici': the range of diseases

Gout and syphilis, which were the first to be closely connected
with courts, and were thus already labelled accordingly, appear
together with stones in the bladder and kidneys and colic in the
title of the earliest monograph on the subject, by Lobera de
Avila (1544). Pains to the gut ('griping') and gout are, according
to Hippolytus Guarinonius (1610), frequent complaints among
the nobility.[79] The list of diseases compiled by Waldschmiedt,
who took up the subject again in a monograph of 1689, looks
rather different. First and foremost, it is far more extensive. He
classifies as court diseases, first, chronic complaints which have
their origins predominantly in the intestines and stomach: he
then goes on to mention disorders of the spleen, uterus, and
liver, 'scorbutic' and 'hypochondriacal' illnesses, shortness of
breath originating in the stomach, pains in the head and heart,
amenorrhoea, and piles, but also colic and kidney disease, by
which is certainly meant kidney stones. In a wider group of
court diseases, Waldschmiedt also includes, rosacea, scabies,
tooth decay, receding gums, and bad breath.[80] Syphilis is not
mentioned by him in this connection.

The same is true of Ramazzini, who otherwise agrees with
Lobera in pinpointing especially gout, colic, and kidney disorders as diseases typical of the court. In his work on the diseases
of workers and craftsmen, there also appears a rare sidelight on
the illnesses of servants. He had observed not a few servants at
court who complained of pain caused by the stone, and he
agreed with their own attribution of this to the 'constant standing'.[81] Ramazzini believed that his three court diseases were all
related, and could develop into one another or be present in
one and the same patient. He also considered that gout and kidney stones were hereditary.[82] Away from the palace, military
campaigns brought the threat of epidemics, in particular ma-
lignant fevers and dysentery, in consequence of the putrid air,
lack of food, and infected water. The prince should thus keep
away from the foot soldiers as far as possible, and on long

marches take his own supply of water in glass vessels.[83]

Although Ramazzini's treatise was frequently reprinted and much quoted, his trio of court diseases did not establish a standard classification any more than Lobera's quartet had done. Other authors mostly went their own way, and in some cases widened the spectrum of court diseases considerably. For Alberti, the most important of court diseases was still the excess of blood which Galen had observed among the rich, and which could lead to diseases of the head, chest, stomach, and extremities, as well as many kinds of fever. Apart from this, he refers to the frequent incidence of catarrh in the head and chest, and disorders of the bowel and abdomen.[84] In Carl's view, the upper classes and the rich suffer from their earliest youth onwards from innumerable fevers, haemorrhages and painful diseases, stomach disorders, various 'fluxes', and pains in the limbs.[85] Their womenfolk are more prone to miscarriages and other obstetric complications.[86] Even the lists of typical court diseases given by Langhans and Tissot, despite many generalities, diverge significantly from one another.

Langhans specifies nervous and hypochondriacal illnesses, rheumatic troubles and gout, obstructions of the liver and spleen, dropsy, skin rashes, apoplexy, piles, and, in women, disruption of menstruation and white discharges.[87] Tissot lists the total undermining of the nervous system and digestion, constipation, acidification of the body fluids, a tendency to feverishness, enhanced susceptibility to air and weather, headaches arising from stomach disorders, sensitivity of the eyes, smallpox, gout, tuberculosis, obstruction of the internal organs (particularly of the liver and stomach exit), formation of gravel in the kidneys, and, finally, nervous diseases; and in women, again, menstrual disorders, premature births, and the white flux.[88] In Mai's view, there were essentially ten different manifestations of the unhealthy 'sharpness' of the bodily fluids of those at court: headaches and migraine; corpulence; sudden death; piles; pains in the joints, particularly gout; damage to the bladder; ascites; various women's diseases; psychic illnesses; and carbuncles and skin rashes.[89]

This survey shows that between the sixteenth and the end of the eighteenth century no fixed and generally accepted canon of court diseases had been established. Indeed, syphilis, the earliest real 'court disease', later on ceases to feature among the wide range of *morbi aulici*. Admittedly in 1840, the most recent author, Rohatzsch, refers to syphilis as 'mal du cour', and remarks that it was particularly rife at smaller courts because of the general boredom that prevailed there.[90] In contrast, arthritis and gout, especially of the feet, seen since the Middle Ages as a disease of the wealthy ruling classes, had from the outset been assigned a secure place among the court diseases, which it retained throughout.[91] The same applies to digestive disorders, and to diseases of the stomach and bowels in general,[92] and holds true to a certain extent for apoplexy and for piles; whereas kidney stones, for example, tend to fall into the background in the course of time, while nervous diseases and gynaecological problems are given greater prominence. Other diseases are considered especially prevalent at courts only by a single author. Tissot, for example, mentions smallpox and tuberculosis, and Johann Storch identifies oedema of the legs as amongst the most important, ascribing its prevalence to the 'protracted periods of enforced standing' as well as to long rides and much travelling. Indeed, he considers standing equally one of the chief causes of gout, in contrast to current aetiology which dealt purely in terms of humoral pathology.[93]

To recapitulate, the spectrum of diseases covered by the term *morbi aulici* is shifting and hard to define. The reasons for this are obvious, and, moreover, are frequently articulated by the authors themselves: diseases considered court diseases also afflict people other than courtiers, in so far as they live under similar conditions.[94] Thus, courtiers and the rich are often classed together, and Juncker draws a comparison between courtiers and scholars, because both take too little exercise. Langhans expressly emphasizes that the rich and the ruling classes are constituted exactly the same as the poor. 'The diseases afflicting the people of the court and the beau monde have therefore much in common with the diseases of the lowliest people.' However, because 'their causes are very different, the same disease in one kind of person is far harder to relieve, and far more dangerous than in the other'.[95] That the rich and high-ranking made extremely difficult patients was an unchallenged commonplace of medicine at this period. In 1701 Ramazzini devoted an academic oration to the thesis that medical intervention had greater success with simple folk than with those of high rank, or princes, and in 1731, Alberti wrote a dissertation entitled *On the Difficulty of Health-care for the Rich*.[96]

The counterfoil: the healthy peasant

When the discussion of court diseases began, there was an absence of contrasting glimpses of other spheres of life. The first references to these other life-styles are brief and usually incidental. Ramazzini, for example, observes that gout is hardly ever seen among the peasants in the countryside or among artisans in towns because they take sufficient exercise. According to Alberti, country dwellers are so healthy without recourse to medicaments because physical labour ensures adequate excretion, and, according to Juncker, artisans, peasants, and carters are less afflicted by noxious 'phlegm', because they eat more frugally and undergo much physical exertion. Bacmeister is convinced that, because of the totally wrong diet eaten there, disease is much more prevalent at courts than in the cottages of the peasants and the poor.[97] Well before the middle of the eighteenth century, such marginal notes give way to an idyllic detailed portrayal of the healthy countryman. The first example of this is provided by Johann Samuel Carl. He draws a picture of country dwellers who fall ill far less than the rich, despite living in rugged, even miserable, conditions. They overcome disease more easily, live longer, and have more children because they live in moderation and peace, and observe the correct balance between work, food, and sleep.[98] The constant 'sickliness' so prevalent among the 'high-ranking and the wealthy' is scarcely to be found among them, and the great variety of haemorrhages, fevers, and painful complaints which plague the *jeunesse dorée* are unknown. Disease remains unfamiliar to them well into their sixties, seventies, or even eighties. Gout, hypochondria, kidney stones, and apoplexy are only rarely observed among the fortunate country dwellers, and, despite coarse food, sour beer, and cold drinks, they complain far less than the upper classes of stomach ailments, and their womenfolk suffer less from white discharges, menstrual irregularities, and miscarriages.[99] Among a thousand peasants, in Carl's opinion, a doctor would find little employment, and would be kept busier at a court of only fifty to a hundred souls.[100]

Langhans's picture of his native Switzerland is remarkably similar.[101] For Tissot, though, the ideal is already under threat. In the wake of Rousseau, he attacks the progressive alienation from the simple life, which inevitably entails a corresponding increase in disease, and which has recently begun to affect even the peasants. He looks back to a time when they were all as healthy as nowadays only a few savages are, but since many of them, employed as servants and soldiers, have brought city habits back to the villages, they have become much more susceptible to disease. None the less, Tissot considers that the peasantry is still the class of society that enjoys the best conditions to ensure continued health. In common with many other authors, the comparison he draws on the basis of the six non-naturals between the man of quality and the countryman comes down completely in favour of the latter. Although the upper classes live in spacious high-ceilinged rooms, they spend most of the time cooped up in them, and also must breathe in the polluted urban air, which they poison further by smoking. On the other hand, the peasants spend a lot of time working in the fresh air, so that the disadvantages of their cramped low rooms, whose stink and lack of cleanliness Tissot does not attempt to deny, hardly have any detrimental effect on them.[102] By contrast, according to Carl, at court, faulty diet is already present in childhood, and lays the foundation for many kinds of diseases. He contrasts the children of simple working folk, who grow up healthy on a diet of bread and water, milk, soup, cheese, and beer, with those of the upper classes, who are fed on meat and wine, fat, and spices, even on tea and coffee, but no bread, for fear of developing a 'peasant ruddiness'. 'What, then, do well-born children look like? Girls and boys alike resemble nothing so much as dainty wax dolls, delicately coloured with a touch of rose-petal tint.'[103] In Langhans's opinion, small children at court are given too many sweet foods, instead of milky dishes, vegetables, fruit, barley, and rice, and too much gruel and broth, which produce acidosis, wind, and other digestive disorders, while the older children get too much meat and highly spiced food, which leads to 'extremely virulent, acute, putrid and inflammatory bilious fevers' as well as to other chronic and debilitating diseases.[104]

There is also general agreement that peasants are at an advantage over courtiers in regard to other points of health theory. As far as physical activity is concerned, Ramazzini, Alberti, and Juncker had already drawn attention to this, and Langhans is equally convinced that the excellent health enjoyed from the outset by peasant children is based on plenty of exercise as well as on the general frugality of their life-style.[105] Tissot writes that, in contrast to the custom at court, peasants sleep at the right time, without violent emotion or overloaded stomachs, and thus find in their slumbers a restorative effect which their social superiors seek in vain. They have no problems at all with their bodily excretions, and, finally, they are free from vanity, ambition, and other unhealthy passions. To put it another way, while the upper classes are kept in a constant state of tension by the great variety in their environment and the many passions which beset their minds, the peasant, with a few tasks to carry out in his simple world, is spared such excitement.[106] According to Tissot, the various stomach and bowel disorders, which make martyrs of the upper classes 'in consequence of their fashionable amusements, their sensuality and luxurious indulgence', are almost completely unknown in village communities, as are smallpox, gout, and pulmonary tuberculosis.[107] Although he cannot avoid conceding that the scabies is more prevalent there than at court, he nevertheless makes every effort, as may be seen from his earlier remarks about the living quarters of the peasantry, to avoid blurring his ideal picture by qualifications of any sort.[108] Thus, he believes that the 'savages' must still be very healthy on account of the fresh air, and, if peasants should over-exert themselves, then they certainly only do so in the service of rich men! Nevertheless, Tissot does not go as far as to recommend upper-class society to decamp *en masse* to the countryside and live like savages or ploughmen. They should simply take more to heart the value of fresh air, physical activity, and the natural divisions of the day. He also posits a 'happy medium, best calculated to promote health, between the coarse food of the ploughman and the rich but debilitating diet of the wealthy and prominent bourgeois'.[109]

By the eighteenth century, the ideal of a happy rustic life, the contrast between town and country, between princely palace and peasant cottage, was already part of a long tradition, which went back to the ancients' weariness with cities and civilization and the celebration in pastoral of the simple life as lived by peasants and shepherds, which had produced its own literary forms.[110] From the Renaissance onwards, the antithesis between court and countryside became also the key *topos* of moralistic criticism of court life.[111] In the main, health and sickness were aspects of these contrasting life-styles hardly touched upon. The widely read author Antonio de Guevara praises healthy country air, and, in 1616, Aegidius Albertinius lists among the nine 'vices' of courtiers 'great immoderation in eating and drinking'; yet the figure of the peasant as the personification of a country life not only simple and happy but also healthy does not appear in their works.[112] This more specific inference was first drawn by the physician Hippolytus Guarinonius in his monumental work on people's reckless treatment of their own health, published in 1610. In contrast to the 'nobleman', who is 'always thick-witted and sick', the peasants in their isolated villages and mountains

> through hard work keep their health and strength until they are eighty, ninety, a hundred or more, and retain into extreme old age such bodily strength as is not to be found in the offspring of gentlemen while they are still young.

Guarinonius then anticipates a theme which was only examined in detail by medical authors from about 1740, as our quotations from Carl, Langhans, and Tissot show.[113]

The theme developed against a background of an intellectual evolution, whereby the general image of happy rural life, which in the early years of the Enlightenment was still confined within the framework of literary conventions, became, from about 1760, a contributory factor in many widespread and interrelated strands of thought among people as diverse as Rousseau, the agronomists, the physiocrats, and the 'rural educationalists'.[114] These tendencies find clear expression in Ackermann's revision of Ramazzini's work on occupational diseases. Ramazzini himself had in 1700 portrayed the peasant's life fairly realistically. He made no mention of the especially good health of the country people. He observed the relative rarity of gout, but balanced that by including many other diseases, the result of harsh toil and a wretched standard of living.[115] In 1780, Ackermann takes over this chapter on the peasants with a few omissions and amendments, but also adds an introduction extolling the moral and physical health of country folk, undamaged by the temptations of civilization. Thus, we read of the peasants 'feeding themselves from the land, frugally and yet adequately'; we are told that there is

> no other section of the population of Europe less infected by the vices which have made their home among us, by the taste for luxury so destructive of body and soul, and by the dread-

ful consequences of dissipation, lechery and debauchery.[116]

Tissot chooses to emphasize one or other of these divergent perspectives on country life according to the audience he is addressing. In the book he published in 1770 on the diseases of the rich and high-ranking, an almost unqualified idealization of country life is put forward as a model and a corrective. In his earlier and widely read *Avis au peuple sur sa santé*, a health manual for ordinary working people, the emphasis is distinctly different. He discusses a whole series of common causes of illness in the countryside, but also underlines several features of a peasant's life favourable to health, which were meant to serve as an example to town dwellers.[117] However, there were no balancing advantages of life in town – or indeed at court – to draw to the attention of country folk.

The health of the prince and his government

Discussion of ill-health at court must also include the question of whether the health of the ruler had any important bearing on the State he ruled and the stability of the government. Ramazzini, in the course of a first chapter devoted entirely to this topic, refers to the old, classical comparison of State and ruler with the body and the head or heart as the parts on whose health the rest of the body depends.[118] If the ruler is laid low by some disease, the laws and well-being of the State are similarly afflicted; or, as others have it, 'peoples are like the princes who rule over them'.[119] Only a healthy ruler possesses the necessary authority to impose obedience on his subjects.[120] In following the counsels of his personal physician, the ruler is not only promoting the welfare of his subjects, but also giving them a good model for their own lives. Immoderate eating and drinking endangers the mental and physical capabilities necessary for a ruler. Extreme corpulence, to which, in Ramazzini's judgement, rulers were more inclined than other people, not only makes them mentally sluggish, but loses them the respect of their subjects. The people despise, even hate their ruler; and a direct threat to the stability of the regime is posed by the infertility which often accompanies obesity.[121]

The decisive argument which Ramazzini and Alberti use to try to persuade the ruler to take to heart the exhortations of the medical profession is an appeal to his own interest in the maintenance of stable government. Half a century later, this is superseded by a very different argument: Langhans postulates a certain obligation on rulers towards their subjects:

> Do not such people, on whose health, good spirits, and long life the well-being of so many of their fellow men depends, deserve that we should beg them in the most pressing terms to take care of these things, and exhort them to forsake, or change for the better, a way of life which often leads not only to their own ruin but also to the ruin of an entire state.[122]

The shift in perspective which this passage implies will be examined in fuller detail in the pages which follow.

The middle-class doctor and life at court

Most works on court diseases or the health of princes were written by doctors who were, at least part time, body-physicians. Their office thus afforded them an intimate acquaintance with life at court. Down to the early years of the eighteenth century, they accepted this way of life as a fixed phenomenon which was not only unalterable but also self-justifying. It did not occur to them to make a candid and radical condemnation of court lifestyle. Instead, they confined themselves to prudent advice as to how its detrimental consequences might be mitigated. In his health guide written for Duke Eberhard of Württemberg in 1538, Johann Stockar points out to his noble readers that it would be a good thing if, in accordance with the rules of health, they were to confine themselves to a single dish at each meal; but he immediately goes on to add that, since the duke is not used to this, and it is appropriate to 'the dignity of a prince' to have a variety of delicacies upon the table, they should at least try to start with easily digestible dishes first and eat the less digestible ones afterwards.[123]

A century and a half later, Waldschmiedt speaks pityingly of court life as a 'splendid misery'. Those unfamiliar with the court envy those who live there, but, in reality, they live a wretched life exposed to innumerable unhealthy influences. In the eyes of a doctor, there can be no more regrettable sight. Indeed, many causes of disease, such as staying awake at night, suppression of the processes of excretion, compression of the abdomen and chest, keeping the head uncovered, and violent emotions, especially fear, grief, and ambition, are unlikely ever to be eliminated from life at court.[124] The general over-supply of food and drink at court seems to Georg Ernst Stahl 'right and fitting', and Ramazzini well understands that princes, in defiance of medical advice, must devote themselves to governmental duties until midnight, and then compensate by sleeping late in the morning. His aim is simply to ensure that rulers should at least make their evening meal earlier and more frugal, and not to go to sleep straight afterwards.[125]

In Alberti, however, such extremely allusive and indirect disapproval of the unhealthy life of the court is already being replaced by frank criticism. He does not shrink from observing that courtiers can hardly be said to carry out their duties satisfactorily, but rather give themselves over to feasting, idling, and dancing with such abandon that one might think that they wished to kill themselves as swiftly as possible. Many actually carouse the whole night through, and sleep in the daytime.[126] A generation later, Langhans, the city physician of Berne, sarcastically describes a noble lady spending all day and half the night in sumptuous meals, at the gaming table, or pursuing sexual intrigues.[127] Coming from a republican Swiss who was not himself a body-physician, this is perhaps not particularly surprising. All the more striking, though, is the unusually sharp, not to say cynical, tone adopted at the end of the century by Franz Anton Mai, personal physician to the Elector Palatine. He makes no bones about comparing the frequency of sudden death at court with that in fattened-up geese, and sums up his impressions of life at court by saying that one would think that one were in a madhouse, describing with relish the repellent symptoms of disease that princes display in consequence of their luxurious life-style.[128]

The attitude of doctors towards rulers thus undergoes a distinct change in the course of the eighteenth century: humble discretion gives way to a growing self-assertiveness, understanding for a way of life unhealthy but legitimate in view of the rank of the ruler rapidly disappears, cautious criticism of court life turns into undisguised polemic. There is also a change in the arguments used by doctors to convince rulers of the value of a healthy life-style. Ramazzini and Alberti had still been appealing to rulers' self-interest when they pointed out the connection between their personal health and the stability of their rule. Langhans reverses the argument, positing the right of the subjects to a healthy ruler, and making the responsibilities owed to his subjects the basis of a ruler's duty to maintain his own health. This new line of argument did not, it is true, strengthen the doctor's position at all: for good health, which for the less exalted ranks of society was of great importance, indeed essential to survival, while it might be necessary for hunting and fighting, did not otherwise figure particularly in the value system of the nobility. In Christian Gotthilf Salzmann's novel *Carl von Carlsberg*, the hero's mother, an officer's wife, addresses the following harangue to her son, who wants to marry a middle-class girl and enthuses about her healthiness:

> What does health matter to a nobleman when he is considering marriage? If you want to make a good match, you must go for lineage and money. Let the bourgeois and the peasants value their good health, for they have nothing better to prize. But for anyone of good family, health is a mere trifle.[129]

So when Langhans demands of rulers that they should take care of their health because their subjects have a right to expect them to be fit for their duties, he is, in the spirit of the Enlightenment, implicitly making them subject to bourgeois values.

The change I have outlined hints at a shift of emphasis in the eighteenth century in the relationship between the physician and his highly placed patients, at least at the level of basic attitudes. Is it possible to conclude from such general statements that there was a corresponding change in the personal interaction of doctor and patient? Claudia Huerkamp has suggested that, well into the nineteenth century, an educated doctor's patients contained a preponderance of his social superiors or at least equals, and that he remained in a position of subordination and total economic dependence on them, not least because of the limited range of effective treatments available to him. The patient remained in control. Not until fundamental progress in diagnosis and therapy had greatly altered and enhanced the authority of doctors and produced a massive increase in demand for medical services, were the roles to be reversed, and the 'modern' doctor–patient relationship created.[130]

This scenario requires modification in various respects, to say nothing of the fact that the factors mentioned by Huerkamp could not have come into play before the second half of the nineteenth century. Doubtless there is evidence that highly placed patients continued to treat doctors as servants into the nineteenth century – although the clientele of academically trained doctors was by no means drawn so exclusively from the nobility and *haute bourgeoisie* as is maintained. Thus, we read, for example, in Georg Ernst Stahl's textbook of practical medicine, published by Johann Storch in 1745, that

> sometimes great men and wealthy people hold their doctors in no higher esteem than a day labourer, so that it is a question of 'Before I give the doctor his money, he must wait for it, and put everything right: it won't hurt him if he sits up a night or two.'[131]

Even after 1800 doctors are still stressing their complete financial dependence on their patients, taking exception to the fact that their colleagues sometimes allow themselves to be treated like lackeys by noblemen, and complaining that their patients ignore their advice on the basis of their own reading and amateurish dabbling in medical knowledge.[132]

These statements are witness to the fact that doctor and high-ranking patient retained their old roles into the early part of the nineteenth century, but also – and this should not be overlooked – that these laments about their conditions included a revolt against the original subordinate position of the doctor, which they were no longer willing to accept unquestioningly. It is no coincidence that these complaints surface in the eighteenth century, just when doctors are taking up a sharper and more uncompromising position in their assessment of life at court. The doctor, both as a professional man and as a citizen, is beginning to lay claim to a new sovereignty in relation to his high-ranking patients, and individual doctors begin to act accordingly. The rationalist theologian Karl Friedrich Bahrdt attacked the famous Johann Georg Zimmermann for having failed to take the necessary measures in treating Frederick the Great before his patient's death; and set out in contrast what would have been the real duty of a physician:

> You should have told the king, not by hints, but in so many

37

words, that he was killing himself, and rendering all forms of therapy ineffective. You ought to have taken courage and said straight out to the king, as befits a man of honour, 'Yes, Sire. I can help you, I want to help you. Of course, I don't yet know how advanced is the incipient destruction of the mechanics of your body....But the certainty, and even the possibility, that my treatment will work, Sire, rests on one condition which depends on your own free will. I must be the one to give orders in your kitchen. And I must be present midday and evening, and allowed to make sure that you are served nothing other, and no more, than what I have prescribed after the most careful consideration.... But if it is not possible to grant this, I must tell you frankly, without further discussion, that I can be of no use to you at all, and that I would be acting dishonestly, were I to allow myself to continue to accept payment from you for so much as another hour.' Thus, Sir, should you have addressed this patient, and, if he had refused to listen to you, you should have gone back home and left him to another doctor.[133]

When in 1784 the eminent Berlin doctor Ernst Ludwig Heim fell into disfavour with the Princess Amalia for no very solid reason, he decided never to visit the palace again, and certainly

never to accept any more 'Highnesses' as patients. To an upright man, the honour may well be a matter of indifference, and, as for the money, one must earn it in bitterness, bowing and scraping, and telling untruths to get it. There is nothing like my own kind of people: that is where I wish my practice to be in future.[134]

When, five years later, a lady-in-waiting sent him word that the princess wished to speak with him, he 'declined to appear before her Royal Highness, unless he received an order through a footman'. Then the lady-in-waiting appeared in person with a polite request, whereupon he complied, and was received most graciously by the princess for an interview which lasted three-quarters of an hour.[135]

In 1820, Prince Karl zu Schwarzenberg, the victor in the Battle of the Nations at Leipzig in 1814, invited Samuel Hahnemann, who practised in Leipzig, to come to Prague to treat him homeopathically for hemiplegia following a stroke. Hahnemann excused himself on grounds of age from travelling so far, and pleaded that he had existing patients to whom he owed a sacred duty to remain at hand.[136] He suggested instead that he begin treatment by sending written instructions, until the prince was in a position to come and consult him in Leipzig. In the event, the seriously ill prince undertook the strain of the journey himself in order to be able to consult Hahnemann personally.[137]

The striking sense of professional freedom and independence which emerges from these episodes was probably shared by at least some other German doctors of the period. Indeed, the Frankfurt doctor Salomon Friedrich Stiebel praised these very attitudes in a poem he composed in 1839 to celebrate a colleague's golden jubilee in the profession. The first stanza contains the line:

Our art of healing is, above all others, free.

and the third:

What the courtier dare not say,
The doctor freely tells the prince.[138]

All the examples in this section support the conclusion that Claudia Huerkamp's explanation of the doctor's movement from subordinate to a dominating position *vis-à-vis* his socially superior patients is both oversimplified and telescoped in time. Since the practical factors she adduces (progress in diagnosis and therapy and a growing demand for medical treatment) only began to take effect in the second half of the nineteenth century, they cannot have been at work in the early stages of this process in the eighteenth and early nineteenth century, although they certainly became decisive later, after other forces had set the change in motion. These forces are to be sought in the Enlightenment, in the self-image of the bourgeoisie moulded by it and proud of its emancipation. Initially the doctor liberated himself as citizen from the role of servant in relation to highly placed patients: only later did a growing professional capacity and greater calls on his services bring him a still further increase in self-confidence and prestige which secured him the dominant position in the modern doctor–patient relationship.

Health doctrines and the early modern state

Finally, there still remains for discussion the place of the theme of court diseases within the evolution of dietetics as a specialized branch of medicine, a process whose origin can be traced back to Antiquity, yet was not completed until modern times. It is noticeable that throughout Antiquity and the Middle Ages this speciality only covered individual stages of life – unweaned infants, children, the old – or transient situations – pregnancy, convalescence, travel, wet-nursing – but was not yet applied to distinct occupations or entire life-styles. The only partial exception to this was the case of intellectual workers. It is no coincidence that this was the first profession whose harmful consequences were of interest to the doctors of Antiquity. From the fifteenth century onwards, there developed a specialized literature on the health of intellectual workers.[139] Some of these writings explicitly included those holding administrative or political office,[140] but these were the only narrower target groups mentioned until, in the eighteenth century, some concentrated on the clergy and religious.[141] In the sixteenth century, there developed, alongside a corresponding body of literature for princes and courtiers, one for soldiers. Beyond these three groups, no specialized medical literature of comparable scale was built up in early modern times. This is particularly true of those occupations involving physical work, which entered the purview of doctors quite early, but only hesitantly. It is significant that Ramazzini's first comprehensive survey, published in 1700, went on being revised and enlarged well into the nineteenth century, whereas only a very few individual studies in occupational medicine of a similar kind appeared during these years.

During the period starting in the sixteenth century when the internal structure of the early-modern State was being systematically built up, the educated doctors were part of the small but influential academic elite, and, in so far as they practised as body-physicians or court doctors, lived in close proximity to the centres of political power. We may venture the hypothesis that they were trying to contribute in their own way to this development of the State by setting out guidelines for the health of those groups on whom the State depended – the ruling princes, the noblemen at court, the military, and the intellectual workers. Ramazzini expressly underlines that 'it is of great moment for the benefit of the state that there should be enough wise and educated people', and therefore that it is important 'that the health of the educated should, as far as possible, be maintained in a good condition, and should be restored if it suffers any setback'.[142] The 'educated' referred to all those who filled posts of importance for the stability of the State, whether as lawyers in the civil service or the courts, as theologians in the Church, teachers in schools or universities, or doctors in the provision of medical care, 'the pillars of the state in the spiritual and secular realms'.[143]

If this interpretation could be confirmed, this previously unnoticed concern to safeguard the health of the people on whom the State depended would sit very logically alongside the efforts of doctors to set up a State health-care service, which have so far been elucidated only in broad outline.[144] Taken together, they would provide a new and more comprehensive picture of the contribution of the medical profession to the development of the early-modern State.

Notes

1. Bernardino Ramazzini, *De principum valetudine tuenda commentatio* (Padua, 1710), reprinted in *Opera omnia, Medica et Physiologica* (Geneva, 1717), pp. 697–782.
2. Bartolomeo Ramazzini, *Bernadini Ramazzini Vita...*, reprinted in ibid. pp.I–LV, XLIV.
3. Bernardino Ramazzini, *De morbis artificum diatriba* (Modena, 1700), reprinted in *Opera omnia*, pp. 470–687.
4. Ibid., p.629; in the German translation, Bernhard Ramazzini, *Untersuchung von den Kranckheiten der Künstler und Handwerker* (Leipzig, 1718), p. 371.
5. Ramazzini, *De principum valetudine tuenda*, p. 773. Later in the century this connection became the subject of independent treatises: for example, Christian Gotthilf Barth, *De morbis ex vitae genere* (Leipzig, 1764); Friedrich Gotthelf Jaessing, *De morbis ex vitae genere* (Leipzig, 1774).
6. Hippocrates, *De diaeta*, ed. Robert Joly (Berlin, 1984), p. 124, 4–17.
7. Ibid., p. 194, 17–21 and p. 200, 23–8.
8. Cf. Rüdiger Vischer, *Das einfache Leben. Wort- und motivgeschichtliche Untersuchungen zu einem Wertbegriff der antiken Literatur* (Göttingen, 1965), p. 44.
9. Hippocrates, *De aere aquis locis*, ed. Hans Diller (Berlin, 1970), pp. 14, 72, 17–74.
10. Cf. R. Vischer, *Das einfache Leben*, pp. 54, 58, 64, 67, 72, 81,

84–5, 87, 92, 113, 150, 159.

11. Cf. Heinrich Buess, 'Die Erforschung der Berufskrankheiten biz zum Beginn des industriellen Zeitalters', in E. W. Bader (ed.), *Handbuch der gesamtem Arbeitsmedizin*, vol. 2, 1 (Berlin, Munich, Vienna, 1961), pp. 15–36.

12. Galen, 'De methodo medendi', in Karl Gottlob Kühn (ed.) *Galeni opera omnia*, vol. 10 (Leipzig, 1825), pp. 783–4.

13. Cf. in general, Werner Friedrich Kümmel, 'Der Homo litteratus und die Kunst, gesund zu leben. Zur Entfaltung eines Zweiges der Diätetik im Humanismus', in Rudolf Schmitz and Gundolf Keil (eds), *Humanismus und Medizin* (Weinheim, 1984), pp. 67–85.

14. The following example taken from a quite different area may clarify this development. Whereas, in the earlier Middle Ages, there had existed special lists of questions for use in confessing monks, and Benedictines in particular, women, the sick and the dying, in the first half of the fifteenth century, Antonius of Florence demanded specialized lists for married people, judges, lawyers, proctors, and notaries, for university graduates, schoolboys, doctors, apothecaries, merchants, knackers, actors, musicians, craftsmen, peasants, priests, canons, nuns, and so on. Cf. Johannes Geffken, *Der Bildercatechismus des fünfzehnten Jahrhunderts* (Leipzig, 1855).

15. For details, see Kümmel, 'Der Homo litteratus', pp. 72–5.

16. Edwin Rosner, 'Ulrich Ellenbog und die Anfänge der Gewerbehygiene', *Sudhoffs Archiv*, vol. 38 (1954), pp. 101–10. This is the earliest treatise on occupational medicine in the strict sense.

17. Edwin Rosner, 'Hohenheims Bergsuchtmonographie', *Medizinhistorisches Journal*, vol. 16 (1981), pp. 20–52.

18. Peter Assion, 'Burkhard von Horneck', in K. Ruh (ed.), *Die deutsche Literatur des Mittelalters. Verfasserlexikon*, vol. 1 (Berlin, New York, 1978), col. 1137–9, 1138.

19. See Claus Uhlig, *Hofkritik im England des Mittelalters und der Renaissance. Studien zu einem Gemeinplatz der europäischen Moralistik* (Berlin, New York, 1973). The quotation is found on p. 211.

20. Ibid., pp. 219, 227.

21. Constantinus Africanus, 'De omnium morborum, qui homini accidere possunt, cognitione et curatione', in *Opera* (Basle, 1536), pp. 1–167, 137; cited by Luis Lobera de Avila, *Libro delle quatro infermita cortigiane, che sono catarro, gotta, artetica, sciatica: mal di pietre, & di reni: dolore di fianchi, et mal francese..* (Venice, 1558), fol. 43v.

22. Gaspar Torrella, *De dolore in pudendagra* (1500), in Aloysius Luisinus, *Aphrodisiacus, sive de lue venerea...*, vol. 1–2 (Leiden, 1728), vol. 1, col. 501–28, 502 B. A further example for Granada in 1609 is given by Iwan Bloch, *Der Ursprung der Syphilis. Eine medizinische und kulturgeschichtliche Untersuchung* (Jena, 1901), p. 87, fn. 1.

23. Cf. K. H. Rohatzsch, *Die Krankheiten der höheren Stände und Klassen...* (Ulm, 1840), pp. 75–6.

24. Luis Lobera de Avila, *Libro de las quatro enfermedadas cortesanas que son. Catarro. Gota arthetica sciatica. Mal de piedra y de*

rinones & hijada. E mal de buas... ([Toledo], 1544); cited in the Italian version of Pietro Lauro (Venice, 1558), cf. above n. 21.

25. Gottfried Wilhelm Ploucquet, *Initia Bibliothecae Medico-Practicae et Chirurgicae sive Repertorii Medicinae Practicae et Chirurgicae*, vol. 5 (Tübingen, 1795), p. 629; *Idem, Literatura Medica digesta sive Repertorium Medicinae practicae, Chirurgiae atque Rei obstetriciae*, vol. 3 (Tübingen, 1809), p. 137 (s. v. 'Morbus Aulicus. Nobilium'); Johann Samuel Ersch, *Literatur der Medicin seit der Mitte des 18. Jahrhunderts bis auf die neueste Zeit* (Leipzig, 1822), p. 290 ('Krankheiten der Vornehmen und Reichen'); Wilhelm Engelmann, *Bibliotheca Medico-Chirurgica et Anatomico-Physiologica* (Leipzig, 1848), p. 719 (s. v. 'Reiche und Vornehme, Diätetik der Krankheiten derselben'; in the index 'Hofleute, Krankheiten derselben' [p. 698]). Neither catchword appears in the *Supplement* for 1848–67 (Leipzig, 1867).

26. For the survival of ancient dietetics outside academic medicine, see Werner Friedrich Kümmel, 'Georg Groddeck und die Gesundheitslehre der "alten" Medicin', in Helmut Siefert, Frieder Kern, Beate Schuh, and Helmut Grosch (eds), *Groddeck Almanach* (Basle, Frankfurt, 1986), pp. 110–14.

27. Cf. Andreas Körtgen, *Die Gesundheit des Fürsten. Diätetische Vorschriften für eine herausgehobene Menschengruppe von der Antike bis zum Anfang des 20. Jahrhunderts* (Frankfurt, Berne, 1982).

28. For example, Antonio Benivieni, 'De regimine sanitatis ad Laurentium Medicem', ed. Luigi Belloni (Turin, 1951); Johann Stockar, *Ain grundtlichs warhaftigs Regiment/wie man sich mit aller speyss/getranck/und früchten halten sol...An Hertzogen Eberhardt von Wirtemberg...* (s. l., 1538).

29 Friedrich Hoffmann, *Consultationum et Responsorum Medicorum Centuriae tres*, in *Opera omnia*, vols. 1–6 (Geneva, 1748), vol. 4, pp. 1–440. The nobility form c. 10 per cent of the cases; cf. for example *Sectio* I, No. 13 (pp. 19–20), No. 36 (pp. 62–4), Sectio III, No. 12 (pp. 178–9), No. 13 (pp. 179–81), No. 26 (pp. 198–9). Many useful examples are given by Wilhelm Treue, *Mit den Augen ihrer Leibärzte. Von bedeutenden Medizinern und ihren großen Patienten* (Düsseldorf, 1955).

30. Cf. Ramazzini, *De principum valetudine*; Michael Alberti (Praeses), *De diaeta principum*, Med. Diss. (Halle, 1728, Resp.: Johann Cristoph Mentzel); Ivon Johannes Stahl (Praeses), *De longaevitate serenissimorum principum naturaliter possibili...*, Med. Diss. (Erfurt, 1730, Resp.: Mathias Friedrich Joseph Landau); Johann Juncker (Praeses), *De ignobili muco ingrato multorum nobilium hospite*, Med. Diss. (Halle, 1734, Resp.: Clamer Hermann Hoffbauer).

31. Stahl, *De longaevitate*, p. 5.

32. Ramazzini, *De principum valetudine*, pp. 698, 742.

33. For example, Alberti, *De diaeta*, p. 38; Franz Anton Mai (Praeses), *Aulica humorum cacochymia foecunda morborum genetrix*, Med. Diss. (Heidelberg, 1799, Resp.: Johannes Baptista Jonas), p. 24.

34. Michael Alberti, *De morbis aulicis*, Med. Diss. (Halle, 1726, Resp.: Samuel Friebe), p. 13.

35. Alberti, *De diaeta*, pp. 19–20.

36. Ramazzini, *De principum valetudine*, p. 718; Alberti, *De diaeta*, p. 22.

37. Alberti, *De morbis aulicis*, p. 14; cf. also Franz Anton Reis, *De officio medici in itinere principis*, Med. Diss. (Altdorf, 1740).

38. Alberti, *De morbis aulicis*, p. 25; Ramazzini, *De principum valetudine*, p. 715. Cf. also Stahl, *De longaevitate*, pp. 10–11.

39. Stahl, *De longaevitate*, p. 14.

40. Ramazzini, *De principum valetudine*, p. 718.

41. Ibid., p. 716; Alberti, *De diaeta*, p. 20.

42. Ramazzini, *De principum valetudine*, p. 720.

43. Ibid., p. 721; Alberti, *De morbis aulicis*, p. 10.

44. Ramazzini, *De principum valetudine*, p. 726–7.

45. Ibid., pp. 721–3; Alberti, *De diaeta*, p. 25; *De morbis aulicis*, p. 11; Johannes Bacmeister (Praeses) Alberti, *De eo, quod sanitati obest circa diaetam, maxime in aulis*, Med. Diss. (Tübingen, 1736, Resp.: Benedictus Christophilus Duvernoy), pp. 11–14.

46. Ramazzini, *De principum valetudine*, pp. 721, 725, 728; Alberti, *De diaeta*, p. 39.

47. Alberti, *De morbis aulicis*, pp. 11–12; Alberti, *De diaeta*, pp. 28–30; Ramazzini, *De principum valetudine*, pp. 731–2; Bacmeister, *De eo, quod sanitati obest*, pp. 21, 31–3.

48. Bacmeister, *De eo, quod sanitati obest*, p. 31, fn; Ramazzini, *De principum valetudine*, p. 721; Alberti, *De morbis aulicis*, p. 20, emphasizes by contrast the valuable effects of tea, coffee, chocolate, and tobacco in creating a sweat.

49. Körtgen, *Die Gesundheit des Fürsten*, p. 117.

50. Alberti, *De diaeta*, p. 24; cf. p. 29.

51. Juncker, *De ignobili muco*, pp. 22, 27; Ramazzini, *De principum valetudine*, p. 736.

52. Ibid., p. 735.

53. Bacmeister, *De eo, quod sanitati obest*, p. 23; Daniel Langhans, *Von den Krankheiten des Hofes und der Weltleute* (Berne, 1770), p. 107.

54. Juncker, *De ignobili muco*, p. 27; [Simon-André] Tissot, *Von den Krankheiten vornehmer und reicher Personen an Höfen und in großen Städten* (Frankfurt a. M., Leipzig, 1770), pp. 62–3; Alberti, *De morbis aulicis*, p. 16.

55. Langhans, *Von den Krankheiten*, pp. 43–4; Juncker, *De ignobili muco*, p. 19; Alberti, *De morbis aulicis*, p. [30]; Bacmeister, *De eo, quod sanitati obest*, p. 11.

56. Alberti, *De morbis aulicis*, p. [30].

57. Ibid., p. 15, cf. p. 25.

58. Ramazzini, *De principum valetudine*, pp. 736–41: Alberti, *De diaeta*, p. 32; Johann Samuel Carl, *Medicina aulica In einigen nötigen täglich vorkommenden Betrachtungen, Vorstellungen und Anschlägen betreffend die Gesundheitssorge* (vol. 1, Altona, 1740; vol. 2, Frankfurt, Leipzig, 1743), vol. 2, p. 101; Tissot, *Von den Krankheiten*, p. 103.

59. Alberti, *De diaeta*, p. 34; Alberti, *De morbis aulicis*, p. 16.

60. Ramazzini, *De principum valetudine*, p. 742, 744; Alberti, *De morbis aulicis*, p. 17; *De diaeta*, pp. 36–7: Bacmeister, *De eo, quod*

sanitati obest, p. 23; Georg Ernst Stahl, *Propempticon inaugurale de morbis aulicis*, in G. E. Stahl (Praeses), *De frequentia morborum in corpore humano prae brutis*, Med. Diss. (Halle, 1705, Resp.: Erhardus Brunner), p. [38].

61. Ramazzini, *De principum valetudine*, p. 744; Alberti, *De diaeta*, p. 38; Alberti, *De morbis aulicis*, p. 18.

62. Alberti, *De morbis aulicis*, p. 17; Ramazzini, *De principum valetudine*, pp. 744, 749, 763.

63. Mai, *Aulica humorum cacochymia*, pp. 12–13.

64. Lobera de Avila, *Libro delle quatro infermita*, fol. 154r; Alberti, *De morbis aulicis*, pp. 20–1.

65. For example, Langhans, *Von den Krankheiten*, pp. 119, 194.

66. Johann Jakob Waldschmiedt (Praeses), *De morbis aulicis*, Med. Diss. (Marburg, 1686, Resp.: Wilhelm Huldrich Waldschmiedt), pp. 4, 9; Alberti, *De morbis aulicis*, p. 19; Langhans, *Von den Krankheiten*, pp. 69–70; Mai, *Aulica humorum cacochymia*, p. 10. Helmuth Kiesel, *'Bei Hof, bei Höll'. Untersuchungen zur literarischen Hofkritik bei Sebastian Brant bis Friedrich Schiller* (Tübingen, 1979), p. 26.

67. Alberti, *De morbis aulicis*, pp. 26, 18; Alberti, *De diaeta*, pp. 44–6; Ramazzini, *De principum valetudine*, pp. 751, 754.

68. Mai, *Aulica humorum cacochymia*, p. 10.

69. Alberti, *De morbis aulicis*, p. 19; Langhans, *Von den Krankheiten*, pp. 72–3.

70. Ramazzini, *De principum valetudine*, pp. 751, 754–5; Mai, *Aulica humorum cacochymia*, pp. 19, 10; Langhans, *Von den Krankheiten*, p. 102; Alberti, *De diaeta*, p. 45.

71. Alberti, *De diaeta*, pp. 38, 21 (*sensibilis principum natura*), cf. also pp. 22 and 41, and Waldschmiedt, *De morbis aulicis*, p. 10.

72. Carl, *Medicina aulica*, vol. 2, p. 14; cf. also pp. 29, 37.

73. Tissot, *Von den Krankheiten*, pp. 52, 38.

74. Carl, *Medicina aulica*, vol. 1, p. 117; Leopold Fleckles, *Die Krankheiten der Reichen. Diätetische Grundlinien für das höhere und conversationelle Leben* (Vienna, 1834), pp. 11, 78.

75. Langhans, *Von den Krankheiten*, p. 19.

76. Carl, *Medicina aulica*, vol. 1, pp. 321–3; vol. 2, pp. 116, 208.

77. Alberti, *De diaeta*, p. 39; Alberti, *De morbis aulicis*, pp. 31–2.

78. Carl, *Medicina aulica*, vol. 2, p. 95; Tissot, *Von den Krankheiten*, pp. 132, 106ff.

79. Hippolytus Guarinonius, *Die Grewel der Verwüstung menschlichen Geschlechts* (Ingolstadt, 1610), p. 95.

80. Waldschmiedt, *De morbis aulicis*, pp. 5, 13–14.

81. Ramazzini, *De morbis artificum*, p. 598.

82. Ramazzini, *De principum valetudine*, pp. 698, 774–5: for heredity, cf. pp. 733, 755.

83. Ibid., pp. 779–80. Cf. on this theme Johann Michel Segner, *De principum militiam sequentium tuenda valetudine* (Jena, 1734).

84. Alberti, *De morbis aulicis*, p. 8; Alberti, *De diaeta*, pp. 19–20.

85. Carl, *Medicina aulica*, vol. 1, pp. 327, 346; vol. 2, pp. 17 and 180.

86. Ibid., vol. 1, p. 341; vol. 2, p. 128.
87. Langhans, *Von den Krankheiten*, pp. 85ff, 150ff, 163ff, 174ff, 185ff, 191ff, 216ff, 198ff.
88. Tissot, *Von den Krankheiten*, pp. 51–67.
89. Mai, *Aulica humorum cacochymia*, pp. 11–21.
90. Rohatzsch, *Die Krankheiten*, pp. 75–6.
91. Cf. Fleckles, *Die Krankheiten*, p. 149.
92. Rohatzsch, *Die Krankheiten*, p. 39, still describes the stomach as the sole source of the diseases of the upper classes.
93. Johann Storch (ed.), *Praxis Stahliana. Das ist...Georg Ernst Stahls...Collegium Practicum...*, 3rd edition (Leipzig, 1745), p. 1156.
94. Alberti, *De morbis aulicis*, p. 4.
95. Juncker, *De ignobili muco*, pp. 19, 21; Langhans, *Von den Krankheiten*, p. 13.
96. Bernardino Ramazzini, *Oratio III: Felicius curari a Medico popularem gentem, quam Nobiles, et Principes viros*, in *Opera omnia*, pp. 30–44; Michael Alberti (Praeses), *De sanatione divitum difficili*, Med. Diss. (Halle, 1731, Resp.: Elias Trangus).
97. Ramazzini, *De principum valetudine*, p. 777; Alberti, *De morbis aulicis*, p. 25; Juncker, *De ignobili muco*, pp. 9–10; Bacmeister, *De eo, quod sanitati obest*, p. 3.
98. Carl, *Medicina aulica*, vol. 1, pp. 5–6; vol. 2, p. 9; vol. 1, p. 330; vol. 2, pp. 128; 193–4; vol. 1, p. 25.
99. Ibid., vol. 1, pp. 108, 111, 285, 330, 327, 346; vol. 2, pp. 126, 128, 180, 186.
100. Ibid., vol. 1, p. 109.
101. Langhans, *Von den Krankheiten*, pp. 108–9.
102. Tissot, *Von den Krankheiten*, pp. 9–10, 21.
103. Carl, *Medicina aulica*, vol. 1, pp. 325–6.
104. Langhans, *Von den Krankheiten*, pp. 35, 25, 27, 30.
105. Ibid., p. 47.
106. Tissot, *Von den Krankheiten*, pp. 28–30, 37, 39, 42.
107. Ibid., pp. 61, 56–7, 60; Langhans, *Von den Krankheiten*, p. 153, also believes that rheumatic complaints and gout, so common at court, are much rarer among peasants and workers.
108. Tissot, *Von den Krankheiten*, p. 56.
109. Ibid., pp. 24, 27, 88–9, 99.
110. See Carl Joachim Classen, *Die Stadt im Spiegel der Descriptiones und Laudes urbium in der antiken und mittelalterlichen Literatur bis zum Ende des 12. Jahrhunderts* (Hildesheim, New York, 1980), esp. p. 15; Vischer, *Das einfache Leben*, p. 126; Uhlig, *Hofkritik*, pp. 13, 242.
111. Kiesel, *'Bei Hof, Bei Höll'*, p. 321; Uhlig, *Hofkritik*, p. 186.
112. Uhlig, *Hofkritik*, p. 244; Kiesel, *'Bei Hof, bei Höll'*, p. 148.
113. Guarinonius, *Die Grewel*, p. 95; cf. later Fleckles, *Die Krankheiten*, pp. 7–8.
114. Burghard Dedner, 'Vom Schäferleben zur Agrarwirtschaft. Poesie und Ideologie des "Landlebens" in der deutschen Literatur des 18. Jahrhunderts', in K. Garber (ed.), *Europäische Bukolik und Georgik* (Darmstadt, 1976), pp. 347–90, 348.

115. Ramazzini, *De principum valetudine*, p. 777; idem, *De morbis artificum*, pp. 625–31.

116. J. C. G. Ackermann, *Bernhard Ramazzini's...Abhandlung von den Krankheiten der Künstler und Handwerker, neu bearbeitet und vermehret*, 2 vols (Stendal, 1780–3), vol. 1, p. 298.

117. [S. A. A.]Tissot, *Avis au peuple sur sa santé* (Lausanne, 1761), pp. 39–51.

118. Ramazzini, *De principum valetudine*, p. 704; cf. also Körtgen, *Die Gesundheit*, p. 33.

119. Ramazzini, *De principum valetudine*, p. 704; cf. also Alberti, *De diaeta*, p. 11: many other examples are given by Körtgen, *Die Gesundheit*, pp. 38–9.

120. Ramazzini, *De principum valetudine*, pp. 699, 703; Alberti, *De diaeta*, pp. 9, 7; Körtgen, *Die Gesundheit*, p. 34, and Rudolf Hiestand, *Kranker König – kranker Bauer*, in P. Wunderli (ed.), *Der kranke Mensch in Mittelalter und Renaissance* (Düsseldorf, 1986), pp. 61–77, 65.

121. Ramazzini, *De principum valetudine*, pp. 769–71.

122. Langhans, *Von den Krankheiten*, p. VIII.

123. Stockar, *Ain grundtlichs warhaftigs Regiment*, fol. 5v.

124. Waldschmiedt, *De morbis aulicis*, pp. 3–4, 9.

125. Stahl, *Propempticon*, p. [38]; Ramazzini, *De principum valetudine*, p. 744.

126. Alberti, *De morbis aulicis*, pp. 7, 17.

127. Langhans, *Von den Krankheiten*, pp. 55ff.

128. Mai, *Aulica humorum cacochymia*, pp. 14, 10, 11, 13, 16.

129. Christian Gotthilf Salzmann, *Carl von Carlsberg oder über das menschliche Elend*, 6 vols (Leipzig, 1783–8), vol. 2, p. 230.

130. Claudia Huerkamp, *Der Aufstieg der Ärzte im 19. Jahrhundert. Vom gelehrten Stand zum professionellen Experten* (Göttingen, 1985), pp. 131–66.

131. Storch (ed.), *Praxis Stahliana*, p. 86.

132. Cf. Michael Stolberg, *Heilkunde zwischen Staat und Bevölkerung. Angebot und Annahme medizinischer Versorgung in Oberfranken im frühen 19. Jahrhundert*. Med. Diss. (Munich, 1986), p. 250.

133. Wilhelm Treue, *Mit den Augen ihrer Leibärtze*, pp. 364–5, relying on Bahrdt's pamphlet, *Mit dem Herrn von Zimmermann...deutsch gesprochen* (Berlin, 1790).

134. Georg Wilhelm Kessler (ed.), *Der alte Heim. Leben und Wirken Ernst Ludwig Heim's...*, ed. 2 (Leipzig, 1846), p. 281.

135. Ibid., p. 299.

136. Státni oblastní archiv v Treboni, Familienarchiv Schwarzenberg, Orlik. Sig.: Feldmarschall Karl Schwarzenberg I – 26-3 (Report of Schwarzenberg's envoys on their conversations in Leipzig from 9 to 12 March 1820).

137. For a detailed discussion of this case, cf. Walter Nachtmann, '"..Ach, wie viel verliere auch ich an Ihm." Die Behandlung des Fürsten Karl Philipp von Schwarzenberg durch Samuel Hahnemann und ihre Folgen', in *Jahrbuch des Instituts für Geschichte*

der Medizin der Robert Bosch Stiftung, vol. 6 (1989) pp. 93–110.

138. *Der Grünborn. Lieder von Frankfurter Ärztem. Gesammelt zum 50. Stiftungsfeste des Ärztlichen Vereins zu Frankfurt a. M.* (Frankfurt, 1895), pp. 14–15.

139. Cf. Kümmel, 'Der Homo litteratus'; idem, 'Kopfarbeit und Sitzberuf: Das früheste Paradigma der Arbeitsmedizin', in *Jahrbuch des Instituts für Geschichte der Medizin der Robert Bosch Stiftung*, vol. 6 (1989) pp. 53–70.

140. Cf. Guilielmus Gratarolus, *De literatorum et eorum qui magistratibus funguntur conservanda praeservandaque valetudine...* (Basle, 1555; Paris, 1562); also in Henricus Rantzovius, *De conservanda valetudine*, 3rd edition (Frankfurt, 1591), and subsequent editions until 1617; English translation: *A Direction for the Health of Magistrates and Studentes...* (London, 1574); Michael Alberti (Praeses), *De litteratorum et honoratorum sanitate tuenda et restituenda*, Med. Diss. (Halle, 1746, Resp.: Ulrich Christoph Salchow). Cf. also Vopiscus Fortunatus Plempius, *De togatorum valetudine tuenda commentatio* (Brussels, 1670). Cf. Sebastiano de Soto, *Discorso de los enfermidades, per que pueden los religiosos depor la clausura* (Madrid, 1639): Heinrich Bernhard Ascheberg, *De morbis religiosorum eorumque cura praeservatoria* (Erfurt, 1702); Johann Heinrich Salmuth, *Dissertatio medica de morbis concionatorum*, Jena, 1707 (A reference kindly provided by Professor L. W. Forster); Michael Alberti (Praeses), *De mystarum morbis praeservandis*, Med. Diss. (Halle, 1721, Resp.: J. F. Heinigke); Johann Andreas Fischer (Praeses), *De religiosorum sanitate tuenda et restituenda*, Med. Diss. (Erfurt, 1721, Resp.: Friedrich Gotthold Caselius); Johann Ludwig Buxtorf, *Cura valetudinis religiosorum...* (Basle, 1768): Johann Georg Friedrich Franz, *Der Artzt der Gottesgelehrten...* 2nd edition (Leipzig, 1770).

141. The earliest monograph is probably Anton Schneeberger, *De bona militum valetudine conservanda liber* (Cracow, 1564); numerous titles are given by G. W. Ploucquet, *Initia*, vol. 5, pp. 557–61; *Literatura Medica*, vol. 3, pp. 44–6, 149–50; Ersch, *Literatur der Medicin*, cols 162–3; *Index-Catalogue of the Library of the Surgeon-General's Office. United States Army*, ser. I, vol. 6 (Washington, 1885), pp. 642–6; vol. 8 (1887), pp. 1049–53.

142. Ramazzini, *Untersuchung*, pp. 424–5; Ramazzini, *De morbis artificum*, p. 650.

143. Heinrich Caspar Abel, *Wohlerfahrner Leib-Medicus der Studenten...* (Leipzig, 1698), 'Zuschrifft', fol. 5v. Cf. also for physicians, Michael Alberti (Praeses), *De tuenda reipublicae salute per medicorum bona consilia*, Med. Diss. (Halle, 1745, Resp.: Heinrich Berck).

144. See, for this, Friedrich-Wilhelm Schwartz, *Idee und Konzeption der frühen territorialstaatlichen Gesundheitspflege in Deutschland ('Medizinische Polizei') in der ärztlichen und staatswissenschaftlichen Fachliteratur*, Med. Diss. (Frankfurt, 1973).

2

Medicine at the Papal Court in the Sixteenth Century

Richard Palmer

Biographical interest in papal doctors began as early as 1696, when Prospero Mandosio published his Θεατρον, a theatre to display the doctors of the Christian pontiffs. Mandosio's aim was to defend the dignity of medicine against its detractors. Calling on to his stage the papal doctors of the past, he sought to show that they were men of virtue and learning, and, no less important, that they came from good families.[1] Mandosio's book was held in esteem until 1784, when a Prefect of the Vatican Archives, Gaetano Marini, was so outraged by its inaccuracies – many of Mandosio's doctors had never served a Pope at all – that he published two bulky volumes of additions and corrections under the title *Degli archiatri pontifici*. With the Vatican archives at his command, Marini easily exposed the flimsy vaudeville of Mandosio's theatre. However, he was not successful in his second aim, which was to encourage further research. Unremitting in its recital of names, dates, and sepulchral epitaphs, his book was worthy, but dull. Marini recognized as much. In its preface he offered his readers the cold comfort that, suffer as they might, at least they did not have to endure what he had gone through in the course of research: he did not know how his patience had survived so tedious and thankless a task. As for the results, what little could be said of many of the doctors was, he admitted, scarcely worth knowing, and boring to read.[2] Marini's words undervalued his great achievement in making available a wealth of reliable information, but it cannot be denied that his book killed its subject stone dead, and two centuries of almost unbroken silence have ensued.

In looking once more at the theme of medicine at the papal court, the aim here is not to add further biographical details of papal doctors, though additions and corrections to Marini's work could indeed be made.[3] This chapter is concerned less with individuals than with the offices of papal physician and surgeon, their place and function in the palatine household, and their significance for medical careers in a period of change as Renaissance gave way to Counter-Reformation. It is also concerned with the relationship between the Popes, a group of patients whose ailments are recorded in exceptional detail, and the doctors who sought to advise them. While Renaissance Rome is at last attracting much scholarly interest,[4] there is still no adequate study of the papal court. This chapter can therefore make only a preliminary approach to its subject.

Rome and the papal court

'What is Rome without the court?' This question, posed in 1543,[5] was purely rhetorical. The court dominated the life of Rome in every respect, economic, social, political, and intellectual. Rome at this time was a small city. The census of 1526–7 had revealed a population in the order of only 54,000, and the sack of Rome in 1527 had diminished it further.[6] With no manufacturing industry to speak of, Rome relied on the employment offered at court or in the range of service industries, including banking and the fine arts, which the court promoted. The court (*curia Romana*) included the complex bureaucracy which administered the Church throughout the Catholic world, dealing with appointments to office and appeals in legal disputes, and dispensing spiritual favours. By the 1520s centralization and bureaucratization had swollen the numbers at court to over 2,000, including in that figure the papal household (*famiglia palatina*) which was partly distinct in that employment in the Church's civil service did not necessarily mean access to the Vatican palace and membership of the papal entourage.[7]

In addition to its international role in the spiritual government of the Church, Rome was also the temporal capital of the papal states, which extended from south of Rome to beyond Bologna in the north. One of the triumphs of the Renaissance papacy was its successful exploitation of these states as a source of revenue. The resulting income was made to compensate for the spiritual revenues lost in the fifteenth century as a result of the Great Schism and in the sixteenth as a result of the Reformation. By 1600 the papal states were providing nearly 80 per cent of the Pope's income.[8] The worldliness of the Renaissance papacy, most notorious in the pontificate of Rodrigo Borgia, Pope Alexander VI (1492–1503), is partly to be explained in terms of these temporal preoccupations, and in the Renaissance period there was a large measure of similarity between the Roman court and those of other, purely secular, rulers. Although Baldassare Castiglione chose to set *The Book of the Courtier* in the small court of Urbino in the year 1507, he was no less at home in the court of Rome: several of his characters were also members of the papal household, or would later become so.[9] The courtly, erudite culture which he described and idealized was no less the prevailing ethos in Rome than it was in Urbino. Indeed, the career prospects open to humanists in the Roman Curia, the opportunity for scholarship offered by the Vatican library, the lure of the remains of ancient Rome, and the patronage of Popes and Cardinals made the city perhaps the leading centre of Renaissance humanism at the opening of the sixteenth century.

Just as the Popes were temporal as well as spiritual rulers, so the Cardinals saw themselves in secular terms as princes of the Church. While the palatine Cardinals enjoyed the right to live alongside the Pope in the Vatican palace, the remaining members of the college lived separately, maintaining large households of their own and contributing to the new, Renaissance face of Rome through their palaces. The households of twenty-one Cardinals were recorded in the census of 1526–7. On average they contained 134 members, the largest being that of Alessandro Farnese, later Paul III, which numbered 306.[10] The humanist Paolo Cortesi in his *De cardinalatu* (Castel Cortesiano, 1510) argued that a large household and a sumptuous palace were necessary to maintain the dignity of the Cardinalate. He offered serious and useful answers to questions such as 'Why should a Cardinal be rich?', as well as advice on where in the palace a Cardinal should house his gem collection, and where he should position the library to make it most accessible to scholars. Naturally, in Cortesi's ideal, as often in actuality, a Cardinal's household included a physician.[11] Many doctors came to Rome in the service of Cardinals, and their careers benefited from the fact that Rome housed a multiplicity of courtly households as well as the papal court itself.

But, although Renaissance Rome might be headed by a

secular-minded sovereign and worldly-wise princes, in other respects the papal court was different from any other in Europe. It was more clerical and male-dominated than other courts. It was also more cosmopolitan. One of the difficulties of Alessandro Petronio in offering health advice to the Romans in his book *Del viver delli Romani* was the fact that most Romans were actually foreigners.[12] Sixteenth-century Rome was a city of immigrants seeking careers and fortunes, just as it was also a city of innkeepers, pilgrims, and tourists. Even the beggars, Montaigne discovered, knew how to seek alms in French.[13] The patronage bestowed by successive Popes on their fellow countrymen brought to the court a stream of Catalans under Alexander VI, Florentines under the Medici Popes Leo X (1513–21) and Clement VII (1523–34), Milanese under Pius IV (1559–65), and so on.

However, the main difference sprang from the elective nature of the papacy. The college of Cardinals contained princes of the Church, but no crown prince, and each conclave could, and often did, spring a surprise. Rivalries between Cardinals, or, in the early sixteenth century, between the European powers whom they served, sometimes promoted the emergence of compromise candidates or stop-gap Popes. Old age could be an asset to a candidate (since it gave unsuccessful rivals the hope of a second chance), as could ill-health. Pius III and Leo X both benefited from having to be carried into the conclaves which elected them, respectively, in 1503 and 1513. Pius in particular was prematurely aged and seriously ill. His swollen right leg had been surgically incised shortly before the conclave, and similar surgery on his left leg followed the election. His pontificate barely lasted three weeks.[14] The average sixteenth-century Pope was 61·2 years old on election, and his reign lasted no more than 6·3 years. While a hereditary monarchy such as England counted no more than five sovereigns in the course of the century, the Church was governed by eighteen pontiffs. The Popes, in consequence, were men in a hurry, whether to carve out a lasting base for their family's prosperity, as in the case of Alexander VI, or to advance the reform of the Church, as in the case of Saint Pius V (1566–72). Small wonder that they were impatient of medical advice when it involved resting or putting aside the affairs which drove them on.

The transient nature of each pontificate also affected the character of the court. Pietro Aretino, who spent most of the period from 1517 to 1527 in Rome, emphasized the role of fortune in court life in his *Ragionamento ... de le corti*, published in 1538. A patron's favour could pluck a courtier from obscurity, and not always because of merit, but such fortune was capricious, and could be reversed.[15] Giovanni Francesco Commendone, son of a physician in Venice, and later to enjoy an outstanding career as a Cardinal, took up the same theme in his *Discorso sopra la corte di Roma*, written in 1564. He argued that nowhere in the world was more favourable for making one's fortune than Rome. At the court of Rome, more than at any other, ambitious people of every kind succeeded in attaining their ends: there, the door was open to all. Since by his election a Pope was suddenly, often unexpectedly, raised high above his fellows, then anyone could indulge the wildest hopes. However, Commendone also pointed out a more negative consequence of the electoral system. Pontificates were short, and the changes which followed them were radical. Cardinals often elected a man quite opposite to his predecessor, out of desire for change or in reaction to the unpopularity of the previous pontificate. Rome, as a result, was in a constant state of flux.[16] A courtier might rise with the election of his master to the papal throne, only to fall back on the latter's death. The courtiers of Alexander VI thus melted away following his sudden demise in 1503, when, according to the master of ceremonies Johann Burchard, his ugly corpse, blackened, swollen, and only narrowly saved from being desecrated by the people of Rome, was unceremoniously rolled in an old carpet and pummelled into a coffin too small to receive it.[17] Although opposite in character, the pontificate of Gian Pietro Carafa, Paul IV (1555–9), evoked a similar hostility. Upon his death the prison of the Inquisition was broken open, and the Carafa arms torn down throughout the city. His statue was smashed, and its head crowned with a Jew's yellow cap, in mocking allusion to Paul's anti-semitism.[18]

Such reversals of fortune affected the court as a whole, but were most keenly felt in the papal household, for its composition depended largely on the favour of each Pope. Hence the despair in the elaborate, worldly, spendthrift household of Leo X when he was succeeded by the humble and sincerely devout Fleming, Adrian VI (1522–3), a man who brought with him one female servant from the Netherlands to launder his clothes and cook his meals, and who preferred to live in the utmost retirement.[19] Hence, too, the relief felt on Adrian's death, when Rome hailed his physician, Giovanni (Antracino) da Macerata as *liberator patriae*,[20] while the college of Cardinals hastened to elect Leo X's cousin, Giulio de' Medici, as Clement VII.

This, then, was the shifting world in which doctors, like other members of the papal court, sought to make their way, and it was the central determinant in their careers. Of 118 physicians who served the Popes of the sixteenth century, no more than twenty held office under more than one pontificate.[21] Papal doctors were always outnumbered by the has-beens, whose service was no longer required. These were men like Alessandro Petronio, who appears on a list of the household of Paul IV in 1555,[22] but who never again formed part of the papal entourage. The year 1581 found him still in Rome, addressing Gregory XIII in the pointed dedication of his *De victu Romanorum*: 'Although, Holy Father, you are not in need of a doctor or a masseur [*iatrolipta*]...'. On the other hand, the unstable politics of Rome emphasized the importance of the doctors' function: for the ultimate uncertainty in the capital of Catholic Christendom was the health of the Popes, on whom all else depended. If anyone could influence the wheel of fortune at the papal court, then surely it was the doctors.

Papal household and palatine doctors

According to the Roman courtier and poet Francesco Berni, Clement VII made a vow to the Virgin Mary during an illness. On his recovery he set up an inscription:

> This is a vow which Pope Clement
> has paid to Our Lady,
> because, at a stroke, she freed him,
> miraculously, from the hands of eight doctors.[23]

The papal bedside could, indeed, be crowded, for all sixteenth-century Popes employed not one physician but several, as well as at least one surgeon. Most of these, however, also treated members of the papal household.

The household comprised those who lived with the Pope in the Vatican palace, and others who merely ate at the Pope's table. Lists of members of the household (*ruoli di palazzo*) survive in isolated instances from the pontificates of Pius III[24] and Leo X,[25] and in profusion from 1550 onwards.[26] They indicate the composition of the household, which included relatives of the Pope, Cardinals, and other leading prelates, papal secretaries and curial officials, librarians, chaplains, musicians and singers of the Sistine Chapel, artists such as Michelangelo, the *Maestro di Casa* and his staff of domestic officials, and the doctors. All of these were accompanied by their own servants. In addition, there were the palace servants, cooks, waiters, cleaners, gardeners, stable hands, and so on. The size of the household greatly increased in the Renaissance period. By 1503, under Pius III, it had reached 400, and under Leo X, in the years 1514–16, it came to total 683.[27] The household of Julius III (1550–5) totalled just under one thousand in 1550, a figure which was surpassed under Pius IV in 1562.[28]

Six physicians and a surgeon are named in the *ruolo* of Pius III; three physicians and a surgeon in that of Leo X; four physicians and a surgeon in the *ruolo* of Julius III of 1550. For a time under Paul IV in 1558 there were as many as ten physicians and five surgeons. This, however, was exceptional, and in a general pruning of Paul's household in the following year the medical staff was cut by half.[29] The medical posts were by no means equal in honour or rewards. Sometimes a doctor is designated in the *ruolo* as the private physician (*medico secreto*) of the Pope, while another appears merely as doctor to the household (*medico della famiglia*). Most, however, carry no particular designation, and presumably treated Pope and household alike, as did the surgeon Benedetto Giuni, who in 1545 was granted a house in the Borgo as a reward for services to the Pope and household.[30] While it is not easy to compare the doctors' salaries, given the complex nature of the latter in money, kind, and the fruits of offices and benefices, the *ruoli* do indicate differentiations of status. Under Julius III, for instance, Balduino Balduini, the Pope's private doctor, was clearly at the head of the medical corps. The *ruolo* of 1550 allowed him six servants, and stabling at the Vatican for two horses. The physicians Cosimo (Giacomelli) and Nicolò (Visinino) in the same list were each allowed three servants, but Cosimo was allowed stabling for two horses, while Nicolò was allowed none. Ippolito (Salviani) and Benedetto (Giuni), respectively physician and surgeon to the household, were each allowed two servants, but no horses. Their table allowance was also inferior – lamb and mutton but not veal, ordinary wine and bread rather than wine from the special cellar (*cantina secreta*), and the finer, 'papal' bread (*pane papalino*) enjoyed by the other doctors. This seems to reflect a division already apparent in the fifteenth century, when the Pope's doctor ate with him in the main dining room (*tinello secreto*), while the doctor of the household ate in another room with the servants and employees.[31] The household also included a pharmacist. We know that he kept his own pharmacy in the palace, since one of the masters of ceremonies, Ludovico Branca, died there, *in aromataria palatii Apostolici*, in 1587.[32] The pharmacist was required to supply medicines for the Pope and his household according to prescriptions written by the doctors and signed by the Maestro di Casa. The post was a busy and lucrative one, to judge from the 1,158 ducats paid to Papo Egidio, *spetiale palatino*, for the period June–September 1576.[33] His work also extended to veterinary medicines, since at least one pharmacist, Gherardo Gannassi, supplied medicines for the mules which were vital to the household's system of transport.[34]

A papal doctor might reside in the Vatican palace. Simone Castelvetro, for instance, was given a room there in 1590;[35] but more commonly they lived outside, and a house might even be granted as a reward for service. With such a base a doctor might have a certain independence from the court, and even maintain a private practice. When one Giovan Battista was wounded in a brawl in Rome in 1582 he was treated by two physicians and three surgeons. Neither of the former, Alessandro (Petronio) da Civita (Castellana) and Alessandro Butrio, were then in papal service. The three surgeons, however, Giuliano (Cecchini), (Giuseppe) Zerla, and Ludovico Monticoli were all employed by the reigning Pope Gregory XIII.[36] Benvenuto Cellini seems likewise to have been treated by Francesco (Fusconi) da Norcia at a time when the latter was physician to Paul III.[37] A number of papal physicians also served on the medical staff of the hospital of S. Spirito. Placido Fusco, for instance, served the hospital from 1559 to 1574, and was also physician to Pius V (1566–72).[38] The University of Rome also offered important avenues of additional employment for papal doctors, even though it lacked the reputation of other Italian universities such as Bologna or Padua.[39] The Pope was no less the master of the university than he was of the court. A close relationship between court and University was therefore a natural development, and one which found parallels elsewhere, as in Renaissance Ferrara. Three doctors who appear on the list of Leo X's household for the years 1514–16 are thus also to be found in the list of medical professors at the *Sapienza* for the year 1514.[40] A Pope might even use the offer of a joint appointment to attract a leading doctor to Rome. Girolamo Accoramboni, for instance, was summoned from Padua by Paul III to an appointment as papal doctor and professor of medicine.[41] In this way a post at court, like contractual service to a large monastery, could be one of several elements which made up the doctor's employment. This was a factor which helped to offset the insecurity of employment at court.

Papal doctors were well placed to share in the intellectual and cultural life of the court. The humanist aim of recovering the wisdom of the ancient world underlay medical and non-medical learning alike in the sixteenth century. Learned doctors found much to admire in pontiffs such as Leo X, Clement VII, or Paul III (1534–49), open-handed patrons of literature, art, and music, who did much to build up the Vatican library and to make searches abroad for Greek and Latin manuscripts. Paul III, for instance, whose slow speech was attributed to the fact that he would never utter an inelegant word, whether in Italian, Latin, or Greek, received flattering dedications in works by Fracastoro and by papal physicians such as Paolo Belmesseri, Silvio Zeffiri, and Ferdinando Balami.[42] Belmesseri dedicated to him a curious rendering of the first two books of Aristotle's *De animalibus* into Latin elegies;[43] Balami a Latin translation of Galen's *De ossibus*, which he said had been commissioned by Paul's predecessor Clement VII.[44] Clement was also responsible for bringing to court one of the most ardent champions of ancient Greek, as opposed to Arabic, medicine, Matteo Corti. Johann Albrecht von Widmanstadt described how he had explained the Copernican system to Clement in the Vatican gardens in 1533, in the presence of Corti and others.[45] Another leading humanist and translator of Greek medical texts, Agostino Ricci, owed his appointment as physician to Julius III to Cardinal Marcello Cervini (afterwards Marcellus II, 1555), himself a humanist scholar with a Latin translation of Euclid to his credit, as well as a poem on baths and medicinal springs.[46] Doctors also shared fully in the general passion for Antiquity which was a feature of Roman cultural life. The wealthy physician Francesco (Fusconi) da Norcia, who served

Adrian VI, Clement VII, and Paul III, thus owned an impressive collection of classical statuary,[47] while another of Paul's doctors, Tommaso Cadamosti, *antiquitatis studiosissimus*, could take part in archaeological discussions concerning the site of the temple of Apollo.[48]

The opportunity to share in the cultural life of the court was doubtless a strong attraction of the post of papal doctor, as was the chance to attend the Vatican, which, with its decorations by Raphael, Michelangelo, and other masters, was considered the largest and most beautiful palace in the world.[49] It would be wrong, however, to overstress the cultural impact of doctors on the court. While Italian doctors, or doctors educated in Italy, often played a prominent part in introducing Renaissance humanism at the courts of Northern Europe, no such leading role was open to them in Rome. Recent scholarship on Roman humanism has found it possible to ignore the doctors altogether.[50] Baldassare Castiglione himself saw no need to include a doctor among his courtiers in *The Book of the Courtier*, which stressed the superiority of the skilled amateur over the tedious professional. The work was set at the court of Duke Guidobaldo, a man crippled by gout while still in his youth. Fortune, Castiglione implied, could not be influenced by medical skill, and doctors only appear in the book as a butt for sarcastic humour.[51] Writing subsequently of the death of Cardinal Rossi, in a dispatch from Rome in 1519, Castiglione doubted that he had died from poison; more probably 'the doctors, not understanding his illness, have killed him, as they do many others'.[52] Doctors, in this author's view, were servants of the court, not courtiers, and sometimes dangerous ones at that. An examination of the achievements of sixteenth-century papal doctors goes some way to confirm Castiglione's estimate of their standing at court. For while the palatine household did include doctors of the greatest distinction (Giovanni da Vigo and Alfonso Ferri stand out among the surgeons; Gaspare Torrella, Girolamo Accoramboni, Matteo Corti, Andres Laguna, Ippolito Salviani, Arcangelo Piccolomini, Michele Mercati, Andrea Bacci, and Andrea Cesalpino among the physicians), taken as a whole the papal doctors could not be said to be the most outstanding figures in the profession. There is, indeed, justice in Marini's remarks that many of them were obscure, and what little could be discovered about them was boring.

If Rome did not always attract the most celebrated doctors,

this was in part a reflection of current attitudes to court life. Aretino's experience of the courts of Leo X and Clement VII, soured by his conflict with the Datary, Gian Matteo Giberti, found expression in his vitriolic dialogue *Ragionamento ... de le corti*. In it he pictured the boredom and anxieties of servitude, where a courtier might not cough or blow his nose for fear of annoying the Pope, let alone pick up a ducat if he dropped one; where every bow brought the worry of whether it had been done properly. Court life corrupted, breeding pride and arrogance. The competition of courtiers for favour encouraged flattery, envy, calumny, rancour, and quarrels, and ultimately led to disappointed hopes. 'Life', in Aretino's view, 'consists in not going to court'.[53] The inconvenience of court life must certainly have been apparent to the elderly doctor of Clement VIII (1592–1605), who, following behind the court on a journey to the sanctuary of the Madonna della Quercia, was left stranded in the countryside when his carriage broke down.[54] Girolamo Mercuriale was one physician who turned his back on Roman court life. His service in the household of Cardinal Alessandro Farnese provided the perfect humanist, antiquarian ambience in which to prepare his treatise on classical medical gymnastics, *De arte gymnastica* (Venice, 1569). On the other hand one of the few letters written by Mercuriale which survive from his years in Rome hints at a less comfortable arrangement, with the Cardinal using his medical skills as a form of patronage to be dispensed to all and sundry.[55] In 1569 Mercuriale was glad to leave for his first teaching position, at Padua, and he spurned a brief from Pius V ordering him to return to Rome for the sake of the Cardinals.[56] Although he later acted as a consultant in the illness of Gregory XIV in 1591,[57] he never entered papal service, and proved that greater fame could be won away from court.

Above all, however, the uneven celebrity enjoyed by the various papal doctors was due to the system which brought them their appointments. Some were brought to court because of their established reputations, especially those who were also called to chairs at the University. Others, however, were in their masters' service long before the latter were elected to the papacy. Their position was thus due to the conclave's wheel of fortune rather than to outstanding ability. Since medicine depended on the physician's intimate knowledge of his patient, a newly elected Pope would not be likely to change his doctor, even if a more famous practitioner were available. Tiberio Palelli, for instance, served Alessandro Farnese during the latter's youth and throughout his career, and he continued to serve him after his succession to the chair of Peter as Paul III.[58] Julius III's private physician, Balduino Balduini, had likewise been in his service long before he became Pope. In this capacity he had attended the Council of Trent and been present in the conclave from which Julius emerged as Pope.[59] Fortune certainly smiled on the physician Simone Castelvetro when Cardinal Sfondrato fell ill in Modena on his way to the conclave of 1590. The Cardinal emerged from the conclave as Gregory XIV, and soon summoned Castelvetro from Modena to a place at court.[60] Medical reputation, moreover, was not the sole criterion by which a Pope chose his doctors. Cardinal Pietro Aldobrandini sought a range of information about the prospective doctors of Clement VIII. Were they, for instance, persons of breeding who could deal with princes?; were they strong enough for the fatigue of office?[61] Just as Alexander VI included three Spaniards in his medical corps, so Sixtus V (1585–90) preferred doctors from his own native area, the Marches.[62] A Pope might even follow the example of Pius II in the preceding century, and prefer a doctor who was lucky but ignorant to one who was learned but unlucky.[63] Each Pope's choice of his private physician was thus a personal one, as it needed to be in an age when the doctor–patient relationship was fundamental to medical practice.

Doctors and patients

The illness and death of a Pope was not only decisive for life at court and for the careers of courtiers, but might have a wide impact on religious and political affairs: hence the intense anxiety with which Francesco Guicciardini, as governor of Bologna, watched every stage of the mortal illness of Clement VII in 1534. He wrote that every hour felt like a year as he waited for news of Clement's symptoms and of the conduct of his doctors, now sending additional medical advice to Rome along with his own lay opinion, now questioning the wisdom of calling in the physician Scipio Veggi from Milan (should the life of the Pope be in the hands of a subject of a foreign prince?), now despairing of doctors altogether.[64] Diplomatic dispatches are an unfailing source of information on the temperament, diet, life-style, and health of each Pope. Good health itself could call for comment, as in a depressing report on Alexander VI in 1500: 'The Pope is 70 years old and every day grows younger.'[65] However, illness was more obviously newsworthy. To the outside world, prognosis could seem the major function of the papal doctor. It was, for instance, a dire medical bulletin on Pius IV (1559–65) that brought the Council of Trent to a sudden end. In anticipation of Pius's death the final decrees of the Council were framed during the night and rushed through on 4 December 1563.[66] Equally full of information on papal illnesses are the *Avvisi di Roma*, an early, and surprisingly reliable, journalistic enterprise which various Popes tried in vain to suppress.[67] Like diplomatic dispatches, they relayed information which came, directly or indirectly, from the Pope's doctors, and they were rich in clinical detail. Subscribers to the *avvisi* could know how many times Gregory XIV (suffering, as it turned out, from stone), pissed blood during the nights of his last illness in 1591, or how great was the pain in the papal urethra on passing water. In report after report there was a full catalogue of the latest symptoms, the most recent diagnostic opinions, accounts of treatment (which included doses of poppy (*papavero*) to aid sleep, and a diet of asses' and women's milk), and plans for surgical intervention and for the summoning of consultants. The *avvisi* also record Gregory's lingering end, putrefying more than just corpse-like, with the comment of one of the doctors that if the Pope survived another day he would burn his books and give up medicine.[68] Far from maintaining a cloak of secrecy, at least one papal doctor saw his role as explaining papal malaise to the outside world. The jubilant commotion which broke out on the death of the irascible Paul IV in 1559 drew a response from his doctor, the humanist Agostino Ricci. His theme was that if people had understood how Paul's conduct had been influenced by a painful and prolonged illness they would not have given way to blind fury on his death.[69] Several doctors in fact wrote up the medical history of their papal patients, for private circulation, if not for publication.[70]

The main function of a papal doctor was not, however, to supply journalistic copy, but to treat his patients. Like any monarch who employed a personal physician, a Pope expected more than merely medical advice when he was ill. He also required a detailed regimen for health, based on the range of environmental and personal factors which all doctors after Hippocrates took into consideration. Alessandro Petronio believed that the people of Rome needed a careful regimen more than most, since the city stood on an unhealthy site. Hilly to the east and west, Rome was exposed to the north and south winds, which blew along the Tiber. Exposure to the south wind had a particularly pernicious effect on disease patterns in the city. He also believed that Roman food had a peculiar character. It was bulky, but not nutritious, so that it was necessary to eat more, and to take meals more often. Evacuation had to be in proportion – two, three, or four times a day.[71] Fortunate in this respect was Paul IV, whose natural tendency to diarrhoea was reputed in 1555 to be the source of his good health. It purged off all bad humours, so that he had never taken medicines in his life.[72] Other Popes were not so lucky and were commonly reported absent from ceremonies after taking purgatives.[73] Another important environmental concern was the water supply. For much of the century Rome was wholly dependent on the water of the Tiber. Clement VII and Paul III trusted it to such an extent (or so distrusted the water elsewhere) that they carried flasks of it on journeys out of Rome, even to places as far off as Nice.[74] Alessandro Petronio and Andrea Bacci, both of whom became members of the papal household, also reported it to be safe to drink in their treatises on the subject published in 1552 and 1558, though Petronio added the impractical suggestion that it should be stored for 6 months before use.[75] On the other hand Giovanni Battista Modio argued in 1556 that Tiber water was unhealthy, and he urged Paul IV to bring in an alternative supply by aqueducts. Whether or not Modio was influential, this project came to fruition with the restoration of the ancient *acqua vergine* in the pontificates of Pius IV and Pius V.[76]

In addition to environmental matters, every aspect of papal life-style was important enough to warrant medical advice, including diet (both what to eat and when to eat it), sleep, rest, exercise, dress, bathing, where to live, precautions for travel, and so on, all of them considered in relation to variables such as the season. A typical detail from the private accounts of Pius IV records payment to a carpenter for a new papal bed, ordered by Pius's doctor Giovanni Andrea (Bianchi).[77] Diet offered endless scope for discussion. Clement VII always had two doctors present at table, with whom he discussed the qualities of the various foods put before him.[78] The physicians of Pius IV strove to restrain his taste for heavy Milanese dishes, while those of his successor Saint Pius V tried to limit the excessive fasting which diverted his frustrated cook into writing a cookery book.[79] Choice of wines needed careful thought both of kind (Paul IV drank a dark, thick Neapolitan wine, followed by a little malmsey at the end of the meal to rinse his mouth),[80] and of quantity (Gregory XIII took three small glasses of wine and water at lunch and two in the evening).[81] Paul III's health care was also evident in his choice of wines, of which he was a connoisseur,[82] while perhaps the most elaborate sixteenth-century treatise on wine came from the pen of Andrea Bacci, who had previously served as physician to Sixtus V (1585–90).[83]

Perhaps the most surprising aspect of the welter of advice which papal doctors heaped on their patients is how infrequently it was heeded. Contemporary sources rarely described a Pope as obedient to his doctors, except on his deathbed. Pius IV, described for once as *patientissimo et obedientissimo* by his physicians on 9 December 1565, died that night.[84] The conscientious Marcellus II likewise failed to please his doctors until 30 August 1555, when at last he seemed to be resting; he was, in fact, unconscious, having suffered a stroke.[85] Urban VII, with fomentations on his stomach and leeches on his backside, was said to be taking his medicines with patience on 26 September 1590, but he too died the next day.[86] Deathbeds apart, however, neglect of medical advice was almost universal. The energetic, strong-willed Julius II (1503–13) was typical of many sixteenth-century pontiffs who refused to rest from work: when necessary he received Cardinals and envoys in bed.[87] Paul IV was said to have hastened his end by refusing advice to give up his fasts.[88] Saint Pius V (a difficult patient since he looked forward to his dissolution with joy) could not be restrained by his doctors from making the pilgrimage to the seven basilicas of Rome, though he collapsed several times on the way and died soon afterwards.[89]

Popes neglected medical advice for a number of reasons, and not merely from pressure of work or an excess of spirituality. They seem, on the whole, to have treated their doctors' recommendations not as absolute norms, but as a basis for a discussion in which other factors, including their own knowledge of their environment, constitution, and heredity, had a part to play. A few Popes had a smattering of medical knowledge of their own. Pius IV came from a Milanese family which had produced doctors as well as lawyers, and he too had studied arts and medicine for a time at Pavia before turning to law.[90] Paul IV was described in 1559 as debating with his doctors, citing Avicenna and Galen as if medicine were his own field.[91] Sixtus V, who had picked up some medical knowledge while a student at Siena, loved to argue with his doctors (quoting Hippocrates, Galen, and Avicenna) and then ignore their advice. Suffering from fever during his last illness in 1590, he defied them by rising from his bed, eating melon and drinking wine chilled with snow while conferring with the Datary and signing petitions.[92] Paul IV and Pius IV both put more faith in their robust constitutions than in medicine. When Paul's strength broke down at the end he alone refused to believe that death was at hand:

> Although he has dropsy, with swollen testicles, and is suffering from gravel, and although he has one leg swollen and immobile (which they are trying to drain as much as possible), and catarrh which bothers him at times, nonetheless he lives in hope, and says he will live as long as his father, who survived twelve years with this infirmity and was a hundred years old when he died.[93]

His successor Pius IV trusted especially to exercise, taking long walks morning and night. His vigour astonished everyone, as he walked about even in the burning sun, ascended the cupola of St Peter's, or climbed the scaffolding on palazzo Colonna to inspect the work. If he was attacked by fever one day, the next would find him, contrary to doctors' orders, taking his usual walk once more.[94] Sixtus V was reported to have sacked five doctors in 1586 on the grounds that a careful diet should keep the papal family from needing physicians and surgeons.[95] A patient's long experience of an illness or regimen could convince him that he was better placed to evaluate it than was the doctor. Saint Pius V was induced to change his life-style by a new doctor, Giovanni Francesco Marenci, who came from Asti to treat him at the end of 1569. Pius agreed to sleep longer, fast less, drink more, and change his mealtimes. Scarcely a month passed, however, before Pius concluded that the new regimen was having no beneficial effect on his incontinence. When he reverted to his former custom in the spring of 1570, he felt as lively as ever, and declared that he did not intend to seek doctors' advice any more, wishing to live according to his own temperament (*volendo vivere secondo la sua complessione*).[96] Until his death two years later he showed his independence by treating his malady, bladder stone, with his own remedy, a diet of asses' milk. A contemporary described him as 'disobedient to the doctors, taking too much of his old favourite remedy, asses' milk, which so weakened his stomach that he could no longer retain food'.[97]

Underlying the Popes' independence of their doctors was the strength of lay medical opinion in sixteenth-century Italy. The detailed study of the Roman environment and its effect on health by the physician Alessandro Petronio was thus foreshadowed in many respects by the comments of a layman, Paolo Cortesi, in his De Cardinalatu. As well as a long chapter entitled 'De sanitate conservanda', which dealt with life-style and subjects such as medicinal baths, Cortesi included detailed information on how a Cardinal should plan his palace in relation to health factors such as the prevailing winds.[98] Alvise Cornaro's popular *De vita sobria*, written in 1558, together with the longevity of its author, showed how a layman could thrive by understanding his own constitution and developing his own regimen. Everyday experience of the environment could yield conclusions about health and disease which, while not necessarily different from traditional Hippocratic opinion, were the fruit of independent, lay observation. Such observation underlay the rise and development of the Italian Health Offices in the fifteenth and sixteenth centuries, and of the measures which their lay administrators took against plague.[99] Much the same could be said of the anti-malaria campaigns, linked to schemes of agricultural improvement, which were pursued in the sixteenth century by the papacy and other Italian governments. The papal provinces bordering the Tyrrhenian Sea were particularly subject to malaria, and for that reason the direct coastal route from Rome to Pisa, the Via Aurelia, was one that travellers avoided.[100] Much of the Roman Campagna in the Renaissance period was a deserted region of marsh, pasture, and abandoned villages. Especially dangerous were the Pontine marshes, which Sixtus V attempted to drain, with a work-force of 2,000 men, in the years 1586–9.[101] Alexander VI, Leo X, Sixtus V, and Urban VII (1590) all died in circumstances which are suggestive both of malaria and of an advanced lay familiarity with that disease. Leo X suffered recurrent bouts of fever throughout his pontificate. He had to leave his coronation mass because of 'a fit of ague',[102] and paroxysms of tertian fever (*parossismi di terzana*) were frequently reported by ambassadors and duly noted in the diaries of Marin Sanudo.[103] Contemporaries blamed his passion for hunting in the Campagna, and La Magliana, the site of Leo's hunting lodge, was known in the sixteenth century for its bad air.[104] The Portuguese ambassador returned from the papal chase with fever in 1517, and many were said to suffer from Leo's entertainment.[105] Some areas of Rome were also affected, including the Vatican palace, which was low-lying and near the river. Contemporaries understood the seasonality of the disease, and its association with particular types of environment, and they stressed the dangers of staying out of doors after nightfall. The death from fever of Alexander VI was blamed on his lingering after dusk at a dinner party in the country.[106] Sixtus V was also criticized in 1585 for walking about the open corridors of the Belvedere as late as two hours after nightfall, 'even though the air at the Vatican, ordinarily bad, was at such times even worse' (*anchorchè l'aria ordinariamente cattiva del Vaticano sia in questi tempi peggiore*),[107] and by 1590 reference was being made to 'his usual tertian fever' (*la solita sua terzana*).[108] According to the diary of the master of ceremonies, Giovanni Paolo Mucanzio, Urban VII lay awake, tormented by mosquitoes, throughout the first night of his pontificate in September 1590. The following day, 'because the air at the Vatican was not yet healthy', he resolved to move up to the palace on the Quirinal hill. Tradition, however, since he was not yet crowned, prevented his leaving the Vatican, and this was seen as the cause of his death from fever a few weeks later.[109] This lay appreciation of the disease gave scope for preventive measures. Most Popes chose to leave the unhealthy air of the Vatican in the summer season. Paul III was anxious to be out of Rome altogether in September, a month condemned by Horace.[110] San Marco, the Quirinal, and Julius III's Villa Giulia were favourite summer palaces for those who did not wish to move too far from the Vatican, while Gregory XIII and Clement VIII were amongst those who found refreshment more remotely, at their villas at Frascati.

The sixteenth-century Popes also showed their independence of their doctors in their readiness to consider alternative forms of treatment. The private accounts of Paul III for 1543 include a gift to the fathers of SS. Giovanni e Paolo in Bologna, in return for large quantities of distilled water supplied for the Pope's running eyes.[111] Urban VII was willing to take a medicine not prescribed by his doctors, but sent by the Duchess of Olivares, wife of the Spanish ambassador.[112] Julius II, according to Cardinal Gonzaga, was prepared, if all else failed, to try the infallible liquid gold of a Roman charlatan,[113] just as Clement VII, in his last illness, took a quintessence profferred by a Carmelite friar.[114]

In the end, however, papal doctors had their patients entirely at their command, in the post-mortem. The decision to hold an autopsy lay with the college of Cardinals, and at least eight were carried out in the sixteenth century, concerning the deaths of Leo X,[115] Adrian VI,[116] Paul III,[117] Paul IV,[118] Pius V,[119] Gregory XIII,[120] Sixtus V,[121] and Gregory XIV.[122] In the cases of Leo and Adrian the sudden tumefaction of the corpses, which prompted rumours of poisoning, provided the motive for the autopsies. There had, after all, been a previous plot to poison Leo, by way of his anal fistula, in 1516,[123] while, following Adrian's death, his Spanish followers accused the Netherlanders of carelessness in allowing the French near his kitchen.[124] In other instances the doctors themselves seem to have wanted the examination, especially where the death had been preceded by disagreements about diagnosis. This was so in the cases of Pius V and Gregory XIV (1590–1). Whether Pius was suffering from stone was long debated. He had allowed his bladder to be probed while still a Cardinal, but the results had only added to the controversy, and as Pope he would not submit to further examination. At post-mortem three stones were found in his bladder.[125] Gregory XIV was the subject of a similar debate. Two hours after his death, while the body was still warm, an examination was carried out by Ludovico Monticoli, papal surgeon, in the presence of Simone Castelvetro and other papal physicians. Their haste, dictated by the state of the corpse, proved embarrassing. The papal innards had been removed before the doctors realized that no urn was at hand in which to place them, and a pot had to be fetched from the kitchens. The results, all the same, were satisfactory. A stone weighing three ounces was found in the bladder, which itself was ulcerated. In addition the lungs and other organs were disordered, suggesting a diagnosis of phthisis (*mal tisico*).[126] From the doctor's point of view the autopsy thus resolved a medical problem, and it also served as a ritual which confirmed their mastery of their profession. The patient may have died, but, having produced the stone like a rabbit from a hat, the doctors were seen, in the end, to understand the morbific processes at work.

Conclusion: the rewards of office

Much of this chapter has stressed the disadvantages of life as a papal doctor, the insecurity of the office, and the difficult nature of the patients. The Popes tended to be past middle age, with a short life-expectancy. The most their doctors could hope for was a speedy reward for office, and a vindication of their medical opinions at post-mortem. They worked on a public stage, among colleagues with whom they were often in open disagreement, and their reputations were not always enhanced by the experience. The six or eight doctors who gathered around his bed in 1513 were of no benefit to Julius II, a former syphilitic who seemed, for obscure reasons, to have lost heart. For all their various opinions, wrote the master of ceremonies, Paris de Grassis, none could understand the nature of his languor.[127] A diplomatic dispatch on Clement VII in 1529 reported that his fever had passed off, 'so, provided the physicians do not commit any more extravagances, as they in fact did by giving him two doses of rhubarb in three days, it is hoped he will recover.'[128] Clement himself lost faith in his doctors when they disagreed during his final illness in 1534. Francesco Guicciardini commented, 'if he has lost faith in doctors, he has every reason; in this field he errs least who never had faith in them at all'.[129]

Leaving aside the pasquinades which, celebrating the deaths of Adrian VI, and Clement VIII, hailed their physicians as liberators of Rome,[130] there was serious comment that papal doctors were sometimes responsible for the loss of their patients. The death of Pius III in 1503 was followed by recriminations in which it was said that his leg should not have been subjected to surgery, nor should he have been given a controversial internal medicine (*potio pigmentaria*) which sapped his strength.[131] Even before Clement VII's demise in 1534, Guicciardini was blaming Matteo Corti's unnecessary innovations for bringing the Pope to the brink of death, and he claimed that the whole world shared his view.[132] Aretino's *Ragionamento ... de le corti*, written only a few years later, hailed Corti as the killer of the Pope,[133] while Girolamo Cardano made reference to the 'too Galenic Corti' (*nimis Galenicus Curtius*) who killed Pope Clement by altering the pattern of his meals.[134]

In these circumstances it may seem surprising that any doctor sought service in the papal household at all. The rewards of office, however, at least in the Renaissance period, could be considerable. Leo X's chronic anal fistula, which at one point developed five separate openings, was a channel of liquid gold for his surgeon Jacopo da Brescia. To it he owed his elegant house in the Borgo, as he gratefully proclaimed in an inscription: 'Leonis X Pont. Max. liberalitate Iacobus Brixianus chirurgus aedificavit'.[135] Matteo Corti was paid a full 1,000 ducats a year for his ill-fated attendance on Clement VII, a high salary probably designed to match his earning power as a leading university teacher.[136] Even more profitable, however, were the multitudinous curial and church offices which lay in the Pope's gift. In an age when plurality and non-residence were standard practice, a Pope could confer canonries, abbeys, even bishoprics, as a reward for service or a mark of favour. Two of Alexander VI's physicians, Gaspare Torrella and Bernardo Buongiovanni, received bishoprics, respectively in 1494 and 1501.[137] Both continued to practise medicine. Buongiovanni was presumably able to exercise both medical and episcopal functions in investigating the stigmata of the blessed Lucia da Narni, and, as the 'Reverendus episcopus Venusinus', he continued to head the doctors in the list of the household of Alexander's successor, Pius III.[138] Julius III had no sooner become Pope in 1550 than he began to reward Balduino Balduini, his doctor of long standing. Within four years Balduini was made Archdeacon of Tortosa (Spain), Abbot of S. Eufemia (Antwerp), Canon of Cagliari (Sardinia), Prior of Nuestra Señora del Pilar (Saragossa, Spain), Bishop of Mariana (Corsica, a diocese which he never visited), and Bishop of Antwerp. Balduini, in turn, used the Bishopric of Antwerp to confer numerous benefices on another member of his family, Orazio Balduini.[139]

Later in the century, however, the Counter-Reformation, and the enforcement of the decrees of the Council of Trent on clerical residence, began to have an impact on the doctors' chances of making a fortune from Church offices, and on the nature of life at Court. The pontificate of Paul III (1534–49) began a slow transition towards that of Pius V (1566–72), when the spirit of the Council of Trent found full embodiment in the papacy. The new spirit was expressed in Commendone's *Discorso sopra la corte di Roma* of 1564, a reformist treatise which exposed the opportunistic free-for-all at court only to condemn it. Using medical metaphor, which may have come easily to a doctor's son, he described the apostolic seat as the stomach of the universal Church, which needed to be purged before it filled the whole body with evil humours. Amongst other abuses, he denounced the use of ecclesiastical offices and benefices as a means of granting favour or rewarding service.[140] Paul IV and his successors began to look critically at the size of their households. In 1559 Paul reduced his by more than 150, including five physicians and four surgeons.[141] Pius IV removed more than 400 superfluous courtiers in 1564, reducing the total to some 600.[142] Pius V also effected a reduction in 1567, when 150 were dismissed, including three out of six physicians.[143] It would be wrong, however, to over-emphasize the effect of such measures. Recent studies have tended to be sceptical of the impact of the Counter-Reformation in Rome on ecclesiastical wealth and on practices related to office-holding.[144] Montaigne, whose visit to Italy spanned the years 1580–1, could still write that he had never seen so great a court as that of Rome, nor a city so full of rich men, coaches, and horses.[145] Just as the Popes expressed the triumph of the Counter-Reformation in the magnificent architecture of Rome, so the court was still expected to display the dignity of the successors of Peter. In addition, the sale of office, the accepted practice of all *anciens régimes*, continued to account for a large number of places at court.[146] As late as 1587 the household of Sixtus V totalled 830, including four physicians, a surgeon, and two pharmacists, while the medical corps of Gregory XIV in 1590 included six physicians, two surgeons, and a pharmacist.[147]

The change wrought by the Counter-Reformation was felt, rather, in the character of the court, as may be seen from an ambassadorial report written in 1565, during the pontificate of Pius IV:

At the curia they live very simply, partly, as has been said, from want of means, but perhaps not less on account of the good example of Cardinal Borromeo [Carlo Borromeo, Pius IV's influential nephew], for those in subordinate positions adapt themselves to the example of their princes.... No Cardinal or courtier can any longer count on favour, if he does not live, either in reality, or at least in appearance, as he does. At any rate, in public they stand aloof from every kind of amusement.[148]

Under the succeeding Pope, Pius V, the Vatican palace was said to be like a monastery, with no traces of the old court life. Idleness was replaced with philosophical and theological lectures; meals (preceded and followed by prayers) were accompanied by a reading, or taken in monastic silence.[149] Clement VIII at the end of the century demanded a similar simplicity and morality from his suite, and expected them to receive communion at his hands once a month.[150] Gone was the cheerful worldliness, with its banquets, buffoons, and hunting parties, which had typified the Renaissance court of Leo X.

The household's medical corps felt the change of mood in several ways. There were no more Jewish physicians, such as Samuele Sarfadi, who had treated Julius II, or Giacomo Mantini, who had attended Paul III and also taught at the *Sapienza*.[151] Gregory XIII's bull of 1581 reinforced the church's ban on Jewish doctors treating any Christian patient, let alone a Pope.[152] In their place came the doctor of the *Compagnia del Santissimo Sacramento di S. Pietro*, dedicated to the poor of the Borgo near the Vatican palace, who was given a place alongside the other doctors in the palatine household.[153] Morality and religion now became important criteria in choosing a papal doctor,[154] and shortcomings were punished with a firm hand. Giovanni Francesco Manfredi, for instance, physician and Vatican librarian, was thrown into prison by his master Pius IV in 1564, accused of adultery.[155]

Occasionally the chance to impress the Pope at court still brought spectacular success. Simone Pasqua, physician to Pius IV, was made a Bishop in 1561, and, a few years later, a Cardinal. This was, however, a recognition of ability which could be useful in a new career, and not the mere provision of an extra income for a doctor. No sooner was Pasqua made a Bishop than he was packed off to the Council of Trent. Moreover, such instances were increasingly rare: Pasqua was, in fact, the last papal doctor to win a Cardinal's hat.[156] For the majority of doctors, as for courtiers in general, the court was less of a honeypot than it had been in the first half of the century. 'Few', wrote Giacomo Soranzo in 1565, 'want to go on living at court at expense to themselves, and with great inconvenience, without hope of greater reward.'[157] At the close of the sixteenth century the disadvantages of court life remained, but the prizes were less attainable.

71

Richard Palmer

Notes

I am grateful to David Chambers, Nicholas Davidson, and Christopher Gatiss for their advice, and to Msgr Charles Burns for kind assistance at the Vatican.

1. Prosper Mandosius, θεατρον in quo maximorum christiani orbis pontificum archiatros Prosper Mandosius ... spectandos exhibet. I have used the edition published by Gaetano Marini at the end of vol. 2 of his *Degli archiatri pontifici* (See note 2).
2. Gaetano Marini, *Degli archiatri pontifici* (2 vols, Rome, 1784), vol. 1, preface, pp. xviii–xix.
3. Marini, for instance, recorded only two of the eight doctors of Pius III. See P. Piccolomini, 'La famiglia di Pio III', *Archivio della Società Romana di Storia Patria* (hereafter ASRSP), vol. 26 (1903), pp. 143–64, especially p. 145.
4. Peter Partner, *Renaissance Rome 1500–1559* (London, 1976); John D'Amico, *Renaissance Humanism in Papal Rome* (Baltimore and London, 1983); Charles L. Stinger, *The Renaissance in Rome* (Bloomington, Indiana, 1985).
5. Ludwig von Pastor, *The History of the Popes from the Close of the Middle Ages*. The sixteenth-century Popes are dealt with in vols 5–24 of the English translation (London, 1923–51). On N. Sernini's question 'What is Rome ... ?' see vol. 11, p. 349.
6. Partner, *Renaissance Rome*, pp. 82–3. Not until 1580 did the population reach 80,000, with a further rise to around 100,000 at the end of the century.
7. Stinger, *Renaissance in Rome*, p. 123.
8. Michael Mallett, *The Borgias: The Rise and Fall of a Renaissance Dynasty* (London, 1969), pp. 22–41; Stinger, *Renaissance in Rome*, pp. 99–102.
9. Baldassare Castiglione, *The Book of the Courtier*, translated by George Bull (Harmondsworth, 1967).
10. D'Amico, *Renaissance Humanism*, pp. 46–7.
11. Paulus Cortesius, *De cardinalatu libri tres* (Castel Cortesiano, 1510). Cf. Kathleen Weil-Garris and J. F. D'Amico, *The Renaissance Cardinal's Ideal Palace: A Chapter from Cortesi's De Cardinalatu* (Rome, 1980), and D'Amico, *Renaissance Humanism*, pp. 45–56, 226–9.
12. Alessandro Petronio, *Del viver delli Romani et di conservar la sanità* (Rome, 1592), pp. 195–6. Cf. Partner, *Renaissance Rome*, pp. 75–6.
13. Pastor, *History of the Popes*, vol. 20, p. 559.
14. Paolo Piccolomini, 'Il pontificato di Pio III', *Archivio Storico Italiano*, series 5, vol. 32 (1903), pp. 102–38.
15. Pietro Aretino, *Ragionamento ... de le corti del mondo, e di quella del cielo* (Venice, 1539). I have not seen the first edition, 1538.
16. Pastor, *History of the Popes*, vol. 16, p. 58 *et seq.*
17. *At the court of the Borgia, being an account of the reign of Pope Alexander VI written by his Master of Ceremonies Johann Burchard*, ed.

72

and trans. by Geoffrey Parker (London, 1963), pp. 224–6.

18. Pastor, *History of the Popes*, vol. 14, p. 415.

19. Pastor, *History of the Popes*, vol. 9, p. 71.

20. Marini, *Degli archiatri*, vol. 1, pp. 322–3.

21. My calculation is based on Marini's incomplete list of papal physicians. Papal surgeons were more secure in their office. Of sixteen surgeons, eight served under more than one pontificate. Giacomo Rastelli served six successive Popes from Clement VII to Pius IV.

22. This list is printed in Gaetano Moroni, *Dizionario di erudizione storico – ecclesiastica*, vol. 22 (Venice, 1843), pp. 66–73.

23. Marini, *Degli archiatri*, vol. 1, p. 330.

24. Piccolomini, 'La famiglia di Pio III'.

25. Alessandro Ferrajoli, 'Il ruolo della corte di Leone X', ASRSP, vol. 34 (1911) pp. 363–91; vol. 35 (1912), pp. 219–71, 483–539; vol. 36 (1913), pp. 191–223.

26. Biblioteca Apostolica Vaticana (hereafter BAV), *Fondo ruoli*, contains over a hundred lists from the second half of the century. For a list of Pius IV (1559–65), see T. von Sickel, 'Ein Ruolo di famiglia des Papstes Pius IV', *Mittheilungen des Instituts für österreichische Geschichtsforschung*, vol. 14 (1893) pp. 537–88.

27. Piccolomini, 'La famiglia di Pio III'; Ferrajoli, 'Il ruolo della corte'.

28. BAV, *Fondo ruoli*, 1, a list of May 1550; von Sickel, 'Ein ruolo'.

29. BAV, *Fondo ruoli*, 33, the list of 1558 with deletions made in January 1559. The revised version, dated March 1559, survives as *Fondo ruoli*, 34.

30. Marini, *Degli archiatri*, vol. 1, p. 391.

31. See the list of the household of Pius II of 1460, Marini, *Degli archiatri*, vol. 2, pp. 152–6. The earliest list of Julius III's household (1550) also distinguishes the *tinello secreto* from the *tinello minore*.

32. Leone Caetani, 'Vita e diario di Paolo Alaleone de Branca, maestro delle ceremonie pontificie 1582–1638', ASRSP, vol. 16 (1893), pp. 5–39.

33. Archivio di Stato di Roma, *Camerale primo*, reg. 1350, f. 120r.

34. Ibid., reg. 1357, f. 42v (April 1587); a similar payment to Antonio Pasquin, ibid., reg. 1359, f. 16r (January 1588).

35. Marini, *Degli archiatri*, vol. 1, p. 471.

36. Bruno Gatta, 'Il diario di Lelio della Valle (1581–1586)', ASRSP, vol. 105 (1982), pp. 237–59.

37. Benvenuto Cellini, *Autobiography*, translated ... by George Bull (Harmondsworth, 1956), pp. 153–9. Cf. Marini, *Degli archiatri*, vol. 1, pp. 325–9.

38. Pietro Savio, 'Ricerche sui medici e chirurghi dell' Ospedale di Santo Spirito in Sassia sec. XVI–XVII', ASRSP, series 3, vol. 25 (1971), pp. 145–68. Cf. Marini, *Degli archiatri*, vol. 1, pp. 444–6.

39. Under Leo X in 1514 there were sixteen medical chairs at the *Sapienza*. As refounded after the sack of Rome, however, chairs were fewer. No more than three, four, or five medical teachers are named in each of the *ruoli* between 1535 and 1548. See F. M.

Renazzi, *Storia dell' Università di Roma* (4 vols, Rome, 1803–6), pp. 235–47, and P. Tacchi–Venturi, 'Un ruolo inedito dell' Archiginnasio Romano sotto Paolo III', ASRSP, vol. 24 (1901), pp. 260–5.

40. Ferrajoli, 'Il ruolo della corte'; Renazzi, *Università di Roma*.

41. *Dizionario Biografico degli Italiani*, hereafter DBI, (Rome, 1960–, in progress), vol. 1, pp. 111–12; Marini, *Degli archiatri*, vol. 2, pp. 279–80.

42. Pastor, *History of the Popes*, vol. 12, pp. 528, 537.

43. DBI, vol 8, pp. 17–19.

44. DBI, vol. 5, pp. 307–8; Marini, *Degli archiatri*, vol. 1, p. 315.

45. Marini, *Degli archiatri*, vol. 2, p. 351.

46. Pastor, *History of the Popes*, vol. 14, pp. 11–18; Marini, *Degli archiatri*, vol. 1, pp. 397–9.

47. Pastor, *History of the Popes*, vol. 13, p. 387; Marini, *Degli archiatri*, vol. 1, p. 327.

48. Marini, *Degli archiatri*, vol. 1, p. 354.

49. This was the view of the Venetian ambassador Mocenigo in 1560, who likened the palace to a small town in which it was difficult to find one's way (Pastor, *History of the Popes*, vol. 13, p. 367).

50. For instance, D'Amico, *Renaissance Humanism*, and Stinger, *Renaissance in Rome*. Studies of humanism in general tend to neglect its impact on the professions and higher university faculties.

51. Castiglione, *Book of the Courtier*, pp. 41–2, 161, 182.

52. David Chambers, *Cardinal Bainbridge in the Court of Rome 1509 to 1514* (Oxford, 1965), p. 134.

53. Aretino, *Ragionamento*, especially p. 30, 'Vita è il non andare a Corte'.

54. J. A. F. Orbaan, 'Un viaggio di Clemente VIII nel Viterbese', ASRSP, vol. 36 (1913), pp 113–45.

55. Italo Paoletti, *Gerolamo Mercuriale e il suo tempo* (Lanciano, 1963), p. 25.

56. Printed in Marini, *Degli archiatri*, vol. 2, pp. 311–13.

57. BAV, *Cod. Urb. Lat.* 1059, part 1, *Avvisi di Roma*, f. 204r, 10 April 1591: 'et come sia in Roma il Mercuriale chiamato da Bologna, et altri medici che si aspettano di fuori, si farà Collegio delli piu periti in questa arte'.

58. Marini, *Degli archiatri*, vol. 1, p. 364.

59. Ibid., pp. 393–7; *DBI*, vol. 5, pp. 539–40.

60. Marini, *Degli archiatri*, vol. 1, pp. 471–2.

61. *Le carte Strozziane del R. Archivio di Stato in Firenze, inventario*. Serie prima, 2 vols (Florene 1884, 1891), vol. 2, pp. 334–5. A letter from Cardinal Pietro Aldobrandini to Iacopo Aldobrandini, Nunzio in Naples, 1604.

62. Marini, *Degli archiatri*, vol. 1, pp. 236–80, 462–8.

63. *Memoirs of a Renaissance Pope: The commentaries of Pius II*, an abridgement, trans. by F. A. Gragg, ed. L. C. Gabel, (London, 1960) p. 39.

64. E. Teza 'Guicciardini alla morte di Clemente VII da lettere inedite, appunti', *Atti dell' Istituto Veneto di Scienze, Lettere ed Arti*,

series 6, vol. 7 (1888–9), pp. 897–932.

65. Eugenio Albèri, *Relazioni degli ambasciatori veneti al Senato*, series 2, vol. 3 (Florence, 1846), p. 11. A *relazione* of Paolo Capello, 'Il papa ha anni settanta; ogni dì si ringiovanisce'.

66. Pastor, *History of the Popes*, vol. 15, pp. 361–2.

67. Jean Delumeau, *Vie économique et sociale de Rome dans le second moitié du XVI ᵉ siècle*, (2 vols, Paris, 1957–9), vol. 1, pp. 25–36.

68. BAV, *Cod. Urb. Lat.* 1059 part 1, ff. 174r–228r; part 2, ff. 529v–559r.

69. BAV, *Cod. Barb. Lat.* 2567, ff. 26r–28v, Augustini Ricchi in hystoriam egrotationis Pauli Quarti ... praefatio. Partly printed in Pastor, *History of the Popes*, vol. 14, p. 486.

70. For instance, 'De Pii V ... morbo, quo obiit. Jo. Francisco Marenco Albensi ejus medico', printed in Marini, *Degli archiatri*, vol. 2, pp. 318–23.

71. Petronio, *Del viver delli Romani*, pp. 1–14, 37, 209.

72. Pastor, *History of the Popes*, vol. 14, appx. 9, pp. 432–3, a letter of 23 May 1555.

73. For example, BAV, *Cod. Urb. Lat.* 1042, f. 56v, an *avviso* of 11 May 1571 on Pius V. Leo X was said by Paolo Giovio to take a weekly purge with pills of aloes. See L. Gualino 'La fistola di Leon X', *Bollettino dell' Istituto Storico Italiano dell' Arte Sanitaria*, vol. 6 (1926), pp. 125–39, 157–68, especially p. 158.

74. Petronio, *Del viver delli Romani*, p. 41 *et seq.*; Pastor, *History of the Popes*, vol. 13, p. 403.

75. Petronio, *Del viver delli Romani*.

76. Ibid., and Pastor, *History of the Popes*, vol. 16, pp. 436–7; Vol. 17, p. 125.

77. Archivio di Stato di Roma, *Camerale primo*, 1299, reg. B., f. 19r, 20 May 1564.

78. Albèri, *Relazioni*, series 2, vol. 3, p. 127. A *relazione* of Marco Foscari, 1526.

79. Pastor, *History of the Popes*, vol. 15, p. 88; vol. 17, pp. 57–8.

80. Ibid., vol. 14, p. 66.

81. Ibid., vol. 19, pp. 38–9.

82. Ibid., vol. 11, p. 29.

83. Andrea Bacci, *De naturali vinorum historia, de vinis Italiae et de conviviis antiquorum* (Rome, 1596).

84. Pastor, *History of the Popes*, vol. 16, p. 400.

85. Ibid., vol. 14, p. 52.

86. BAV, *Cod. Urb. Lat.* 1058, f. 494r, an *avviso* of 26 September.

87. Pastor, *History of the Popes*, vol. 6, p. 433.

88. Agostino Ricci (see note 69), f. 27v.

89. Pastor, *History of the Popes*, vol. 18, p. 454.

90. Ibid., vol. 15, p. 66.

91. BAV , *Cod. Urb. Lat.* 1039, f. 55r, an *avviso* of 24 June 1559.

92. Pastor, *History of the Popes*, vol. 21, p. 52; vol. 22, pp. 178–9.

93. BAV, *Cod. Urb. Lat.*, 1039, f. 58v, an *avviso* of 8 July 1559.

94. Pastor, *History of the Popes*, vol. 15, pp. 85–7.

95. J. A. F. Orbaan, 'La Roma di Sisto V negli *Avvisi*', ASRSP,

Richard Palmer

vol. 33 (1910), pp. 277–312, especially p. 286, an *avviso* of 5 February 1586.

96. BAV, *Cod. Urb. Lat.* 1041, ff. 198r, 221r, 248v–258r, 291r, *avvisi* December 1569–April 1570. Cf. Pastor, *History of the Popes*, vol. 18, pp. 450–4. On Marenci's appointment, Marini, *Degli archiatri*, vol. 1, pp. 441–3.

97. 'Relatione dell' infermità e morte di Papa Pio Quinto', published on pp. 200–7 of 'Le pape Saint Pie V', *Analecta Bollandiana*, vol. 33 (1914), pp. 187–215.

98. Cortesius, *De cardinalatu*, ff. 70–83 (*de sanitate conservanda*); Weil-Garris and D'Amico, *The Renaissance Cardinal's palace*, p. 74 *et seq.*

99. Richard Palmer, 'The control of plague in Venice and northern Italy 1348–1600', unpublished Ph.D. thesis, University of Kent at Canterbury, 1978.

100. Mallett, *The Borgias*, p. 22. On the subject in general, Angelo Celli, *Storia della malaria nell' agro romano* (Città di Castello, 1925).

101. Pastor, *History of the Popes*, vol. 21, p. 103.

102. *Calendar of State Papers, Venetian*, ed. Rawdon Brown, vol. 2 (London, 1867), p. 96.

103. Marin Sanudo, *I diarii* (58 vols, Venice, 1879–1903), for example vol. 22, cols 372, 443, 475; vol. 26, col. 7; vol. 29, cols 164, 172–3, for the period 1516–20. On Leo's health in general, Gualino, 'La fistola di Leon X'.

104. Petronio, *Del viver delli Romani*, pp. 301–2.

105. *Calendar of State Papers, Venetian*, vol. 2, p. 425, 17 October 1517.

106. Pastor, *History of the Popes*, vol. 6, p. 132.

107. Orbaan, 'La Roma di Sisto V', p. 283, an *avviso* of 22 May 1585.

108. BAV, *Cod. Urb. Lat.* 1058, f. 441r, an *avviso* of 29 August 1590.

109. BAV, *Cod. Barb. Lat.* 2804, f. 441r. 'Aiunt Sanctitatem suam primam noctem sui Pontificatus insomnem fere totam pertransiisse et molestas sibi fuisse musculas nonullas quas zampanas vocant, et quia adhuc apud Vaticanum aer salubris non erat, die sequenti, que fuit Dominica XVIª eiusdem mensis septembris ex Vaticano ad montem Quirinalem transmigrare statuit ... '

110. Pastor, *History of the Popes*, vol. 11, p. 29.

111. A. Bertolotti, 'Speserie segrete e pubbliche di Papa Paolo III', *Atti e Memorie delle RR. Deputazioni di Storia Patria per le Provincie dell Emilia'*, new series, vol. 3 (1878), pp. 169–212, especially p. 186, 3 June 1543.

112. Pastor, *History of the Popes*, vol. 22, p. 232.

113. F. Gregorovius, *Storia della città di Roma nel medio evo* (4 vols, Rome, 1900–1), vol. 4, p. 407, a letter of 20 February 1513.

114. Marini, *Degli archiatri*, vol. 1, p. 358.

115. See the diary of the master of ceremonies, Paris de Grassis, British Library, *Add. MS.* 8444, ff. 225v–228r; Gualino (see note 73);

E. Rodocanachi, *Le pontificat de Léon X* (Paris, 1931), pp. 274–7.

116. Pastor, *History of the Popes*, vol. 9, p. 216. Cf. C. W. Simon and M. T. Arco, 'Das Ende Adrian VI', *Medizinische Monatsschrift*, vol. 13 (1959), pp. 303–6.

117. *Calendar of State Papers, Venetian*, vol. 5 (London, 1873), p. 274. A dispatch of Matteo Dandolo to Venice, 13 November 1549.

118. Ricci (see note 69).

119. See notes 70 and 97.

120. Pastor, *History of the Popes*, vol. 20, p. 636, an *avviso* of 12 April 1585.

121. BAV, *Cod. Urb. Lat.* 1058, f. 500r, an *avviso* of 29 September 1590.

122. BAV, *Cod. Barb. Lat.* 2804, f. 421r–v, the diary of the master of ceremonies Mucanzio.

123. Rodocanachi, *Le pontificat de Léon X*, p. 115.

124. Pastor, *History of the Popes*, vol. 9, p. 216.

125. See note 70.

126. Mucanzio (see note 122); BAV, *Cod. Urb. Lat.* 1059, parts 1–2, ff. 174r–559r, *avvisi* March–October 1591.

127. British Library, *Add. MS.* 8442, f. 280r–v. The passage is quoted in Marini, *Degli archiatri*, vol. 1, p. 283, where the word *Gallicus*, describing Julius's old ailment, is omitted.

128. *Calendar of State Papers, Venetian*, vol. 4 (London, 1871), p. 200, Gasparo Contarini to Venice, 20 February 1529.

129. Teza, 'Guicciardini', p. 902.

130. On Adrian, see note 20. On Clement, BAV, *Cod. Ferrajolus* 287, part xiv, f. 5r: 'Al fiscio per la medicina da cavalli data a Papa Clemente ... Rodulpho Silvestrino fisico clarissimo liberatori urbis et orbis S.P.Q.R. benemerito posuit.'

131. Piccolomini, 'Il pontificato di Pio III', pp. 116, 123.

132. Teza, 'Guicciardini', p. 907, 16 August 1534 – 'mi è parsa una strana fantasia quella del Corte a volere, con una inventione nuova et senza necessità alcuna, fare notomia della persona d'un papa'; p. 909, 5 September 1534 – 'Maestro Matteo, al quale el mondo attribuisce l'havere condotto Sua Santità a questi termini'.

133. Aretino, *Ragionamento*, p. 21. 'Il Macerata che ci levò dinanzi Adriano, e il Corte, che mandò a porta inferi Clemente'.

134. Marini, *Degli archiatri*, vol. 1, p. 339.

135. On Leo's fistula, Gualino, 'La fistola di Leon X'. On Jacopo da Brescia, Marini, *Degli archiatri*, vol. 1, pp. 317–19. On his house, C. L. Frommel, *Der Römische Palastbau der Hochrenaissance*, vol. 2, *Katalog* (Tübingen, 1973), pp. 49–52. Further details of Jacopo's house are in his will, BAV, *Cod. Ferrajolus* 424, ff. 273r–275v, 18 September 1520.

136. Marini, *Degli archiatri*, vol. 2, p. 273.

137. Ibid., vol. 1, pp. 243–6, 257–80.

138. Piccolomini, 'La famiglia di Pio III'.

139. Marini, *Degli archiatri*, vol. 1, pp. 393–7; DBI, vol. 5, pp. 539–40.

140. Pastor, *History of the Popes*, vol. 16, pp. 58–65, especially

p. 61; DBI, vol. 27, pp. 606–12.

141. BAV, *Fondo ruoli*, pp. 33–4.

142. Pastor, *History of the Popes*, vol. 16, p. 81.

143. Ibid., vol. 17, pp. 140–2.

144. A. V. Antonovics, 'Counter-Reformation Cardinals: 1534–90', *European Studies Review*, vol. 2 (1972), pp. 301–28. Barbara M. Hallman, *Italian Cardinals, Reform and the Church as Property* (Berkeley, Los Angeles, and London, 1985).

145. Cited in Delumeau, *Vie économique ... de Rome*, vol. 1, p. 11.

146. Pio Pecchiai, *Roma nel Cinquecento* (Bologna, 1948), p. 282.

147. BAV, *Fondo ruoli*, pp. 67, 100.

148. Albèri, *Relazioni*, vol. 4. (Florence, 1857), p. 138, the *relazione* of Giacomo Soranzo, 1565. English translation as in Pastor, *History of the Popes*, vol. 16, p. 79.

149. Pastor, *History of the Popes*, vol. 17, pp. 55, 140–3.

150. Ibid., vol. 23, p. 40.

151. Marini, *Degli archiatri*, vol. 1, pp. 290–7, 367–9.

152. Rome, Archivio di Stato, *Università di Roma*, filza 58, a copy of the bull of 30 March 1581.

153. On Demetrio Canevari, for instance, who held this post under Gregory XIV and the three successive Popes, see DBI, vol. 18, pp. 59–60.

154. See note 61.

155. Marini, *Degli archiatri*, vol. 1, pp. 435–9; vol. 2, pp. 302–10. Cf. Pastor, *History of the Popes*, vol. 15, p. 75.

156. Marini, *Degli archiatri*, vol. 1, pp. 433–5.

157. Albèri, *Relazioni*, series 2, vol. 4 (Florence, 1857), p. 136.

3

The Court Physician and Paracelsianism

Hugh Trevor-Roper

Paracelsianism is one of the great intellectual phenomena of the sixteenth century. In retrospect, we see it as a medical phenomenon, but in its origin it was much more than this. Though its permanent result was medical – the insertion of chemistry into medicine – it began as a total movement, a philosophy, a new *Weltanschauung,* with revolutionary implications. Seen in his context, in the intellectual history of his time, Paracelsus was a kindred spirit, and a rival, to his contemporary, Martin Luther. Both were products of the spiritual crisis of Germany in the early sixteenth century, and they shared many German, and many personal, characteristics. Like Luther, Paracelsus was a violent, intemperate man, of strong language and rough manners, and he addressed himself primarily to the German world: he wrote in German for Germans. His medical teaching was the application, within his own special field, of a general philosophy, indeed cosmology, which far transcended that field; and this philosophy, he claimed, as Luther claimed for his, was true Christianity, restored to its original purity, free at last from the corrupt incrustations of the Middle Ages. In Luther's eyes, that corruption came from the paganism of the Roman Church; in those of Paracelsus, it came from the paganism of Aristotle and his medical disciple Galen.

Philosophically, and in its political implications, Paracelsianism was far more radical than Lutheranism – at least than Lutheranism after the German Peasants' Revolt of 1525. It had a revolutionary messianic content which it never entirely lost: it continued to provide some of the dynamism of German Protestantism when Lutheranism had run out of steam. In this Paracelsus is comparable not with Luther but with Luther's

79

other German rivals – Sebastian Franck, Caspar Schwenckfeld, and, later, Valentin Weigel and Jakob Boehme: men who preserved something of the radical mysticism of the early Luther and continued it, through the Thirty Years War, till it settled into Pietism.

This revolutionary content of Paracelsianism must not be forgotten even if we are concerned only with its medical application; for it affected the reception of its medical teaching. It alarmed the established classes, just as the initial revolutionary content of Lutheranism had done when it became apparent in the Peasants' Revolt. So long as Paracelsian medical ideas were inseparable from their revolutionary premises, they were bound to be suspect to conservative rulers. On the other hand, if they could be separated from those premises, and judged, and vindicated, purely empirically, the grounds for suspicion were taken away. The external history of Paracelsian medicine – the history of its dissemination – is thus, to a large extent, the history of its disengagement from Paracelsian cosmology: a disengagement which (combined, of course, with its proven effectiveness in some cases) rendered it acceptable among the conservative classes. That separation was never absolute: there were always occasions when Paracelsianism returned, as it were, to its revolutionary roots. But this was not the Paracelsianism patronised by princes – except in those cases (for there were some) when princes themselves became revolutionary.

The effective dissemination of Paracelsian ideas and practices began in the generation after the death of their author in 1541. Paracelsus himself seems to have shown remarkably little interest in the publication of his works. A wild, disorderly charismatic genius, perpetually on the move, he scattered his ideas and his manuscripts without apparent concern for their preservation. However, his disciples treasured these documents as declarations of saving religious truths, or at least as manuals of profitable medical practice. They published the truths, or some of them, and they applied the practice. However, since both the truths and the practice were heretical, they inevitably ran into opposition: the religious truths were suppressed by the religious establishment, the medical ideas and practice were opposed by the medical establishment. For Paracelsianism, as a medical system, was a doctrine for the depressed classes of the medical world, for the apothecaries and surgeons. It was an affront to the traditional establishment, the Galenist physicians organized in colleges and faculties. Thus, from the start, patronage was necessary to overcome this opposition.

Where could such patronage be found? It could come from various sources. There was the private patronage of rich individuals. There was the patronage of city corporations: many German cities appointed a Paracelsian physician as their *Stadtphysicus*. Other such physicians were maintained, just as heretical chaplains could be, in the private households of the nobility. Still others maintained themselves by general practice – but precariously, at a low social level, always at the mercy of the established medical corporations which had the right to expel unqualified practitioners from the cities of their jurisdiction. And then there were the armies of warring Europe. Paracelsus himself had been an army doctor, and so were many of his followers. The battlefield was perhaps the greatest laboratory for the new experimental science of Paracelsian surgery, as were the city slums for the Paracelsian apothecaries, the physicians of the poor.

Thus, in the generation after Paracelsus, in spite of official disapproval, his ideas circulated. They circulated mainly in the German world, to which they were addressed; and because they were apparently disorderly and certainly revolutionary, they were taken up, vulgarized, and distorted by a host of so-called 'spagyrists' – empirics, not to say quacks, who gave them a bad name. However, even in those years, thanks to certain enthusiastic disciples, they made their way in lay society, and here and there they even won the attention, and favour, of that most valuable of all protectors (as Luther knew), a prince.

For obviously, for any heresy, the ultimate protection, at that time, was princely power. A Renaissance prince could defy the entrenched authority of a medical faculty or corporation. He could give protection against the law. He could pay for the publication of books and guarantee them against censorship. He could provide resources – a laboratory, a professorial chair in his private university, a team of researchers, international contacts. And he could also provide power, wealth, and fame: to be in charge of the health of a prince, to have protected him against assassination by poison (one of the most important functions of a royal doctor in the age of ideology and despotism), to be also (for with Paracelsians, one function merged in the other) his alchemist, capable – at least potentially – of creating wealth by chemical transmutation, was a responsibility which, of itself, brought in rewards; though it also entailed risks, as Dr Lopez, the too-political Portuguese Jewish physician of Queen Elizabeth, and some of the unsuccessful alchemical doctors at the court of Württemberg, were to discover.

The part played by the princes in the fortune of Paracelsianism began, naturally enough, in Germany. Paracelsus himself was far too independent a character to acknowledge any patron. Although he was received by Ferdinand, King of Hungary, afterwards the Emperor Ferdinand I, he was never a royal doctor. His association with city governments in Basel and Strasbourg was turbulent and brief. He preferred a life of vagabondage, among peasants and miners. However, in the years after his death, his disciples found princely patrons, and soon the fashion spread from court to court. Royalty has often shown a preference for unconventional doctors; the princes of the Renaissance were themselves, in many respects, radicals: intellectual heretics, innovators not traditionalists in practice; and anyway, Paracelsianism itself, thanks to its commentators, was coming to meet them. In the generation after the death of the Founder, we find it quietly disowning his revolutionary ideas and exchanging his disordered peasant clothes for a more courtly dress.

One of the first, perhaps the first, prince to take up Paracelsianism was the great humanist and patron of printing and the arts, Ottheinrich, Duke of Neuburg, afterwards Elector Palatine and head of the senior branch of the house of Wittelsbach. His court physician was Adam von Bodenstein, who had been converted to Paracelsianism by his own experience and became the first great propagandist of Paracelsus, publishing over forty of his works. Ottheinrich also had chemical interests. He employed a chemist, Hans Kilian, who made a large collection of Paracelsian manuscripts. These were stored in the Elector's castle of Neuburg on the Danube, and remained there after 1545, when the Elector was driven out of his little Danubian principality and forced to take refuge in the Palatinate, at Weinheim on the Rhine.

The Elector was driven out because he had become a Protestant. From the beginning, the heresy of Paracelsianism was closely linked to the other new heresy of Protestantism. It was, or became, a heresy within that heresy. The connection was not exclusive, however. Sometimes family tradition was stronger than doctrinaire consistency. The junior branch of the Wittelsbach family, the ducal house of Bavaria, would also become patrons of Paracelsianism. Indeed, at the end of the century, it was a younger son of that family, Ernst von Wittelsbach, Elector of Cologne, a vigorous politician of the Counter-Reformation, who would finance the first publication of the complete works of Paracelsus. That was a remarkably bold step in 1590–1605, when the Catholic Church was condemning all forms of Platonism, hermeticism, and so on. However, the Elector of Cologne was a powerful prince and could afford to be eccentric. The editor of this great edition was the Elector's court physician, Johann Huser, a Paracelsian from Breslau; and he based it on the 141 volumes of manuscripts which Ottheinrich had collected and which had remained at Neuburg. He was just in time, for within a few years the growing opposition of the Roman Church would reach its climax and the works of Paracelsus would be put on the Roman Index. Later, when the Wittelsbach Palatinate had fallen into pious Roman Catholic hands, Ottheinrich's great collection would be solemnly burnt.

Ottheinrich also employed, as librarian and physician, a German doctor from Danzig, Alexander von Suchten. It was while at his court that Suchten too became a Paracelsian – indeed, the most distinguished of the early Paracelsians. Afterwards (in 1554) Suchten was employed as *Archiater*, i. e. chief physician, by Sigismund Augustus, King of Poland; but his religious views got him into trouble in Poland – he had already been condemned in Rome and deprived of his canonry of Frauenberg – and he returned to Germany and published his offending Paracelsian works at Basel. One of his offences may have been his scientific proof that the transmutation of base metal into gold is impossible. This was not acceptable doctrine to German, or other, princes.

The year 1570, when Suchten published his first volume, may be taken as the year when Paracelsianism became respectable. It was then that Paracelsian books began to come out in a steady stream, presented not in barbarous German but in civilized Latin, addressed to, and sponsored by, learned men. In 1571 the venerable Winther von Andernach, the teacher of Vesalius, having been converted by one of Paracelsus's disciples at Strasbourg, published his *De Medicina Veteri et Nova*, in which he announced his respect for 'the new medicine'. Even more important, in the same year a Danish physician, Peder Sorensen, *alias* Severinus – 'Severinus the Dane' as he was called (to distinguish him from the other Italian Severinus, Marco Aurelio Severino – published at Basel his *Idea Medicinae Philosophicae*. This was an academic presentation and vindication of Paracelsianism. Severinus had studied Paracelsianism in Germany. Now he went back to his native Denmark and was appointed court physician to the King of Denmark – a position he was to hold for thirty years. There he became an important person in an important court of the northern Renaissance; for the court of Denmark was now rich with the tolls of the Sound, elegant new buildings were rising in Copenhagen, and the royal observatory of Tycho Brahe at Uranieborg was known throughout Europe. When European scholars visited Denmark, the persons they liked to boast of having met were the great astronomer Tycho Brahe, Niels Hemmingsen, the Danish oracle on witches, and Peter Severinus, 'Severinus the Dane'.

Denmark, of course, was within the German *Kulturgebiet*. Paracelsianism was still a very German phenomenon. However, German ideas were carried across the German cultural frontier by two means in particular: by religion and war. French, English, Polish, and Hungarian Protestants studying medicine abroad tended to go to German universities. Army doctors accompanying the cosmopolitan French and imperial armies learned German techniques. By these two means Paracelsian ideas came to France and, particularly, to the royal court of France. Indeed, we can say that the French court, though Catholic, was the first royal court to patronize such ideas; and it patronized them more continuously than any other. The ideas reached it when the army doctors returned to Paris after the peace of Câteau Cambrésis of 1559 which wound up the wars of Charles V and François I and established international peace for a whole generation. They also reached French society – particularly in the south – through returning Huguenots who had discovered them while seeking religious truth in Protestant Germany.

It is just after the Peace of Câteau Cambrésis that we find in Paris a group of successful army doctors meeting regularly at the home of one of them, the Piedmontese physician Leonard Botal. Botal had made his name as a specialist in gunshot-wounds, and was to become *premier médecin* to the Queen Mother, Catherine de Médicis. The others included Honoré Chastellan, the present *premier médecin* to the Queen, Jean Chapelain, *premier médecin* to her son, the young King, and the famous surgeon Ambroise Paré. All these men were Catholics; none of them was a Paracelsian. However, the court of Catherine de Médicis was liberal, tolerant, open to new ideas, and all of them were interested in these new doctrines. The driving force among them was Jacques Gohory. He was a real, indeed an enthusiastic Paracelsian, and was to become the chief propagandist of Paracelsian ideas in France. He would found an academy and his arboretum would be the precursor of the *Jardin des Plantes*, the centre of chemical teaching in Paris in the next century.

From this circle in Paris came the royal doctors of the Valois court in its last thirty years. They were not Paracelsian, but they can be described as semi-Paracelsian: they were open to chemical and other heresies. As such they were deeply suspect to the medical establishment of Paris, which was entrenched in the Faculty of Medicine of the University. Since the court of Catherine de Médicis was also suspect to the religious establishment – as too favourable to Huguenots, too eager to tolerate Huguenots, allied with Protestants abroad, in Germany and Holland, against ultra-Catholic Spain – this only added to the deep distrust with which the court was regarded by the defenders of orthodoxy. So three powerful institutions of society – the Parlement of Paris, representing the legal establishment, the Sorbonne representing the theological establishment, and the Faculty of Medicine representing the medical establishment – found themselves allied as the defenders of tradition in law, religion, and medicine against a dangerously liberal royal court. This was the background to the spectacular test case which the Parlement of Paris, in alliance with the Sorbonne and the Faculty, brought in 1578 against Roch le Baillif, a Huguenot, and a bigoted Paracelsian, who held the useful title of *médecin ordinaire du roy*. Like many test cases, it solved nothing, but gave great publicity to the Paracelsians who, from now on, established themselves firmly in French society.

If this was true in the court of the last Valois kings, who were Catholic, what was to be expected in the court of a Bourbon king, a Huguenot, whose power base was the heretical Huguenot Languedoc? Henri of Navarre, the political leader of the Huguenots, was the indisputable heir to the crown of France. His little court at Nérac was a Huguenot court and his court physicians, who were all Huguenots, were either real Paracelsians, trained in Germany or Switzerland, or semi-Paracelsians from the suspect, semi-Huguenot University of Montpellier. When he finally found himself King of France, Henri IV abjured his Protestantism, but he did not abjure his medical preferences, and when his court was established at Fontainebleau, the Medical Faculty of the University saw with dismay that he relied on a close partnership of three doctors who were triply suspect: for all of them were Huguenots, immigrants from Calvinist Geneva, and professed Paracelsians. They were Jean Ribit, sieur de la Rivière, *premier médecin*; Joseph Duchesne (in Latin *Quercetanus*), sieur de la Violette, the most famous chemical doctor of his time; and Theodore de Mayerne, a protégé of Duchesne. The fear and hatred which this situation inspired in the Paris Faculty, dominated as it was by rigid Galenists, led to a fierce struggle and a long and bitter public controversy, in the course of which the Faculty formally declared the royal doctors to be charlatans and forbade them to practise in Paris or apothecaries to prepare medicines for them.

The battle between the Faculty of Medicine and the royal doctors of Henri IV lasted several years, and tempers grew very violent. It engaged outside doctors: Huguenot doctors from Orléans joined in, and the great Saxon chemist Andreas Libavius, whom the orthodox had hoped to enlist on their side (for he hated Paracelsian radicalism), finally came down on the side of the heretics. In the end, a compromise was reached, which settled nothing except the dust. The King of France continued to employ Paracelsian doctors (although after 1608 they had to be Catholics): Jean Héroard, the *premier médecin* of Louis XIII, a converted Huguenot, was a Paracelsian. The Faculty continued to rage against them, but less violently because it had now no hope of victory. The private feelings of its leaders are vividly displayed in the letters of Gui Patin, Dean of the Faculty. Patin's mordant eloquence rises to a high pitch of detestation whenever he touches his *bêtes noires*: royal doctors, the University of Montpellier, doctors from the heretical Languedoc, the home of crooks and charlatans, and a whole series of dreadful chemical doctors: du Chesne, Mayerne, Francois Vautier, *premier médecin* of the Queen Mother Marie de Medicis – a chemical doctor from Montpellier – and the even more dreadful Paracelsian Huguenot protégé of the execrable Cardinal Richelieu, 'le gazetier' (for he was a journalist, the founder of French journalism) Théophraste Renaudot.

By following the French court we have moved forward

rather rapidly in time. Let us go back to the 1570s, the period of the Paracelsian breakthrough into the courts of Europe. First, however, let us guard against too simple a view. Paracelsianism was a complex system of thought, unsystematically expressed, imperfectly published, and often misunderstood. It was open to different interpretations according to time, circumstance, and inclination, and by 1570 these differences were becoming apparent. In particular, it was becoming clear that if it was to capture the royal court, it must shed, or at least suspend, its revolutionary content – or rather, escape from its revolutionary context: its religious and ideological messianism, its insistence that the Prophet Elijah was to return – *Elias Artista*, Elijah as alchemist – to create a new 'chemical' transformation of the world. We may observe that, in the whole of the sixteenth century, it was only the medical and never the specifically religious works of Paracelsus that were published: these circulated in manuscripts, but, until the nineteenth century, they remained the private possession of obscure German sects, and it is only since the end of that century that they have been published. Of course Paracelsus's religious views emerged incidentally in his medical works; but there they could be taken or left at choice. Meanwhile, his medical ideas became detached from his total philosophy and could be absorbed piecemeal into more orthodox medicine.

This leads to difficulties of definition. How can we define a Paracelsian doctor in the later sixteenth century? The easy definition is an iatrochemist, 'a chemical doctor'. But not every chemical doctor acknowledged Paracelsus as his master. Andreas Libavius, the Saxon founder of modern chemistry, who seemed a Paracelsian when viewed from Galenist Paris, was a pugnacious anti-Paracelsian in public controversy. Peter Severinus, the greatest publicist of Paracelsian ideas, would be praised highly by Francis Bacon, who was critical of chemical philosophers and contemptuous of Paracelsus himself. There were many eclectic physicians who respected Paracelsus and borrowed from him without swallowing his whole philosophy, and who are most safely described as semi-Paracelsian. We must therefore use the term with some caution.

Nor is the definition of royal doctors clear and constant. Physicians specifically defined as *Archiater, Leibarzt, Premier Médecin*, are beyond dispute: these were the real court physicians. However, the more general title of *médecin du roi, medicus regius, à consiliis medicis,* may indicate only a tenuous and occasional connection, like the modern term 'purveyor to Her Majesty'. Some of those who used such terms cannot be proved to have attended their patron professionally. Even those who can were often transients at court. They also had other non-medical interests, and we cannot be quite sure in which capacity they were most valued. A medical man of the Renaissance was expected to be a Renaissance man, a universal philosopher – like Paracelsus himself. Ficino, Rabelais, Servetus, Cornelius Agrippa, Nostradamus, Giordano Bruno, John Dee were all medical doctors, but we do not think of them as such. William Gilbert, the discoverer of magnetism, and Lancelot Browne, the orientalist, were physicians to Queen Elizabeth. Many doctors were better known as Greek scholars, mathematicians, mineralogists, botanists, poets, historians, than as physicians, and we cannot be sure in which capacity they had been discovered, or were valued by their patrons. Perhaps the award of the title of physician to the prince was sometimes no more than a recognition of distinction in other fields, an encouragement to technological research or a reward for tributary odes, like the titles of honour which the Emperor Rudolf II gave to his artists. And then we must always remember that chemistry is not yet distinct from alchemy, nor alchemy from the transmutation of metals. All princes were greedy of gold, and men who thought of themselves as Paracelsian physicians were sometimes seen by princely patrons as useful for more vulgar purposes of which Paracelsus himself, that uncompromising radical idealist, would never have approved.

With all these reservations, however, we can still say that, after 1560, there is a perceptible tendency in princely courts to prefer Paracelsian or semi-Paracelsian doctors, sometimes in direct defiance of the official medical establishment. There is also, at least in Catholic countries, a hardening of the orthodoxy of that establishment. I have remarked that, by the turn of the century, Platonism, Hermetism, and ultimately Paracelsianism itself were condemned by Rome. The Jesuits in particular hated it, and it was they who, increasingly, controlled education in Catholic countries. However, some Catholic rulers refused to toe the line: the Wittelsbachs in Bavaria and Cologne; the Medici in Tuscany as in France (where two of the family – Catherine de Médicis the widow of Henri II and Marie de Médicis the widow of Henri IV – were Queens Regent); above all the Emperor Rudolf II, the crowned Hermetist who broke all the rules and turned his capital, in semi-Protestant Prague, into the headquarters of a Hermetic international. Among Rudolf's physicians were the two Martin Rulands, father and son, both Paracelsian enthusiasts: the father was the author of the most famous dictionary of Paracelsian terms. The imperial example no doubt encouraged other German princes. In 1604 the Huguenot and Paracelsian *médecin ordinaire* of Henri IV, Joseph Duchesne, gave a list of the German princes who were patrons of Paracelsian medicine. They were the Emperor, the King of Poland, the Elector of Cologne, the Duke of Saxony, the Margrave of Brandenburg, Heinrich Julius Duke of Brunswick, Maurice Landgrave of Hesse, Ferdinand Duke of Bavaria, 'all the princes of Anhalt'.

Indeed, these first years of the sixteenth century saw Paracelsianism at its height in the courts of Europe and, particularly in those of Germany. In the rest of Europe it was the modified Paracelsianism of Severinus, but in Germany it was closer to its original form: these were messianic years in which it would resume – if it had ever shed – its religious radicalism. So it mingled with Rosicrucianism and became the doctrine of Protestant revolt. This was not quite what its patron the Emperor Rudolf intended, but it was not without some reason that the revolution, when it came, began in his capital, Prague.

Among the Paracelsian physicians who haunted the court of Rudolf II were three men of particular interest. One was Joan Baptista van Helmont, the Belgian who was to become the great revisionist of Paracelsianism. He travelled through Germany, studying, in the years 1599–1605. If he was not a court physician that was not because the princes were not interested in him: both the Habsburg Emperor and the Wittelsbach Elector of Cologne tried to engage him as their court physician, but like Paracelsus himself, he was an austere idealist, not to be trapped by princes. He refused and returned to his private researches in Belgium, where he was persecuted for them by the Jesuits. The second was Oswald Croll, the *Leibmedicus* of Christian, Prince of Anhalt-Bernberg, who in turn was the adviser, indeed the Mephistopheles, of Frederick, Elector Palatine, soon to be, by a disastrous gamble, the Winter King of Bohemia. If any one man provoked the Thirty Years War, it was he. Christian of Anhalt was himself an amateur as well as a patron of Paracelsian chemistry: on a secret diplomatic visit to Paris he surprised the French court physicians by swallowing poison and then correcting it by his own home-made antidote. The third was the Pole Michael Sedziwoj, or Sendivogius, who claimed to have discovered the philosophers' stone and whom a modern Polish scholar has credited with the discovery of oxygen. He was a very mysterious character, and his life is encrusted with romantic myth. He was employed by both the Emperor Rudolf II and the King of Poland. Croll and Sendivogius were the two most famous Paracelsians of the time. Their books were best sellers. Croll's *Basilica Chymica*, dedicated to Christian of Anhalt, went through numerous editions and translations, and an English enthusiast described Sendivogius's *Novum Lumen Chemicum* as second only to the Bible in importance. Both were also secret political agents: Croll from the Prince of Anhalt to the Emperor, Sendivogius for the Emperor and the King of Poland.

For these Paracelsian court doctors formed a freemasonry. They were widely travelled men: they had contacts throughout Europe, they were accustomed to secrecy, their princes trusted them, and they trusted one another. When Henri IV of France conducted secret negotiations with Maurice the Learned, Landgrave of Hesse, who was his main ally among the German princes, the secret diplomatic intermediaries were their two Paracelsian physicians, the French Huguenot Joseph du Chesne and the German Mosanus. The Landgrave was the most effective patron of Paracelsianism in Germany. He too was himself a chemist, as well as being a poet, a musical composer, a surgeon, a linguist, a philosopher, a theologian, and a patron of drama, and he institutionalized the study of chemistry, founding the first official chair of the subject at his University of Marburg in 1609. The first professor was his own Paracelsian chief physician, Johann Hartmann.

I have left to the last the reception of Paracelsianism at the court of Great Britain. The first British monarch to employ Paracelsian court physicians was James VI and I. He showed his preference first as King of Scotland, then, after 1603, as King of England. The impulse came from other royal courts: first, when he was in Scotland, from that of Denmark, then, when he was in England, from that of France.

The man who first introduced the sophisticated form of Paracelsianism into England was an Anglicized Scotsman, Thomas Muffet, who went from Galenist Cambridge to the University of Basel in 1578 and there became a convert to the Paracelsianism which was gaining ground there – though not yet in the university: indeed, he shocked the examiners of his doctoral thesis by his aggressive denunciation of Galen. After his return to England he accompanied Lord Willoughby of Eresby on an embassy to Denmark to present the Order of the Garter to King Frederick II, and there he met the more sober Paracelsian Severinus, to whom he dedicated his first published work. Returning to England, he had a very successful career both in medicine and in politics. He sat in Parliament for a borough controlled by Sir Philip Sidney's brother-in-law, the Earl of Pembroke, and was physician to the *avant-garde* statesmen and courtiers of Queen Elizabeth – the supporters of the Earl of Leicester and a forward policy in Europe – Sir Francis Walsingham, Sir Philip Sidney, the Earl of Essex, Sir Francis Drake. However, the Queen herself clung to established ways and Muffet died in 1604, too soon to profit by the more liberal attitude of the next King.

Already, as King of Scotland, James I had shown his interest in Paracelsian medicine. In 1589–90 he too went to Denmark to marry a Danish princess, and there he met not only Severinus – and Hemmingsen (who taught him a thing or two about demonology) – but also a Scottish doctor, Thomas Craig, whom he brought back with him as his 'chief mediciner' to Scotland. When James became King of England in 1603 Craig followed him to London, and soon other Paracelsians were added to the medical establishment at court. However, James's great scoop was the acquisition, in 1610, of the most famous Paracelsian doctor in Paris, Theodore de Mayerne.

Mayerne was the last survivor of the three Huguenot Paracelsians from Geneva who had served Henri IV and whose heretical views had precipitated the great medical battle of 1603–8. Henri IV would have made him his *premier médecin* in 1609 if he had been willing to become a Catholic; but he was not. When Henri IV was assassinated in 1610, Mayerne decided to emigrate to England. He had already prepared the ground and King James was so delighted that he gave him very generous terms. In England Mayerne discovered Muffet's apothecary and acquired from him all Muffet's papers. He consciously became Muffet's heir, and published Muffet's learned and beautifully illustrated book on insects. He was enormously successful at the English court, the first physician to be knighted.

91

At the same time, being fond of money and a very skilful operator, he contrived to retain his position (and salary) as *médecin ordinaire* to the Crown of France – at least until 1628 when the two countries were at war and his French appointment was stopped. That upset him greatly, and he wrote agonized but ineffectual letters to the French ministers, including Cardinal Richelieu, whom he had cured of venereal disease (but he was too tactful to dwell on that) and who therefore, he thought, owed him something. Like so many of his colleagues – like du Chesne and Mosanus and Croll and Sendivogius – Mayerne was used by his patron as a secret agent abroad. On one occasion he was expelled from France, which caused a terrible international scandal: it took years to settle down. Clearly he was suspected of being in secret communication with the Huguenot grandees, who were all his patients, and were then plotting rebellion.

The suspicion was not unreasonable, for Mayerne remained always a Huguenot, deeply involved with the Calvinist international. His two wives were Dutch – one the sister of the Dutch ambassador to France, one the daughter of the Dutch ambassador to England. One of his sisters married an Italian Protestant who was James I's secret envoy to the Duke of Savoy, another went to Heidelberg in the train of James I's daughter, the Winter Queen of Bohemia, and then married a French Huguenot. He himself bought a feudal castle the Pays de Vand in Switzerland, not far from Geneva, and used it as a listening post for Protestant Europe. He was an international Protestant busybody as well as one of the most famous and successful doctors in Europe. He wrote out with his own hand royal instructions for British ambassadors, skilfully inserting into them orders to forward his own economic interests, and took it upon himself to recommend his foreign patrons as generals to be employed by the King of Britain. He was painted by Rubens; became enormously rich, and enormously fat; and married his daughter to the heir of a Huguenot duke. He lived to be 83, and when he died, in 1655, he was, I suppose, the last of the Paracelsian court physicians; for by that time Paracelsianism had lost its identity: its ideological content had dissolved, disintegrated, with its whole intellectual context, in the Thirty Years War. Its permanent contribution, the use of chemistry in medicine, had by then been quietly accepted into the medical tradition of Europe.

92

When we look at the Paracelsian royal doctors as a class, is there any general judgement that we can make? Not, I think, as physicians. As physicians they were a very miscellaneous group, and of course they were never exclusively royal doctors: they were physicians who happened to attract royal patients and so became part of the court; but they also had other patients, other activities, in which they no doubt prospered the more because of their court connection. If they illustrate anything it is rather the interest of princes than it is the history of medicine. They were not necessarily the greatest of medical men, or even of royal doctors: after all, the two greatest medical men of the period, Vesalius and Harvey, were also royal doctors, one to the Emperor Charles V, one to Charles I of England; and they were not Paracelsians. However, these Paracelsian court doctors undoubtedly helped to promote chemical medicine. However, they show that the Renaissance princes were, or could be, innovators in this area of patronage, as in others; and they illustrate the success of the Paracelsian challenge to medical orthodoxy.

We may also note that they fall into two main classes, distinguishable by nationality: the Germans and the non-Germans. Severinus in Copenhagen, La Rivière and Duchesne in Paris, Mayerne in England, are all explicitly Paracelsians: they declare themselves to be such. They are, however, very different from the Paracelsians at the German courts, who are far more deeply committed to the specifically German ideology of Paracelsus – even, in the case of Croll and Sendivogius, to its radical implications. We may also note how many of these doctors were engaged in secret diplomacy. That may or may not be connected with their Paracelsianism: royal doctors were always, potentially at least, political confidants. They did, however, distinguish themselves by the nature of their rewards. Royal doctors always prospered. They received royal grants, of land, of sinecures, sometimes, in Catholic countries, of benefices. Alexander von Suchten, while a good Catholic, was canon of Frauenberg. The Piedmontese Botal, court physician to Catherine de Médicis, though a layman, was the happy absentee abbot of a distant abbey. But there were also other assets which Paracelsian royal doctors, being chemists, naturalists, and mineralogists, were particularly qualified to exploit. Sendivogius was commissioned to build copper and iron foundries at Krzepice in Poland and was put in charge of another foundry

93

in Silesia. Mayerne invested in coal-mines in Scotland, tried to corner the coal trade to Paris and to exploit minerals in Derbyshire, sought a monopoly of English oyster-beds, and obtained a monopoly of distilling. This was an unforeseen, but not illogical, development from Paracelsus's experience in the mines of the Fugger at Villach and the interest of his disciples in mineral waters and baths. Perhaps a group of scholars will prefer the non-Paracelsian, non-chemical, Aristotelean, and far greater Dr Harvey, who replaced Mayerne as chief physician at the court of Charles I, and who never, as far as is known, showed any such vulgar interest in money but concentrated on his enquiries into the circulation of the blood and the generation of animals.

4

Prince-practitioning and the Direction of Medical Roles at the German Court:

Maurice of Hesse-Kassel and his physicians

Bruce T. Moran

Among physicians rendering medical service at European courts in the sixteenth and seventeenth centuries, by far the largest number cared for households at the smaller, less prominent courts of German territorial princes. The modest size of princely courts in comparison with those of royal patrons often encouraged occupational versatility among court attendants in order to respond to the personal interests and needs of the prince. The requirement for multiform talent especially affected the roles and responsibilities of physicians. Besides practising *physic*, physicians at smaller courts at times held administrative posts. They provided valuable ambassadorial services, and, because many doctors had studied mathematics in addition to medicine,[1] they could assume functions as diverse as making medically relevant astrological prognostications[2] to overseeing practical building and engineering projects. Given such a variety of activities within the confines of the territorial court, there must certainly be a sense in which the authority of the prince often proved to be role directive. But how far did that authority extend? Could the court, for instance, influence the practice of a particular kind of medicine or lead physicians to confront situations and to develop skills which might have been otherwise ignored?

Answering questions like these must begin with an examination of individual cases. The approach most preferred would be to study the activities of a large number of physicians within an equally extensive range of princely courts, allowing the survey to establish a kind of quantitative portrayal of physician involvement and experience relative to princely demands. Such a study, resting as it must on the accumulation of a vast amount of archival detail, is presently unrealizable. Nevertheless, an entrance, albeit a narrow one, into understanding the influence of the court in directing physician roles can still be found by concentrating on a particular case study – one in which the fine structure of a relationship between the prince and his physicians can be reconstructed. Admittedly such a microstudy can tell us little about relationships at other courts, but it will still be useful as an indication of the possibilities and potential of courtly authority in the legitimation of medical ideas and in orienting the focus of medical activity.

One of the most interesting of the German courts from the point of view of medical patronage, as well as with respect to the nurturing of humanist learning, is the court of the German Landgrave Maurice of Hesse-Kassel (1572–1632). From his court at Kassel, Maurice acquired a wide reputation as both patron and practitioner of medicine and chemical pharmacy. Aside from his attention to the sciences, he became also an enthusiastic participant in arts and letters. He composed music, published philosophical commentaries, wrote occasional verses and plays, and, for his court school, the *Collegium Mauritianum*, edited both a French–German lexicon and a Latin grammar.[3] Maurice tied his claim to personal erudition to assumptions of aristocratic privilege, and rested his certainty of intellectual authority upon the same divine foundations as supported his noble rights. Having joined one of Germany's many erudite societies in the early seventeenth century, the literary and partly political *Fruchtbringende Gesellschaft*, Maurice faced the problem of choosing a pseudonym, a requirement of all members of the society. Without straying far from his original sobriquet 'the learned', Maurice distinguished himself as *Der Wohlgenannte*, 'the well named'.[4] Nor were the prince's intellectual talents celebrated only within local German circles. They were noticed in one of the most widely read books of courtesy in the early seventeenth century, Henry Peacham's *The Complete Gentleman* (1622).

> But above others who carrieth away the palm for excellency, not only in music, but in whatsoever is to be wished in a brave prince, is the yet living Maurice, Landgrave of Hesse, of whose own composition I have seen eight or ten several sets of motets and solemn music set purposely for his own chapel, where, for the great honor of some festival, and

many times for his recreation only, he is his own organist. Besides he readily speaketh ten or twelve languages. He is so universal a scholar that, coming, as he doth often, to his university of Marburg, what questions soever he meeteth with set up, as the manner is in the German and our universities, he will extempore dispute an hour or two, even in boots and spurs, upon them with their best professors. I pass over his rare skill in chirurgery, he being generally accounted the best bonesetter in the country.[5]

Peacham almost missed referring to Maurice's medical skills, and ignored altogether what had become by the early 1620s an all-absorbing intellectual commitment at the Kassel court to hermetic philosophy, defined there as theoretical and practical understanding of alchemical secrets and insight into the preparation of useful medicines. With Paracelsian physicians and alchemical adepts Maurice carried on an extensive correspondence, out of which developed a circle of hermetic-alchemical contacts and protégés. Through such letters there passed to the prince alchemical-pharmaceutical recipes, laboratory reports concerning the preparation of chemical medicines, and expositions of both alchemical and medical texts.[6] The privileged intellectual position of the prince as the focus of information within the Kassel circle also affected his definition of medical roles at court and dominated his thinking in making hermetic appointments to his university faculty in Marburg. Adding hermetic dimensions to traditional academic disciplines at Marburg brought elements of Paracelsian natural philosophy, Cabala, and alchemy to the faculties of philosophy and theology. However, it was with the hermetization of the medical faculty that Maurice's personal direction of academic roles had the greatest effect, leading to the creation of an entirely new university discipline – the laboratory study of *Chemiatria*, that is, chemical medicine.

To lead the new discipline Maurice chose a physician recently appointed to the Marburg medical faculty, Johann Hartmann (1568–1631).[7] Yet Hartmann had begun neither his university career nor his career at court in the medical arts. He appeared first in Kassel in 1591 after having studied mathematics at Wittenberg and other universities, and gained the recommendation of Maurice and his father, Wilhelm IV, to fill a recently vacated position at Marburg as professor of mathematics. Although lecturing at Marburg, Hartmann was never far from the court in Kassel. In 1594 Maurice turned to him for advice in editing the optical works of Friedrich Risner (died 1580) and later arranged for a two-year separation from the university to allow Hartmann to work further on the project in Kasssel. What Hartmann's experiences were at court are not known. However, by the time of his return to Marburg in 1601 it had become clear that advancement under Maurice's patronage would require intellectual talents apart from the strictly mathematical. Writing to the prince's secretary in 1603, Hartmann referred to his earlier appointment at the Kassel court, alluding to the prince's patronage as the 'earthly sun' that had shone upon him two years earlier, and expressed his fear that that sun should now have been eclipsed.[8] The direction of patronage at court had changed since Maurice's father, the astronomer-prince Wilhelm IV, supported and participated in projects of astronomical measurement and instrument-building at Kassel.[9] Maurice's interests had turned away from mathematics and astronomy and towards the study of alchemy and hermetic medicine. In winning the court's patronage, Hartmann grew aware of the need to change the basis of his own intellectual appeal so as to remain in closer step with the prince's preference. Referring to skills that would add to his versatility, Hartmann confided that the wise man knew that one should possess 'different bows to reach one's goals – a strong bow [presumably medicine and practical alchemy] for a far goal, and one of lesser strength [most likely mathematics] for a goal not so distant'.[10]

Hartmann was certainly no stranger to the study of medicine, but only began formal preparations for a medical degree after his return to Marburg from Kassel. Readings in medicine were directed by his colleague in the medical faculty, Johann Wolf. At the same time he studied the alchemical treatises of Basil Valentine and sought a correspondence with Johann Thoelde, the editor of the Basilian texts just then beginning to be published in northern Europe.[11] Not until 1606 did Hartmann complete his studies in medicine and receive the first fruits of Maurice's medical-alchemical patronage – an appointment to a medical professorship at Marburg, which he held concurrently with his professorship in mathematics until 1609. In that year Maurice, encouraged by his court physicians, sanctioned an addition to the medical curriculum at Marburg and, consistent with his practice of determining roles at court and personally appointing positions at Marburg, named Hartmann *Professor Publicus* of *Chemiatria*.

The significance of the appointment in establishing a continuity of medical knowledge between the Galenic and spagyric-Paracelsian traditions was not lost on the Leipzig Paracelsian physician and alchemist, Joachim Tanckius (1557–1609). At the beginning of a collection of alchemical writings, published posthumously in 1610, he declared that it would be a fine thing if the potentates of Europe knew that along with Aristotle and Galen, the *chemicos Authores* should also be read so as not to remain at the shell of natural things [*in corticibus rerum naturalium*] but to arrive at the nucleus and core of nature. He then reminded his readers that such a collation of philosophy, traditional medicine, and chemistry had been achieved by Maurice of Hesse, who had brought learning together by founding a new academic profession, and he invited other princes to follow Maurice's example by adding the study of chemical medicine to the medical curricula of their universities. This would be more easily accomplished if court physicians no longer proved a hindrance to the advancement of hermetic medical learning, but, like the court physicians at Kassel, became its willing supporters and advisers.[12]

Tanckius's reference to physicians affecting princely interest in chemical medicine is especially fitting in light of the problem of understanding the direction of medical influence at court. Court physicians were generally not reserved in rendering judgements on what they considered to be the correct theoretical basis and practice of medicine, whether approving of the traditional Hippocratic-Galenic remedies or endorsing Paracelsian cures. With respect to the court at Kassel, however, the medical interests of court physicians were always secondary to those of the prince. At Maurice's insistence, the Kassel - *Leibmedici* were required to accept the relevance of chemical medicines as part of medical therapy, and were each directed to contribute to the court's alchemical-pharmaceutical projects. Some participated personally in laboratory procedures. Others tested and evaluated the chemical medicines which were produced in the court's own laboratories, or which were received from other sources. Maurice's personal activity in making chemical medicines, his influence over court physicians in bringing them also into the laboratory for purposes of preparing chemical remedies, and his part in establishing the discipline of *Chemiatria* at Marburg are each recognized by the hermetic-anatomist Heinrich Petraeus, professor of anatomy and surgery at Marburg, and, like Hartmann and numerous others there, a personal appointee of the prince. Many German princes closely supervised their territorial universities, although most limited their involvement to the theological faculty. Maurice's influence was much more widely felt. Writing in the preface of a surgical handbook commissioned by the Landgrave in 1617, Petraeus extolled the dimensions of his prince's medical-pharmaceutical skill, and observed also the medical authority of his patron both at court and within the university.

> But one thing I must mention, namely that Your Grace ... has diligently practised and questioned in the [medical] arts, has prepared medicines with his own hands, especially the ingenious chemical sort, which his servants have used for the good of their health. He has thereby improved his understanding of medicine to such an extent that he himself is able to converse with the most experienced Masters and occasionally comprehends a matter better than they.... In addition he has followed the example of his father, Wilhelm IV, and has had the most learned and most experienced physicians at his court in Kassel. For these he has provided the opportunity to increase their art and experience in his well known princely laboratory .... Your Grace has also propagated this wonderful and necessary art for posterity, supporting, loving, and protecting the medical faculty of Your university ... and especially You have raised and extended the true chemical art, which until now had remained hidden, and have caused it to be taught publicly and to be practised in a laboratory built for this purpose.... In advancing further the study of medicine Your Grace has ordered that not only executed criminals be delivered for anatomical study, but has also ordered that when anyone should die in the state of a special illness, the *medici* be permitted to dissect and inspect the same. For this purpose You have ordered the construction at Your university of a public anatomical theatre.[13]

Laboratory activities at court and university gained their theoretical justification from within a hermetic-Paracelsian context. Maurice trusted firmly in the correspondences and natural analogies of an integrated hermetic universe. Yet in his dealings with hermetic doctors, the mystical-eschatological elements of Paracelsian philosophy were of far less importance than acquiring practical procedural information on the making of useful spagyric medicines, and procuring operational insights into the articulation of alchemical recipes. Paracelsians like Joseph Duchesne (*Quercetanus*), Heinrich Nollius, Johann Poppius, and Benedict Figulus were encountered at the Kassel court as laboratory adepts. And although Maurice provided an annual stipend to the well-known Paracelsian and Rosicrucian advocate Michael Maier (c. 1568–1622), appointing him in 1618 *Medicus und Chemicus von Haus aus*, Maier's chief responsibility was to correspond with the Landgrave as an alchemical consultant. Of those physicians with specific medical duties at court, however, three stand out most prominently. Two were among the prince's earliest physicians, Hermann Wolf (1562–1620) and Jacob Mosanus (1564–1616). A third, Johannes Rhenanus, while associated with the court for many years, only became the prince's personal physician following Maurice's abdication of power in 1627. Defining the activities of each in the service of the prince will indicate much about role versatility among physicians at the Kassel court and will also help to illustrate Maurice's central position in directing and co-ordinating the responsibilities of his *Leibmedici* in pursuit of his own hermetic ideal.

Before coming to Kassel, Hermann Wolf had studied medicine at Basel and later at Marburg where his brother Johann (1578–1616) had already joined the medical faculty. After first being named professor of physics at Marburg, he also entered the medical faculty there, and, several years later, when plague touched many of the cities and towns in Hesse, was taken into the service of the court.[14]

Whatever Wolf's experience had been at Marburg, Maurice's own interests and the needs of the court now established the direction of his professional activities. Wolf, to be sure, cared for the princely household and diligently supplied Maurice with reports concerning the health of individual family members.[15] Yet besides medical talents, Wolf's mathematical skills also appealed to the prince, and Maurice sought to apply them by adding to his physician's regular medical duties the task of supervising the completion of the court's architectural and building designs. Over almost twenty years, Wolf's medical reports were thus interwoven with descriptions of building projects in Kassel and throughout Hesse. In them the assessment of materials and plans for the construction of locks along the Fulda and Werra, discussions concerning the construction of mills and bridges, descriptions of improvements and renovations within and surrounding the princely palace, and reports on progress in the building of Maurice's theatre for the dramatic arts, the Ottoneum, accompany news of the plague, and follow descriptions of the illnesses and treatment of those attached to the princely family.[16]

If, however, Wolf was less often found making medicines than inspecting construction projects at the command of the prince, he still was required to play a role in Maurice's alchemical-medical information system by communicating alchemical processes,[17] and as a consultant on chemical remedies. Most importantly, he also became a trusted confirmational source in evaluating the efficacy of medicines received and produced at court. This latter responsibility was not without its risks. After having obtained both written works and prepared medicines from the Italian spagyricist and court physician to the dukes of Mecklenburg-Gustrow, Angelo Sala (1576–1637),[18] Maurice sent to Wolf Sala's treatise *Anathomia Vitrioli*,[19] requesting his physician's opinion concerning the safety of Sala's preparations made from vitriol, and wondering about the possible use of Sala's so-called *spiritus vitriolis humididus* in the treatment of the ailing Landgravine Juliana. Wolf found that each of the proposed medicaments was supported by Paracelsus. Maurice, however, in this case, required more than simple textual confirmation. After testing the *spiritus vitriolis* personally without vomiting or suffering other disturbing side-effects, Wolf recommended that the medicine was safe to administer.[20] The testing of medicines provided by the prince was the responsibility of court physicians at Kassel. The task seems most often, however, to have fallen to Wolf. Whether the medicaments were of the prince's making, or came to the court from elsewhere, Maurice expected from him reports concerning their taste and physical effects. Besides the *spiritus vitriolis*, Maurice entrusted his physician with a medicine produced from lead, the *clyssi ex Saturnia*, requiring him to establish its correct dosage and use.[21] In 1619, as Wolf himself lay ill, Maurice prescribed an *essentia Perlarum*, which Wolf took with six drops of *aurum potabile Angelicanum*. He felt better as a result and was dutifully thankful for the Landgrave's pharmaceutical understanding.[22] Another of Maurice's medicines, *essentia lunarum*, Wolf however considered to be potentially dangerous, but wished, nevertheless, to test the substance on his own person. Reference to the courageous act comes in one of the last letters in his long correspondence.[23] He died a few months later without the benefit of Maurice's further successful medicinal intervention.

In 1599, a year after Wolf joined the court, another physician, Jacob Mosanus, gained entrance at Kassel. Mosanus studied medicine at the University of Cologne and there acquired a medical degree in 1591. His father, also a physician, had in the meantime established a medical practice in England which had, on several occasions, run foul of the London College of Physicians.[24] Jacob's initial design was to follow his father into practice in London. Nothing, however, came of the plan, since Mosanus's application in 1592 for a licence to practise in the city received a critical review by the College and was denied. Whether from a distrust of foreign physicians, or from genuine misgivings, he was instructed to read Galen more thoroughly and to devote himself to a four-year practice in his own German provinces.[25] Between this time and 1598, when he published an English translation of a medical treatise written by Christoph Wirsung,[26] his activities are unknown, although part of that time may have been spent in Strasbourg and in the Netherlands in the company of the alchemist Jan Cornelius van Amsterdam, whom he helped transcribe an alchemical treatise attributed to Isaac Hollandus.

Mosanus had already begun attempting the preparation of chemical medicines while in England. Nevertheless, the decision to return to Germany and to accept a position as one of Maurice's physicians opened up avenues of practical learning in chemical pharmacy which, without the agency of the court, would most likely never have been made accessible. Besides assigning to him medical duties, Maurice used Mosanus as a personal envoy and, in 1604, commissioned him with an ambassadorial errand to the French court. Along the way Mosanus was also to make contact with the well-known French Paracelsian and royal physician, Joseph Duchesne (*Quercetanus*) (c. 1544–1609), in order to encourage and help arrange a visit by Duchesne to the court in Kassel. The desired meeting offered an invaluable opportunity to learn more about specific elements in Duchesne's Paracelsian pharmacy. Writing to

Maurice from Strasbourg on his way to Paris, Mosanus reported in English:

> I do heare that Quercetanus is sometymes at Paris, other
> whiles at Genff, however it be, I will (God willing) speake
> with him before my retourne, and I doubt not but that I shall
> obtaine many fine physical and medicall matters of him; for
> I doe heare wonders of him, how cunning a physician and
> chemist he is.[27]

The Paris visit produced the desired results, and Duchesne
arrived in Kassel later that same year. At a laboratory especially
equipped for the visit, he demonstrated and explained many of
his procedures in the presence of Maurice, his physicians,
Mosanus and Wolf, and Johann Hartmann, who was still at that
time a medical student in Marburg. The demonstrations had
the greatest influence on Mosanus, and replicating them became the primary focus of his laboratory activity thereafter –
so much so that he could report shortly after the French physician's return to Paris that he had already attempted to make almost all the medicaments whose recipes Duchesne had left at
Maurice's court. Most of the processes had been reproduced
without great difficulty. A few, however, like the preparation of
an alchemical compound called *viridellus*, produced from the
calx of silver and a 'certain tincture', one of several recipes that
Duchesne had prepared himself in Kassel, resisted duplication.[28] Another procedure left in Kassel, the elevation of gold,
Mosanus admitted giving up all hope of understanding, announcing his frustration by likening Duchesne to Oedipus,
without whose help he could never solve such an enigma in all
eternity.[29]

In transmitting recipes for making chemical medicines,
Duchesne's relationship with the Kassel court was not
altogether one-sided. Mosanus also shared his own processes
and preparations,[30] and also reported on his personal laboratory experiences.[31] In 1606 those experiences included, again
on Maurice's command, a two-month residence in Coburg with
Andreas Libavius (1540–1616), one of the most accomplished
interpreters of chemical-alchemical *praxis* in the early seventeenth century. Through Mosanus Maurice hoped to bring Libavius's procedural techniques into use within his own court
laboratories. Although little has come to light concerning their

brief encounter, the two, on Mosanus's account, discussed a wide range of topics, as much medicine as Libavius's own laboratory procedures.[32] Despite missing details, it is nevertheless clear that contact with Duchesne and Libavius, greatly expanded the store of Mosanus's laboratory talents. Because of those skills he became increasingly occupied with the articulation of processes in the Kassel court laboratory, and, apart from the duties imposed upon him as physician at court, assumed also the role of organizational liaison between the Landgrave and those at work in the court's various spagyric and alchemical projects.

Of all Maurice's physicians Mosanus clearly won the most respect and affection from members of the prince's family. Maurice's sons and daughters found in him a sympathetic elder companion and even playmate.[33] Like Wolf, Mosanus was expected to provide medical supervision, and treatment when necessary, for all members of the court, including the young pupils at the Landgrave's court school. The close contact between Maurice's family and the often untidy and sickly boys in the school always worried the Kassel physicians and led both Mosanus and Wolf to explore ways of separating the two.[34]

In plague years Maurice lived apart from his court and family, retreating most often to his residences in Melsungen and Rotenburg. At such times, one of the court physicians remained behind in Kassel while the other travelled with the prince and his company.[35] During such periods, the letters passing between physicians and the prince became more frequent. Maurice wished to be informed during his absence both of the health of his family and of other related medical matters, especially concerning the progress of pharmaceutical preparations in the court laboratory. Most correspondence took place in the form of quickly composed in-house memoranda; but to this sort of communication Mosanus in particular added his own detailed letters, discussing questions of general anatomy, the making of medicines, and describing his own most recent spagyric accomplishments. Although only one side of the correspondence remains, it is nevertheless clear that Maurice, in his letters, not only displayed a sophisticated degree of medical learning, but often reported on successes communicated to him from others working in laboratories supported by the court. This, of course, never failed to elicit hearty praise from Mosanus as a necessary prelude to answering the Landgrave's latest

105

spagyric-alchemical enquiries, and describing the progress of
projects under way in his own laboratory.[36]

In acting as laboratory consultant, Mosanus needed always
to conform to the procedural priorities of the prince. On the
other hand, he might also seek to influence Maurice's judgement, and to attract his patron's attention as much as possible
to the methods and experiences resulting from his own laboratory efforts. This meant, of course, distracting the prince at
times from the enthusiastic promises of alchemical petitioners.
With the arrival in Kassel, for instance, of the Scottish alchemist
Rampsaeus [Ramsey] in 1611, Mosanus grew alarmed that
Maurice might become preoccupied with making the Philosophers' Stone, with whose production Ramsey seemed entirely
concerned. In attempting to deflect Maurice's interest in Ramsey and his alchemical processes, Mosanus delicately argued
that while the Philosophers' Stone was the most eminent of all
medicines, other medicines too should be praised for their virtues and not be overlooked. No one can doubt, he added, that
Paracelsus possessed the stone, yet even he exalted other
medicaments possessing spiritual powers.[37] Like Paracelsus,
the preparation of such medicaments was the role Mosanus felt
called upon to perform at court, at least according to his own
self-perception of courtly service.[38] However, the discovery of
new medicines, and the understanding of the Universal Medicine itself, he argued, followed from the knowledge and skill
obtained in creating medicaments of lesser effect. In Mosanus's
view, therefore, attainment of the alchemist's Philosophers'
Stone should advance by degrees, being attempted gradually,
through knowledge obtained in the production of ever-more-
useful and powerful medicinal remedies.

That Mosanus saw the perfection of a Universal Medicine
and the preparation of the *aurum potabile* as also a goal of his
own laboratory work is clearly suggested by his correspondence. At times alchemists willing to part with operational secrets aided the endeavour. To Duchesne he confided in 1605
that the servant [*famulus*] of the well-known alchemist Alexander Seton (died 1604) was with him at Kassel describing two
methods, the one by dissolving gold, the other by sublimating
its calx, through which the 'oil of gold' could be obtained.[39]
Nevertheless, obtaining the Universal Medicine was not to be
expected without great effort, and Mosanus was not reluctant
to advise the prince that of such mysteries one might expect to

acquire knowledge in two ways: one could either await the coming age of Elias the Artist, when all secrets of nature would be revealed, or one could learn things, albeit slowly, through the accumulation of experience.[40]

Clearly, Maurice believed that waiting for the coming Elias was not necessary to comprehend the structure and relationships of nature required to make useful medicines and to attain knowledge of the universal. Instead he relied upon his own textual and procedural understanding, and also upon the organization of his hermetic-alchemical circle to bring together the discoveries and talents of numerous independently working laboratory informants in order to broaden and sharpen his own privileged perspective. That the prince should possess such an advantaged position in regard to hermetic learning was frequently emphasized in the *encomia* coming to Maurice, praising him, in the words of the Paracelsian alchemist Benedict Töpfer (*Figulus*), as a predestined *maecenas* of alchemy and the true hermetic art.[41] Mosanus was no less fulsome in his own letters, and at one point sought to link Maurice's medical learning to a type of intellectual nobility first attained by ancient kings.

> That Your Grace has so exactly explained anatomy and physic is an achievement much to be praised and worthy of such a prince. For he is doing that which the most famous kings and princes used to do, who not only defended themselves and their own from the incursions and plunder of external enemies, but endeavoured with all their strength to liberate the same from the harm and injury of internal diseases.[42]

The kings and princes to whom Mosanus refers include Alexander, Mithridates, and Solomon. Placing his patron in their company amounted to a contrived rhetorical device designed to preserve the prince's favour by reflecting Maurice's self-image as a chosen, privileged figure standing in a line of chosen philosopher (hermetic) kings.

Mosanus's death in 1616 and Wolf's in 1620 brought about the appointment of new physicians at court. Maurice chose Ludwig Combach (1590–1657), who had recently graduated in medicine at the University of Padua after having visited Paris, Montpellier, and Geneva, and whose brother, Johann, taught in the Marburg theological faculty. Although Ludwig later pub-

Bruce T. Moran

lished several alchemical writings, including an edition of the
works of George Ripley (Kassel, 1649) and a treatise concerning an alchemical *Liquor Alcahest* (Venice, 1641), for purposes
of laboratory consultation Maurice preferred to turn to another
physician tied closely to the court, Johannes Rhenanus. In contrast to the roles of Wolf, Mosanus, and Combach, Rhenanus's
activities were confined almost exclusively to the laboratory,
Maurice himself paving the way for his medical- alchemical
education and ultimately sculpting the talents of his protégé to
fit the hermetic contours of his court circle. In this instance, the
relationship between prince and physician-alchemist rested
upon familial connections.

The first to study medicine in the Rhenanus family was
Johannes's father, Martin, who became physician to the Archbishop of Bremen (Johann Adolph von Holstein) before starting a private medical practice in Kassel. From his father, Martin
Rhenanus had learned practical assaying and metallurgical
skills before beginning his medical training. The combination
of talents pleased and interested Maurice who, in 1594, named
him *medicus extra ordinarius* with the assigned duties of caring for
the prince's health and tending to the health of court advisers
and servants. Taking advantage of the full spectrum of his
physician's ability, Maurice also required, as a condition of appointment, Martin's willing laboratory participation in the
court's alchemical-spagyric projects.[43]

With Martin's death, Maurice assumed the care of the Rhenanus family, providing his physician's widow with financial
support and granting the eldest son, Johannes, an annual allowance which would enable him to begin studies at the medical
college in Marburg just at the time when the new discipline of
chemiatry had been added to the medical curriculum. Studying
with Hartmann, Rhenanus advanced in his readings with remarkable speed and obtained his medical degree in 1610. His
dissertation, a description of chemical procedures and instruments, *Dissertatio Chymiotechnica*,[44] he dedicated to his benefactor, the Landgrave.

What effect Maurice's financial assistance may have had in
actually determining the course of Rhenanus's studies is not
clear. Nevertheless, those studies were perfectly suited to the
prince's own interests. After completing courses in medicine
and chemiatry at Marburg, Rhenanus accepted Maurice's invi-
tation to combine a private practice in Kassel with the super-

108

vision of the prince's chemical laboratory. There Rhenanus served the court in alchemical-spagyric projects known, for the most part, only to Maurice.

Besides laboratory work, much of which was based on an interpretation of the medieval alchemical writings of Raymond Lull, Rhenanus further harmonized his activities with the intellectual values of the court by adding literary and poetical efforts to his practical alchemical-pharmaceutical duties. The coincidence of poetry, alchemy, and medicine was by no means an oddity in the early seventeenth century. Especially alchemical descriptions, heavily laden with symbolic and metaphorical content, lent themselves as *exempla* of a special literary genre, as did the mystical fantasies of many Rosicrucian, Cabalist, and Paracelsian authors. Both Michael Maier and another physician at the Prague court of Rudolf II, Matthias Borbonius, appealed to patrons by producing poetic-emblematic volumes.[45] Another physician, Adrian Mynsicht (1603–38), *Medicus* and *Chemicus* at the court of the Duke of Mecklenburg-Schwerin, and author of one of the most frequently reprinted works of chemical pharmacy, the *Thesaurus et Armentarium medico-chymicum*, published in 1631, was named in that same year imperial poet-laureate. Rhenanus never rose to such heights. Nevertheless, he knew the full range of Maurice's interests in the arts, and in one surviving instance found a way to discuss the main problem of his alchemical-pharmaceutical labours (the problem of combining theory and practice) by referring to the central problem, as he saw it, of German playwriting, which, he believed, had never adequately adapted poetry to action.

Rhenanus made his observations as part of a comparison of English and German plays that he attached to a dramatic work of his own called *Speculum Aistheticum*, which he completed and dedicated to Maurice in 1613.[46] In his preface to the Landgrave, he acknowledges that the English know how to combine composition (i.e. the poetic content of a play) with action, whereas German plays had been confined up until then to rhyming verses and concerned primarily with prose, without emphasis at all upon the activity of the players. In England, however, actors not only understood the techniques of performance (i.e. stage activity) but allowed themselves to be instructed as well in poetry, and it is, Rhenanus concludes, this combination of performer and poet that brings life to English comedies. To see if the same poetic content could be borne as much in German as in other languages, he announces that he has written a comedy which is, on the one hand, full of action and should, on the other, be sufficient to show that 'our German language is just as [poetically] complete as any other'.[47]

The description is not completely honest. Rhenanus's comedy, in which the tongue (*Lingua*) contends with five other human senses, is, in fact, not originally a German play at all, but is rather a translation of an English play which had been published, without a known author, in 1607 with the title *Lingua: Or, The Combat of the Tongue, And the Five Senses for Superiority. A Pleasant Comaedie.*[48]

Despite the apparent deceit, there is something symmetrical about Rhenanus's reasons for composing the work when viewed against the background of his own alchemical labours, and in relation to Maurice's own patronage values. The necessity of unifying an understanding of poetry with action, in this case within a dramatic structure, must have been readily conceived as central also to any laboratory task which had to join a theoretical understanding of the operations of nature with practical application. The distance between Rhenanus's application of skills in the laboratory as a physician-chemist and the central focus of his attempts as a poetic author is thus by no means great. Most remarkably, the play ironically turns at one point to confront the translator's alchemical involvement.

> *Heuresis*: I see no reason to the contrary, for we see the quintessence of wine will convert water into wine; why therefore should not the elixir of gold turn lead into pure gold?
> *Mendacio*: Ha, ha, ha, ha! He is turned chemic, sirrah; it seems so by his talk ...
> *Anamnestes*: These chemics, seeking to turn lead into gold, turn away all their own silver.[49]

The lines may have chaffed, but the fiction was comic; not so the reality of alchemical failure within the court's own laboratories. The play's reference to the loss of silver was tragically real at the Kassel court, where Rhenanus's requests for both silver and wine (the source of the Lullian fifth essence) were always especially large, and where the expenses for these and other alchemical projects became, with the compounding of Maurice's political difficulties in the early years of the Thirty Years War, increasingly burdensome. Nevertheless, Maurice never lost confidence in his final deliverance from personal and political adversity by means of the ultimate and crowning alchemical successes that he hoped would result from those who played laboratory roles in the theatre of his hermetic-alchemical circle.

Maurice was not rescued from political disaster by alchemical intervention, nor by Rhenanus or any other of his physicians and alchemical laborants. Nevertheless, Rhenanus remained a valuable figure in the prince's company, especially in the turbulent days preceding Maurice's abdication, and thereafter during the Landgrave's more solitary years following his departure from government. Where Combach and Hartmann, who had been called back from Marburg as *Leibarzt* in 1621, now attended the new court in Kassel, Rhenanus continued as Maurice's personal physician and alchemical consultant, still communicating news of promising alchemical recipes, and testing processes that had come to him from outside contacts.[50] Of added importance now was his role as political liaison when Maurice, excluded from Kassel by imperial successes in Hesse and by the consequent resignation of his political leadership, lived away from the city, primarily at his smaller residences in Melsungen and Eschwege. Through Rhenanus came at frequent intervals news of the advance of Tilly's army, reports of the impact of its arrival in Kassel, and assessments of the disposition of the Hesse *Ritterschaft* which had been called upon to approve the division of cities in Hesse-Kassel among Maurice's sons.[51] To Maurice, however, whose political involvement had been reduced to passive observation, nothing at the moment mattered so much as the removal of his laboratory materials and chemical-alchemical library from Kassel to Melsungen. In obtaining for Maurice his books, manuscripts, instruments, and at least 'a half part' of the chemical materials left behind in the Kassel apothecary,[52] Rhenanus served his prince in one final role, that of supplicant on behalf of his own exiled patron.

The reward for engaging in specific medical-laboratory roles at court could be reckoned in wealth and influence. Rhenanus's annual income, for instance, was, in 1630, increased from 320 to 420 Florins, reflecting the assumption of various new duties on behalf of the displaced prince.[53] Moreover, court physicians were able to take an active hand in deciding medical policy in Hesse and by so doing could promote their own financial interests. Perhaps the most striking instance of Maurice's consent to

111

the authority of his physicians in organizing medical practice within his principality is the construction of a medical ordinance (*Medizinalordnung*) announced in 1616. In composing the ordinance Maurice relied upon the advice of a group of physicians at court, including Rhenanus, and consulted the Marburg medical faculty only after the document had already been formulated. The resentment of the Marburg medical professors at being overlooked in favour of court physicians in drawing up the ordinance is clear from comments returned to the Landgrave.[54] Most disconcerting was the intended establishment of a general *Collegium Medicum* to which all physicians in Hesse would be required to belong. In their response, the Marburg professors worried that such an organization would deprive them of their traditional privileges and of their rights of medical examination, control of which had always been a university function. Further, since the ordinance allowed for the election of a *Dekan* to oversee the operation of the *Collegium*, they insisted that such an office be reserved for a member of the Marburg medical faculty. The deeper purpose of the ordinance in diffracting medical authority in Hesse is indicated in Maurice's response that on this point there would be no argument. The office of Dekan would be open to all within the *Collegium*.

In many ways the Hessen *Medizinalordnung* is similar to other ordinances in the late sixteenth and early seventeenth centuries, and bears a close resemblance in parts to the Nuremberg ordinance of 1592. Nevertheless, in certain features it is unconnected to any pre-existing medical canon.[55] In reflecting the increased influence of court physicians at Kassel, one of the most significant departures concerns the prescribed relationship between physicians and pharmacists. While securing distinct occupational realms between the two groups, and although expressly forbidding physicians to sell medicines directly, the ordinance still allowed physicians to make chemical *compositiones* or other types of medicaments and to sell them indirectly through an apothecary. The only additional constraint upon physicians was that the apothecary could not be forced to sell more than a certain quantity of physician-made medicines each year.[56] Maurice seems to have been aware of the potential for economic discontent that this part of his *Medizinalordnung* might arouse. Nevertheless, in endorsing, however hesitantly, plans redounding to the economic benefit of chemical physicians at court, he found perhaps the most effective way to encourage the performance of the laboratory-medical roles that each had been guided to play on his behalf.

Acknowledgements

I wish to express my thanks to Dr Hartmut Broszinski and to the staff of the Murhardsche Bibliothek und Landesbibliothek der Stadt Kassel for their kind assistance and direction in preparing this study. I am grateful also to the Alexander von Humboldt Foundation through whose support research at the Kassel library was made possible.

Notes

1. A useful study of the relationship between medicine and mathematics is David Eugene Smith, 'Medicine and mathematics in the sixteenth century', *Annals of Medical History* (April 1917), pp. 125–40.

2. On physicians and the practice of astrology in the medieval period, see Lynn White Jr, 'Medical astrologers and late medieval technology', *Viator*, vol. 6 (1975), pp. 295–308. Wolf-Dieter Müller-Jahncke offers a most interesting treatment of the theory and practice of astrological medicine in the sixteenth and seventeenth centuries in his *Astrologische-Magische Theorie und Praxis in der Heilkunde der Frühen Neuzeit (Sudhoffs Archiv, Zeitschrift für Wissenschaftsgeschichte, Beiheft 25)* (Franz Steiner Verlag, Stuttgart, 1985). A descriptive account of medical-astrological role direction at one German court is Liersch, 'Dr Peter Cnemlander, Leibarzt und Astrolog des Markgrafen Johann von Cüstrin', *Schriften des Vereins für Geschichte der Neumark*, vol. 16 (1904), pp. 219–40.

3. The range of Maurice's studies was summarized by Johann Combach in his funeral oration on behalf of the Landgrave, 'De Exitu, Vita ac Virtutibus, Illustrissimi ... Mauritii ... a Johanne Combachio' in Mausolei Mauritiani pars altera ... (Johannes Saurius, Kassel, 1635), pp. 55–107. A good general account of Maurice's intellectual interests in the arts and sciences is Christoph von Rommel, *Geschichte von Hessen* (Kassel, 1835–7), vol. 6, pp. 399–433. A list of Maurice's written works is found in Friedrich Wilhelm Strieder, *Grundlage zu einer Hessischen und Schriftsteller Geschichte seit der Reformation bis auf gegenwärtige Zeiten* (Göttingen [and Marburg], 1781–1868), vol. 9, pp. 188–200.

4. F. W. Barthold, *Geschichte der Fruchtbringenden Gesellschaft* (Alexander Dunker, Berlin, 1848), p. 325. See also Klaus Conermann et al., *Fruchtbringende Gesellschaft* (VCH, Leipzig, 1985), vol. 1, sig. V.iv; vol. 2, pp. 85–7; vol. 3, pp. 23–45.

Bruce T. Moran

5. Henry Peacham, *The Complete Gentleman, The Truth of Our Times, and the Art of Living in London*, ed. Virgil B. Heltzel (Cornell University Press, Ithaca, 1962), pp. 111–12.

6. I have attempted to outline the gross parameters of Maurice's hermetic-alchemical circle in 'Privilege, communication, and chemiatry: the hermetic-alchemical circle of Moritz of Hessen-Kassel', *Ambix*, vol. 32 (1985), pp. 110–26. See also Kolbe, 'Beiträge zur Geschichte der Medizin in Hessen', *Zeitschrift des Vereins für Hessische Geschichte und Landeskunde*, vol. 11 (1867), pp. 1–21.

7. Information concerning Hartmann's life begins with Theophilus Newberger, *Auss dem CXXI Psalm Davids, als dess weiland, Ehrenvesten ... Herrn Johannis Hartmanni ... Verbliechener Leichnam am 11. Decembris dess 1631 Jahrs in seine Ruhstatte in der Haupt: Kirche ... gesetzt worden ...* (Johann Saurn, Cassel, 1632). More recent references include Th. Kunzmann, 'Der Weberssohn Hartmann von Amberg', *Bayerische Heimat*, vol. 22 (1941), pp. 125–6. Rudolf Schmitz and Adolf Winckelmann, 'Johann Hartmann (1568–1631) "Doctor Medicus et Chymiatriae Professor Publicus", Eine Biographische Skizze', *Pharmaceutische Zeitung*, vol. 111 (1966), pp. 1233–41. W. Hubicki, 'Uczniowie z Polski na Studiach Chymiatrii w Marburga w Latach 1609–1620', *Studia i Materialy z Dziejów Nauki Polskiej*, vol. 12 (1968), pp. 79–103, and my 'Court authority and chemical medicine', *Bulletin of the History of Medicine*, vol. 63 (1989) pp. 225–46.

8. Murhardsche Bibliothek der Stadt Kassel und Landesbibiliothek [hereafter referred to as MBK] 2° MS Chem 19, vol. 2, 155r–156r.

9. On the projects of Wilhelm IV and the direction of roles at his court, see Bruce T. Moran, 'Wilhelm IV of Hesse-Kassel: informal communication and the aristocratic context of discovery', in T. Nickles (ed.) *Scientific Discovery: Case Studies* (D. Reidel, Dordrecht, 1980), pp. 67–96. *Idem*, 'German Prince-practitioners: aspects in the development of courtly science, technology, and procedures in the Renaissance', *Technology and Culture*, vol. 22 (1981), pp. 253–74.

10. MBK: 2° MS Chem 19, vol. 2, 155r–156r.

11. On Hartmann's relationship with Thölde, see Hans Gerhard Lenz, 'Johann Thölde: ein Paracelsist und "Chymicus" und seine Beziehung zu Landgraf Moritz von Hessen-Kassel', unpublished dissertation, Marburg University, 1981, pp. 53–7.

12. Joachim Tanckius, *Promptuarium Alchemiae ...* (Leipzig, 1610), Vorrede.

13. Henricus Petraeus, *Encheiridion Cheirurgicum: Handbuch oder Kurtzer Begriff der Wundartzney, Auff Gnedigen Dess Durchleuchtigen, Hochgebornen Fursten und Herrn, Herrn Moritzen, Landgraven zu Hessen ...* (Paul Egenolph, Marburg, 1617).

14. Strieder, *Grundlage*, 17, pp. 281–5.

15. Hessisches Staatsarchiv Marburg [hereafter referred to as HSM] 4a. 39. 54.

114

16. HSM: 4a. 39. 54.

17. MBK: 4° MS Chem, 88.

18. On Sala, see Robert Capobus, *Angeles Sala, Leibarzt des Johann Albrecht II ... seine wissenschaftliche Bedeutung als Chemiker im XVII. Jahrhundert* (Berlin, 1933).

19. *Angeli Salae Vincentini Veneti medici Spagyrici Anatomia Vitrioli in duos tractatus divisa ... accedit arcanorum compurium ... sylva* (Geneva, 1613). First published in 1609.

20. MBK: 2° MS Chem 19, vol. 2, 41r–42r.

21. MBK: 2° MS Chem 19, vol. 2, 43r–v.

22. MBK: 2° MS Chem 19, vol. 2, 48r–v.

23. Ibid.

24. Sir George Clark, *A History of the Royal College of Physicians of London* (Oxford, 1964), vol. 1, p. 142.

25. Ibid.

26. *Praxis Medicinae Universalis, or a general Practice of Physicke, written ... in the German Tongue, and now ... translated ... and augmented by J. Mosan* (London, 1598).

27. HSM: 39. 55.

28. Staats-und Universitätsbibliothek Hamburg [hereafter cited as SuUBH] Sup. ep. (4°) 30: 13v, March 1605. Several of Mosanus's responses to specific questions of the Landgrave regarding the production of Duchesne's medicines are found in MBK: 2° MS Chem 11, nr. 1, 68r.

29. SuUBH: Sup. ep. (4°) 30: 14v–15r, 8 May 1605.

30. SuUBH: Sup. ep. (4°) 30: 13r–14r, 11 March 1605.

31. SuUBH: Sup. ep. (4°) 30: 15r–16r, 22 September 1606.

32. Ibid. Mosanus also draws attention to Libavius's published attack against the crazed writings (*maniographi*) of one of Duchesne's earliest antagonists at Paris, Jean Riolan, who represented in his censuring of essences, magisteries, oils, and waters the judgement of the Parisian medical faculty concerning Paracelsian medicine. However, while defending the chemists, Libavius also condemns Paracelsus and his medicine, being in the matter, Mosanus correctly concludes, one with the Parisians themselves. On Libavius's position regarding Paracelsus's medical system, see O. Hannaway, *The Chemists and the Word* (Johns Hopkins Press, Baltimore, 1975), chapters 4 and 5.

33. To pass the time on Epiphany Sunday 1611, Mosanus arranged for Moritz's children to take part in a processional play in which each of the children portrayed a member of court and Mosanus himself played the role of court chancellor. MBK: 2° MS Chem 19, vol. 5, 271r.

34. MBK: 2° MS Chem 19, vol. 5, 267r–268r. The Kassel residence of Johann Hartmann was to serve for a time as a temporary dormitory. HSM: 4a. 39. 54. (15 April 1605).

35. When not occupied with the family, Mosanus copied and composed medical and alchemical treatises. One tract describing the causes of the plague, its historical occurrences, treatments, and the celestial, atmospheric, and terrestrial signs of its approach

based heavily on the works of Galen and Avicenna still survives, MBK: 4° MS Med 11, 57r–120r, as do various collections of alchemical-medical recipes in Mosanus's hand: MBK 2° MS Chem 8; 9; 11 (vol. 1, 75r–v; vol. 2, 44r–v). MBK 4° MS Chem 1; 40; 54; 55; 57; 60; 88 (88r–99r).

36. HSM: 4a. 39. 45.

37. MBK: 2° MS Chem 19, vol. 5, 278r–279r.

38. MBK: 2° MS Chem 19, vol. 5, 273r–274v.

39. SuUBH: Sup. ep. (4°) 30, 12v–13r, 10 June 1605.

40. MBK: 2° MS Chem 19, vol. 5, 280r–281r.

41. MBK: 2° MS Chem 19, vol. 1, 241r–242v.

42. MBK: 2° MS Chem 19, vol. 1, 1r–2r.

43. HSM: 4B. 266: 'auch sich sonsten uff unsser begeren in Alchimistisch und andern der gleichen Sach darinnen er geubtt, sich willig gebrauchen lassen.' At the same time Maurice appointed a medical student, Conrad Curss, as 'laboratory assistant in spagyric medicine'. See also Irmgard Dübber, 'Zur Geschichte des Medizinal-und Apothekenwesens in Hessen-Kassel und Hessen-Marburg von den Anfängen bis zum Dreissigjährigen Krieg', unpublished dissertation, Marburg University, 1969, p. 180.

44. *Dissertatio Chymiotechnica, in qua totius operationis chymicae methodus practica clare ob oculos ponitur ... sub praesidio ... Johannis Hartmann ...* (Marburg, 1610).

45. On Borbonius and Maier at Prague, see R. J. W. Evans, *Rudolf II and His World* (Clarendon Press, Oxford, 1973), pp. 206–7.

46. MBK: 4° MS Theater 2. Speculum Aistheticum: Das ist eine schone und lustige comoedia darin alle Sensus so wol Innerliche als eusserliche, sambt ihren eygenschaften und Instrumenten erclaret, und gleichsam in einem spiegel vor augen gestellt wereden.

47. Ibid. Cf. Phillip Losch, *Johannes Rhenanus ein Casseler Poet des Siebzehnten Jahrhunderts* (Marburg, 1895), pp. 5–6.

48. Printed at London by G. Eld for Simon Waterson. Losch, *Johannes Rhenanus*, pp. 19–21.

49. W. Carew Hazlitt, *A Select Collection of Old English Plays* (London, 1874), vol. 9, p. 411.

50. HSM: 4a. 39. 64.

51. Ibid.

52. Ibid.

53. HSM: 4a. 39. 64.

54. Dübber, 'Zur Geschichte des Medizinal- und Apothekenwesens in Hessen', pp. 243–68.

55. Ibid., pp. 269–71.

56. A brief sketch of relations between physicians and pharmacists is supplied by Rudolf Schmitz, 'Das Verhältnis von Arzt und Apotheker in historischer und aktueller Sicht', *Pharmaceutische Zeitung*, vol. 109 (1964), pp. 1911–15.

5

The Literary Image of the *Médecins du Roi* in the Literature of the Grand Siècle

Laurence Brockliss

Introduction

In Act II, Scene I of Shakespeare's *All's Well That Ends Well*, the King of France lies dying from an unspecified fistula. Given up for lost by the court physicians, the king sadly watches the departure of his troops for the Italian wars, convinced he will not live to see their return. Help, however, is at hand in the form of Helena, daughter of a famous doctor now deceased, who has inherited her father's skill and has come to the French court in search of the man she loves, Bertram, Count of Roussillon. Gaining access to the stricken king, Helena promises to restore his health, but finds her offer initially repulsed:

> The congregated college have concluded
> That labouring art can never ransom nature
> From her inaidable estate.

The king, therefore, will not 'prostrate our past-cure malady to empirics'. Nevertheless, Helena eventually persuades him to take her proferred potion by insisting that she has divine assistance in her art and that she is willing to forfeit her life if she fails. In consequence, the king recovers and as a reward grants Helena's request that she should marry Bertram.

Shakespeare's account of Helena's triumph has long been of interest to literary scholars, for it is another example from the Bard's plays of the 1590s and early 1600s of role reversal. Helena, like Portia in *The Merchant of Venice*, takes on the male professionals and soundly beats them (a tribute to Gloriana in the winter of her years, perhaps).[1] However, the scene recounted above is also of particular significance for historians of early-modern medicine. To the best of my knowledge, it is the only occasion in the European literature of the late-sixteenth and seventeenth centuries that a dramatist, poet, or essayist publicly criticizes the court physician in the performance of his official functions. Indeed, considering how court-oriented the literature of the period was, it is surprising how few and far between are the references of any kind to the Royal Aesculapius. Surprisingly, too, the dramatists of the period seldom used the court physician as an actual character. Admittedly, Shakespeare introduces some half-dozen court doctors into his plays (or rather doctors attending on royalty for only Dr Butts in *Henry VIII* is given an official title).[2] However, they all have merely walk-on, undeveloped parts, and their function is to help the action along, not determine it. Only Cornelius in *Cymbeline* shows any vitality, as he tricks his murderous patroness into accepting an anodyne sleeping-draught in place of the poison she seeks (Act I, Scene V). Furthermore, in *All's Well That Ends Well*, where the role of the court physicians *is* essential to the plot, there is no attempt to dramatize their gloom or stage a professional confrontation with Helena. The 'congregated college' remain out of sight in the wings; their pessimism is merely reported.

The absence of the court physician from the literature of the late-sixteenth and seventeenth centuries is all the more perplexing in that the medical profession *tout court* was a continual butt for the *literati* of the period. To virtually every dramatist, poet, and essayist, the simple physician and his associates were figures of fun. At best, the physician was a pompous and verbose quack, deluding himself as well as others in his belief that he could successfully counter disease. At worst, he was a deceitful and murderous charlatan. Moreover, the *literati* made little attempt to disguise the fact that their barbs were aimed at particular individuals. Certainly there was a stock stage physician, but he was often through dress and speech given a recognizable persona. Often, too, the physician under attack held a royal appointment. Molière, for instance, in *L'Amour Médecin* (1665), poked fun at a number of court physicians, especially the notorious antimony pedlar, François Guénault (d. 1667). On the play's first performance there could be no doubt that Guénault was guyed in the guise of Dr Macroton. In case the audience failed to draw the necessary conclusion from the character's

slow drawl and ponderous periods, the actor was unambiguous-
ly equipped with a look-alike mask.[3] Even when royal physicians were openly ridiculed, however, they were attacked only
in their general, not their official, practice. We see Macroton at
the bedside of the malingering daughter of Sganarelle, not in
attendance on royalty.[4]

In part, the absence of the court physician must be explicable
generically. Following the Aristotelian conventions, the court
in the literature of the period was predominantly presented in
the tragedy, a dramatic genre which was judged to require a
royal or noble caste of characters as it dealt with the grand
human passions. The less socially elevated might appear in such
dramas but only in occasional attendant parts. The court physician, therefore, was unlikely to make a frequent appearance.
Aristotelian conventions, too, help to explain the unsavoury
literary image of the medical profession in general. When
physicians, surgeons, or apothecaries did appear, then it was
usually in the comedy, picaresque novel, or satirical poem, literary genres where a large majority of the characters were either
fools or villains. Admittedly, many members of the contemporary educated elite were genuinely suspicious of the ethics and
learning of the medical profession. It was not just a literary creation; witness the venom of Montaigne at the end of the sixteenth century.[5] Nevertheless, it is clear that among the *literati*
public and private attitudes could differ profoundly. On several
occasions in his satires the poet Boileau savaged Guénault and
other physicians (for example, Satire IV, 1s. 31–2). Yet his
correspondence reveals that several medical men were close
personal friends whose advice on his ailments he sought and
heeded.[6]

Literary convention, however, cannot completely account
for the court physician's infrequent appearance. Too many *literati*, especially in England, ignored the rules for this to be a
convincing solution. A better explanation, perhaps, lies in
authorial circumspection. In an age when faction-fighting at
court could be deadly and the junior branches of the royal
houses of Europe were not unknown to covet their seniors'
inheritance, the court physician was in a strategically important
position to further opponents' designs. To question the competence of the royal doctor directly, therefore, was a political
statement which no sensible writer, concerned for his freedom,
to say nothing of his life, would presumably lightly have made.

One could risk the ire of the court physician by ridiculing him as an incompetent general practitioner. There is evidence that Guénault for one took Molière's parody in good part. [7] However, nobody in their right mind would risk offending the court faction to which a royal doctor belonged by indicating its creature in his official capacity as a murderous swine. This must have been especially the case when the sinister potential of the court physician was only too well known to a classically educated elite through the histories of Tacitus and Suetonius.[8] Presumably, then, it was felt best to keep the court physician *qua* court physician out of one's art altogether, lest, whatever guise the latter appeared in, some court peacock or other felt his feathers had been wantonly ruffled.

Whatever the truth of the matter, the unwillingness of the late-sixteenth and seventeenth century *literati* to discuss the court physician in public has made it clearly impossible to provide a portrait of the literary image of the royal doctor of the period from conventional sources. Whether the country chosen for study be England, France, or Spain, the harvest from perusing the output of contemporary dramatists, poets, and essayists would be disappointingly meagre. Any attempt, therefore, to construct the literary image of the court physician during these years must adopt an alternative approach. Two possibilities present themselves, and both require extending the definition of literature beyond the customary sense of the word in English. In the first place, a study could be undertaken of contemporary ballads, broadsheets, and medical pamphlets, where dangerous and scurrilous sentiments were frequently propagated in seventeenth-century France and England under the shelter of anonymity. However, a study of the 'low literature' of the age, although almost certain to produce interesting results, could not be swiftly completed. Uncovering informative sources could take a lifetime. A much more convenient approach would be to examine the private literary remains of the period: diaries, memoirs, and correspondence. Not intended for the public gaze, they have yet frequently come into the public domain through the energetic editorial work of nineteenth- and twentieth-century scholars. Their value lies in the freedom (apart from the obvious cultural constraints) with which their authors usually speak and their accessibility as a source.

It is this second approach which is deployed in the following chapter on the image of the court physician in seventeenth-century France. In the court of *Le Grand Siècle* many members of the aristocracy, the Church, and the lay professions entrusted their private thoughts to paper and much of what they wrote down has survived to be scrutinized by the historian. Indeed, more than is certainly the case in England, the literary critic has sometimes found this material interesting, too. Although in general forming a literature that can be described as neither 'high' nor 'low', a handful of these posthumously published biographical remnants are literary masterpieces: one thinks in particular of the *Mémoires* of the Duc de Saint-Simon. French literary style in the reign of Louis XIV was developed as much in the private *étude* as in the pulpit or on the stage. In order to do justice to the richness of this source in the space available, the present chapter is based on the information provided by only five particularly useful memorialists. Each covers a particular part of the period and in all but one case speaks in a distinctive socio-professional or sexual voice. Thereby it becomes possible to view the court physician across time from a variety of perspectives. Unfortunately one important voice is absent: the ecclesiastical one. Although several French clerics left detailed private accounts of their life and times, none mysteriously paid any attention to the *médecins de cour*. Bossuet, for instance, left a vast correspondence which, it might be thought, would have yielded a plethora of details about the physicians surrounding Louis XIV. Bossuet, however, says virtually nothing about his own maladies, let alone those of the royal family.[9]

To understand what follows, a few remarks about the organization of the royal medical service during this period is needed. The king's health in seventeenth-century France was officially presided over by the *premier médecin du roi* and his eight subordinates, the *médecins par quartier*, who served, as their name suggests, in rotation. In addition, when required, the king could also summon his *médecins ordinaires*, physicians living outside the court and whose title was chiefly honorary. Besides the king's personal physicians, the queen and other members of the royal family had their own much smaller establishment of doctors. To carry out the physicians' instructions there were comparable hierarchies of surgeons and apothecaries. All these posts were theoretically in the king's free gift, but like all offices in seventeenth-century France they could eventually be purchased by those with capital and connections. To what extent their purchasers could sell or transfer them like other office-holders, however, is difficult to say. All that is known for certain is that there was a definite market in these medical offices in the mid-seventeenth century. Physicians attending the king's family lost their posts when their charges died. Physicians attending the king, however, usually remained in office when there was a change of monarch. Only the *premier médecin du roi* was definitely required to resign his position.[10]

The reign of Henri IV: Pierre de L'Estoile

Pierre de L'Estoile (c. 1540–1611) was a Parisian *avocat* who left a diary of the reigns of Henri III and Henri IV. He was an ardent *politique* who wrote in a vivacious, infectious style about the day-to-day lives of himself, his family, and friends, while recording many of the often-rumoured events that took place at court and in the capital.[11] L'Estoile's general view of the medical profession was more balanced than some of his contemporaries. While being sceptical at times of the prescriptions of the individual physicians whom he patronized and prepared to challenge their wisdom, he recognized all the same that once in the hands of a medical practitioner he was a passive instrument: 'il ne faut appeler un médecin (dit-on), qui ne le veut croire'.[12] On the other hand, he suspected that the medical profession was going downhill and that a growing number of doctors were neither knowledgeable nor well meaning. He felt, too, that even a good doctor would not be guaranteed to cure his or anybody else's malady. Health was a gift from God. 'Le grand médecin en est là-haut, qui seul y peut, comme il me l'a fait assez connaître, et par ci-devant et à cette heure plus que jamais.'[13]

L'Estoile seems to have known a number of court physicians personally, especially the *médecin ordinaire*, Michel Marescot (d. 1605), who was an intimate friend.[14] In the light of his appraisal of the profession as a whole, his assessment of the character and competence of the *médecins de cour* suggests that he thought that they were *la crème de la crème*. As a group, the court physicians were honourable and dedicated men, who did credit to their calling. Thus, Alibour (d. 1594), *premier médecin du roi* of Henri IV in the early 1590s, is described as 'ce bon homme de médecin, fidèle serviteur de Sa Majesté'.[15] Similarly, André Du

Laurens (1558–1609), *premier médecin* in 1606, is said to have had 'la réputation d'un homme de bien et bon médecin'.[16] His successor, Petit, too, is called '[un] homme très habile en son art'.[17] Even the libertine, the sieur de la Rivière, Du Laurens's predecessor, made a good end: 'duquel on ne peut dire autre chose, sinon que le proverbe de telle vie, telle fin, est failli en lui, et que ça a été le bon larron que Dieu a regardé pour lui faire miséricorde'.[18]

The *médecins du roi*, however, did not just evoke L'Estoile's sympathy because, unlike many of their colleagues, they were men of probity. They deserved it the more, his diary suggests, because the life of the court physician was not to be envied. It is quite clear from the account of Marescot's relations with Henri IV that the *médecin du roi* could be a royal intimate, licensed to engage in repartee with his royal master and comment on the contemporary political situation. When Marescot treated the king in October 1598, for example, Henri IV asked the physician for his views on the religious temperature in the capital. Was it true that the Parisians were murmuring against the king's decision to call the Huguenot, Casaubon, to a chair at the University of Paris?

> A quoi ledit Marescot répondit qu'il n'en avoit point ouï parler, et qu'à Paris on ne se battait plus qu'à coups d'Evangiles, à qui se ferait le mieux. Ce que le roi lui dit 'qu'il trouvait très bon et que c'était son intention que celle-là'.[19]

On the other hand, L'Estoile produces no evidence that the position of royal confidant brought with it any real political power. On the contrary, all the evidence points to the powerlessness of the *médecin de cour*.

In the first place, the court physician was exploited by his royal patron. A simple *médecin ordinaire* could be sent off at a moment's notice to the provincial wilds to treat a sick relative or favourite. Thus, in 1603 Du Laurens was dispatched posthaste to Lorraine to bring succour to the purportedly gravely ill Duchesse de Bar, Henri's Protestant sister, a malady which L'Estoile hints was totally fictitious, a fit of Huguenot pique.

> On disait que la cause de son mal provenait d'un dédain qu'elle avait conçu, de ce qu'on ne lui avait voulu permettre de faire enterrer un de ses officiers, à raison de la religion

en laquelle il était mort.[20]

Even the *premier médecin du roi* received small consideration. When Du Laurens eventually gained this elevated position, he was treated by Henri IV as a glorified valet. Each night the physician had to get up in the early hours and read to his royal master the exploits of *Amadis de Gaule* in order to put the king to sleep, a task that L'Estoile suggests hastened the physician's death.[21]

All the time, too, the court physician was surrounded by calumnies, and on one occasion was possibly the victim of deadly violence. When the 'faithful servant' Alibour died on 24 July 1594, it was immediately rumoured that he had been poisoned on the command of the king's mistress, Gabrielle d'Estrées, on account of 'une parole libre qu'il avait dite à Sa Majesté tenant son petit César' (Gabrielle's royal bastard).[22] In consequence, L'Estoile waas convinced of the rectitude of Petit's decision in September 1609 to retire to Guyenne after only a month as *premier médecin*. Only a courtier (i. e. in L'Estoile's eyes a lackey) could survive at court and Petit was a lover of liberty, rich enough to give up his post without discomfort.

Si que, se retirant de la cour avec ses bonnes grâces [celles du roi], il avait échangé la peine (qui souvent passe le profit) à la tranquillité, et le vain honneur de la cour (qui n'est que vent) à un repos pour le reste de ses jours.[23]

The age of Richelieu and Mazarin: Gui Patin

Of all the many private accounts of the age of the Cardinal-Dukes, the most prejudiced and scurrilous is contained in the collection of letters of the Paris physician, Gui Patin (1601–72). A sample of this correspondence was published as early as 1683 at Frankfurt by his son Charles, but the fullest edition appeared in 1846.[24] Patin regarded Richelieu and Mazarin as tyrants, and he vented his spleen at their expense in a vitriolic prose. However, the Cardinal-Dukes were simply his political enemies. Patin had as deeply held views on religion and medicine as he did on matters of state and he personalized the issues in exactly the same way. Often labelled wrongly as a libertine because he was Gassendi's physician in the early

1650s, he can be more accurately seen as an austere Augustinian Christian with Jansenist sympathies. In his medical opinions, he held to an old-fashioned and uncompromising Galenism, especially in therapeutics. His bitterest foes, therefore, were the Paris physicians who treated their patients with Paracelsian and chemical drugs. Above all, Patin's *bête-noire* was antimony, in his eyes a murderous purgative if applied to the delicate constitution of Frenchmen, but unfortunately in the mid-seventeenth century the favoured remedy of many of his colleagues.[25]

Patin shared L'Estoile's conviction that the court physician lived an uncertain and often dangerous existence. In fact, in the years when Richelieu was establishing his ascendancy, the *médecins de cour* had to sail exceptionally close to the prevailing political wind, if they wished to survive. Three court physicians, Patin's letters reveal, were definitely sunk in the aftermath of the Day of Dupes (10 November 1630), the day on which Richelieu found himself temporarily ousted from the king's affection by the Queen Mother, Marie de Médicis, and her creature, Marillac. The first, Charles Guillemeau (d. 1656), simply lost his office for backing the wrong horse; he had been a *médecin* to the subsequently exiled Marie de Medicis.[26] The two others, Semelles and François Vautier (1592–1652), however, had both ended up in the Bastille. Semelles, Patin claimed, had been guilty of casting a horoscope saying Louis XIII would die in September 1631, and was thereby, we can presume, judged guilty of aiding and abetting the anti-Richelieu faction of Gaston d'Orléans, the king's brother and, at that date, heir. Besides being imprisoned, Semelles had had his goods confiscated and been deprived of his post as *médecin par quartier*.[27] François Vautier, on the other hand, had been a client of Richelieu's rival, Marillac, and his access to the king had been used by the *garde des sceaux* to try to unseat the Cardinal. As a result, Vautier had been locked away for the rest of the reign. Nevertheless, unlike his two contemporaries in misfortune, on the death of Louis XIII in 1643 Vautier had bounced back into courtly favour.

> Enfin la scène et le théâtre de la cour étant echangées, il devint premier médecin du roi [in 1646], moyennant 2000 écus qu'il donne au cardinal Mazarin ... à la charge, comme on dit, qu'il seroit là son espion. Voyez la politique: il avoit été

prisonnier du père douze ans, et on lui commit la santé du fils.[28]

Admittedly, the late 1620s and early 1630s seem to have been a unique period of uncertainty, but attendance at court was still a thankless task in the age of Mazarin. In a letter of 30 November 1655 Patin reveals that the eight *médecins par quartier* had not been paid their salary for ten years. At the same time, if it was their turn for duty they had to follow the king wherever he went.

Si le roi est à Narbonne ou en Flandre, il faut aller faire là son quartier, coucher sur de la paille, et peut-être mourir dans une grange, comme fit M. Akakia l'an 1630, en Savoie, âgé de quarante-deux ans, qui laissa dix enfants vivants.[29]

The lot of the *premier médecin du roi* was scarcely better, for Antoine Valot (d. 1671), Vautier's successor in 1652, was complaining in 1658 that he, too, had received no pay. Moreover, in the early years of his tenure, he had to suffer the additional indignity of a factional attempt to remove him. Valot, like Vautier, was Mazarin's man, and when the king fell ill in the autumn of 1655, the Queen Mother (an intriguing comment, this, on her supposedly close relations with the Cardinal) did her best to have him replaced by her own favourite physician, Guénault, on the grounds of incompetence. Despite the hostility of both the king and Anne of Austria, however, Valot survived thanks to the patronage of the Cardinal, although it was only three years later, after two further attempts to unseat him, that he was really secure.[30]

Unlike L'Estoile, however, Patin was totally unsympathetic to the trials and tribulations of the court physician. If the job was thankless, the financial rewards were high (something L'Estoile never mentions). Buying a court office was admittedly very expensive. Claude Séguin (d. 1681), *premier médecin de la reine-mère* in the 1650s, for instance, bought the position of *médecin ordinaire du roi* for 50,000 *livres* in 1643; seven years later he sold it to Marin Cureau de la Chambre (d. 1669) for a 30 per cent profit.[31] However, the high cost reflected the money that could be made from the position. Vautier, despite his misfortunes in the 1630s, supposedly told one of Patin's friends in 1648 that counting his revenue from his office as *pre-*

mier médecin du roi, the income he received from a royal abbey, and the money he had in the bank, he was worth 25,000 *écus de rente*.[32] The court physician, therefore, was playing for high stakes in a vicious, unstable society, and he must accept the consequences. The court was 'le vrai pays des anthropopagues'.[33]

Moreover, the large majority of court physicians were just as unsavoury as their aristocratic clients. Service at court tended only to attract those who were themselves greedy and morally flexible. Guillemeau, for instance, is said to think only of his pocket; Séguin is called avaricious; Valot is accused of doing everything to attract money.[34] However, the worst indictment is laid against the *médecin ordinaire* of Louis XIII, Gui de la Brosse, founder of the Paris Jardin des Plantes. When the latter died in 1641, Patin confidently entrusted him to the fond keeping of the devil as 'un fourbe' and 'un athée'. Even while dying, he assured his correspondent, la Brosse 'n'a eu plus de sentiment de Dieu qu'un pourceau, duquel il imitoit la vie, et s'en donnoit le nom'.[35] The few court physicians, too, who were initially honest were soon drawn into the mire by the corrupting atmosphere of the place. Witness Patin's judgement on Charles Bouvard (1572–1658), Louis XIII's *premier médecin* in the 1630s: '[il] a autrefois été un fort excellent homme; mais la cour l'a corrompu, comme elle a fait de plusieurs autres'.[36] Only Jacques Cousinot (c. 1585/90–1646), the short-lived *premier médecin* of Louis XIV, escaped without censure.[37]

In addition (and this undoubtedly prejudiced his view of their moral qualities), Patin despised all but a few of the court physicians of his day because they were his ideological opponents. Vautier and Valot were both convinced supporters of Paracelsian remedies. So, too, were a number of the less elevated *médecins de cour* who appear in the Patin correspondence, such as Guénault (whose predilection for antimony has already been noted), De la Brosse, D'Aquin *père* and Charles de l'Orme (1584–1678), the single-minded promoter of the mineral waters of Bourbon L'Archambault.[38] Only Bouvard, Nicolas Brayer (a candidate for court office in the 1660s), Cousinot, and Guillemeau were on the side of the angels, good Galenists to a man, whatever their moral failings. Guillemeau, for instance, was described in October 1656 as 'un courtisan recuit et rusé'. Nevertheless, 'il a toujours été du bon parti, et dans les sentiments de la méthode de la saignée, de la paucité des remèdes, de l'antimoine et de toute la chimie'.[39] However, this certainly

could not be said of most *médecins de cour*, who were in
consequence murderers as well as venal hypocrites. Moreover,
some of them could not even offer the excuse that they erred
in all honesty, holding fast to a respectably scientific therapeutics, albeit (in Patin's eyes) an erroneous one. This might be the
case of a Guénault, like Patin himself, a graduate of the Paris
faculty. However, there were physicians at court who were
downright charlatans. Valot only had a degree from Reims
(where doctorates, it was well known, could be swiftly obtained
by the ignorant and the unscrupulous).[40] D'Aquin *père*, on the
other hand, had no medical qualification at all. Before his elevation through the good offices of Vautier and Valot, he had
been simply 'garçon apothicaire de la feue reine-mère [Marie
de Médicis]'.[41]

Patin was more than ready to provide chapter and verse in
support of his accusations of murder. Guénault, the great promoter of antimony, had in 1649 killed off his nephew with the
drug *inter alia*, and then his own daughter four years later.[42] In
1637 the young Séguin had caused the death of the Duchesse
de Longueville by sending her to drink the waters at Forges.[43]
In 1661 D'Aquin *père* in England had poisoned the Princess of
Orange with 'un breuvage' given her 'fort mal à propos'.[44]
Finally, Valot had gone one better and in 1669 carried off the
princess's mother, the king's aunt, Henrietta Maria of England,
with a laudanum pill, thus deservedly becoming the subject of
the following vicious lampoon:

> Le croirez-vous, race future,
> Que la fille du grand Henri
> Eût en mourant même aventure
> Que feu son père et son mari?
> Tous trois sont morts par assassin,
> Ravaillac, Cromwell, médecin.
> Henri d'un coup de bayonette,
> Charles finit sur un billot,
> Et maintenant meurt Henriette.
> Par l'ignorance de Valot.[45]

Patin, however had scant sympathy for the victims of the
court physician either. The courtier and the empiric deserved
one another. In a world where everything was sold, the igno-
ramus and the charlatan would thrive. It was only to be ex-

pected, then, that the *premier médecin* of the king would be the worst physician in the kingdom. The court physician was an 'asinus inter simias'.[46] It should be no surprise, therefore, that 'les grands sont malheureux en médecins'.[47] 'Il faut de tels médecins aux princes, genus hominum quod decipit et decipitur'.[48]

The age of Colbert and Louvois: Madame de Sévigné

Published for the first time by the chevalier de Perrin in 1734, the correspondence of Marie Rabutin Chantal, Marquise de Sévigné (1626–96), has long been recognized as a literary classic, the most detailed and lively seventeenth-century account of maternal devotion. More recently, the correspondence has attracted the earnest attention of the medical historian, for both Madame de Sévigné and her adored daughter, Madame de Grignan, were incorrigible hypochondriacs. Of all the literary remains of *Le Grand Siècle* none provides a fuller picture of contemporary medicine from the point of view of the patient.[49] It might be thought, then, that of all the sources at our disposal for constructing the literary image of the court physician, the Sévigné correspondence would be the most useful. Unfortunately, this is not the case. Certainly, Madame de Sévigné was on the fringe of the court, if not actually part of it. Certainly, too, she knew many court physicians personally, for she belonged to the Parisian high aristocracy who consulted only the most fashionable and socially prestigious medical men. However, her correspondence reveals only the occasional glimpse of the medical world of the court. Her *grande passion*, it must be concluded, simply permitted no distractions. Her gaze was focused fixedly on the day-to-day lives of herself and her family. She had no interest in faction-fighting at court and little in the health of the king and the royal family (at least not as to want to pass any news to her daughter in Provence). Her letters convey the social prejudices of her class, but not political opinions. None the less, for the period of the *Colbertiste* ascendancy, the snippets of information that the Sévigné correspondence provide about medicine at the court of Louis XIV are still invaluable, all the more so in that the letters are the work of a woman. They offer one of the few opportunities in seventeenth and early-eighteenth-century France to look at the court physician from the female perspective. (Another, of course, is the correspondence left by Elisabeth-Charlotte, Duchesse d'Orléans.)[50]

What the Sévigné collection suggests above all is the continuing precariousness of life at the top for the *médecin de cour*. This, however, was no longer the result of the perpetual struggle between the factions for position and place, which in Patin's eyes explained the instability of the era of Richelieu and Mazarin. Rather, it stemmed from the absence of any clearly defined and hierarchically organized medical college. There was, admittedly, always a *premier médecin du roi*, now Antoine d'Aquin (1632–96), who served from 1673–93. A number of other physicians, too, were officially in charge of the health of the ever-growing royal family.[51] However, D'Aquin and his colleagues had no monopoly of consultation. There was a state of open competition. Anyone who could get the ear of the king (qualified or unqualified) could end up treating a royal invalid; there was no professional control. As a result, the court was swarming with visiting quacks, making wild claims for their cures and often being allowed to try their luck. The most famous was the Englishman, Tabor or Talbot, who appeared in Paris in the autumn of 1679 with his quinine wine. When a year later the *dauphine* fell ill due to a quartan ague, Talbot boasted 'sur sa tête' that he would cure the disease in four days. D'Aquin and the other official doctors were elbowed unceremoniously out of the way and the Englishman successfully effected the cure.[52]

When medicine was so obviously customer-led, medical stars could wax and wane very rapidly. *Médecins de cour* who had bought their posts were definitely no longer dismissed when they fell from favour. The one physician whom Madame de Sévigné records as losing his place was one Guilloire in 1671, *médecin* to the king's niece, Mademoiselle (princesse d'Orléans), who was purportedly too bold in his opposition to her marriage to the Comte de Lauzan.[53] Rather, the *médecin de cour* whose reputation was suspect was simply ignored. Not surprisingly, as a result, whatever their status, court physicians were treated shabbily. When D'Aquin was worsted by the bumptious Talbot, the *premier médecin* was taunted cruelly to his face by the highly uncivil Duc de Gramont:

> Talbot est vainqueur du trépas,
> Daquin ne lui résiste pas;
> La Dauphine est convalescente;

Que chacun chante, etc.
[a parody of a song from a popular play].[54]

This anarchic condition of court medicine was almost certainly nothing new. Patin gives an example of the limited powers of the *premier médecin du roi* at an earlier date, when the Queen Mother in October 1655 refused Valot's request to call D'Aquin *père* and Vesou to help him treat the king, and had another court physician, Guénault, summoned instead on the grounds that the latter had already seen the king through the *petite vérole* (of 1647).[55] It is only in the Sévigné correspondence, however, that the absence of professional control appears to be total. Perhaps, then, order was better maintained in the era of the Cardinal-ministers, when the *premier médecin du roi* and his allies retained a quasi-medical monopoly in return for praising their patrons' greatness in the royal bedchamber. A medical free-for-all was arguably the unexpected price of Louis XIV's personal monarchy.

Whatever the truth of the matter, Madame de Sévigné herself definitely aped the medical consumerism of her royal betters, as did doubtless her aristocratic acquaintances. While Louis XIV in the prime of life exchanged his doctors as frequently as his mistresses, Madame de Sévigné took up and laid down her medical counsellors as if they were suits of clothes. In the course of two decades, she hired and fired at least a dozen qualified practitioners and a half-dozen fashionable quacks. Moreover, she and her family could be just as callous as the Duc de Gramont. They treated physicians as domestic servants, to be petted or kicked as the mood took them. In the mid-1690s the wife of Madame de Sévigné's nephew, Madame de Coulanges, was being treated by the Italian empiric, Carette (Nicolas Cevoli, *dit* the marquis del Caretto), highly regarded at court for the miraculous cures he effected with his elixir. At one moment in June 1694 Carette's stock was so high in the Coulanges household that he was sharing the family table. At the next, in August, it had suddenly declined, after his patient suffered a relapse. In consequence, Carette became the victim of a cruel practical joke. Deliberately invited to a society garden party at Vaugirard, outside Paris, he was encouraged to pay serious court to certain young ladies present. Then, having become successfully entranced, he was made to look suitably foolish for his temerity. Finally, to add insult to injury, Madame de Coulanges begged Carette to continue as her medical adviser.[56]

Madame de Sévigné's judgement on the capacity of the court physicians of her day depended entirely on their success in treating her friends and relations. Thus, the Englishman Talbot was a consistent medical hero, for in November 1679 he had cured her uncle and former guardian, the *abbé* de Coulanges, of 'ce rhume qui nous fait peur'.[57] Ever thereafter quinine was a miraculous remedy, inevitably guaranteed to succeed. The empiric Carbrières, on the other hand, who appeared at court at the same time as Talbot on the recommendation of Cardinal du Bouillon, and stayed there throughout the 1680s as a specialist in dealing with apoplexy, was treated with disdain. Witness Madame de Sévigné's letter to her relation, Bussy-Rabutin, of 5 April 1687:

> Mon beaux-frère de Toulongeon a failli à mourir depuis huit ans. Il y avoit longtemps qu'il avoit la goutte aux genoux. Il s'avise il y a trois ou quatre ans, d'aller avec sa femme trouver le prieure de Cabrierès [*sic*] pour qu'il leur fît faire des enfants. Il prit aussi de ses remedes pour guérir sa goutte. A la vérité ce charlatan ne leur fît point faire d'enfants, mais en récompense, il guérit mon beau-frère de sa goutte aux genoux, et il la lui mit dans la tête, où il y a de temps en temps des douleurs insupportables; et c'est de cela qu'il vient d'être à l'extrêmité.[58]

To find favour with Madame de Sévigné, too, the court physician had to have the right bedside manner and prescribe simple, painless remedies. Because of the difficulty of locating her veins, the marquise had a particular abhorrence of phlebotomy. It was for this reason that she was so impressed with Madame de Maintenon's protégé, the up-and-coming Gui-Crescent Fagon (1638–1715) later *premier médecin du roi*, who came to examine her failing daughter in 1678. Fagon was exceptionally thorough; the consultation lasted two hours and he concluded that Madame de Grignan had a lung disorder. Throughout, Fagon was firm but suitably pliant and deferential, contradicting De Grignan when she declared her thinness was nothing (thereby pleasing her mother), but accepting that his patient had an aversion to milk. To build her up, therefore, he suggested 'demi-bains' and refreshing 'bouillons'. This was the first time Madame de Sévigné had encountered the *médecin des enfants du roi* (the royal bastards), and she was convinced that he deserved his fame: 'Il parle avec une connoissance et une capacité qui surprend, et n'est point dans la routine des autres médecins qui accablent de remèdes: il n'ordonnent rien que de bons aliments.'[59] Madame de Sévigné's account of this consultation doubtless helps to explain Fagon's rapid promotion at court in subsequent years, beginning with his appointment as physician to the *enfants de France* (the royal grandchildren) in 1683. He was authoritative, concerned, and knew exactly the kind of remedy his client appreciated![60]

The age of the European wars: Saint-Simon

The most detailed account of medicine at the French court in *Le Grand Siècle* comes from the pen of Louis de Rouvroy, second Duc de Saint-Simon (1675–1755). This is understandable given Saint-Simon's immersion in the world of Versailles, and given the fact too that his *Mémoires*, first published in 1829, were not just the hastily written jottings of a diarist, but a journal carefully edited with the benefit of hindsight.[61] Not that Saint-Simon for all his attention to detail and accuracy could be described as more objective than other observers of the court scene. The literary greatness of his *Mémoires* lies in the coherence brought to the rambling narrative by his twin aristocratic and Augustinian prejudices. Saint-Simon, like Fénelon and a number of other court critics in the years after 1690, believed that the reign of Louis XIV had degenerated into a tyranny. Patin's despotism of the Cardinal-ministers had been replaced by the despotism of the 'bourgeois' minister-secretaries. Preventing outside access to the king and feeding him selective information, the descendants of Colbert and Louvois effectively determined royal policy, while the natural servants of the monarch and nation, the great aristocracy, were left in the political wilderness. At the same time, the court was the centre of decadence, squalor, and intrigue, which Louis's own infidelities and the elevation of his bastards only helped to promote. The king had been guilty of turning the social and moral order upside-down and the state of France in the War of Spanish succession was God's chastisement on an errant ruler.[62]

Saint-Simon's picture of the organization of the medical life of the court is strikingly different from that of Madame de

Sévigné. Whereas D'Aquin's control of the health of the king and his entourage was superficial, the power of Fagon, his successor as *premier médecin du roi* in 1693, was complete.[63] In the final decades of the reign, instead of anarchy and free competition, the watchword was order. Not only did Fagon monopolize treatment of the king but his was the final judgement whenever a member of the royal family fell ill. Moreover, Louis expected courtiers to address themselves to Fagon as well if they fell sick, and he was very annoyed if they did not follow his physician's advice *à la lettre*.[64] Court medicine, then, was 'Fagon-ized'. As a result, the only physicians allowed to treat the royal family were those with official posts, who served as Fagon's lieutenants. If others were summoned, then they came only on Fagon's bidding. Not surprisingly, quacks and empirics disappeared altogether. After 1693 no unqualified physicians got near to Louis himself until the king lay dying on 25 August 1715, when one Le Brun 'une espèce de manant fort grossier' was permitted to administer an elixir for curing gangrene. 'Le roi étoit si mal et les médecins tellement à bout, qu'ils y consentirent sans difficulté, en présence de Mme de Maintenon et duc de Maine.'[65]

Fagon's power over the king, after the previous era of patient-controlled medicine was truly remarkable. According to Saint-Simon the *premier médecin* had the ability totally to blind Louis with science. Through his 'raisonnements de médecine' Fagon could always persuade his royal patient to do as he wished. Both the king and Madame de Maintenon, we are told, 'le prirent pour bon, et ne se doutèrent de rien'.[66] Furthermore, Fagon was ready to thwart the royal will, if he felt it necessary. He put the good of his patients before any personal considerations and generally got his way. Thus, in 1706, when the king was about to set out for Fontainebleau with his pregnant granddaughter-in-law and favourite, the Duchesse de Bourgogne, Fagon and his lieutenants forbade the trip because the princess was near her time. 'Cela fâcha fort le Roi; il dispute; les autres étoient bien instruits; il n'y gagna rien.'[67]

Inevitably, a man with such a sway over the king was a powerful figure at court. Few dared mock Fagon openly in the way Gramont had done D'Aquin. Inevitably, too, Fagon had tremendous independent political influence, something previous royal physicians seem not to have had. Fagon and his own protégé, Georges Mareschal (1658–1736), *premier chirurgien du roi* from 1703, were permanently attached to the royal bed-chamber. Fagon in particular was a man 'qui voyait tout et savoit tout'.[68] Those who sought favours from the king, therefore, were advised to press their suits through the good offices of one or the other. Saint-Simon certainly did so. In 1707 he tried to get both Mareschal's and Fagon's support for the promotion of D'Aguesseau as *premier président* of the Paris Parlement, a candidate who needed much backstairs propulsion given his Jansenist background.[69] Then, in 1709, when forced to retire from court under a cloud, he used Mareschal as his intermediary to get back into favour.[70]

Saint-Simon himself undoubtedly disliked Fagon's medical monopoly. On several occasions he talked of the *premier médecin* 'tyrannizing' the profession (an interesting choice of verb given the duke's views of the political scene), and he took pleasure in recounting the times when Fagon was worsted or humiliated. One successful tormentor was the empiric Le Brun. 'Ce manant ... le malmena fort brutalement, dont Fagon, qui avoit accoutumé de malmener les autres et d'en être respecté jusqu'au tremblement, demeura tout abasourdi.'[71]

Arguably, Saint-Simon saw Fagon's position as analogous to that of the minister-secretaries: his power prevented a balanced assessment of the health of Louis and his family by denying access to alternative viewpoints. Saint-Simon definitely thought the monopoly was dangerous. In 1711, for instance, when the *grand dauphin* (Louis's son) was struck down with smallpox, the latter's own *premier médecin*, Jean Boudin (d. 1728), suggested that help should be sought from physicians in the capital because the *médecins de cour* had never seen the *maladie de venin*. Fagon, however, rejected the plea; outside intervention, he claimed, would only engender vexatious disputes; and that was the end of the matter, although the heir to the throne was clearly ailing fast.[72] Again, in 1715, Fagon's predominance, Saint-Simon suggests, prevented the final malady of the king being effectively treated in time. Mareschal, it seems, had grasped that Louis was seriously ill many months before Fagon and the other physicians. He spoke to the *premier médecin* on several occasions about his concern, but 'fut toujours durement repoussé'. Madame de Maintenon was just as uninterested in the surgeon's fears, declaring that Fagon was the expert. As a result, Louis's illness was allowed to drift. Fagon, therefore, was ultimately responsible for his master's death. 'Il ne vouloit ni raison ni réplique, et continuoit de conduire la santé du Roi comme il avoit fait dans un âge moins avançé, et le tua par cette opinâtreté.'[73]

Nevertheless, despite this dislike of Fagon's medical autocracy, Saint- Simon generally approved of the *premier médecin*. On three major counts he passed the Saint-Simonian test of respectability. In the first place, there could be no doubting his medical expertise: he was '[un] grand botaniste, bon chimiste, habile connoisseur en chirurgie, excellent médecin et grand praticien'. Fagon was the greatest physician of his age. Second, the *premier médecin* never abused his position. 'Il aimoit la vertu, l'honneur, la valeur, la science, l'application, la vérité.'[74] In consequence, he never used his influence over the king to advance anyone who did not deserve promotion. It was for this reason that he had taken up the case of D'Aguesseau, although worried by the latter's Jansenist connections. Finally, and most importantly, Fagon was a good courtier, discreet and deferential. If anything, he was over-pliant. While always forcefully putting his point of view when it was a case of making a diagnosis, he could keep irritatingly silent on other occasions when his judgement would have been decisive. When the new *dauphin* (Louis's grandson, the Duc de Bourgogne) and his wife in turn died of smallpox in 1712, the rumour circulated that they had been poisoned on the orders of the Duc d'Orléans, to enhance his chances of gaining the throne (he was the king's nephew and only the future Louis XV, the great-grandson of the Roi du Soleil stood in his path). Much to Saint-Simon's annoyance (the duke was his friend and patron), Fagon did nothing to scotch this foul slander. While Mareshal leapt to defend the duke's honour, speaking to the king with a 'virtueuse liberté', Fagon stayed aloof from the political quarrel, doubtless (although Saint-Simon only implies this) because he knew that his own patron, Madame de Maintenon, suspected the worst.[75]

Fagon was not the only *médecin de cour* to receive the Saint-Simonian seal of approval. This positive image was duplicated in a number of other less detailed character sketches, such as those of Adrien Helvétius (1662–1727), J. B. Duchesne (1616–1707), and Claude Jean-Baptiste Dodart (1664–1730).[76] Above all, the image was repeated in the case of the *premier médecin* of Philip V of Spain, the expatriate Irishman John Higgins, whom Saint-Simon encountered while ambassador to Madrid during the Regency. He, too, was learned, pious, and deferential, and by implication a greater credit to his profession even than Fagon himself for his character was far more open. Not only was Higgins detached from all ambition and never involved in court intrigue, but he would always speak honestly to the king when asked to comment on matters of state. Higgins, Saint-Simon believed, had even greater power over Philip than Fagon had over Louis (his grandfather), for the King of Spain was a hypochondriac. The fact, then, that Higgins never exploited his position in the way Coctier had done as *médecin* to the hypochondriac, Louis XI of France, in the late-fifteenth century emphasized the more the Irishman's probity.[77]

Two *médecins de cour*, however, were painted in a far less attractive light. The first was Jean Boudin, whom we have already encountered in his office as *premier médecin* of Monseigneur, the *grand-dauphin*. At first sight, Saint-Simon tells us, Boudin, son of an *apothicaire du roi*, was an attractive figure. He was vivacious and witty and one of the few people able to manipulate Fagon. After becoming a hit in high society, however, success spoiled him. He became impertinent and began to behave in a manner above his station. At the same time, he neglected his profession, no longer taking the trouble to see his patients, and spending his days in a vain search for the philosophers' stone.[78] In the end his avarice and singular lack of discretion led to disastrous consequences. It was Boudin, only recently advanced on the death of the *grand dauphin* to the post of *premier médecin* to the wife of his son, who thoughtlessly published abroad in 1712 the fears that his mistress had been poisoned: 'Boudin, outré d'avoir perdu sa charge et une princesse pleine de bontés pour lui, même de confiance, et ses espérances avec elle, répandit comme un forcené qu'on ne pouvait pas douter qu'elle ne fît empoissonée.'[79]

The second, much more heinous blackguard, was Pierre Chirac (1650–1732), *premier médecin* to the Duc d'Orléans from 1715 but in his service for considerably longer. Like Fagon, Chirac, in Saint-Simon's eyes, was the greatest doctor of his day. 'C'étoit le plus savant médecin de son temps.'[80] Like Fagon, too, he was a good courtier; but in Chirac's case the deference and the courtliness were all show. In reality, Chirac was eaten up by avarice and ambition. Perhaps even 'la religion lui étoit inconnu'.[81] Certainly, according to Saint-Simon, he was known to cause the death of his patients deliberately. In 1719, the Duchesse de Berry, Orléan's dissolute daughter, had been given up for dead by her official doctors, including Chirac, when she was revived by an elixir administered by a Montpellier graduate, turned empiric, Joseph Garus (d. 1722). Chirac, who had presumably been unable to prevent the admittance of this outsider (he clearly lacked Fagon's authoritative touch!), feared a consequent loss of face. Against Garus's express orders, therefore, he gave the duchess a purgative that as good as killed her. 'Chirac, voyant avancer l'agonie traversa la chambre, et, faisant une révérence d'insulte au pied du lit, qui étoit ouvert, lui souhaita un bon voyage en termes équivalents, et de ce pas s'en alla à Paris.'[82]

Why did Saint-Simon single out these two physicians for such an unceremonious mauling? The answer must surely be that they alone had offended the duke personally. Boudin's intemperate tongue, we have seen, started the rumour that threatened to have his patron charged with high treason. In Saint-Simon's opinion, even if poison had carried off the heir to the throne and his wife, the *médecins* should have argued in favour of death by natural causes to save the king's peace of mind.[83] Chirac, on the other hand, had made the duke look a fool. When Fagon's successor as *premier médecin*, Louis Poirier, died suddenly in 1718, Saint-Simon supported Chirac's request to be made *intendant* of the Jardin des Plantes (in the gift of the Regent). Chirac had told the duke that he wanted to re-equip the Jardin at his own expense. The *premier médecin* of the Duc d'Orléans, however, had done no such thing. On the contrary, Chirac took away all the choice plants and left the Jardin 'en friche'.[84]

The portraits of Boudin and Chirac are therefore almost certainly overdrawn and should be discounted. They must not be allowed to mask the fact that Saint-Simon found the *médecins de cour* as a group sympathetic, whatever his doubts about 'Fagonization'. Arguably, he wished to portray the royal physician as a well-mannered, honest professional, a representative of order in a court of moral chaos. Interestingly, too, Saint-Simon's positive appraisal was not limited to the physicians but extended to their surgical colleagues. None of our other sources really acknowledged the existence of the court surgeon. One of the most intriguing lacunae of the Sévigné correspondence is the absence of any letter by the Marquise concerning the famous operation of the fistula (1686). The only time the man who conducted the operation, the great Félix, is referred to in his official capacity as *premier chirurgien du roi* is in a letter of 1689, where he is disdainfully depicted in the humiliating position of phlebotomizing the king's *premier valet*.[85] Saint-Simon, on the other hand, continually recounts the deeds of his successor, Georges Mareschal. Indeed, in some ways, the latter is the medical hero of the *Mémoires*.

As a practitioner, it seems, Mareschal could do no wrong, a skilful lithotomist who included among his successes, Fagon, the Comte de Toulouse (a royal bastard) and the Duc de Gramont.[86] As a man he is described as 'droit et parfaitement vrai',[87] so uninterested in money that he would only accept 10,000 *écus* for operating on the Comte de Toulouse on the king's express command. Moreover, Mareschal, unlike Fagon, was not afraid, as we have seen, to speak his mind on other than medical matters. Not only did he defend the reputation of the Duc d'Orléans but he did his best to stop the poison story from spreading at the beginning. He feared foul play himself, Saint-Simon reports, but insisted that the autoptic signs were equivocal and that the death of the *petit dauphin* and his wife should be taken as natural.[88] Not surprisingly, it had been Mareschal a few years earlier who had had the courage to tell the king of the state of public opinion during the 1709–10 dearth. The general belief, he had told His Majesty, was that the *gens de finance* were exploiting the situation. 'Le roi parut touché, n'en sut pas mauvais gré à Mareschal.'[89] If the *premier chirurgien du roi* had a fault, it was that he was a little 'grossier', not knowing the force and measure of his terms (apparently he would call the Duc d'Orléans 'his friend'). Nevertheless, he was 'tout à fait respectueux et parfaitement éloigné de se méconnoitre'.[90]

Saint-Simon's attention to the *premier chirurgien du roi* doubtless reflected the power that Mareschal could wield in the closet alongside his patron Fagon. It also reflected the fact that Mareschal had always been closely attached to the Saint-Simon family,[91] and had successfully reinstated the duke in the king's favour (see above). It would be interesting to know if earlier *premier chirurgiens du roi* had enjoyed a similar position at court, and if they too had developed the same kind of rapport with their opposite numbers which Mareschal and Fagon purportedly had.[92] Unfortunately, neither question can be conclusively answered from the texts under study. However, the fact that the literary sources are almost silent about the royal surgeons and that Saint-Simon has virtually nothing to say about Félix, although the latter was in office for the first ten years of the period covered by the *Mémoires*, suggests that their profile at court was low.[93] It seems reasonable to assume, therefore, that in the person of Mareschal the *premier chirurgien du roi* made a quantum leap in courtly status. In some ways, Mareschal was even closer to the king than Fagon, for Saint-Simon tells us that he slept every night in the vicinity of the royal bedchamber.[94] Fagon, on the other hand, locked himself away in his apartment and could be difficult to rouse. In 1711 when one of the royal bastards, the Duc de Maine, collapsed at Marly (close to Paris), the *premier médecin* 'à qui deux heures à peine suffisoient pour s'habiller par degrées, n'y vint qu'au bout de quatre'.[95]

The age of Fleury: Etienne Barbier

Saint-Simon's account of the medical world of the court is so rich that any other source necessarily represents an anticlimax. It seems useful, however, to close this chapter with a brief forage into the first half of the eighteenth century to see whether 'Fagon-ization' was a lasting or transient phenomenon. To give the chapter a certain symmetry, too, it seemed appropriate to select as the final literary witness another professional diarist. Etienne Barbier (1689–1771), like L'Estoile, was a Paris *avocat*, who kept a detailed journal of events at the court and in the capital during the Regency and the first part of the reign of Louis XV.[96] Unlike L'Estoile, however, Barbier reveals virtually nothing about himself and his family in his day-to-day record. He was much more the ice-cool observer, viewing the activities of the great and good with a detached irony. As a result, it is difficult to assess his personal feelings about the events he describes. He offers many judgements, but they are nearly always presented as the opinion of others or the public in general. This is particularly true in the case of the court medical scene. Barbier offers us a coherent and definite image but only once provides a personal commentary to his description.

Barbier's portrait of medicine at the court of Louis XV takes us back to the age of Madame de Sévigné. Again, we enter a world of medical anarchy where the *premiers médecins* do not enjoy omnipotence. Two examples effectively illustrate this point. In August 1721 the king was suddenly taken ill and, as was customary, the *médecins de cour* held a *conseil de santé*. It was not, however, the advice of the *premier médecin*, C. J. B. Dodart, which was adopted but that of a *médecin du roi par quartier*, J. Cl. Adrien Helvétius (1685–1755).[97] A similar *conseil* was held in 1752 when the *dauphin* was ailing of smallpox, which led to the unconventional decision being taken to bleed the patient *after* the appearance of the pustules (he had already been bled before). Once more the driving force behind this decision was not the *premier médecin*, now François Chicoyneau (1672–1752), but one of his subordinates, Jacques Du Moulin (1666–1755), who had started his career as a surgeon.[98] In Fagon's day only the view of the *premier médecin* would have won the day.

Yet if 'Fagon-ization' did not survive its creator, the situation did not revert totally to the *status quo ante*. The official *médecins de cour* might again have competed amongst themselves to gain the ascendancy at the royal bedside, but at least Barbier's portrait suggests that they were united enough to keep out the empirics and quacks who had besieged the court in Madame de Sévigné's day. Moreover, there is no evidence that the royal physicians were once again subjected to the open ridicule of the court aristocracy, sceptical of their skills, and hostile to their pretentions. The era of Fagon, it appears, had ensured that their status in the court hierarchy had been accepted. Admittedly, by the 1740s Barbier depicts their position as again being under attack, but the opposition now came from a different quarter. Their opponents were no longer the ducs de Gramont of this world, but their own immediate subordinates, the court surgeons.

This battle in the mid-eighteenth century between the physicians and surgeons for supremacy at the court, Barbier realized, was part of a wider struggle between the two wings of the medical profession. It was a battle, he believed, that the surgeons would undoubtedly win. Writing in 1743, the year of a royal edict which separated the Paris surgeons from the Paris barbers and insisted that future masters of the art should be MAs, Barbier predicted that within fifteen years the world would be turned upside-down and the surgeons would be at the apex of the medical profession. The chief reason for this, he suggested, was 'la perfection de leur art, qui a été porté à un haut degré, qui leur a attiré l'approbation et la confiance des grands et du public, et qui leur a fait obtenir l'établissement d'une académie royale de la chirurgie [in the 1730s]'. But this, he also insisted, was not the only cause. The surgeons' advance was facilitated by the political victory in the *cabinet du roi*, where the *premier chi-rurgien du roi*, François Gigot de La Peyronie (1678–1747), had greater influence than his opposite number, Chicoyneau. At a critical moment, in other words, the physicians had as their chief representative before the king a political lightweight. La Peyronie, Barbier tells us, was 'un homme d'esprit et entrepre-nant et fort supérieur par le crédit et l'intrigue à M. Chicoyneau ... qui est un homme tranquille'.[99] It is hard to imagine a Fagon being elbowed so easily aside.

The extent of the rivalry between the two branches of the profession at court is illustrated by Barbier's account of the mis-carriage of the *dauphine* in January 1749. This was the princess's second miscarriage and both king and public were apparently very alarmed. Rumour had it that Louis blamed the *médecins de cour*, but Barbier suspected that 'ce bruit se répand-il ici [at Paris] de la part des chirurgiens'. Certainly, his account reveals that the surgeons at court had gained the royal ear. Originally, the princess had been in the hands of the *accoucheur*, Jarre, ac-ting on consultation with his medical colleagues. After the mis-carriage, however, the *médecins de cour* must have been dropped from the case, for two other famous Parisian *accoucheurs*, Nicolas Puzos (1686–1753) and one Bourgeois, were summarily called to Versailles to assist in the *dauphine's* recovery.[100]

As members of the royal family miscarried and died with pre-dictable regularity in the first half of the eighteenth century, the surgeons had plenty of opportunities to accuse the *médecins de cour* of incompetence. Barbier definitely felt the attack was un-just. When a princess died in July 1746 after giving birth, he for once dropped his guard, and expostulated against the rumours that were flying around.

> On jure beaucoup contre les médecins à l'ordinaire sans songer que ces sortes d'évenements humains sont dans les déstinées supérieures à tout. Mais ils n'ont personne au des-sus d'eux pour leur faire à cet égard leur procès.[101]

Barbier's sympathies probably reflected no more than a pro-fessional solidarity. He was the member himself of a profession with its own subordinate branches. Victory for the surgeons might encourage *procureurs* and *notaires* in turn to challenge the *avocats'* monopoly of the Bar. Undoubtedly, Barbier, in contrast to L'Estoile, held no brief for the *bon médecin* thrown into the courtly lion's den. On the contrary, his continual, slightly deprecating references to the wealth to be gained in court medical service suggests that he felt that the *médecins* and *chirurgiens de cour* enjoyed a comfortable and enviable billet. On one occasion, he seems to have found the rewards almost scandalously high. In February 1738 the *dauphin* was suffering from a small abscess on the cheek, accompanied by a slight fever. A small operation was performed and the heir to the throne was perfectly cured. However, in recognition of their sterling contribution to the survival of the dynasty 'M. Silva, médecin, a eu la noblesse, et M. Dumoulin [then a surgeon] six milles livres de pension'.[102]

Barbier's remarks about the fruits of courtly medical office are reminiscent of the gibes of Gui Patin, although their tone is never so acerbic. Neither Madame de Sévigné nor Saint-Simon had mentioned the rewards of medical service, the first doubtless because she took such little interest in the court physicians in their official capacity anyway, the second because to do so would have tarnished the positive and deferential image that he wished to convey. Barbier's comments, then, remind us that the *médecins* and now, too, the *chirurgiens de cour* were playing for high stakes.[103] More than that, his journal emphasizes that the stakes had increased. The Cardinals' medical men were paid for their dubious services in *rentes* and misappropriated ecclesiastical revenues. Silva, on the other hand, was ennobled, as indeed were many other court physicians and surgeons in the first half of the eighteenth century.[104] Those, too, who failed to extract the honour from a grateful crown, used the wealth which they accumulated at court to buy their way in. Du Moulin, for instance, entered the nobility by buying the office of *sécrétaire du roi*. Assuming he paid the going rate of 120,000 *livres*, he had still put aside enough by his death in 1755, according to Barbier, to be worth 100,000 *livres* in *rente*.[105]

Conclusion

Although the five authors under discussion wrote from a variety of social, ideological, and even sexual perspectives, they present a surprisingly coherent picture of the world of the court physician in seventeenth- and early-eighteenth-century France. All agree that except for the period of 'Fagon-ization', the life of

143

the *médecin de cour* was somewhat precarious. To survive and prosper at court, it was insufficient to be recognized as the re-incarnation of Jean Fernel. More importantly, the court physi-cian had to wear the mask of Polonius. Even in the eighteenth century he had to know how to intrigue, fawn, bow and scrape, and servilely carry out the commands of his royal master or mistress. In 1601 Du Laurens had been sent off post-haste to Lorraine to treat the king's sister in a fit of pique. In 1714, Louis XIV peremptorily ordered Adrien Helvétius to go off to Spain to minister to the dying wife of Philip V. Helvétius thought the journey pointless and remonstrated against the royal com-mand, but he went nevertheless. Plus ça change ... [106]

On the other hand, the security of the court physician defi-nitely improved as the period progressed. In the first half of the seventeenth century the court physician was part lackey and part entertainer, closely identified with the faction that had brought him to the royal notice. Shabbily treated, his fall from grace could be swift and painful when his patrons were ousted. From the moment Louis XIV began his personal rule, however, the court physician's star began to wax. Significantly the last *médecin de cour* to share the fate of his master was Fouquet's doc-tor, the anatomist Jean Pecquet (1622–74), flung in the Bastille in 1664 some three years after the fall of the finance minis-ter.[107] Thereafter, if entrance to the court required patronage, the *médecin de cour* could survive his patron's disgrace. D'Aquin, for instance, was a client of Madame de Montespan, Louis's most fecund mistress. Nevertheless, as Saint-Simon reveals, he 'n'avoit rien perdu de son crédit par l'eloignement final de la maîtresse' in 1683, surviving in office another ten years. In fact, in the late-seventeenth and early-eighteenth centuries the *médecins de cour* were only 'retired' when their royal charge died (hence Boudin's grief) or if they did something utterly stupid. Thus, D'Aquin was only finally felled by La Maintenon in 1693 and replaced by her protégé, Fagon, because the *premier médecin* had already stumbled. D'Aquin was notorious for the demands that he made on the king on behalf of his family, and he finally went too far. When the archiepiscopal see of Tours fell vacant, '[il] avoit l'effronterie de vouloir faire son fils [a relatively minor ecclesiastic] tout d'un coup archévêque, *al despetto* de tous les abbés de la première qualité et de tous les évêques du Royaume'.[108]

At the same time, too, this new security was accompanied (or perhaps, rather, followed) by a rise in the status of the *médecin de cour*. Once Fagon had become *premier médecin* and the empirics had been ejected, the titular *médecins de cour* seemed to gain a stable and recognized position in court society. Presumably, this was not just the result of Fagon's obviously powerful personality, his ability to browbeat an ailing and aged king, to say nothing of his morganatic wife. Rather, it suggests a growing confidence in and respect for the qualified medical practitioner among the great aristocracy as a whole. The official *médecins de cour* had arguably convinced a large part of Versailles society that they were indispensable experts. Saint-Simon for one drew a sharp dividing-line between the licensed physician or surgeon and the uncertified quack. He had little time for the likes of Carette,[109] and was highly suspicious of the amateur lithotomists who plied their trade in the capital. When his father-in-law died in agony in 1702 after being operated on by the fashionable Frère Jacques (who lithotomized twenty patients a month, so it was said), Saint-Simon was scarcely surprised. This layman 'bizarrement encapuchiné en gris' had a good operating technique but no capacity to grasp that there were different varieties of stone requiring different treatments.[110]

Of course, the impression conveyed by the five literary sources under discussion can only be tentative at this stage. Before it is accepted as authentic, it needs to be verified by the study of many other similar literary remains. Nevertheless, the very fact that a pattern has emerged from the sources explored to date is encouraging. It adequately demonstrates that the study of the literary image of the court physician is not some deconstructionist game but a serious historical enterprise. Such a study may be of little value, admittedly, in constructing an accurate portrait of prominent medical personalities, although some literary witnesses are clearly more reliable than others; Saint-Simon is definitely a more credible witness than Gui Patin, for all his bias. On the other hand, a literary approach can be highly rewarding in uncovering the general ambience in which these individuals flourished. Indeed, in the case of seventeenth-century France, without a recourse to literary evidence, virtually nothing would be known about the world of the court physician at all before the reign of Louis XIV. With little usable material in the surviving records of the royal household (Archives nationales, series 0), it is the literary sources to which we must often turn simply to recover the physicians' names.

Laurence Brockliss

Appendix

The literary image of the médecins du roi in the literature of Le grand siècle

Table 5.1 Premiers médecins du roi, *1593–1752*

Jean d'Alibour (or Aillebourt):	1593–4
Jean Ribit, sieur de la Rivière:	1594–1605
André du Laurens:	1606–9
? Petit :	1609
Jean Hérouard:	1610–28
Charles Bouvard:	1628–42
Jacques Cousinot:	1643–6
François Vautier:	1646–52
Antoine Valot:	1652–71
Antoine d'Aquin:	1672–93
Gui-Crescent Fagon:	1693–1715
Louis Poirier:	1715–18
Claude J. B. Dodart:	1718–30
Pierre Chirac:	1730–2
François Chicoyneau:	1732–52

Table 5.2 Premiers chirurgiens du roi, *1653–1747*

François-Félix Tassy:	1653–78[a]
Charles-François Tassy dit Félix:	1678–1703
Georges Mareschal:	1703–33
François Gigot de la Peyronie:	1733–47

a. Félix père replaced Jean-Baptiste Bontemps.

Notes

1. I owe this thought to Dr Nigel Smith, Keble College, Oxford.
2. Sir William Butts, d. 1545, is accredited with helping to introduce medical humanism to England: see *Dictionary of National Biography* (hereafter DNB), III, pp. 555–6.
3. Henri, Duc d'Aumale, *Histoire des Princes du Condé pendant les 16ᵉ et 17ᵉ siècles* (Paris, 1883–96), VII, p. 198, n. 1: letter of the Comte de Langeron to Pierre Desnoyers, secretary to the Queen of Poland, 18 September 1655. Guénault will be referred to on several occasions below. A graduate of the Paris faculty in 1615, he ended his days as physician to Louis XIV's queen. Biographical details in J. A. Hazon, *Notices des hommes les plus célèbres de la faculté de médecine*

146

1110–1750 (Paris, 1773), p. 108; *Dictionnaire de Biographie Française* (Hereafter DBF), 16, pp. 1434–5.

4. Similarly, in Shakespeare's, *Merry Wives of Windsor*, John Caius (1510–73), only appears as Dr Caius, a French physician. By 1600–1, too, when the play was written, Caius, a relatively safe target because of his alleged Catholicism, was long dead.

5. According to Montaigne those who were treated by doctors were sick first and cured last. See Merleau-Ponty, *Montaigne et les médecins*, thèse pour le doctorat en médecine (Paris, 1903), p. 22. Montaigne's sceptical attitude was aggravated by his failure to find relief for his stone by taking the waters in Italy in 1580–1.

6. See especially Boileau's letters to Racine in 1687 while undergoing treatment for his lost voice at the spa of Bourbon L'Archambault: printed in Boileau, *Oeuvres complètes*, ed. Françoise Escal (Paris, 1966), pp. 733–51.

7. 'M. Guéneau [*sic*] a traitté cela de raillerie.' Langeron to Desnoyers, see note 3 above. Guénault perhaps had little choice in his response; since the late 1620s he had been physician to the family of Molière's protector in the 1660s, Louis II de Bourbon, prince de Condé.

8. Neither Suetonius nor Tacitus were studied widely in the seventeenth century in the *collèges de plein exercise* where future members of the hierarchy and the parlements were educated; nevertheless it is evident that Tacitus in particular was well known in court and government circles: see E. Thiau, *Raison d'état et pensée politique à l'époque de Richelieu* (Paris, 1966).

9. When Bossuet does refer to court physicians, moreover, he is laconic. For example 28 May 1696, letter to the *abbé* Bossuet: 'M. d'Aquin, ancien premier médecin, s'est tué aux eaux par son art, en agissant contre l'avis de ses confrères des provinces.' Ch. Urbain and E. Levesque (eds), *Correspondance de Bossuet* (15 vols, Paris, 1909–25), VII, p. 411. D'Aquin will be discussed below.

10. For a discussion of the royal medical service, see P. Delaunay, *La Vie médicale au 16e, 17e, et 18e siècles* (Paris, 1935), pp. 192–237. At present no detailed list of court physicians exists for the seventeenth century. The *premiers médecins du roi* in this period are listed in the appendix.

11. Pierre de l'Estoile, *Journal pour le règne de Henri III (1574–89); Journal pour le règne de Henri IV, tome I (1589–1600); Journal pour le règne de Henri IV, tome II (1601–1609)* eds L. R. Lefèvre and A. Martin (3 vols, Paris, 1935–58). Details concerning the publication of the diary are given in L. G. Michaud (ed.), *Biographie universelle ancienne et moderne*, 2nd edn (45 vols, Paris, 1843) 13, pp. 155–6.

12. L'Estoile, *Journal*, III, 331: 22 April 1608. L'Estoile had called in Jean Duret (d.1629) to treat his son for measles. Duret had ordered a phlebotomy against L'Estoile's opinion and will. Jean Duret, a Paris graduate, was the son of Louis, the famous Hippocratic commentator. He is the subject of a short and doubtless scurrilous notice in Tallemant des Réaux, *Les Historiettes*,

ed. G. Mongrédien (8 vols, Paris, n. d.) I, p. 264.

13. L'Estoile, *Journal*, II, p. 269: 4 September 1607; the editors have modernized the orthography.

14. Marescot was a Paris graduate in 1566. For his life, see Hazon, *Notices des hommes*, pp. 66–8.

15. L'Estoile, *Journal*, III, 522: 24 July 1594. Jean d'Alibour or Aillebourt (1532–94) replaced Marc Miron as *premier médecin* of Henri IV in 1593; brief biographical details in DBF, I, p. 934.

16. L'Estoile, *Journal*, III, p. 501: 16 August 1609. Du Laurens is famous for his *Historia anatomica*, 1st edn (Frankfurt, 1595). He was a graduate of Montpellier in 1583. See DBF, 12, 70.

17. L'Estoile, *Journal*, III, p. 502. Nothing is known about this physician that is not related in L'Estoile.

18. Ibid., III, p. 174: 5 November 1605. This is Jean Ribit, sieur de la Rivière, c. 1546–1605, born near Geneva. He has been usually mistaken for Roch Le Baillif, sieur de la Rivière, a Paracelsian from Normandy. The proper identification was first made in H. Trevor-Roper, 'The Sieur de la Rivière, Paracelsian Physician of Henri IV' in A. Debus (ed.), *Science, Medicine and Society in the Renaissance* (2 vols, London, 1972), I, pp. 217–50.

19. L'Estoile, *Journal*, II, p. 543: 30 October 1598. Isaac Casaubon (1551–1614) held the chair in Greek at the Paris Collège Royal from 1600–10; this was an institution, founded by François I in 1530, independent of the university.

20. Ibid., III, p. 2: 13 January 1601.

21. Ibid., II, pp. 375, 532–3: September 1608 and September 1609.

22. Ibid., II, p. 422. Further details about this bizarre episode are to be found in *Memoirs of Maximilien de Béthune, Duc de Sully*, Eng. trans. (5 vols, London, 1812), II, pp. 31–2. Sully is otherwise silent about the *médecins du roi*.

23. L'Estoile, *Journal*, III, pp. 502, 533: 16 August 1609; September 1609.

24. G. Patin, *Lettres*, ed. J. H. Réveillé-Parise (3 vols, Paris, 1846). An attempt to publish a complete edition was begun by P. Triaire, but got no further than the first volume: *Lettres de Gui Patin 1630–1672* (Paris, 1907).

25. A useful biographical notice on Patin as a physician appeared in Hazon, *Notices des hommes*, pp. 112–18. He graduated from Paris in 1629. More recent studies include F. R. Packard, *Guy Patin and the Medical Profession in Paris in the Seventeenth Century* (London, 1924). For the debate over the utility of antimony, see L. W. B. Brockliss, 'Medical teaching at the University of Paris 1600–1720', *Annals of Science*, 35 (1978), pp. 239–45.

26. Réveillé-Parise (ed.), *Lettres*, II, pp. 427–8: Patin to Falconet, 23 March 1663. Guillemeau was a graduate of the Paris faculty in 1627, so can only have held his position for a few years when he was disgraced. A brief biographical notice can be found in DBF, fascicule XCVII, p. 214, but fuller details can be gleaned from the Patin correspondence itself.

27. Triaire, *Lettres*, p. 23: Patin to Belin, 28 October 1631. The truth is more complex; Semelles or Senelles (dates unknown) seems to have been caught carrying letters containing the horoscope.

28. Réveillé-Parise (ed.), *Lettres*, III, p. 429: Patin to Falconet, 23 March 1663. Vautier was a graduate of Montpellier in 1612; see the notice in J. Astruc, *Mémoires pour servir à l'histoire de la faculté de médecine de Montpellier* (Paris, 1767), pp. 372–5.

29. Réveillé–Parise (ed.), *Lettres*, II, pp. 227–8: Patin to Spon, 30 November 1655. This is presumably Jean Akakia, Paris graduate in 1612, who died in Savoy 'à la suite de roi' in 1635: see DBF, I, 1057. There were many Paris physicians called Akakia in the late-sixteenth and early-seventeenth centuries.

30. Réveillé-Parise (ed.), *Lettres*, II, pp. 209, 217, 360; III, pp. 64–5: letters to Spon, 19 October 1655, 2 November 1655, 4 December 1657; letter to Falconet, 1 November 1656. Biographical details on Valot in Michaud (ed.), *Biographie*, 42, pp. 510–11.

31. Réveillé-Parise (ed.), *Lettres*, II, p. 5: Patin to Spon, 3 May 1650. Séguin was a Paris graduate, who took his degree at the same time as Patin (1629); he has been the subject of no biographical notice. On the *érudit* Marin Cureau de la Chambre, see DBF, 9, pp. 1391–3.

32. Réveillé-Parise (ed.), *Lettres*, I, pp. 396–7: Patin to Spon, 29 May 1648. Given the high seventeenth-century rates of interest, this would suggest that Vautier had a fortune of at least 600,000 *livres* or a sterling equivalent of c. £24,000. This figure did not include the value of his private medical practice.

33. Ibid., II, p. 360: Patin to Spon, 4 December 1657.

34. Ibid., II, p. 166; III, p. 153: letters to Spon, 9 April 1655 (on Guillemeau); to Falconet, 19 September 1659 (on Séguin and Valot).

35. Ibid., I, pp. 81–2: Patin to Belin, 4 September 1641. For a more appreciative assessment of the botanist, see Rio C. Howard, 'Gui de la Brosse: the founder of the Jardin des Plantes', unpublished Ph. D. dissertation, Cornell University, 1974.

36. Réveillé-Parise, (ed.), *Lettres*, II, p. 243: Patin to Spon, 3 March 1656. Bouvard was a Paris graduate in 1604. Biographical details in DBF, 7, pp. 69–70.

37. Cousinot was always lionized by Patin as one of the stars of the Paris faculty; he had graduated in 1618. On his death Patin bought his library: letter to Belin, 12 November 1653 (Réveillé-Parise (ed.), *Lettres*, I, p. 200). There is a biographical notice on Cousinot in DBF, 9, pp. 1081–2.

38. On learning incorrectly of De l'Orme's death in 1658, Patin's epitaph in a letter to Spon (18 June) was short and to the point: 'Il n'étoit pas ignorant, mais grand charlatan et effronté courtisan' (Réveillé-Parise (ed.), *Lettres*, II, p. 398). De l'Orme's contribution to the popularity of the spa at Bourbon is stressed in Tallemant des Réaux, *Les Historiettes*, 4, pp. 180–2.

39. Réveillé-Parise (ed.), *Lettres*, II, p. 256: Patin to Spon, 24

October 1656. For Brayer, a Paris graduate in 1628, see Hazon, *Notices des Hommes*, p. 118.

40. Réveillé-Parise (ed.), *Lettres*, II, p. 498: Patin to Spon, 25 March 1664. Patin himself had helped to remodel the Reims statutes in 1660 but until the close of the *ancien régime* degrees were always fairly easy to obtain from the faculty. For Patin's involvement, see A. Jacquinet, *Le Centre universitaire médical de Reims (1550–1666)* (Largentière, 1950), pp. 10–12. Valot may well have been a graduate of Reims. Astruc, *Mémoires*, pp. 380–2, says that he failed to find any evidence associating Valot with Montpellier.

41. Réveillé-Parise (ed.), *Lettres*, II, p. 298: Patin to Spon, 24 April 1657. Louis-Henri-Thomas d'Aquin (dates unknown) was the son of a Jewish rabbi of Avignon and the father of Valot's successor in 1672. Patin says that he had been one of Gassendi's doctors (ibid., II, p. 107: to Spon, 30 January 1654).

42. Ibid., I, p. 423; II, p. 80: letters to Spon, 8 January 1649 and 21 October 1653.

43. Ibid., I, p. 47: Patin to Belin, 16 September 1637.

44. Ibid., II, p. 455: Patin to Spon, undated, 1661. At this date D'Aquin *père* was in England in attendance on Henrietta-Maria.

45. Ibid., III, p. 706: Patin to Falconet, 18 September 1669. Bossuet preached the sermon at Henrietta-Maria's funeral. There is no hint in the text that the doctors hastened her demise.

46. Ibid., III, pp. 103–4: Patin to Falconet, 10 September 1658.

47. Ibid., I, p. 222: Patin to Belin, 14 March 1657.

48. Ibid., II, p. 298: Patin to Spon, 24 April 1657.

49. For an idea of the medical value of this source, see the collection of essays in *Madame de Sévigné, Molière et les médecins de son temps*, Actes du Centre Méridional de Rencontres sur le XVIIe Siècle (Marseilles, 1973).

50. Various collections of the duchess's letters exist: for example in a French translation (she wrote in German), *Correspondence de Mme duchesse d'Orléans, née princesse palatine* ed. and trans. G. Brunet (2 vols, Paris, 1857). Her correspondence has recently been analysed in Elborg Forster, 'From the patient's point of view: illness and health in the letters of Liselotte von der Pfalz (1652–1722)', *Bulletin of the History of Medicine*, 60, 3 (1986), pp. 297–320.

51. Antoine d'Aquin (1632–96), graduate of Montpellier in 1648, *premier médecin de la reine* in 1667 (on the death of Guénault). Biographical details in J. Lévi-Valensi, *La médecine et les médecins français au XVIIe siècle* (Paris, 1933), pp. 611–14; DBF, 3, pp. 186–8.

52. Mme de Sévigné to Mme de Grignan, 8 November 1680: see M. Monmerque (ed.), *Lettres de Madame de Sévigné, de sa famille et de ses amis* (14 vols, Paris, 1862), VII, pp. 128–9. On Sir Robert Tabor or Talbot (1642?–81), see DNB, XIX, pp. 289–90.

53. Monmerque (ed.), *Lettres*, II, pp. 123, 142: Mme de Sévigné to Mme de Grignan, 20 March and 3 April 1671. He significantly received a 5,000 *livres* viaticum. There is no biographical notice on Guilloire.

54. Ibid., VII, pp. 128–9: Mme de Sévigné to Mme de Grignan, 8 November 1680. In the same letter the marquise says that she wishes Molière were still alive to depict D'Aquin's rage at being worsted.

55. Réveillé-Parise (ed.), *Lettres*, II, p. 205: Patin to Spon, 19 October 1655. Louis at this date was 17. For an account of his different maladies, see the diary kept by his *premiers médecins* from 1647–1711, published by J. A. Le Roi under the title, *Le Journal de la santé du roi Louis XIV* (Paris, 1862). The diary is analysed in Ch. Daremberg 'Louis XIV, ses médecins, son tempérament, son caractère et ses maladies'; see his *La Médecine: histoire et doctrine* (Paris, 1865), pp. 198–253.

56. Monmerque (ed.), *Lettres*, X, pp. 167, 175–7: M. de Coulanges to Mme de Sévigné, 23 June and 4 August 1694. On Cevoli, see *Dizionario biografico degli Italiani* (Rome), 24 (1980), pp. 338–40.

57. Monmerque (ed.), *Lettres*, VI, pp. 27–8: Mme de Sévigné to Mme de Grignan, 24 November 1679.

58. Ibid., VII, pp. 39–40. Cabrières was prior of Saint-Geniez-de-Malgoirez. His particular protector at court was Louvois.

59. Ibid., V, pp. 444–6: Mme de Sévigné to the Comte de Grignan, 27 May 1678. For the marquise's horror of phlebotomy, see M. Gérard, 'Les médecins dans la correspondance de Madame de Sévigné', in *Madame de Sévigné, Molière et les médecins de son temps*, p. 90. Biographical details about Fagon can be found in Lévi Valensi, *La Médecine*, pp. 624–32; also P. Eloy, *Fagon, archiâtre du grand roi* (Paris, 1918). He graduated from Paris in 1664.

60. Of course these qualities would have counted for nothing without the favour of Mme de Maintenon. Fagon seems to have first encountered her (by design?) at the spa of Barèges on the edge of the Pyrenees in 1673, where she had gone with the duc de Maine, the young bastard son of the king, in the hope of curing his rickets. Fagon's initial patron had been Valot who had obtained him a post at the Jardin des Plantes and encouraged his botanical interests.

61. On the construction of the memoirs, see Gonzague Truc, (ed.), *Mémoires de Saint-Simon* (7 vols, Paris, 1948–61), I, intro., p. ii.

62. For a statement of Saint-Simon's political views, see especially his 'Lettre anonyme au roi' (c. 1712), in Truc, *Mémoires*, III, pp. 1238–79. The duke's political theory is analysed in J. P. Brancourt, *Le Duc de Saint-Simon et la Monarchie* (Paris, 1971).

63. Unlike Vautier and Valot, D'Aquin did not die in office but was ousted; his fall is discussed below, in the final section.

64. Truc, *Mémoires*, II, pp. 1032–3: comments on the death of the king's valet, Mansard.

65. Ibid., IV, p. 94. On 31 August the king was given the specific remedy of the late *abbé* François Aignan (c. 1644–1709), a Swiss Capuchin and graduate of Padua installed at the Louvre in the late 1670s. The remedy was given on the insistence of the duchesse de Maine, wife of the royal bastard. 'Les médecins

consentirent à tout, parce qu'il n' y avoit plus d'espérance.'
Biographical details on Aignan in DBF, I, pp. 871–2.
    66. Truc, *Mémoires*, II, p. 393: remark 1704.
    67. Ibid., II, p. 653.
    68. Ibid., II, p. 392. For Mareschal's elevation, see II, p. 189;
Fagon, says Saint-Simon, had used his influence to get the surgeon
the post. On Mareschal, see Michaud, *Biographie universelle*, 26,
pp. 516–17.
    69. Truc, *Mémoires*, III, p. 788. This was Henri-François
d'Aguesseau (1688–1751), later Chancellor of France.
    70. Ibid., III, pp. 341–2, 348–50, 405–6.
    71. Ibid., IV, p. 934.
    72. Ibid., II, pp. 811–12. Boudin graduated at Paris in 1683. He
had a successful career at court, ending up as *premier médecin* to
Louis XV's queen, Marie Leczinska: biographical details in Hazon,
Notices des hommes, p. 160.
    73. Truc, *Mémoires*, IV, p. 879.
    74. Ibid., I, p. 108: from a lengthy character sketch of the *premier
médecin*.
    75. Ibid., III, pp. 1220, 1226.
    76. Ibid., II, p. 105; III, pp. 77–8; V; p. 963. The first is famous
as the popularizer of the use of ipecacuanha; the second was *premier
médecin* of Louis XIV's grandson, the duc de Bourgogne, from
1699; and the third eventually became *premier médecin* of Louis XV
in 1718. Dodart was a Paris graduate. Biographical details on
Dodart and Helvétius are to be found in DBF, II, p. 418; Michaud,
Biographie universelle, 19, pp. 84–6. There is no biographical notice
on Duchesne.
    77. Truc, *Mémoires*, VI. pp. 1026–9, 1080. Higgins was a
Montpellier graduate; see Astruc, p. 393.
    78. Truc, *Mémoires*, II, 105, pp. 747–8.
    79. Ibid., pp. 1203, 1210. Boudin's passionate advocacy of
poisoning reaped a financial reward. On royal command he
continued to receive his annual salary of 9,000 *livres* (see II, p.
1226). Be it said in his defence that he was predisposed towards the
diagnosis, having apparently learnt of a plot to poison the *petit
dauphin* and his wife before they were struck down (II, p. 1143).
    80. Ibid., V, p. 963: comment 1718. On Chirac, see N. F. J. Eloy,
Dictionnaire historique de la médecine ancienne et moderne (4 vols, Mons,
1778), I, p. 621; DBF, 8, pp. 1167–8. Chirac had been attached to
Orléans from 1706 when he had served as a *médecin de l'armée* in the
duke's campaign in Savoy. He was a Montpellier graduate in 1683.
    81. Truc, *Mémoires*, V, p. 964.
    82. Ibid., VI, pp. 366–9. On Joseph Glarus and his elixir ('un
excitant'), see DBF, 15, p. 582. Glarus's widow sold the secret to
Orléans in 1723 for an annual pension of 1,000 *livres*.
    83. Ibid., II, pp. 1202–3.
    84. Ibid., V, p. 963. Louis Poirier was a Paris graduate. He was
not the obvious choice for *premier médecin* on the death of Louis
XIV. According to Saint-Simon (V, p. 72), Chirac had the best

reputation but was excluded because he was the doctor of the regent, Orléans (*sic:* fears of foul play?). Boudin, too, had the better claim given the court offices he had held, but he was understandably disliked by the duke. Poirier was thus a compromise candidate, although he was well placed, being already the young dauphin's doctor when the latter inherited the throne. There is no biographical notice on Poirier.

85. Monmerque (ed.), *Lettres*, IX, p. 235: Mme de Sévigné to Mme de Grignan, 12 October 1689. 'Je ne sais lequel je plains le plus, ou de celui qui l'a soufferte [the phlebotomy], ou d'un premier chirurgien du Roi qui pique une artère.' On Charles François Tassy, *dit* Félix, see DBF, 13, pp. 900–1.

86. Truc, *Mémoires*, II, p. 189; III, p. 1103; VI, p. 117.

87. Ibid., III, pp. 23–4: comment 1709.

88. Ibid., III, pp. 1202–7.

89. Ibid., III, pp. 84–5.

90. Ibid., III, p. 1207: comment 1712.

91. Ibid., II, p. 189: comment 1703. When Saint-Simon was phlebotomized inexpertly in 1704, the king sent Mareschal to treat him.

92. Ibid., IV, p. 879. Before Mareschal rejected Fagon's complacent diagnosis of the king's final disease, Saint-Simon says that the two had never disagreed professionally.

93. Félix is only mentioned in passing on two occasions in Saint-Simon: Truc, *Mémoires*, II, pp. 75, 97.

94. Ibid., III, p. 305: remark 1709.

95. Ibid., III, p. 818.

96. E. J. F. Barbier, *Chronique de la Régence et du règne de Louis XV 1718–63* (8 vols, Paris, 1857–8). On Barbier, see DBF, 5, pp. 320–1.

97. Ibid., I, pp. 146–7. Helvetius, a Paris graduate, was the son of Adrien, mentioned above; biographical details in Michaud, *Biographie universelle*, 19, p. 86.

98. Ibid., IV, pp. 266–7. Information on Chicoyneau and Du Moulin can be found in DBF, 8, pp. 1138–9, and Eloy, *Dictionnaire historique*, II, pp. 108–9. Chicoyneau was a Montpellier graduate in 1693.

99. Ibid., III, p. 447. For La Peyronie and the mid-eighteenth-century quarrel between the physicians and the surgeons, see Toby Gelfand, *Professionalizing Modern Medicine, Paris Surgeons and Medical Science and Institutions in the 18th Century* (Westport, Conn., 1980), ch. 4. Barbier's comments on the novel influence of La Peyronie are supported from other sources: see the remarks on the *premier chirurgien* in Gelfand, *Professionalizing Modern Medicine*, pp. 60–2.

100. Barbier, *Chronique*, IV, pp. 345–6. I can find no biographical notices on either Jarre or Bourgeois. For Puzos, an important obstetrical innovator, see Michaud, *Biographie universelle*, 34, pp. 570–1.

101. Barbier, *Chronique*, IV, pp. 168–70.

102. Ibid., III, p. 123. On J. B. Silva (1682–1777), see Michaud, *Biographie universelle*, 9, pp. 348–9.

103. If Barbier's account is reliable, then clearly the royal surgeons were now in high esteem. Mareschal, it will be recalled, had received only a single payment of 30,000 *livres* for lithotomizing the Comte de Toulouse in 1712. Du Moulin's pension, given that he lived until 1755, was much more lucrative.

104. The ennoblement of court physicians and surgeons was virtually unknown before the end of the seventeenth century. According to Hazon, *Notices des hommes*, pp. 66–8, Michel Marescot was elevated to the nobility as early as 1595, but he seems to have received the honour for his services as a spy (L'Estoile understandably does not confirm this assertion). In the reign of Louis XV, the ennoblement of both the *premier médecin* and the *premier chirurgien* seems to have been *de rigueur*. Louis XIV, interestingly, ennobled Félix and Mareschal, but not Fagon. Such favouritism must have been of great importance in raising the status of surgeons generally and arguably gave them the confidence to challenge the physicians' monopoly of medical practice in the mid-eighteenth century. Saint-Simon says nothing about the elevation of Félix and Mareschal. Undoubtedly, such a bitter opponent of bourgeois *arrivisme* would have considered their ennoblement an affront to the dignity of his social order.

105. Barbier, *Chronique*, III, p. 123. Secretaryships to the king were honorary offices attached to the royal chancellery. For their prominent role in upward social mobility in eighteenth-century France, see D. Bien, 'La Réaction aristocratique avant 1789: l'exemple de l'armée', *Annales, économies, sociétés, civilisations*, 29, 1 (1974), pp. 44–8. Eloy, *Dictionnaire historique*, II, pp. 108–9, gives Du Moulin's fortune on his death as 1·5 million *livres*.

106. Truc, *Mémoires*, IV, p. 273.

107. Monmerque, (ed.), *Lettres*, I, pp. 476–81: Mme de Sévigné to M. de Pomponne, 21–26 December 1664. Fouquet's trial lasted until 1664. Pecquet emerged from his ordeal none the worse; he was Mme de Sévigné's physician in the early 1670s. On Pecquet, the anatomist, see *Dictionary of Scientific Biography* (New York, 1974), X, pp. 476–8; he was a Montpellier graduate.

108. Truc, *Mémoires*, I, p. 107; IV, p. 1045. Saint-Simon's account is supported by that of the *abbé* Le Gendre, canon of Notre-Dame and secretary to the archbishop of Paris, Harlay; see Le Gendre, *Mémoires* ed. M. Roux (Paris, 1865), pp. 212–13.

109. For example, ibid., II, p. 508.

110. Ibid., II, pp. 116–7. The real name of the lithotomist was Jacques Baulot (1657–1719): see DBF, 5, pp. 931–2.

6

Court physicians and State Regulation in Eighteenth-century Prussia:
The emergence of medical science and the demystification of the body

Johanna Geyer-Kordesch

As the monarchs in Brandenburg-Prussia succeeded one another from the *Große Churfüst* Friedrich Wilhelm (1620–88) to Friedrich III (1657–1713), who became the first 'König in Preußen' (1710, as Friedrich I), to Friedrich Wilhelm I (1688–1740), so the style of their governing changed. The *Große Churfürst* is said to have laid the foundation for the state of Brandenburg-Prussia; Friedrich I made it a monarchy full of the pomp and circumstance of absolutist courts; and Friedrich Wilhelm I achieved its bureaucratic, financial, and military consolidation. Friedrich Wilhelm, the *Soldatenkönig*, made Friedrich the Great's Prussia possible, the Prussia of legend, of whose power one had to be mindful in conflict-laden early-modern Europe.

The nature of absolutist monarchy points to centralized power, but this does not mean that the methods of imposing political will were straightforward. Of course, no elective forces were brought to bear. However, lobbying, the right word at the right moment, the rivalry between court factions, even private relations, for example those of queen to king, or the influence of servants and of friendships, made for intricate networks of gaining power – or of losing it.[1] Added to these possibilities of influence, official institutions exercised the will of the State. This was implemented through royal decrees, ministerial authority, and administrative bureaucracies.

The most far-reaching reorganization of medical power in Brandenburg-Prussia was a result of the organizational and financial reforms under Friedrich Wilhelm I,[2] and on these I shall concentrate. Friedrich Wilhelm ascended the throne in 1713 and died in 1740. The most powerful medical men at his court were his *erste Leibmedici*, Andreas von Gundelsheim (1668–1715) and Georg Ernst Stahl (1659–1734). Andreas von Gundelsheim held the post for twelve years (1703–15) and Stahl for nineteen (1715–34). These first among the court physicians never retired, as no one not deposed ever retired, but died in office. In contrast to titular court physicians, the first court physicians could exercise direct administrative power.[3]

Court physicians were part of the intrigues of power by virtue of their access to the person of the king, the royal family, and patients at court. They were also professionally a part of the medical organization of Prussia. But power at an absolutist court is never a simple matter. I will try and assess three aspects of its implementation in regard to medicine. Only the first is relatively easy to describe because it is mainly institutional and structural and has, of course, been written about often.[4] Institutional change in medicine was implemented through court edicts, the founding of medical boards, and official medical training in the form of teaching lectures offered in Berlin. This official road to change regulated access to the medical profession. It defined who could be said to be a physician. This is the classic process of professionalization,[5] usually seen as the ascendancy of the learned doctor over 'quacks' and healers, these now increasingly lacking the 'correct' credentials, although, as far as general practice was concerned, empiric healers still predominated over learned doctors.

Eighteenth-century medical professionalization depended on two additional factors. While the State issued rules for the 'correct' credentials of its medical men, these were not necessarily the qualities for which patients consulted doctors.[6] Therefore one of the important political differences determining the relative power of healers and learned doctors was the access of the latter group to the monarch and the court. Only learned doctors or court physicians were able to make use of prestigious institutions, such as the Academy of Sciences, or to influence the king and his ministers. Implementing medical change was to the advantage of the learned physician. He alone was part of the institutional network as it was represented by state finances and absolutist politics. Although this explanation holds true for the general development of institutional change, it should not be thought to be smooth or inevitable. Court physicians were not one of a kind, and the Prussian example contains inner vicissitudes. Two of the most powerful court physicians, Gundelsheim and Stahl, were not in favour of the 'modern' medicine allied to the 'new' science.[7] They were overpowered, so to speak, by a general trend implemented through institutional interests. This does not mean, however, that they did not hold their own in other respects. Despite the push toward institutionalized professionalization, Gundelsheim, as a representative of a traditional 'first physician to the king', and Stahl, as a representative of a theory opposed to the mechanical philosophy anchored in 'modern' medicine, were closest to what was actually practised as medicine. This essential tension is one of the main characteristics of medicine at its centres of power in the eighteenth century, as I hope to make clear.

Three basic developments intersect in Berlin: the regulatory agency of the court and the *collegium medicum*, the establishment of new leading interests in medicine (anatomy and surgery), as they become institutionalized and officially taught, and a medical opposition preferring what patients also preferred at the time – a view of the body not identical with Enlightenment science. The texture of court life enhanced all these tensions since factions vied with one another and Stahl, at least, could, on the basis of what his patients wanted, ignore the rise of institutionalized medicine.

The institutional changes which were effected in medicine in Prussia in the course of the eighteenth century must be seen in conjunction with the rise of medical science. The 'scientific revolution' of the seventeenth century in the neighbouring countries of England and the Dutch Republic began to influence medicine decisively in the last quarter of the seventeenth century. The 'discovery' of the circulation of the blood, the reliance on new scientific instruments such as the microscope, and the methodological discussions in science, in particular Cartesian ideas, as well as the interests which Leibniz pursued, were in evidence both in Holland and in Brandenburg-Prussia at the universities and in relevant publications.[8] The new science was obviously a leading theme in intellectual discourse; but it was not, outside of some universities and the correspondence of the scientifically aware, proscriptive for medical practice, neither as to legal expectations, nor, as yet, as part of the image of the medical profession. The socio-cultural change which invested the doctor with the scientist's image and which succeeded in attaching him to institutions such as hospitals had not yet been thoroughly effected. This was to be one result of the State's pressure for the regulation of the profession. Governmental interest in Prussia allied itself with scientific medical interests during the eighteenth century against a wider field of medical practice. Medical practice itself, however, was still oriented toward a more diffuse therapeutics in which medical ideas were not separate from cultural notions in respect of religion, the body, and nature.

Specified competence lends itself better to regulation. The edicts of the Crown regarding medical practice, issued from 1685 to 1725, achieved just such a stratification and specification when it separated medical doctors from other healers and emphasized their university training. The introduction of state approbation through examinations then linked university medical training to the power of the State. The image of science as it was developed with regard to empirical methods and the scientific value of experiments in the seventeenth century filled the vacuum of what the criteria for medical men as approved by the State were to be. Science guaranteed that definite criteria could be established for medical training, and created an optics for the physician when he examined the body, disease, and the general health of the public.

The preference of seventeenth- and eighteenth-century physicians for *observationes clinicae*,[9] a well-established field of medical enquiry, was not as incisive as the claim of the anatomist and the experimental physiologist to pinpoint specific cause-and-effect relationships. Healing success and therapeutic effectivity constitute a notoriously difficult area for measuring the practical capability of medical advance. Experimental findings operate more directly in the legitimating process. Theoretical approaches to medicine that voiced an interest in influences beyond the doctor's control, such as Thomas Sydenham's and Stahl's advocacy of the healing power of nature,[10] in effect a plea for less medication and a more reticent application of medical treatment, neither appealed to the Enlightenment's cry for immediate usefulness and for human-made scientific intervention, nor necessarily bolstered the image of the doctor. Stahl's medical theory, for example, was immensely critical of the claim that the new methods and paradigms of scientific medicine could solve any of the real problems of medicine, namely those concerned with therapeutics.[11] Anatomy and empirical physiology, iatrochemistry and other monocausal solutions to the problems of illness and disease, on the other hand, seemed to provide specific and rational insights into the mysterious body's functions.[12] Above all, however, these latter provided a show-case for the learned physician's qualifications. The influence of something so uncontrollable as 'nature' or the 'soul' was avoided and this both simplified medicine and made it accessible to the new science. The intentions of science met those intentions of bureaucratic reform within the State which were based on rationalization and hierarchical order. Laurentius Heister, the famous surgeon, mechanist and opponent of Stahl, preferred the doctor to assert himself as *der Herr der Natur*,[13] the master of nature, and thus exemplified the modern scientific trend. Physicians who admitted doubt and were cognizant about how difficult it was to learn to heal, were caught in a double-bind of legitimization. They did not seem entirely progressive and yet their field of vision was no less aware of the basic dilemma of medical advance, the cure of a person's illness. The eclipse of medical doubts as effected by medical science, particularly as it left the unsolved problem of illness in its dark shadow, produced a sunshine of its own: the belief in medical science as the sole representative of medical capability.

It is, indeed, significant that Stahl's theory of medicine was misunderstood and opposed to the extent that it was pushed into the corner of religious sectarianism and 'non-science'. His was a theory which did not subordinate medicine to chemistry, physics, or mathematics.[14] Stahl was the only eighteenth-century scholar in Germany who attempted to formulate a theory of medicine entirely from the premises of *medical* observation.[15] His methodological approach, that of medical experience, precluded the excision of the soul. His main interest concerned *pathological* theory[16] and it was entirely logical there to include the psyche. That the medical theory of his time wished to exclude the soul was not his doing: to do so was a necessary demand of the methods of the new science, whose primary concern was to predicate conclusions on the laws of matter and the laws of mechanical motion. To say that one could not understand Stahl, as his medical contemporaries maintained,[17] was to say that one did not wish to understand a medical advance outside of somatic–mechanical–causal principles. Where medicine and science were conflated on these principles, a secular view of nature dear to the Enlightenment and to the enlightened rule of the State ('aufgeklärter Absolutismus') gained ascendancy.

The period from the late-seventeenth to the end of the eighteenth century in Prussia can be seen as a time in which the *content* of medicine was altered. My hypothesis is the following: that such bodies as the state-supported *collegium medico-chirurgicum* helped transfer the view of the body developed by the 'new science' into medical practice. The *collegium medicum* in Berlin was intimately connected with the examinations and teaching at the *theatrum anatomicum*. The idea of 'progress' in science, an idea that the Enlightenment supported, is thus structurally linked with the court and the State. It set the trend for the nineteenth-century emphasis on hospitals, clinical teaching, and scientific research in medicine.

Hence, my second point concerns the displacement of a mentality or way of thinking about the body, the loss of the consensus of a 'trade-off' between the patient's view and the knowledge of the doctor and its replacement by the need to appeal to science. The medical *science* of the eighteenth century was post-Cartesian and mechanistic and rested upon two assumptions: first, the dualism between body and soul, and second, rationalistic and empirical proof as the methodological basis of medical knowledge. Scientific medicine was embraced mainly by university-trained physicians. It thereby also exemplified a process of increasing isolation: that process which we call 'specialization' and which establishes authority. However, professionalized specialization in medicine was, in this period, still at odds with other ideas concerning the nature of the body.

I

The first milestone along the road to institutionalizing professional medical power in Brandenburg-Prussia with regard to the healing arts was the Edict of 1685, which regulated medical practice for the *churfürstliches Land*.[18] It justified its regulation of medical qualification by an attack on malpractice by non-physicians. As an eighteenth-century source records, the edict was issued because

> various gross excesses had occurred, perpetrated partly by
> barber-surgeons and surgeons. In particular, complaints
> were made that the *Raths-Apotheker* on the Friedrichswerder,

Lienemann, and the *Amtsbarbier* Giese had cheated several people of health and life through untimely purgation and vomiting cures, and a French surgeon, Gerway, had helped a nobleman of the aristocracy to an early grave through a mercury cure ('Salivation').[19]

The same risk to the people's health through various representatives of the healing arts was mentioned in the introductory paragraphs of the Edict of 1685 and used directly to explain its implementation.[20] Such considerations had been part of earlier petitions, in particular a formal letter from the *Leibmedici* (court physicians) in Berlin of August 1661, in which the *Churfürst* was asked to found a *collegium medicum*.[21] The petition of 1661, however, never reached a legally binding form.[22] In 1685 the enlarged and codified Edict was issued by the Crown. Its intention was to regulate medical practice especially in regard to qualifications, specialized areas of competence, the efficacy of treatment and remedies, and expected costs for the patients.

This concern for the people's health also allowed the monarchy, in the same edict, to form a regulatory body that was different in kind from the traditional and loosely organized *collegia medica* found in some cities.[23] The *collegium medicum* it created was bound to the authority of the court; it was a centralized body with power over provincial medical boards, and it was invested with enforcing powers.[24] In particular, it could demand: first, that all physicians, that is, licentiates and *doctores medicinae*, had to register their qualifications with this body; and second, that the *collegium* would extend its approbation to them, otherwise they were not to practise (this was at this time more governmental wish than reality). Similar systems of control were set out for the inspection of apothecary shops, for the practice of 'barbers, barber-surgeons, midwives, oculists and lithotomists ('Bruch- und Steinschneider')'.[25] In other words, an official system of control was ordained, centred in Berlin.

If one looks at the composition of the *collegium medicum* in Berlin of 1685, its members are all *Leib- und Hofmedici*.[26] This firmly establishes the context of a far-reaching development; the control of medical matters through physicians bound to the court. They were to have a firm hand in the inspection of all other medical personnel. In all subsequent edicts – which never disestablish the regulations of 1685 – the *collegium medicum* exercises institutional power and is primarily composed of court physicians. Until 1715, when Stahl became its *praeses*, and was personally made responsible to the king and his advisers for all medical matters in Brandenburg-Prussia,[27] in effect another increase in the power available to the first court physician and to learned doctors, the *collegium* was headed by jurists who were part of the administration.[28] Other learned doctors in Berlin, who were not court physicians did not usually belong to the *collegium medicum*, as can be verified, for example, by a 1695 list of those practising in the city.[29]

The frequent reissuing of the medical edicts shows the widening supervisory and investigative powers of the *collegium medicum*.[30] It seems, on the one hand, despite several petitions, to have been unsuccessful in regard to the control of medical healers by physicians but, on the other hand, it broadened its scope as it persuaded the Crown to issue successive royal decrees on enforcing its dictates, particularly through the courts of law. After the accession to the throne of Friedrich Wilhelm in 1713, changes were rapid, all involving an increase in administrative control. The decree of 1713 made plain once more that the *collegium medicum* wanted: (1) examinations for those medical men (*medici bullati*) who had not publicly disputed but obtained their degrees from the *Comes Palatinus* (licentiate or doctorate); (2) no remedies issued by apothecaries without the approval of a doctor; (3) no 'internal cures' by surgeons or 'Wundärzte'; and (4) the elimination of medical practice by 'quacks' ('abgedankte Soldaten, Weise-Mütter, Laboranten'), who could be punished by law when in violation.[31] The decree of 1716 saw the sharpening of the juridical basis for bringing contraventions of the edict before the courts.[32] In 1717 the *collegium* reminded the king that doctors were sending in their *disputationes* but were neither submitting to examinations nor sending in all their papers.[33] The decree of 1718 then ordered all graduates to submit to examinations by either the *collegium* in Berlin or the provincial *collegia*.[34] An *Adjunctus collegii medici* from Berlin was to be present at the provincial examinations. In effect, this meant the institutionalization of the power of the *collegium*, that is, of the court physicians in Berlin, to approve all learned doctors. After May 1718, all examined doctors and surgeons had to swear to uphold the regulations contained in the official edicts (primarily the regulations contained in the Edict of 1685 and, later, the more comprehensive Edict of 1725).[35] In 1723, the *collegium medicum* separated the responsibility for 'internal cures' from general practice, especially that of the surgeons, and delegated the responsibility for these specifically and exclusively to physicians who had both received a degree (doctorate) and who had completed an examination (approbation).[36]

The actual enforcement of the medical edicts outside Berlin took time. The extent to which an informal toleration of medically competent healers (to judge from the patient's choice of practitioners) still existed is exemplified by the case of the first woman doctor in Prussia, Dorothea Christiane Erxleben-Leporin (1715–62).[37] Her case illustrates that, by the middle of the eighteenth century, administrative control of the medical profession outside Berlin was strong enough to be used successfully by approbated physicians against those they wished to exclude from practice. Dorothea Erxleben-Leporin, who had learned medicine from her father, a progressive doctor who was convinced of the right of women to education, practised for a number of years in the town of Quedlinburg without formal qualification. In 1753, her medical colleagues denounced her for her lack of proper credentials.[38] This drove her to complete a doctorate in medicine at the University of Halle, which she officially received in 1754. In effect, her case shows the tightening of control. The biography of the medical doctor Johann Storch (1681–1751) exemplifies similar tendencies.[39] Storch's father did quite well as a knowledgeable empiric, but he insisted that his son, whose medical reputation established itself toward mid-century, should receive university training and a medical degree.

By the middle of the eighteenth century, then, it is apparent that the *collegium medicum*, whose control via a succession of edicts and royal decrees had expanded into an effective network of regulation, had successfully established a hierarchy of power in the medical world, and, perhaps most effectively, wrought an alliance between bureaucratic control vested in the State (the Crown) and those physicians who by virtue of their university education had access to the court. A *system* of control over medical qualification and admission to practice had emerged between 1685 and 1750 which united state power with the medical reform desired by learned physicians. This is perhaps not surprising in view of the Prussian monarchy's tendencies towards centralization. The enforcement of medical professionalization went hand in hand with the increasing intervention of government into the lives of the governed. However, there is another aspect integral to this change in the medical profession which interests us here. With the increasing state demand for formally verifiable medical competence – and thereby the exclusion of practitioners vying for patients on a 'free-market' basis – the content of medical knowledge itself was altered.

II

The medical edicts implemented the monarchy's legal regulation of medicine. However, legislation in the form of decrees does not create the medical qualities it stipulates. Other developments in Berlin dovetailed with legal changes. In 1700 the Academy of Sciences was founded by G. W. von Leibniz and D. E. Jablonsky under the patronage of the *Churfürstin* Sophie Charlotte and the *Churfürst* Friedrich III (Friedrich I).[40] Leibniz was the driving force behind the scientific ideals to be adopted by the society. He did not want 'mere inventions' to be discussed.[41] An internationalist, Leibniz was well aware of the developments in the 'new science' and the mechanical philosophy, but also critical of them and of the societies in Paris and London.[42] For the Berlin Academy, he specifically envisioned scientific contributions which were to be applied to useful projects for economic betterment.[43] His was a true quest for modernization in the now familiar mode of the blessings that attach to scientific methods and discoveries.

At first medicine was not included among the sciences that were to be propagated under the patronage of the Society.[44] Jablonsky was aware of the founding of the *collegium medicum*, but very optimistically, in view of later events, he wrote that the Society wanted to avoid meddling with a board, the *collegium medicum* organized by the State, adding that the common ground of science would soon 'bring the best men to join us'.[45] The 'best men' were a great problem. Eleven years passed before, on 29 January 1711, the first meeting of the *physikalisch-medizinische Section* took place.[46] In the minutes of this meeting the installation of a *theatrum anatomicum* in the *Observatorium* is mentioned.[47] The 'best men', however, were not happy with one another. In 1711 Friedrich Hoffman (1660–1742), Stahl's colleague as professor of medicine at the University of Halle, was active in Berlin, but, in the Society, Theodor Dietrich Krug von Nidda, one of the court physicians who had been involved with the Society since its inception, but who seemed to lack scientific verve – he never published anything of note – disliked Hoffmann's competence and energy.[48] Krug von Nidda's role in the Society's medical section seems to have been relatively negligible, but he nevertheless applied brakes to various discussions on new members and insisted that Society funds be earmarked for projects not at all akin to Leibniz's ideas of scientific progress.[49]

A much more powerful enemy to the Society was Andreas von Gundelsheim, the first court physician. Gundelsheim's interests in medicine were not those of the Society.[50] He was an expert in the cure of fevers and in botanical remedies.[51] He had accompanied Joseph Pitton de Tournefort (1656–1708) on botanical and scientific excursions to Greece, Asia Minor, and Africa to record and collect native plants, herbs, and minerals. He was recruited to the Prussian court as 'Hof- und Leibmedicus' in 1703 by Frederick I and raised at the same time into the ranks of the minor aristocracy. It is not clear why he did not like the Society, but perhaps his botanical expertise, his knowledge gathered on practical expeditions, and a need to defend his position as first physician to the king combined to enable him to scorn the Society. In Friedrich Hoffman he had his first powerful rival, a medical man whose advocacy of Cartesian philosophy and of the 'modern' principles of mechanical medicine were well known and who had published on a number of medical subjects. A scandal involving the rivalry between Hoffmann and Gundelsheim ended with the return of Hoffman to Halle in 1712.[52] These tensions indicate that outside of the general tightening of control over medical qualifications through the edicts, an intense fight was emerging over medical science. The Society, weak as it was in the beginning, was marshalling a campaign, whose beginning can be dated to Hoffmann's influence on Jablonsky, over the *theatrum anatomicum* and other innovations that, he considered, the Society *should* be contributing to medical advance.

On 6 February 1711, Jablonsky wrote to Leibniz about Friedrich Hoffmann. Jablonsky set much hope in Hoffman, stating:

...the members (of the Academy) show a great desire to contribute something meaningful; in particular Hof-Rath Hoffmann, in whom we set a great deal of hope: he as well as others do not think the work of the society to be merely the collection of various treatises ... but more like that of the Royal Society ... And the above named Herr Hoffmann suggested in the first meeting that a Theatrum anatomicum might be installed in the Observatorium along with the necessary instruments, and that he would himself, with the help of some other members undertake dissections (*Anatomien*) of the whole and of special parts (*Glieder*), through which the planned Amphitheatrum Naturae et Artis of the Society would be enriched, hopefully, also one or another useful Inventum come to light etc.[53]

The *theatrum anatomicum* was not a product of the Academy, it seems, although after 1717 the Academy was responsible for its upkeep.[54] The sources are at variance about its origins. Gundelsheim did not like the Academy and did not want the king's favour transferred to the Academy, at least in the opinion of A. von Harnack, its later official historian.[55] Another source describes the founding of the *theatrum anatomicum* in the royal *Marstall* by the monarch in 1713.[56] Christian Maximilian Spener, the son of the Pietist Philipp Jacob Spener, equipped it with the necessary instruments and held, as the first Professor of Anatomy, the first dissection of 'a male subject' in 1713 and another in 1714.[57] C. M. Spener was another of the 'modern' physicians who had travelled and represented mechanist views: he had been to Strasbourg and then studied at the Dutch academies, where he presumedly became adept at anatomy. He became court physician in 1701 and was a member of all the important societies (Leopoldina; Prussian Academy of Sciences) and also of the *collegium medicum* in Berlin. It is indeed ironic that this 'modern' physician could do little for his father in 1705 when the latter was seriously ill and that the greatest enemy of mechanism and of the primacy of anatomical knowledge, Stahl, was called to the bedside of P. J. Spener to save his life.[58]

With the establishment of the *theatrum anatomicum* in Berlin, at which regular dissections proceeded after 1719, the power of the Crown together with its regulatory agency, the *collegium medicum*, effected a change whose consequences became tangible by mid-century. Although the *collegium medicum*, the *theatrum anatomicum*, and the Academy of Sciences were initially separate bodies with different aims, they had one important thing in common: their power was actively supported by the Prussian Crown. What they wished to achieve could be managed by virtue of their relation to the king. As the *theatrum anatomicum* gained favour, it provided the basis for exactly that extension of medical training which corresponded with the reform ideas of the 'modern' physicians – namely the training of doctors along specific lines of medical knowledge.[59]

The Academy's position in medical matters was the least secure. At first Friedrich Wilhelm I disapproved of what he thought was its drone-like existence, and Gundelsheim and Stahl disliked the old-guard court physicians who held sway there. However, after 1717, when the king ratified the charter of the Academy on condition of its financing the *theatrum anatomicum* and the partial salaries of physicians who were added to a teaching staff, the Academy's medical section was incorporated into the general professionalization of medicine in Berlin. By 1724, when the *collegium* became the *collegium medico-chirurgicum*, all the essentials for medical advance had been integrated: control of medical qualification through examinations and approbation, courses to instruct those deficient in medical knowledge, and a selection of medical men, all connected to the court as court physicians, who were installed to teach therapeutics, anatomy and physick, botany, chemistry, surgery, physiology and pathology, and mathematics.[60] The 'modern' medical supervision and teaching in Berlin was a product of the ideas of the men who planned, persuaded the king, and who rose with the importance of their profession; the learned court physicians. In 1727, the founding date of the Berlin Charité, Johann Theodor Eller, after 1734 Stahl's successor as first court physician, added clinical teaching to the rest.[61]

Stahl's position in regard to the establishment of the *collegium medicum* and the teaching at the *theatrum anatomicum* had been dutifully correct. He not only fulfilled his obligations, but was also actively interested in the qualitative and regulatory reform of medicine in Prussia.[62] No one not interested in reform would have been invested, as Stahl alone had been, as *praeses* of the *collegium*, without having a direct administrative superior in medical matters, as was the case before and after his term of office. This did not preclude, however, his disagreement with the Society over how it wished to allocate funds, the type of medical teaching it supported, where this meant the primacy of anatomical knowledge, or with the predominant trend towards a somatically oriented medical science. Stahl stood his ground, but he was a man caught in other forces.

III

The medical practice of the first court physician never included surgery and had little to do with anatomy. While the institution-alization of professional medicine in the 'modern' teaching sense established itself in Berlin, different perceptions of the body and a different interaction between patient and doctor determined 'medicine'. Thus, the linearity of 'progress' within institutionalized change was a result of the alignment of the State with the 'modern' ideas of learned physicians influenced by the 'new' science. The healing arts, on the other hand, notwithstanding the practice of learned medicine, were at the same time more flexible in their boundaries and their subject.

The 'modern' emphasis on anatomy and surgery was evalu-ated as the vanguard of more exact knowledge in the scientific 'discovery' of the body. It was not devoid of a dogmatic element. The shift of emphasis to anatomy and surgery dictated a man-ner of perceiving which was closely tied to mechanism because both emphasized structural components. What a muscle or the heart looks like, of what tissues it is composed, how other parts of bodily 'matter' influence physiological change, and an oper-ative knowledge of how these parts relate are essentials in anat-omy and surgery and in a somatically oriented physiology. The 'new' mechanical philosophy supported this type of 'exact' knowledge. All adherents to the post-Cartesian division of soul and matter, from Hermann Boerhaave through Friedrich Hoffmann to Albrecht von Haller and Gerhard von Swieten, quickly mastered the first principle of 'seeing' physiology in terms of the matrix of somatic structural components, be they fibres, nerves, muscles, the heart, or the circulation of the blood. A succinct statement of this view is given in Laurentius Heister's 'Abhandlung von der Vortrefflichkeit der mechani-schen Arzneylehre', printed in his *Practisches Medizinisches Handbuch* (Leipzig, 2nd edn 1763; 1st edn 1744):

> I understand mechanical medicine to be that science of heal-ing (*Arzneywissenschaft*) which investigates and explains the wise Creator's artful preparation and construction of the human body *as we learn it from anatomy* [my emphasis] and can then explain its effects as they flow from the solid and liquid parts, as well as from the physical, mechanical and chemical discoveries and observations according to mechanical prin-

ciples. The human body is nothing but a very artful machine or construction [Gebäude = building] which again is composed of small machines [mechanical elements]. This is proven by anatomy as well as by the famous Barhave [*sic* = Boerhaave] in his *Institutiones Medicae*, and by many other medical and mechanical writers, namely, Borellus, Bellinus, Steno, Lowerus, Pitkarn, Friedrich Hoffmann, Berger, Guilelminus, Lancisius, Keil, Mead, Michelottus, Mezinus, Schreiber, Hamberger [names spelled as in original] etc., who have thrown off the yoke of worldly recognition and have not admitted anything as truth other than that which the senses through verifiable experience and observations have proven and understood, that is, have derived and demonstrated from the construction of our bodies, in its healthy as well as its ailing condition, through the process of reasoning (*Vernunftschlüsse*).[63]

In this very classical statement of the creed of 'mechanical medicine', all the elements of 'modern' medicine are named: the primacy of anatomical knowledge which goes hand in hand with experimental physiology, the reliance on the scientific discoveries in physics and chemistry which are to aid medicine, the step-by-step approach of rational induction which is to guide the 'new' science of the body. The programme taught through the lectures at the *theatrum anatomicum* is here encapsulated. This is the voice of the new science. However, while mechanical philosophy was useful to science, it had few answers for internal illnesses and did not match the reality of the perception of illness or of the body by patients or in concurrent systems of medical thought. 'Reason' and 'method' are not really at issue in the perception of a body which is ill.

As already indicated in the introduction, it is a mistake to assume that 'science' replaced 'superstition'. The conflation of the 'new' science and medicine was asserting itself against medical theories and medical practice which had advanced and developed in a different context and with different goals. The idea that the 'Dark Ages' were replaced by science is one way of leaving out these other medical concerns. One method of recording this different medical geography is to look at medical ideas and medical practice as advocated by medical men just as important as those engaged with the 'new' science.

A way into this other context of medical life is signposted by the theory of Stahl, by the connection his followers make through Stahl's theory with a different interpretation of nature, and by tracing the lay practitioner's and patient's interest in medicine. The actual healing practices to which patients turned – at court as well as elsewhere – speak for a major concern with the diagnosis and context of illness.[64]

This context, in which medical knowledge and healing enter a no less 'advanced' relation to medical epistemology than its 'scientific' counterpart, shows its interpretative pattern in the *observationes clinicae*. This genre of medical literature was more prevalent, and more of a guide to medical thinking, than any anatomical lessons, at least for the eighteenth century. Lay practitioners and doctors, adherents of the Stahlian school in particular, turned to the extensive literature of the *observationes clinicae* to guide them to diagnosis and to interpret and manage disease. The *observationes clinicae* (observations at the bedside) provided information on the conceptualization of the body that determined medical practice. This appeal of the *observationes* accentuates, on the one hand, the epistemological quality of empirical knowledge, as doctors delved more intensely into the description and intellectual management of what they recorded and 'saw'; and, on the other hand, it means that the historian has to recognize the discursive quality of a transfer in medical knowledge which chose language and 'signs', not inductive science, as its medium. A detailed description of ailments, medical theory, therapeutics, and remedies, all tied to concrete cases, was, for example, the subject of the correspondence between Stahl, his student, the physician Christian Friedrich Richter, and Karl Hildebrand, Baron Canstein, an influential nobleman in Berlin.[65] In this sense 'medicine' was the object of a discussion of symptoms, of the daily progress of an illness and of the remedies applied and their effects. The case itself was thus a 'story', an individual experience, 'told' in order to be related to the experience of the physician, whose expertise could best interpret the pattern of 'disease'. Thus, medicine was in every sense still a very empirical discipline, in which the doctor, as a knowledgeable healer to whom the patient appealed, could assess, direct and medicatively manage the empirical progression of semiotic indications. To be a trained doctor was to recognize the pattern. Fevers made this clear: they were, in the Stahlian view, neither an illness, nor a symptom, but a 'movement' of nature effected in the body (with specific periodicity) and in aid of the body's self-curing strategies.[66] If the doctor was knowledgeable enough, he could temper, support, and alter nature's 'movement'.

Barbara Duden in her book. *Geschichte unter der Haut*,[67] has examined the cases that Johann Storch, a follower of Stahl, who practised for most of his life in the town of Eisenach, recorded in his published works. The cases are legion (eight volumes alone on *Weiberkranckheiten*) and Duden sought to trace the conceptualization or 'picture' of the body as it was expressed in the descriptions of 'ailments' that Storch recorded. The cases of Storch are so fresh in the telling that the language and thinking of Eisenach are not translated into medical *termini*, but retain the flavour of their original sources. Duden's interesting conclusions bear comparison with the general orientation of Stahl's medical theory, thereby letting the historian weave together a broader texture of the concerns of 'internal' medicine. In essence, this represents an opposition to mechanism and anatomy because it presupposes a different relation between knowledge and healing.

Duden finds that in patients' descriptions the body is not only inscrutable ('undurchsichtig' = not transparent),[68] 'ein Ort verborgenen Geschehens' (a place of concealed actions),[69] but also 'ein Raum überraschender Wandlungsmöglichkeiten' (a space full of surprising possibilities of change).[70] 'The internal (das Innere) is only palpable (greifbar) as a place where invisible 'flowing' ('unsichtbares Fließen') can be experienced.'[71] This description of the body, which Duden supplies as a result of her investigation on Storch's cases, could not be more apt in the language she finds for it.

Although Duden did not extend her analysis to the medical ideas and background of the eighteenth century, her findings can be joined to the views and medical reform envisioned by the Stahl school. Along with the emphasis on observational medicine as it primarily relates to illness diagnosis, many of the doctors who turned to Stahl's medical theory were also aware of a different interpretation of nature.[72] Their concern was to relate illness and health not to the 'new' science's methodology, but to an encompassing vision in which cosmos and person were related. Illness was one aspect of the changeability within nature. It was not a mechanical derangement of substances, defined as a disease, but a state of illness involving the body and soul with specific semiotic signs.[73] Illness involved the soul and the state of the soul and reflected on the state of nature. Advance in medicine was directed at case-studies, the comprehension of illness as it became visible in the 'language' (semiotics) of the body.[74] This trend in medical 'discovery' was born of a different view of nature, one alien to the new scientific thinking. The 'new' science equated spiritual concerns with beliefs outside the pale of 'natural laws'.[75] None the less, it is to this idea of nature that we must turn, if 'change' and 'illness' as parts of nature are to become comprehensible. As Duden has documented, it was the non-scientific form of thinking which pervaded the cultural normality of the 'language' between patient and doctor.

From the works of Johann Samuel Carl, a student of Stahl's and an important member of anti-orthodox religious circles,[76] we learn about the mentality which affirmed nature as a cosmographic unity, itself composed of body and soul. Only from this perspective does it make sense to speak about the relation of inward being and outward being, about change and 'flowing' (*Fließen*), about the visible and the invisible, and about 'circulation'. This dialectic of natural being presents the basis for medical advances curious about 'change' as it relates to an encompassing expression of life. It seeks to define particulars as a form of the whole. These are by no means mysterious since they can express themselves in patterns which are open to diagnosis. Carl writes:

> Wir wissen ja / daß zum theuersten in der Natur principia spiritualia moventia seynr / und daß alle Cörperliche Bewegungen zu einem endlichen geistlichen Zweck hinzielen / daß alles Creatürliche ein Ausdruck nach seinem elementischen Wesen des reinen unsichtbaren geistlichen und göttlichen Wesens und Haushaltung seye; aus welchen Bildern Iconismis wir zum Erkänntniß des Wesens / Archetypi, des Unsichbaren / geleitet werden; daß die gantze äussere Creatur in den Menschen einfliesse / alle actus vitales in die animales und diese in die Rationales, und diese in die Spirituales; damit nur der Mensch seine Letztere Wiederbringung durch solche richtige Circulation von dem Sichtbaren zu den Unsichtbaren wieder finde. Dieses glauben wir nicht allein nach denen äusserlichen buchstäblichen Zeugnissen; sondern wissens / sehens / betastens durch greifliche fundamenta documenta et experimenta; ja könnens

andern durch gantz analytische und mathematische Demonstrationes beweisen. Wie solte denn ein so grober Knoten des Atheismi und Epicureismi sich verstecken / daß wir doch im Herzen gedenken und sprechen könten: Es sey kein Gott.[77]

We know that the *principia spiritualia moventia* are most precious in nature and that all bodily movements are directed towards a final spiritual goal; that everything which is made, is, in its constitution as formed from the elements, an expression of the pure, invisible, spiritual and godly being and economy; that from these expressions (images), *Iconismis*, we are led to the knowledge of that being, the archetypes, of the invisible; that the whole of outer nature flows into man, all vital movements into animal movements (*animales*), and these into the rational and these into the spiritual; so that man is able to return through this true mode of circulation from the Seen (visible) to the Unseen (invisible) in order to be restored in the fullness of time.[78] This we believe not solely because it is in accord with the witness of outer, literal (*buchstäblich*) testimony, but because we know, see, touch, through apprehensible *fundamenta, documenta et experimenta*; yes, we can demonstrate it to others through wholly analytical and mathematical evidence. It is not possible for such a roughly made knot of atheism and epicureanism to disguise itself well enough that we would not be able to recognize it in our hearts and to voice its fundamental assumption: that there is no God.

The language that Carl uses is difficult to translate because he employs an imagery that underscores his world view, an understanding of cosmography that is alien to new scientific thinking. He unites paradoxes instead of seeking to isolate them. The language is not that of a scientific reduction to cause and effect, but of complementary movements, whose aim is transmutation, the change effected not by the separateness, but by the unity of being. The key word is 'circulation' and this means more than change. It means that what we are conditioned to see as boundaries are not to be accorded a dividing status, but have rather the quality of an interface, or of a permeable membrane. Carl thus unites the 'movement' of the *principia moventia* in the spiritual with the 'movement' of bodies, the German 'Cörperlich' containing both the meaning 'body' and 'matter'. He does not separate expression (outer nature) from inner nature. Thus 'Ausdruck' (expression) is what constitutes the outer form and because it is also shape and expression it can be described as a 'Bild', an image, whose pictorial nature contains the language of the 'Innermost', the archetypes, of the Unseen. Nature (seen) thus unites with Being (unseen). All of Nature, all the 'movements', perceived as interchanges of describable acts, the vital, animal, rational, and spiritual, contribute to the change or transmutation into the spiritual, whose final form of completion is achieved in the 'Letztere Wiederbringung' (the final restauration of all things, which in enthusiast circles was not merely spiritual, but a reincarnation).[79] Carl's whole cosmographic conception is antagonistic to the material and empirical thinking whose constraints the 'new' science adopted. The word 'reductionist' acquires a very concrete meaning when seen from Carl's perspective: mechanistically and materially defined cause-and-effect relationships of the kind necessary to Newtonian physics or laboratory experiment cannot hope to include or decipher the influences postulated in a universe defined as primarily spiritual. In the cosmography of Carl there is no dualism between matter and spirit; thus the *principia moventia*, seen as active and form-giving influences, direct what is incarnate or present in the elements, the vital and non-vital forms of Nature. Spiritual change is not divested of its unity with bodily habitation. One flows into the other.

Carl here represents the theosophical answer to the mechanization of the universe as it was preferred and advanced by the new science. His was the counterargument to the premiss of a science based solely on the laws of matter, of nature conceived according to Newton, in particular to its negation of the 'place' of the spiritual.[80] Carl's *caveat* against the 'new' science states that: (1) nature is the outward sign of the *principia spiritualia moventia*; (2) all of nature, in particular all living things, is dynamic – that is, composed of 'actions' that define the 'Gestalt' nature attains; (3) the *telos* of an action is invisible and spiritual and *not* material; (4) by seeing nature as an outward manifestation of the *dynamis* of elemental being it becomes the expression of the *pneuma* or being of God, who is 'unseen' ('unsichtbar'); (5) visible nature shows us (or lets us read) the archetypes of the invisible.

The relationship of outward and inward, visible and invisible, always a *dynamic* relationship, means, according to Carl, that 'all outward creation *flows* (*fliessen*) into men/women (*Mensch*)': that is, all vital actions flow into the actions of the body (*actus animales*) and into rational actions (*actus intellectus*) and these into spiritual actions. The acts of dynamic Nature (outward and inward) are therefore interrellated, circular, and not linear, and therefore not to be described in terms of mechanistic natural philosophy. This is *not* just a matter of faith because the visible 'alphabet' or 'signs' of nature ('buchstäbliche Zeugnisse') are existentially in accord with the knowledge of the senses (*fundamenta, documenta et experimenta*). This 'material' proof is methodologically identical with analytical and mathematical demonstrations.

Carl's objection to the 'new' science is based on a claim of scientific observation and not to be confused with a non-scientific criticism founded on solely religious assumptions. In his sceptical view the 'new' science is castigated for the separation of Creation from the Creator; the 'new' science is seen as fundamentally atheistic. According to Carl, mechanical movements and the dissection of bodies into parts destroy the idea of 'circulation', as well as the idea that actions form matter and that matter is not 'static', but 'takes shape'. The circular 'flow' of creation cannot work with the reduction of nature to mechanical laws of energy. Neither is 'matter' in living things immutable, nor is it subject to the explanatory device of a mechanical cause-and-effect model.

In view of this 'organic' or circular (all points touching) interpretation of Nature (and body and soul), the Stahlian school never denied the relevance of emotions and imagination in the interplay of health and illness.[81] The content of 'internal medicine', with which most learned doctors concerned themselves, saw the 'body' in terms of flow and change, the medical view of which is primarily concerned with signs related to process or 'movement'.

This interpretation brings together the theories or ways of viewing the body–mind unity that is inherent in the medical thought of Johann Baptist von Helmont, Johann Conrad Dippel, Stahl, Carl, and others who never adhered (even if they were not overtly antagonistic) to the mechanical philosophy and its medicine. It seems possible, thus, to trace a wider opposition to the 'progress' of medicine as it developed from post-Cartesian dualism and mechanism and its emphasis on

175

anatomy, surgery, physics, and chemistry, and to admit to a
diversity in medical views as they actually seemed to exist. One
thing is also certain: that the first court physician, Stahl, in his
nineteen years in practice in Berlin, considered the 'new'
science negligible for medicine.

Thus, an interesting basic tension in eighteenth-century medicine can be discerned: between, on the one hand, the intentions manifest in the political and institutional power of medical
progress which tended to materialize the body, dissect it, view
its components, and to control it in accordance with Heister's
adage, that the doctor is the 'master' (Herr) of nature, and, on
the other hand, a medical, but also non-medical, view of the
body that held greater cultural sway – that is, a body caught up
in time and 'flow', whose signs and signals were integrated into
a diversity of languages, based on a perceptual exchange between the observational experience ('training' of the physician)
and the patient's modes of conceptualizing suffering.

In eighteenth-century medicine, Heister's physician as master of nature stands in contrast to Stahl's physician as the servant of nature. The anatomical paradigm with its functional
searching out of somatic construction excludes the vagaries of
feeling, the indefiniteness of pain, in so far as it crystallizes and
pin-points the dysfunctional. Medicine only becomes a master,
an absolutist monarch, when it subjugates the increasingly un-
mysterious body. The court physicians of Prussia who aligned
themselves with the 'new' science identified themselves with
and used the power of the State to regulate credentials and to
teach the 'new' science. They helped to achieve the advance of
demystification which is the essence of the scientific view. The
'servants of nature', on the other hand, were conscious of a different paradigm; their 'circular movement' included the soul
and its invisible 'flowing', perceiving the 'inward' nature of the
body as capable of altering its 'outward' state. For them nature
was in a sense still alchemical, the bodily coagulation of the inward archetype. Looking at these fundamental tensions, we
find that the institutional power of modern medicine, beginning with the Edict of 1685, was well invested with a legal and
social base for its professional criteria by the end of the eighteenth century. The road not taken in institutionalized medicine
found affiliates among all those who still spiritualized the nature of humanity, whether religious sectarians, the mad, the ro-
mantics, mesmerists, or those disaffected with authority, in

essence that sector within absolutist states which remained beyond its control, although the State did its confining best.

Notes

1. Family relationships and informal influence played a large
role at the Prussian court. Gossip is legion in the reports of the
agents of other states: see, for example, Richard Wolff, 'Vom
Berliner Hofe zur Zeit Friedrich Wilhelms I., Berichte des
Braunschweiger Gesandten in Berlin 1728-1733', *Schriften des
Vereins für die Geschichte Berlins*, Heft XLVIII and XLIX, Berlin
(1914); or the reports of Count Friedrich Heinrich von Seckendorff
to the Viennese court in the Haus-, Hof- und Staatsarchiv, Vienna.
A well-read piece of court gossip was the letters and memoirs of
Baron von Pöllnitz: *Lettres et mémoires du Baron de Pollnitz, contenant
les observations qu'il a faites dans ses voyages et le caractère des personnes
qui composent les principales cours de l'Europe*, 5th edn, 2 vols
(Frankfurt, 1738); the largely untrue and acid tales of the court in
Berlin of the daughter of Friedrich Wilhelm I, Friederike Sophie
Wilhelmine, are another case in point: *Mémoires de Frederique Sophie
Wilhelmine Margrave de Beireuth*, 1706–1742, 2 vols, 5th edn (Berlin,
1910).

2. See especially: Carl Hinrichs, 'Der Regierungsantritt
Friedrich Wilhelm I', and 'Die Preußische Zentralverwaltung in
den Anfängen Friedrich Wilhelms I' in his *Friedrich Wilhelm I. König
in Preußen, Eine Biographie* (Darmstadt, 1968 (reprint)). Hinrichs
does not specifically analyse medical aspects.

3. This is particularly true for Stahl. See Moritz Pistor,
*Grundzüge einer Geschichte der preußischen Medizinalverwaltung bis Ende
1907* (Brunswick, 1909), p. 11.

4. Pister, *Grundzüge*; F. L. Augustin, *Königlich preußische Medizinal-
verfassung* (Potsdam, 1818–38); Ludwig von Rönne and Heinrich
Simon, *Das Medicinal-Wesen des Preußischen Staates*, I. Theil (Breslau,
1844); Manfred Stürzbecher, *Beiträge zur Berliner Medizingeschichte,
Quellen und Studien zur Geschichte des Gesundheitswesens vom 17. bis zum
19. Jhd.* (Berlin, 1966), pp. 6–64 (bibliography given in footnotes
therein).

5. For a recent discussion see: Claudia Huerkamp, *Der Aufstieg
der Ärzte im 19. Jahrhundert* (Göttingen, 1985).

6. For an overview and literature to this problem, see Roy
Porter (ed.), *Patients and Practitioners: Lay Perceptions of Medicine in
Pre-industrial Society* (Cambridge, 1985), especially the introduction.

7. Andreas von Gundelsheim was an expert in botany and
fevers: see Johann Peter von Ludewig, *Hallische Gelehrte Anzeigen ...
nunmehr zusammen gedruckt ...* (Halle, 1743), p. 867ff; for Stahl's
medical theory, see *Theoria medica vera* (Halle, 1708).

8. See my forthcoming book, *Georg Ernst Stahl: Pietismus, Medizin
und Aufklärung in Preußen im 18. Jahrhundert* and its chapter on 'Die

mechanische Medizin'.

9. As an example of the importance of this unfortunately vastly neglected area of medical advice and the exchange of medical knowledge, I can point to the continuous re-publication of Georg Ernst Stahl's *Observationes clinicae*, the first of his medical works to be translated into the German vernacular. No scholarly studies of the frequency in publication or the extent of the literature on medical cases for the seventeenth and eighteenth centuries exists.

10. Thomas Sydenham, *Observationes medicae morborum acutorum historiam et curationem* (London, 1676); Georg Ernst Stahl, *Theoria medica vera* (Halle, 1708); G. E. Stahl, *De autocratia naturae spontanea morborum excussione et convalescentia* (Halle, 1696).

11. Georg Ernst Stahl, *Untersuchung der übel-curirten und verderbten Kranckheiten* (Leipzig, 1726).

12. This was the case the 'progressive' physicians in the wake of Cartesian philosophy made for themselves. See J. Geyer-Kordesch, 'Fevers and other Fundamentals: Dutch and German medical explanations c. 1680 to 1730', in W. F. Bynum and V. Nutton (eds), *Theories of Fever from Antiquity to the Enlightenment* (London, 1981), pp. 99–120.

13. Robert Herrlinger, 'Heister contra Stahl, Eine zeitgenössische Polemik um Grundauffassungen der barocken Medizin', in *Ärztliche Praxis*, Nr. 49 (Dez. 1951), p. 10.

14. Stahl, *Theoria medica vera*: 'De vera diversitate corporis mixti et vivi ... ', *passim*.

15. G. E. Stahl, *Negotium Otiosum* ... (Halle, 1720), the Latin text of the debate between G. W. von Leibniz and Stahl reiterates Stahl's claim to the *difference* between his theory based on medical observation and the claims of Leibniz for universal laws of physics and mathematics to which Leibniz thought medicine must subordinate itself, if medicine was to be a science. See also my forthcoming book, *Georg Ernst Stahl*, especially 'Negotium Otiosum: Stahl contra Leibniz'.

16. This is emphasized by Stahl from the first: see *De moto tonico vitali*... (Jena, 1692); *Problemata practica febrium pathologiae et therapiae* ... (Halle, 1695); *De mutatione temperamenti cum epistola de fatis doctrinae temperamentorum* (Halle, 1712).

17. This became increasingly common, especially because of Albrecht von Haller's opposition to Stahl's inclusion of the soul in his medical theory. See Albrecht von Haller, *Bibliotheca anatomica* (Zürich, 1774–7), Bd. I, p. 697; *Bibliotheca medicinae practicae* (Berne and Basel, 1776–88), Bd. II, p. 518; *Elementa physiologiae* (Lausanne, 1757–66), Bd. I., p. 2ff.

18. Stürzbecher, *Beiträge*, p. 24ff; Pistor, *Grundzüge*, p. 2ff.

19. Georg Gottfried Küster, *Des Alten und Neuen Berlins* ... (Berlin, 1756), Theil I, p. 469.

20. Stürzbecher, *Beiträge*, p. 27. (The text of the *Medizinalordnung* of 1685 is reprinted there.)

21. Ibid., p. 8ff.

22. Ibid.

23. Manfred Stürzbecher emphasized the difference between city physicians who organized themselves in a *collegium medicum* and the Berlin *collegium medicum* which was invested with regulatory powers: Stürzbecher, *Beiträge*, p. 34. He does not specifically analyse these differences, however.

24. The following explanation of the content of the Edict of 1685 is taken from its publication in L. von Rönne and H. Simon, *Das Medicinal-Wesen*, p. 13–14.

25. Ibid., p. 13.

26. Küster, *Des Alten* p. 470ff.

27. Pistor, *Grundzüge*, p. 9.

28. Ibid., p. 8.

29. Küster, *Des Alten*, p. 473.

30. Pistor, *Grundzüge*, p. 9ff; von Ronne and Simon, *Medicinal-Wesen*, p. 15ff.

31. Pistor, *Grundzüge*, p. 8.

32. Von Ludewig, *Hallische Gelehrte Anzeigen*, p. 474.

33. Pistor, *Grundzüge*, p. 9.

34. Ibid.

35. Ibid., p. 10.

36. Ibid., pp. 10–11.

37. Heinz Böhm, *Dorothea Christiane Erxleben, Ihr Leben und Wirken* (Quedlinburg, 1965).

38. Ibid., p. 15.

39. See for details: J. Geyer-Kordesch, 'Medical biographies of the 18th century: reflections on medical practice and medical education in Germany', in W. Eckart and J. Geyer-Kordesch (eds), *Heilberufe und Kranke im 17. und 18. Jht., Die Quellen- und Forschungssituation* (Münster, 1982), p. 133ff.

40. Adolf Harnack, *Geschichte der Königlich Preussischen Akademie der Wissenschaften zu Berlin* (Berlin, 1900; reprint, Hildesheim, 1970), Bd. I (1), p. 112ff.

41. Ibid., p. 77.

42. Ibid., p. 95.

43. Ibid., p. 77, p. 81ff.

44. Ibid., p. 77.

45. Ibid.

46. Ibid., p. 176.

47. Ibid., pp. 176–7.

48. Ibid., p. 179, reference 3.

49. See J. Geyer-Kordesch, 'German medical education in the eighteenth century: the Prussian context and its influence', in W. F. Bynum and Roy Porter (eds), *William Hunter and the Eighteenth-century Medical World* (Cambridge, 1985), p. 198ff.

50. Harnack, *Geschichte*, Bd. I (1), p. 183.

51. Von Ludewig, *Hallische Gelehrte Anzeigen*, p. 867ff.

52. Adolf Harnack mentions Hoffmann's return to Halle and the Berlin rivalry: *Geschichte*, Bd. I, (1), pp. 182–5. Archival material in Merseburg and Halle suggests there were juridical consequences. The 'rivalry' has not been analysed.

53. J. Kvacsala, 'D. E. Jablonsky's Briefwechsel mit Leibniz', in
Acta et Commentationes imp. Universitatis Jurievensis (Juriew (=Dorpat),
1897), p. 125.

54. See J. Geyer-Kordesch, 'German medical education', p. 199ff.

55. Harnack *Geschichte*, Bd. I (1), p. 193ff.

56. Küster, *Des Alten*, p. 176ff.

57. Ibid., pp. 175–6.

58. Peter Schicketanz, *Carl Hildebrand von Canstein's Beziehungen
zu Philipp Jakob Spener* (Witten, 1967), pp. 66–75.

59. The specific medical subjects taught at the *theatrum
anatomicum* under the official direction of the *collegium medicum*
were printed: 'Lektionsverzeichnisse 1724–1751'. The archival
sources for the 'Acta betreffend die Lektion der Professorum auf
dem Theatro Anatomico 1723': Archive of the Akademie der
Wissenschaften, Berlin, German Democratic Republic, AAW XIV
25.

60. Küster, *Des Alten*, p. 177.

61. See Johann Theodor Eller, 'Von der Stiftung und
Errichtung dieses Hauses', in *Nützliche und auserlesene Medicinische
und Chirurgische Anmerkungen* (Berlin, 1730), p. 5ff.

62. See J. Geyer-Kordesch, 'German medical education', p. 196ff.

63. Laurentius Heister, 'Abbhandlung von der Vortrefflichkeit
der mechanischen Arzneylehre', in *Practisches Medicinisches
Handbuch*, (Leipzig, 1763), p. 9.

64. Illness, diagnostic patterns, the efficacy of treatment and the
value of remedies fill various correspondences: the letters
exchanged by Karl Hildebrand von Canstein with the medical
followers of Stahl, the brothers Richter in Halle; the reflections of
D. G. von Natzmer and Heinrich Julius Elers in their diaries and
letters; the advice of Frau von Natzmer to her son by her first
marriage, Count Nikolaus Ludwig von Zinzendorf, on matters
concerning his health.

65. Archive of the Francke'schen Stiftungen: AFSt C 285.

66. Stahl, *Theoria medica vera:* 'De febre, seu febribus in genere',
p. 924ff.

67. Barbara Duden, *Geschichte unter der Haut, Ein Eisenacher Arzt
und seine Patientinnen um 1730* (Stuttgart, 1987).

68. Ibid., p. 125.

69. Ibid.

70. Ibid., p. 126.

71. Ibid.

72. This is particularly true of those medical doctors who were
also religious radicals: Johann Samuel Carl, Christian Friedrich
Richter, Johann Jacob Reich, Christian Weißbach, Samuel
Forbinger, Michael Alberti, Johann Daniel Gohl, Johann Juncker.
To disavow the radical connections of these men is to
conventionalize their contribution to medicine.

73. Stahl's *Theoria medica vera* reflects the concern with *vital*
processes, especially in its cohesiveness as a medical explanation.
The physiology (p. 256ff: 'de vita et sanitate') is based on the

explanation of blood flow, secretions, excretions, temperament. The pathology is based on the particular patterns of change in the disease process.

74. See, for example, the cases given in Christian Friedrich Richter's *Höchst-Nöthige Erkenntnis des Menschen* (Leipzig, 1709).

75. See the concerted attack on prophecy, inspiration, and the imagination in general in the 'revolt against enthusiasm', particularly: Truman Guy Steffan, 'The social argument against enthusiasm', in *Studies in English*, 21 (1941), pp. 39–63.

76. Hans-Jürgen Schrader, 'Johann Samuel Carl', in *Schleswig-Holsteinisches Biographisches Lexikon*, Bd. 5 (Neumünster, 1979) pp. 60–4.

77. Johann Samuel Carl, *Decorum Medici, von denen Machiavellischen Thorheiten gereiniget, und nach dem Maaß-Stab des Christenthums eingerichtet, mir und meinem Auditoribus zum Unterricht* (Büdingen, 1719), p. 11.

78. The 'Letztere Wiederbringung' was an important element of the radical Protestant view of nature. We know too little about its precise meaning for the period in question. The work of Walter Pagel on Paracelsus and Johann Baptist von Helmont gives valuable insights. The biblical reference here is to either *Acts* 3:21 or *Eph.* 1:10. Luther translates *Acts* 3:21 'bis auff die Zeit/da herwiedergebracht werde/alles ... ' The *Vulgate* translates *Eph.* 1:10 with 'in dispensatione plenitudinis temporum, instaurare omnia in Christo, quae in caelis, et quae in terra sunt, in ipso'.

79. Ibid. Even less sectarian Pietists, such as Hermann August Francke, seem to have emphasized the *bodily* resurrection in 'the fullness of time'. Francke's grave in Halle carries the inscription from Job 19: 25–7 in the full Lutheran translation, including 'Und werde darnach mit dieser meiner Haut umgeben werden/und werde in meinem Fleisch Gott sehen ... '

80. See also Michael Alberti's defence of the soul: *Medicinische und Philosophische Schrifften von unterschiedenen Materien ... aufs neue herausgegeben mit einigen Tratactgen vermehret* (Halle, 1721).

81. See, for example, the introduction to Richter, *Höchst–Nöthige Erkenntnis*; M. Alberti, *De Therapia imaginaria* (Halle, 1721); M. Alberti (praes.)/Abraham Levin (resp.), *De vi imaginationis in vitam et sanitatem naturalem* (Halle, 1740).

7

Medicine at the Court of Catherine the Great of Russia

J. T. Alexander

Medicine hardly figures among the activities ordinarily associated with the imperial Russian court in the reign of Catherine the Great (1762–96). Brilliance, splendour, luxury, opulence, refinement – or passion, pleasure, display, intrigue, favouritism, avarice, frivolity, depravity, hypocrisy, exploitation – these are the epithets commonly invoked to praise or to malign Catherine II and her court. Popular histories seldom mention such mundane matters as medical services or medical practitioners in the 'barbaric splendour' of the 'gorgeous' court centred on St Petersburg and its suburban palaces.[1] Perhaps as a function of these widespread, deeply rooted stereotypes, medicine in the context of the Russian court is fated to be trivialized, to be seen as insignificant or purely decorative. This chapter aims to question such superficial contentions.

It is no simple matter to reconstruct the place and role of medicine at the Catherinian court. First, there are no modern studies of either medicine or the court in that period, nor did any individual practitioner achieve sufficient eminence to merit a full-scale biography.[2] In addition, the sources for such studies appear to be quite scattered and scarcely processed. Third, medical affairs at court, the health of the sovereign in particular, were considered such sensitive subjects that they were deliberately concealed from prying eyes and have left, as a result, scant documentary traces. The official court registers often omitted any mention of the presence of medical practitioners; hence there is no informed record of Catherine's own health history, a subject that few biographers have even touched upon.[3] All these considerations mean that one must often rely upon indirect testimony to glean some notion of what went on at court in matters medical. Some of that testimony amounts to little more than hearsay evidence or recorded gossip and speculation. Rarely did the official Russian press discuss such topics, whereas foreign press reports were invariably speculative. Even though Catherine in private correspondence and in the several different drafts of her so-called memoirs refers frequently to questions of health and, occasionally, to questions of treatment, her testimony can hardly ever be directly checked against other sources. Besides, it must often be discounted because of her own sceptical, sometimes sardonic, appreciation of medical knowledge and practice. Another complication stems from the foreign background of nearly all court medical practitioners in Catherinian Russia, a factor which led them rarely to record their observations at the time and which largely isolated them from the broader Russian medical context.[4] Indeed, one wonders whether there may not have been an implicit prohibition on court practitioners discussing their practice outside the court. All these problems of sources and circumstances must needs contribute to the tentativeness and sketchiness of the following foray into this neglected subject. Considering its state of historiographical neglect, though, even negative findings may yield greater than ordinary value.

In a sense, both the court itself and court medicine centred on Catherine (1729–96). From her arrival in Russia in 1744 aged fourteen, Princess Sophie of Anhalt-Zerbst, soon to become Grand Duchess Catherine, encountered court medical practitioners as a patient, as a member of the Russian court, and as an interested bystander and observer of the health of Empress Elizabeth (1709–61) and of Grand Duke Peter (1728–62), her husband-to-be, the heir presumptive to the throne, and the future Emperor Peter III (1761–62). Even before she set foot in Russia the young German princess had imbibed a sceptical attitude toward medical practitioners from her French governess, from reading such satirical authors as Molière, and from the ministrations of folk empirics such as the local hangman, who supposedly treated her spinal curvature with a harness and applications of spittle. Catherine professed to be no better impressed by Russian court medical practices, particularly the repeated blood-lettings she received for treatment of a pulmonary illness that severely afflicted her within a few weeks of arrival. The imperious Elizabeth overruled the objections of Catherine's mother and insisted on numerous blood-lettings, which Catherine somehow survived.[5]

Some months later, now officially betrothed and designated Grand Duchess of Russia, Catherine witnessed the travails of her fiancé in barely surviving a severe attack of smallpox, which left permanent facial scars and, perhaps, permanent sterility. Both results doomed her marriage, thereby imperilling her future in Russia. Little wonder that Catherine preserved such a vivid horror of smallpox for the rest of her days. Several times she thought she herself had been exposed to smallpox, but in each instance the tell-tale symptoms failed to develop. Indeed, she grew into a young woman of robust health and vitality that carried her through bouts of dental abscess, periodic depression, and several miscarriages.[6] The care she received for these conditions left her feeling thankful to her physicians, albeit sceptical of their treatments. In particular, she remembered thankfully the care she received from Dr Antonio Ribeiro Sanches and Dr Hermann Kau-Boerhaave. Sensitive to the injustice accorded Sanches, who had left Russia in 1747 after being denounced as a crypto-Jew, Catherine in the early months of her own reign awarded him an annual pension of 1,000 rubles.[7] His well-known book on Russian steambaths was published in Russian translation in 1779.[8]

The political potential of court practitioners was dramatized to Catherine in the stature accorded the chief imperial physician (archiater) Count Armand Lestocq as a consequence of his role in the *coup d'état* of 1741 that had placed Elizabeth on the throne. His primacy conferred immense influence in all manner of affairs, yet it did not shield him from abrupt disgrace in 1748 – arrest, interrogation, torture, imprisonment, and exile – as a result of accusations that he had plotted to poison the empress.[9] This putative plot may also have involved the grand ducal 'young court', hence Catherine's guarded references to it in the various drafts of her autobiographical recollections.[10] It was another Elizabethan error that she later sought to set right: only days after mounting the throne, Catherine pardoned Lestocq (1692–1767), awarded him and his wife an estate in the Riga district, and granted him his former salary of 7,000 rubles annually instead of a pension.[11] As grand duchess, Catherine had also observed the importance of court practitioners as sources of information on the crucial question of Elizabeth's declining health, tapping an unnamed surgeon for that purpose.[12]

Upon Catherine's abrupt accession to the imperial throne

with the *coup d'état* of 28 June 1762, the status of court medicine appeared in some disarray. Within a month she reappointed Dr Karl Kruse (1727–99), who had resigned amid Peter III's brief tenure and who may have been present at his murder on 7 July 1762, and surgeon Villim Villimovich Foussadier (1709–73) to serve her son and heir, Grand Duke Paul, and surgeon Ivan Roeslein to her own service.[13] When archiater Dr James Mounsey (1710–73) retired on 22 July 1762, she granted him a year's salary and a pension of 1,000 rubles annually, but did not hasten to appoint a successor, possibly to avoid appointing another foreigner in the chauvinistic atmosphere following the downfall of Peter III's 'Prussian' regime.[14] Dr Johann Lerche (1703–80), a Prussian from Potsdam with four decades' experience in Russia, served as acting archiater for more than a year. Mounsey's resignation opened the way to a complete reorganization of the administration of medical affairs in 1763, by which time Catherine's initial reform programme began to emerge.

Actually, one problem of court medicine seized Catherine's nervous concern earlier and more forcefully than the larger issue of general medical reform. In August 1762 Catherine consulted Dr Kruse concerning Paul's fragile health and was told that he was underweight from a sour stomach, vomiting, and diarrhoea.[15] While travelling to Moscow for her coronation in September 1762, she overtook her 7-year-old son, halted *en route* with a fever. Although he felt better upon seeing his mother, he experienced a relapse soon afterwards, before rejoining her for a triumphal entry into the 'first-crowned' capital on 13 September. Catherine was officially crowned in the Kremlin's Assumption Cathedral on 22 September, but her enjoyment of the coronation festivities was beclouded when Paul's third attack of fever within a month kept him bedridden and intermittently delirious for the first two weeks of October.[16]

In this matter Catherine's concerns were both maternal and political, inasmuch as Paul was her sole legitimate heir (her bastard son by Grigorii Orlov, eventually named Aleksei Bobrinskoi, was kept out of sight and apparently raised mainly abroad after his birth on 11 April 1762). Moreover, in staging her coup she had publicly pledged to protect Paul's rights to the throne – rights that Peter III had allegedly planned to violate. Paul's health had been weak from infancy, whereas Catherine's uncertain hold on power made her doubly fearful of appearing to be negligent of his well-being. Further episodes of fever and measles in early 1763 were among the main reasons why she tarried in Moscow until June 1763. Indeed, just before she left for Petersburg, she established in Paul's name the first public hospital (*Pavlovskaia bol'nitsa*) in Moscow. This action furnished a good, practical example of how personal concerns could be turned to public benefit in matters of health policy.[17]

The reorganization of court medicine sprang directly from Catherine's abolition of the office of archiater and her replacement of the Medical Chancery with a more diversified institution, the Medical College. In formulating this reform, publicly proclaimed on 12 November 1763, the empress drew upon varied advice, from court and non-court medical practitioners, and from experienced officials such as Grigorii Teplov and Baron Alexander Cherkassov. The last two were considered among the best-educated men in Russia, with considerable experience in state service and in scientific affairs at home and abroad. Cherkassov had spent almost ten years in England and Scotland, studying humanities at Cambridge and medicine at Edinburgh, though he took no degree. Catherine had known him years before her elevation to the throne and later warmly dedicated one version of her memoirs to him. Her confidence in his administrative abilities was underlined by his appointment as the first president of the Medical College, in which post he served until 1775. He appointed the other, professional members of the new medical administration.[18]

The medical reform of 1763 fundamentally changed the status of court medicine in Russia by separating its practitioners from the rest of the highly centralized state medical administration, and by abolishing the office of archiater, which had supervised all medical affairs since Petrine times. By contrast, the Medical College had no jurisdiction over court practitioners. They were placed directly under the sovereign, not under any particular agency and only vaguely under the slowly bureaucratizing court administration; whereas the Medical College itself was headed by a non-professional administrator – unlike the archiater, who had always been a foreign-educated physician. The Medical College was subdivided into a College of Medical Arts, staffed by six professional practitioners of varied ranks and specialities, and a business office that the president administered. In concept the medical reform of 1763 apparently aimed to achieve some functional specialization: to free court practitioners from other duties and, perhaps, to insulate them from political pressures. At the same time the new Medical College and its single regional department, the Moscow Office, were to provide a broader, better articulated, and more assertive administration of medical affairs outside the court, that would seek to train more native practitioners and to establish more hospitals and other treatment facilities. There was no thought, it seems, of establishing any hospital for the court, whose servitors were presumably expected to be treated at home.

Catherine II devoted considerable attention to her court, which became almost legendary for its opulence. It is difficult to calculate the cost of the Catherinian court, however, simply because it is so difficult to define the institution. In the narrow sense, the imperial Russian court comprised the empress and her attendants under the jurisdiction of the Chief Court Chancery and the Cabinet of Her Imperial Majesty. The Reverend William Tooke, who spent several decades in Petersburg during Catherine's reign, offered this summary of the institution:

> The court is composed of the great officers of state, of senators, actual privy-counsellors, princes, counts, barons &c. whose names may be seen in the Russian court-kalendar, one cup-bearer, one master of the horse, one high chamberlain, one master of the hunt, one court-marshal, one court-master, one master of the stables, twenty-three actual chamberlains, nine gentlemen of the bed-chamber, eight adjutant-generals, (of whom two are field-marshals, five generals in chief, and one lieutenant-general), fifteen ensign adjutants, one mistress of the court, eight state-ladies, one lady of the bed-chamber, six maids of honour.[19]

Tooke's definition was a purely formal one, and it remains rather problematical how involved in court life some of these offices actually were; for it was not uncommon for army officers to hold court ranks, whose exercise their military duties must often have prevented. Furthermore, many courtiers took extended leaves, and some may have regarded their court ranks as purely honorary.

Tooke's numbers of the different ranks are also suspect: a later account found twenty-six chamberlains and twenty-seven gentlemen of the chamber at the end of Catherine's reign.[20] Nevertheless, in its narrowest definition the Catherinian court appears to have been a fairly small institution in terms of number of personnel. It retained strong marks of its recent emergence as a European-type institution in service to the imperial household, exemplified by the German origins of most court ranks and offices. However, the relationship among the various court ranks remained rather vague, and before the nineteenth century there was no standard court uniform.[21]

In a broader sense, the court was much larger; so much so that it is hard to set limits to its reach. St Petersburg was itself pre-eminently a court residence.[22] The court included a whole series of institutions in the highly centralized Russian administrative structure, such as the Court Staff, the Court Stables Chancery, the Chamber-Stallmaster Office, the Workshop and Arms Chamber, the Senior Huntmaster Chancery, the Petersburg and Moscow Court-Inspector's Office, and the Estates Chancery of Her Imperial Majesty. To give some idea of the number of officials employed by these central court administrations and their local branches, a survey of 1755 counted 258 ranked officials, or about 5 per cent of the total officials surveyed.[23] However, that figure did not include many more employees without status in the Table of Ranks. These were commoners who worked in dozens of jobs, from footmen to waiters to cooks, gardeners, and so on. Certainly they numbered many hundreds, but how many is not known. A roster of 1730 listed 625 persons with annual money salaries of 83,571 rubles and 35 copecks, whereas another of 1741 counted 559 persons with annual salaries of 87,426 rubles and 87½ copecks.[24] Presumably, the figures for Catherine's reign were substantially higher in both categories.

Another measure of the court was the expenditures it consumed. A recent estimate places court expenditures in 1762 at 1,753,000 rubles out of total spending of 16,500,000 rubles, figures that rose in 1795 to 10,640,000 and 79,150,000 rubles, respectively. Over Catherine's reign, then (and uncorrected for inflation), court expenditures increased about sixfold, from 10·6 to 13·4 per cent of total spending.[25] Another estimate reckons the increase from 2,550,000 in 1767 to 10,640,000 in 1795, with an additional one million spent in the latter year on science, schools, charity, and medicine.[26] Unfortunately, there are no figures for court spending on medical affairs specifically, but it is safe to assume that the amount rose substantially in the course of Catherine's reign. Tooke's comments about the court late in her reign confirm the general impression of extravagance:

> The annual expenses of the palace were about one million five hundred thousand rubles. Almost two hundred tables were spread there twice a day; and the dishes for them reckoned to amount to two thousand three hundred. Every third day the court-purveyor received the money for making this provision. The waste at court was carried to an inexpressible height. The houses or apartments which the empress caused to be fitted up for the persons to whom she gave quarters, contained frequently in furniture more than three times their value. Twelve hundred candles were every day delivered out to the guard, who never consumed one hundred. The dinner for the officer on guard cost seventy rubles; that it was worth nothing was not the fault of the empress. Every officer about the palace asked for what he would in glasses, decanters, and things of that nature: nothing ever came back; and this happened every day. The quantity of china-ware that was broken is incredible. Whoever broke any was obliged to shew the fragments, but the fragments of four or five pieces would very well serve for a dozen, as he was never required to fit them together. They whose business it was to clean the silver made rapid fortunes. They had a certain substance, which by rubbing brought off much of the metal; the diminution was apparent to every attentive observer. For the four months which the empress passed at Tsarskoe-Selo, twenty-five english miles from town, the Neva-water for her own table (as she would take no other) cost her ten thousand rubles annually.[27]

Closely associated with the court were a host of other institutions, ranging from the four Guards regiments, the Imperial Corps of Pages, the Noble Cadet Corps, and the Smol'nyi Institute for Women, to charitable institutions such as the foundling homes in Moscow and Petersburg, both of which employed several practitioners. There was sometimes confusion about whether the Medical College had the authority to appoint the practitioners to these court-related institutions. In 1764–5, despite objections from the Medical College, the Smol'nyi Institute succeeded in hiring its own choice of practitioners, Dr Johann Heinrich Jaenisch (MD, Jena, 1755), and surgeon Wilhelm Nagel; but to save money no salaries were specified and the practitioners were to serve only when summoned. At the time Dr Jaenisch taught theoretical surgery and medical practice in German (for an extra 200 rubles per year) at the twin Petersburg Admiralty and Infantry hospitals. In opposition, the Medical College favoured a permanent medical staff, with ranks and salaries and housing on par with those of practitioners at the Noble Cadet Corps, and sought to impose its choice of candidates. However, after much wrangling Catherine finally ruled in favour of the institute, authorizing its choice of practitioners, who like others at court were exempted from the Medical College's jurisdiction.[28] This may well have been an exceptional case because of the chaos attendant upon the creation of both the Smol'nyi institute and the Medical College itself. It cannot be assumed that other court-related institutions enjoyed the same autonomy in medical affairs.

Medical practitioners were assigned to serve the employees of many, if not most, of these court institutions. The staff of the Chief Court Chancery in 1773, for example, were supposed to be under the care of one surgeon, one surgeon's mate, and two barbers.[29] It may be indicative of the generally low status of these people that no doctor was assigned to oversee their health. Nor is it by any means certain that such offices were actually provided with the prescribed numbers and types of practitioners. The number of court practitioners in Catherinian Russia therefore remains quite uncertain, depending on which institutions are considered and when. No single office supervised court medical practitioners; consequently no central repository like the Medical College kept a roster of such personnel.

It is also unclear exactly how many persons they served at any one time. According to the regulations of 1786, for instance, the staff of the Cabinet of Her Imperial Majesty (sixty-one persons) and its branches should have been served by one staff-surgeon, one surgeon's mate, and two surgical apprentices, whereas the Senior Huntmaster's Chancery in 1773 was assigned one surgeon and one surgeon's mate.[30]By contrast, when Grand Duke Paul and his wife travelled to Europe in 1781–82, their suite of 89 persons was served by Dr Kruse and surgeon Rozberg.[31] Likewise uncertain is whether such practitioners when actually assigned were expected to be on duty full time, or whether they might have had other duties elsewhere. Presumably their duties varied, and some accepted private patients on occasion. Apparently they were not allowed to charge fees to patients from their assigned institutions.[32]

From the preceding regime Catherine inherited a small court medical establishment that comprised the body-physicians (*leibmedik*) Drs Johann Schilling (degree unknown) and Karl Kruse (MD, Leyden, 1749), body-surgeons (*leibkhirurgus*) Johann Roeslein and Villim Foussadier, surgeons Christopher Paulsohn, Johann Liders, and Christian Ulrich, and court apothecary (*pridvornyi aptekar'*) Maksim Briskorn. In the first months of Catherine's rule they received these monetary rewards: Schilling (1,500 rubles), Kruse (1,500), Foussadier (1,000), Roeslein (1,000), Paulsohn (2,000), Liders (1,000), Ulrich (1,000), and Briskorn (600).[33] A decade later this court medical cadre had expanded in size and expense. Schilling and Kruse each earned 4,000 rubles per year, Roeslein and Foussadier 2,000, and court doctors (*pridvornye doktora*) Karl Eiler, John Rogerson, and Friedrich Allaman 1,000. In addition, court physician (*gofmedik*) Dr Shulinus and staff-surgeon Kliber were assigned to Grand Duke Paul with annual salaries of 2,000 and 700 rubles, respectively. They were assisted by court surgeons (*gofkhirurgi*) Christopher Paulsohn, Johann Bek, Christian Baumgard, Johann Liders, and Mikhail Dreier, all with annual salaries of 820 rubles (600 in salary, 120 for quarters, and 100 for equipage).[34]

Over the next ten years this court medical establishment gradually expanded further. By 1785 it comprised the following practitioners in the various ranks and assignments, as listed in the official court register[35] (hence the russified form of their names):

Body-physicians: Karl Fedorovich Kruz and Ivan Samoilovich Rozherson, actual court councillors
Body-surgeons: Ivan Zakhar'evich Kel'khen, state councillor
Court doctors: Karl Leont'evich Eiler, Georgii Kirner, Ivan Freigang, Veikart, collegial councillors
Court surgeons: Ivan Ivanovich Liders, Khristian Ivanovich Baumgardt, Mikhail Ivanovich Dreier, Ivan Krest'ianovich Zal'tser, court councillors
Staff-surgeon: Andrei Kliber, court councillor

Surgeon: Rozberg
Court Apothecary: Villim Greve, court councillor

Assigned to His Imperial Highness (Grand Duke Paul and family)
Court-physicians: Shulinus, Friderik Alaman
Body-physician: Ivan Filippovich Bek, state councillor.

Besides these practitioners, other specialists were occasionally employed, such as the dentist Skardovik in 1783 at an annual salary of 800 rubles.[36] Judging by names only, Germans predominated among the Russian court medical practitioners, just as they did among the upper strata of medical personnel in the empire throughout the eighteenth century.[37] No doubt some became quite russified. Only a few attained national or international recognition. Thus, Dr Kruse had been elected an honorary member of the Academy of Sciences in 1756 and wrote at least one letter to Linnaeus.[38] Drs Jaenisch, Mohrenheim, and Weltzien, and surgeon Kelchen all published works recognised abroad.[39] Surgeon Johann (Ivan) Bek (1735–1811), who succeeded Foussadier in 1773 as Paul's body-surgeon and served his sons from 1784 as body-physician, appears to have been the single court practitioner to obtain an MD from the Medical College for 'longtime practice and especial knowledge', without defending a dissertation at a university.[40] Like Bek, the Riga-born surgeon Ivan Zakhar'evich Kel'khen or Johann Heinrich Kelchen (1722–1800) served Catherine's court as body-surgeon from the early 1770s and rose to prominence from his activities in the Free Economic Society and from his part in founding and directing the short-lived Kalinkin Medico-Surgical School in Petersburg (1783–1802).[41]

As practitioners these men enjoyed varied reputations. Princess Dashkova praised Dr Kruse for saving her life and credited him and Kelchen for saving her son's life from 'an internal abscess which required a risky and painful operation'. On another occasion, when Kruse and Kelchen were away at Tsarskoe Selo, Dr John Rogerson treated Dashkova's son for 'an aphitic complaint, a prey to burning fever', and he also cured Dashkova's 'rheumatic pains, this time in my intestines'.[42] Several court practitioners were apparently followed into the profession by sons. At any rate, Russian students named Foussadier and Roeslein earned the MD at Leyden in 1765 and

1769, respectively.[43]

The court practitioners' titles and salaries imply certain hierarchical relationships, but these may have been more complex than meets the eye. It is well known, for instance, that medical men received compensation for particular treatments, and like other courtiers their income included payments in kind, especially for quarters and food. For assisting with the birth of Grand Duchess Elena Pavlovna on 22 December 1784, for example, Dr Kruse received 2,000 rubles, surgeon Bek 1,000, operator Mohrenheim 1,000, and apothecary Greve 500.[44]

Different practitioners understood the hierarchy differently. When Dr Melchior Adam Weikard arrived from Fulda at Catherine's court in 1784, he was told that his designation was *kamer-medik*, with access to the empress on par with her first *leibmedik* and first *leibkhirurgus*. The title was unknown in Russia, Weikard learned, so nobody was sure where it stood in relation to the other court practitioners. He himself thought it ranked between *leibmedik* and *gofmedik*. 'But we were all mistaken', he later concluded, 'because each *gofmedik* oversees a particular group, for example the maids of honour, the pages, etc.; hence my charge was to care for persons belonging to the empress' chamber.'[45] This assignment seems quite vague, and indeed the court register of 1784 listed no specific assignments or any such rank as *kamer-medik*; Weikard was grouped with other *pridvornye doktora*.[46] Even so, he maintained that Dr Rogerson, the empress's first *leibmedik*, was so affronted by the new title and appointment that he asked for leave abroad, sold his Petersburg house, and received 2,000 rubles for the journey, but he did not leave because of the complications arising from the death of Alexander Lanskoi, Catherine's current favourite.[47]

Weikard's testimony, one-sided and malicious though it may be, provides some further insights into the inner workings of Catherine's court. He had been recruited by promises of monetary reward: a salary of 2,500 rubles (or 1,500 more than a regular *leibmedik*, figured as 1,000 for salary, 500 for quarters, and 1,000 rubles for the journey to Russia). His brother was physician to the Shuvalov family in Petersburg, and Weikard himself had achieved some European fame with his book, *Der philosophische Arzt* (1773). Though he complained bitterly about the difficulty of finding suitable housing in Petersburg, Weikard was astonished at the splendour of Catherine's court, as proudly asserted by state secretary Adam Olsuf'ev: 'Not at one court, not in Europe, not in Asia, not in Africa is so much spent as with us.'[48] Other visitors such as William Coxe agreed with him, noting:

> The richness and splendour of the Russian Court surpasses description. It retains many traces of the Asiatic pomp, blended with European refinement. An immense retinue of courtiers always preceded and followed the empress; the costliness and glare of their apparel, and a profusion of precious stones created a splendour, of which the magnificence of other courts gives a faint idea.[49]

Weikard received much more than he could eat from a court kitchen better than that which supplied the so-called doctors' table; he was told to give any surplus to his servants. Each day he was provided with some thirty bottles of wine, English beer, and Russian beverages. He professed to be proud of his rank of collegial councillor, which he compared to *Regierungsrath* in Germany or colonel in the military, whereas he sneered at the next lower rank, court councillor, commenting that 'in Russia, where rank alone makes the man, it is almost imperative to have a rank. It is awful to be nothing where almost everybody is something.'[50]

Concerning the importance of favour at court, he waxed sarcastic:

> For the Russian there is nothing more important than a gracious glance or a good reception at court. Court disfavour for him is murderous. The Russian falls ill if his sovereign glances at him ungraciously. For him it becomes worse if she does not enquire about him during his illness and is not informed through others about his health.[51]

Weikard offered a close, somewhat defensive account of the final illness and death of Lanskoi on 25 June 1784, an event that shook Catherine and her court. It was not an auspicious beginning for a medical career in Russia. He criticised Catherine for disputing his diagnosis and prescriptions, for relying on nature, folk remedies, and other practitioners' advice, and implicated surreptitiously administered stimulants in the young man's demise. Dr Rogerson's last-minute prescription of James's Powders, the antimonial nostrum, Weikard dismissed as useless, if not positively fatal. He grumpily acknowledged Rogerson's re-establishment in Catherine's favour as a result of his treatment of the illness triggered by her loss.[52]

John Rogerson (1741–1823) was, in fact, the most prominent court practitioner for much of Catherine's reign. As Anthony Cross and John Appleby have amply demonstrated, Rogerson played a many-sided role in Anglo-Russian intellectual, cultural, scientific, and social relations over a period of fifty years (1766–1816).[53] With an MD from Edinburgh in 1765, Rogerson went to Russia the next year and passed the obligatory examination by the Medical College that authorized him to practise medicine on 5/16 September 1766. He entered court medical service as *pridvornyi doktor* on 18 February 1769 at a salary of 1,000 rubles and rose to *leibmedik* on 18 January 1776 with the rank of Actual State Councillor and a salary of 4,000 rubles.[54] From the Russian press British newspapers hailed his appointment: 'Her Imperial Majesty has been pleased to appoint Mr Rogerson (a Scotchman by Birth) Counsellor of State, and Physician to the Court, in the room of Mr de Schilling, with the same Title, and an Appointment of 4,000 Roubles.'[55] Rogerson soon became a fixture at Catherine's court and in the British community in Petersburg.

His medical reputation was decidedly ambivalent. He was praised for his skill by such patients and friends as Princess Dashkova, while Catherine herself kept him at a distance in matters medical (and once commented privately on his proclivity for gossip-mongering at court), and rivals such as Weikard scoffed at his reliance on blood-letting and James's Powders. Still, Catherine sent him with medicine for the counts Orlov and heeded his advice on one occasion not to venture out in the cold with a sore throat.[56] Her bastard son Bobrinskoi praised Rogerson's assiduous care during the influenza epidemic of early 1782 while mentioning his penchant for card-playing.[57]

Though Rogerson was depicted as a powerless onlooker at the deathbeds of Paul's first wife, Grand Duchess Natalia Alekseevna, in April 1776, and of Lanskoi in June 1784, Catherine herself seemed to credit his assistance in overcoming the illness and depression she suffered for several weeks after Lanskoi's demise.[58] The doctor reportedly concluded that the blood taken from her on 27 July 1784 had been 'extraordinarily inflamed', yet she continued to be tormented by a sore throat, flatulence, and chest pains, all of which Rogerson treated with purges and pills (James's Powders again?).[59] He remained devoted to Catherine, who rewarded him in 1795 with an estate of 1,586 serfs on former Polish territory.[60]

Rogerson was widely known in Russia and abroad. Elected to the Imperial Russian Academy of Sciences in 1776 and to the Royal Society in 1779, he was no scholar himself. Rather, he fostered the scientific work of others by supplying seeds and ore specimens from Russia and Siberia to Scottish botanists and mineralogists. As a close friend of Reverend William Robertson, the head of Edinburgh University, Rogerson brought his historical works to the attention of Catherine, who rewarded Robertson with election to the Academy of Sciences and the gift of a gold snuff-box.[61] Catherine, in turn, used Rogerson in 1777 to negotiate with Melchior Grimm concerning the latter's involvement in her proposed school reform.[62] The empress evidently enjoyed Rogerson's company although his official attendance at court – not once in 1784 and only five times in 1785, for instance – hardly reflected their closeness.[63] He accompanied her on the famous Tauride Tour in 1787 and attended her last illness and death in November 1796.

Something of Rogerson's affability and common sense is reflected in the comments recorded by a visiting Oxford don, John Parkinson, on 13 November 1792:

> Dr. Rogerson, a Scotchman and Physician to the Empress, was of our party at a dinner at Mr. Whitworth's. Dr. Rogers [*sic*] told me that the deaths within a certain time were become two in a hundred fewer than they were in the year: and that Putrid Fevers are now very uncommon. He does not think that the Dysentery which People are liable to be seized with on their arrival here is owing to the water so much as to the Air. He reasoning from the Analysis of the water and from the case of several people who have been seized with it without drinking the water.[64]

If John Rogerson was the most eminent court physician of Catherine's reign, his fellow countryman Matthew Guthrie (1743–1807) represented a quite different sort of practitioner on the periphery of the court. Of humbler professional status (he began Russian service in 1769 as a surgeon), less a courtier and more a scholar than Rogerson, Guthrie served as physician to the Noble Cadet Corps in Petersburg from 1778 to his death.

Little is known about Guthrie's own medical practice in Russia, but he achieved considerable international repute through correspondence with such scientific luminaries as Joseph Priestley, John Howard, James Hutton, and Joseph Black. Elected a Fellow of the Royal Society in 1782, he contributed several papers to the *Philosophical Transactions*, gathered a large collection of precious and rare stones, compiled extensive data on the natural history of the Crimea, published numerous articles on Russia in Edinburgh journals, and translated into English one or two of Catherine's own comedies.[65] Rarely if ever did Guthrie appear at court, and it is not certain that Catherine ever made his acquaintance. Besides, it should be remembered that English (or Scottish) practitioners were comparatively few in Catherinian Russia – barely 4 per cent of the MDs authorized by the Medical College to practise in the eighteenth century.[66]

As far as actual medical practice at the Russian court is concerned, little definite can be said, for secrecy shrouded the specifics of most treatments, particularly when Catherine was the patient. If the empress occasionally mentioned in private how she was treated for certain ailments, no direct documentation has been found from the practitioners who supervised her care. Her oft-repeated scepticism about medical knowledge and practice applied especially to herself. 'Medicines interfere with my work', she once told Dr Rogerson when he offered assistance; 'it will suffice if I just have a look at you'.[67] Instead of the usual pills, purges, and blood-lettings that her physicians prescribed, she preferred to rely on nature, i.e. bed rest, relaxation, dietary moderation or fasting, and mild exercise. Her health had become more robust, she boasted to Madame Geoffrin in 1766, because she ignored her physicians and strengthened her constitution by exposing her body continually and successively to cold and heat.[68] Even so, she experienced the usual afflictions of the age – headache, backache, indigestion, colds, fever – all of which may have been exacerbated by her sedentary mode of life, the huge burden of work that she shouldered almost daily, and the array of psychological pressures under which she laboured. Thus, she described one illness to Nikita Panin in 1768:

> I am quite sick, my back hurts worse than I ever felt since birth; last night I had some fever from the pain, and I do not know what to attribute it to, I swallow and do everything that

they wish; yesterday I took a powder, which was so small that, of course, in all its ingredients it did not amount to a grain; and therefore one could expect little effect from it, as proved to be the case in actual fact. They ascribed to this powder the power of causing perspiration, yet, to my extreme regret, although I even accepted the artfully composed dust, perspiration did not dutifully show itself.[69]

Like everybody else, Catherine sometimes treated herself with natural remedies or popular nostrums. She won some renown for championing the efficacy of 'Bestucheff drops' – also called tincture de la Mothe, a popular iron or nerve tonic which in 1762 was available only at single pharmacies in Petersburg and Moscow. In 1780 the empress purchased the secret recipe and published it in the Russian press.[70] In the 1780s, when she began to suffer more frequent 'indispositions', she swore by the substance, quipping in 1786 that she would take eighty drops at age 80![71] From 1784 and her depression in the wake of Lanskoi's death, her health became the subject of constant rumours, and her death or mortal illness was reported in the foreign press so many times that she joked about it to friends such as Dr Johann Zimmermann, court physician in Hanover, whose book *On Solitude* she credited with helping her out of the hypochondria after her loss of Lanskoi on 25 June 1784.[72] Indeed, she stayed out of public view for three weeks, according to the court register.[73] By contrast, the official Petersburg press first mentioned the matter on 23 July: 'The entire Recovery of our Sovereign from the late Indisposition has dissipated the general Alarm of the Nation for the Days of our august Empress.' On 4 August the same newspaper cautioned that 'The bad state of Health of her Imperial Majesty obliges her still to keep her Chamber' until her entire recovery was reported on 20 August.[74] Rarely did official sources offer even this much information about the health of Catherine or other prominent persons. From the few sources available it seems evident that medical practice at the Russian court was considered much like that elsewhere in Europe.

Were Russian court medicine and its practitioners involved in such general concerns as smallpox epidemics and the question of inoculation against smallpox, and in public-health catastrophes like the bubonic plague epidemic of 1770–2? Given the widespread menace and publicity that smallpox and plague generated in Russia and abroad, it should come as no surprise to find some involvement of court medical circles in such matters of pressing attention. As mentioned above, the empress herself harboured vivid memories of the dynastic damage that smallpox could inflict, hence her apprehension at the start of her reign to protect her son against the scourge. Probably on the advice of court practitioners, she directed Nikita Panin, Grand Duke Paul's *Oberhofmeister*, to keep the young man away from crowds that might include infected persons, and the Petersburg police in November 1765 reaffirmed Empress Elizabeth's prohibition of attendance at court or church by anyone with smallpox or other exanthemata at home.[75] The idea of inoculation or variolation was known in Petersburg by mid-century, and there was a physician-inoculator employed there at the start of Catherine's reign. In 1764 the empress even considered submitting Paul to the controversial procedure. As the British ambassador reported on 14 September 1764 (NS),

> The Great Duke seems every day to gain strength, but still his constitution is so delicate that the probability is certainly against his ever living to have children. He has never had the small pox; there was lately the idea of inoculating him, but it was overruled by those who had the immediate care of him.[76]

Supposedly, Grigorii Orlov, Catherine's favourite at the time, advocated Paul's inoculation, whereas Nikita Panin and unnamed court practitioners – in all likelihood, Drs Kruse and Schilling, first and foremost – opposed it as too risky.

The issue receded for the next few years. Paul's improving health and lengthening years dampened fears, such that in 1767 the 12-year-old grand duke himself made fun of the danger to Sir George Macartney, the new British envoy. Asked whether he would attend a masquerade, Paul referred the query to Nikita Panin with a wry remark:

> You know I am a child and cannot be supposed to judge whether I ought to go there or not, but I will lay a wager that I do not go; Mr. Panin will tell me there is a great monster called the small-pox, walking up and down the ball-room, and the deuce is in it, but that same monster has very good intelligence of my motions, for he is generally to be found

precisely in those very places where I have the most inclination to go.[77]

The possibility of inoculation resurfaced with new urgency in 1767–8 when the Austrian Habsburgs including Empress-Queen Maria Theresa were ravaged by the dread disorder, and, closer at hand, it raged in Petersburg, killing Countess Anna Sheremeteva, Nikita Panin's own fiancée, on 17 May 1768.[78] At that juncture Catherine, apparently in consultation with Baron Cherkassov, undertook to hire Dr Thomas Dimsdale, one of the best-known British imitators of the Suttons' new, improved technique of variolation. Earlier that year, in fact, King George III's physicians and surgeons had publicly endorsed the Suttons' new technique with certain qualifications, concluding:

> The Suttons are undoubtedly in some respects improvers in the art of inoculation, but by applying their rules too generally, and by their not making proper allowance for the difference of the constitutions, have frequently done harm. All their improvements have been adopted by other inoculators, and in the hands of these the art seems to be carried to great perfection.[79]

Dimsdale and his son Nathaniel, a medical student at Edinburgh, were privately received by Catherine, with only Baron Cherkassov and Nikita Panin present, on 28 August 1768 and dined with her that afternoon. The empress made known her intention to be inoculated as soon as practicable, but explained that her plans for herself would be kept secret under the pretext that only the grand duke would undergo variolation. When Dimsdale requested the assistance of Catherine's court practitioners, however, she disagreed, offering this explanation (in French):

> You are come well recommended to me; the conversation I have had with you on this subject has been very satisfactory, and my confidence in you is increased; I have not the least doubt of your abilities and knowledge in this practice; it is impossible that my physicians can have much skill in this operation; they want experience; their interposition may tend to embarrass you, without the least possibility of giving any useful assistance. My life is my own, and I shall with the

utmost cheerfulness and confidence rely on your care alone. With regard to my constitution, you could receive no information from them. I have had, I thank God, so good a share of health, that their advice never has been required; and you shall, from myself, receive every information that can be necessary.[80]

Although the Russian court registers ignored Dimsdale's presence altogether, the British ambassador reported that Catherine's intention was 'a secret which everybody knows, and which does not seem to occasion much speculation': indeed, she privately apprised him of her resolve three weeks before the fact.[81] Her criticism of her own court practitioners notwithstanding, Catherine permitted Dimsdale to consult Dr Shulenius, who had performed 1,023 inoculations in Livonia since 1756 using a pre-Suttonian technique, and Dr Andreas Strenge (MD, Erfurt, 1768), whom Nikita Panin had recently hired.[82] Dimsdale also carried out several trial inoculations on other patients, but when the results of these sapped his confidence, Catherine insisted on pursuing the procedure for the benefit of herself, her son, and the empire. Of course, once her inoculation occurred without incident and the date (12 October 1768) became a national holiday, scores of people begged to be inoculated. Clinics were established in Petersburg and Moscow and other towns; and Dimsdale's treatise explaining his technique was published in Russian translation in Petersburg.[83] Furthermore, the honours Dimsdale and his son received – they were named barons of the Russian Empire, with annual pensions, and the father was appointed Catherine's personal physician – certainly advertised the rewards available to talented court practitioners. Dr Dimsdale went shooting with the empress and treated her for a 'pleuritic fever' in March 1769 that kept her in bed for a week. About this 'fever of cold' the British ambassador commented:

Such events are not suffered to be spoken of here; but Her Majesty was pleased of herself to direct him from time to time to give us accounts of her health, which, I have the pleasure to assure Your Lordship, is now in the way to being perfectly re-established; the fever being greatly abated, and only a cough remaining which, without fever in Her Majesty's case, is not likely to be of any consequence.[84]

Following Catherine's lead, many practitioners joined the inoculation bandwagon. Dr Jaenisch, for example, published several tracts explaining the new procedure and supposedly inoculated 589 youngsters at the Moscow Foundling Home in the period 1773–80.[85] An inoculation clinic operated at Tsarskoe Selo at the empress's expense and another at Vyborg in Russian Finland.[86] Dimsdale returned to Russia in 1781 to inoculate Catherine's grandsons, Alexander and Konstantin. While on the Tauride Tour of 1787 the empress enquired by mail about the inoculation of two other granddaughters and she directed Field Marshal Rumiantsev, the governor-general of Kiev, Chernigov, and Novgorod-Seversk *guberniias*, to promote the introduction of inoculation by the Bureaux of Public Charity in co-operation with *guberniia* and district physicians and surgeons, suggesting that they use monastic buildings for that purpose and tap town revenues to provide free inoculation for the poor. *Guberniia* practitioners such as Dr Gund in Novgorod-Seversk, Catherine concluded, could be paid up to 300 rubles extra to oversee the introduction of variolation in the countryside.[87] In short, inoculation offered a superb example of a medical innovation pioneered at court and then provided to the population at large at minimal cost or free. Still, it remains uncertain how widespread variolation became before Jennerian vaccination superseded it in Russia in the early nineteenth century. Perhaps as many as two million inoculations were performed in Russia by 1800.[88]

In the horrific plague of 1770–2, court medical practitioners played a less visible but no less important role than they did in the smallpox inoculation episode of 1768 and after. In May 1770 Dr Johann Lerche, former acting archiater and then city-physician of Petersburg, was dispatched by Catherine to check for plague in the Russian armies in the Danubian Principalities. To be sure, Lerche was not a court practitioner in the narrow sense of the term, but he was personally known to the empress as a man with special experience and expertise in dealing with plague and other epidemics. In the event, Lerche found himself a step behind the plague's relentless incursion into the Russian Empire at Kiev in September 1770 and on to Moscow in December. Lerche confronted the Kiev epidemic in October, just when it began to abate, and he remained there till the following July, when he was transferred to Moscow just in time to witness a full-blown pestilential disaster.[89] As Lerche vainly strove to combat the 'pestilential distemper' on the spot, his medical colleagues in Petersburg were polled by the empress in mid-March for their evaluation of the initial outbreak in Moscow. Catherine ordered Baron Cherkassov to convene all court physicians, doctors, and staff-surgeons in the capital to decide the nature of the disease in Moscow. This was perhaps the single instance of court and non-court practitioners being consulted jointly. Unfortunately, the results of their consultation are not known. Assuming that they did meet, their opinions must have been divided and indecisive, but the issue seemed moot when this second limited outbreak abruptly subsided in early April 1771.[90] Presumably, Catherine consulted informally with her court practitioners as the plague returned for a third time that summer, although no specific meetings or advice have been pin-pointed. That autumn, at the height of the Moscow epidemic, when it was feared that Petersburg itself might be threatened, low-ranking court practitioners were ordered to check the health of the court personnel under their care and to report any unusual symptoms or sudden deaths. The scare soon passed, however, and no plague deaths were discovered near Petersburg.[91]

As a sort of epilogue to this most fearsome of epidemics in Catherinian Russia, the empress in 1786 rewarded surgeon Ivan Vien, a russified German practitioner who had fought the epidemic in the Ukraine, for the compilation and publication of *Loimologia* (St Petersburg, 1786), the first comprehensive plague tractate in Russian. Surgeon to the Izmailovskii Guards Regiment from 1776 to 1789 (staff-surgeon after 1786), Vien may be considered a court practitioner in the broader sense of the term. Through Catherine's patronage, he later became an important official in the Medical College. Possibly he was consulted by the empress and her councillors about the sporadic plague scares and other epidemic alarms in the late 1780s and 1790s.[92] By contrast, his contemporary rival, Dr Danilo Samoilovich, who also wrote extensively about plague (in French and Russian) and who tried several times to win Catherine's favour and to enter Grand Duke Paul's service, found his importunities repeatedly rejected by the empress.[93] Capitalizing on the sensitive subject of plague with the empress was, obviously, a delicate matter.

To conclude this survey, Catherine II's reign witnessed significant changes in the status and organization of medicine at the imperial court. The number of practitioners employed increased substantially, as did the size, expense, and activities of the court itself. A cosmopolitan cadre of court practitioners served substantial numbers of people, presumably providing medical services of acceptable quality. Court practitioners were occasionally consulted about medical matters outside the court; and there were no medico-political scandals at the Catherinian court comparable, say, to the disgrace of Archiater Count Lestocq at Elizabeth's court. Evidently, Catherine's concern to separate court medicine from political concerns, and from the administration of expanded medical services at large, was largely achieved in fact.

Notes

1. Fitzgerald Molloy, *The Russian Court in the Eighteenth Century*, 2 vols (London, 1905), II, p. v. The essay by M. S. Anderson, 'Peter the Great: imperial revolutionary?', in A. G. Dickens (ed.), *The Courts of Europe: Politics, Patronage, and Royalty 1400–1800* (New York and London, 1977), pp. 262–81, ignores medical matters entirely.

2. W. M. Richter, *Geschichte der Medizin in Russland*, 3 vols (St Petersburg, 1813–17), reprinted, Leipzig, 1965, is now quite outdated and, in any case, ends primary coverage with Elizabeth's reign.

3. Philip M. Dale, *Medical Biographies: The Ailments of Thirty-three Famous Persons* (Norman, Okla., 1952), pp. 91–101, gives only a superficial overview.

4. Edward L. Keenan, 'Muscovite political folkways', *Russian Review*, XLV (1986), pp. 116–17, 162.

5. K. Anthony (ed.), *The Memoirs of Catherine the Great* (New York, 1927), pp. 43, 110, 231–2.

6. Ibid., pp. 59–60, 112, 132–5, 169, 194–5, 207, 212, 236–7.

7. C. R. Boxer, 'An enlightened Portuguese: Dr. Ribeiro Sanches', *History Today*, XX (1970), pp. 270–7; *Sbornik imperatorskogo russkogo istoricheskogo obshchestva*, 148 vols (St Petersburg, 1867–1916), VII, pp. 119, 175–76 – hereafter SIRIO.

8. G. Sanshes, *O parnykh rossiiskikh baniakh*, trans. from French (St Petersburg, 1779).

9. V. V. Fursenko, 'Delo o Lestoke 1748 goda', *Zhurnal Ministerstva narodnogo prosveshcheniia*, n. s. XXXVIII (1912), pp. 185–247.

10. Anthony (ed.), *The Memoirs of Catherine*, pp. 136, 155–6, 163, 167, 250.

11. SIRIO, VII, pp. 126–7.

12. *Correspondence of Catherine the Great when Grand-duchess with*

Sir Charles Hanbury-Williams and Letters from Count Poniatowski, edited
and trans. by the Earl of Ilchester and Mrs Langford-Brooke
(London, 1928), pp. 31–2, 35–6, 46, 59, 110, 161, 167, 179–80, 183.
    13. SIRIO, VII, p. 144; anon, 'Kruze, Karl Fridrikh', *Russkii
biograficheskii slovar'*, 25 vols (St Petersburg, 1896–1918); reprinted
New York, 1962, IX, p. 454 – hereafter RBS; V. A. Bil'basov,
Istoriia Ekateriny Vtoroi, 2 vols (Berlin, 1900), II, p. 128, note 1.
    14. SIRIO, VII, p. 116; XLII, pp. 475–6; John H. Appleby,
'"Rhubarb" Mounsey and the Surinam toad – a Scottish physician-
naturalist in Russia', *Archives of Natural History*, XI (1982), pp. 137–9.
    15. SIRIO, VII, pp. 144–9.
    16. Bil'basov, *Istoriia Ekateriny Vtoroi*, II, pp. 163–5; S. A.
Poroshin, *Zapiski* (St. Petersburg, 1844), pp. 12, 541.
    17. J. T. Alexander, 'Catherine the Great and public health',
Journal of the History of Medicine and Allied Sciences, XXXVI (1981),
p. 190.
    18. Anthony Cross, *'By the Banks of the Thames': Russians in
Eighteenth-century Britain* (Newtonville, Mass., 1980), pp. 117–18. On
Teplov, see RBS, XX, pp. 471–8, and Wallace C. Daniel, 'Teplov,
Grigorii Nikolaevich (1717–1779)', *The Modern Encyclopedia of
Russian and Soviet History*, XXXVIII (Gulf Breeze, Fla., 1984), pp.
240–4. Teplov published a pamphlet protesting the medical
treatment he received: *Rassuzhdenie o vrachebnoi nauki, kotoruiu
nazyvaiut doktorstvom* (St Petersburg, 1774).
    19. William Tooke, *View of the Russian Empire During the Reign of
Catherine the Second, and to the Close of the Eighteenth Century*, 2nd edn,
3 vols (London, 1800), II, pp. 229–30.
    20. N. E. Volkov, *Dvor russkikh imperatorov v ego proshlom i
nastoiashchem* (St Petersburg, 1900), p. 19.
    21. L. E. Shepelev, 'Pridvornye chiny i zvaniia v
dorevoliutsionnoi Rossii v sviazi s ikh znacheniem dlia
istoricheskikh issledovanii', *Vspomogatel'nye istoricheskie distsipliny*,
VIII (Leningrad, 1976), pp. 150–63; Volkov, *Dvor*, pp. 16, 42–3.
    22. J. T. Alexander, 'Petersburg and Moscow in early urban
policy', *Journal of Urban History*, VIII (1982), pp. 145–69.
    23. S. M. Troitskii, *Russkii absoliutizm i dvorianstvo v XVIII v.:
formirovanie biurokratii* (Moscow, 1974), pp. 165, 173.
    24. Ministerstvo imperatorskogo dvora, *Opisanie vysochaishikh
povelenii po pridvornomu vedomstvu, 1723–1730* (St Petersburg, 1888),
p. 94; *Vnutrennii byt russkago gosudarstva s 17- go oktiabria 1740 goda po
25-e noiabria 1741 goda, po dokumentam, kraniashchimsia v Moskovskom
arkhive Ministerstva Iustitsii*, bk I (Moscow, 1880), pp. 3–9.
    25. Arcadius Kahan, *The Plough, the Hammer, and the Knout: An
Economic History of Eighteenth-century Russia* (Chicago, 1985), p. 345.
    26. S. M. Troitskii, 'Finansovaia politika russkogo absoliutizma
vo vtoroi polovine XVII i XVIII vv.', in N. M. Druzhinin *et al.*
(eds), *Absoliutizm v Rossii (XVII–XVII vv.)* (Moscow, 1964), pp. 310,
316. Quoting unspecified sources in Petersburg in May 1784, *The
Scots Magazine*, XL (1784), p. 326, offered 'an account of the
expenditure of the Empress of Russia; on an average of several

J. T. Alexander

years':

	Sterling
Establishment of the palace, kitchen, chambers, etc.	260,000
Wardrobe and expense of the person	300,000
Presents	250,000
New furniture	230,000
Buildings	270,000
Libraries, academies, etc.	67,000
Pensions to men of letters	22,000
Stables and journeys	84,000
Allowance to the Grand Duke and Duchess	250,000
Ditto to their children	67,000

27. Tooke, *View*, II, pp. 233–4.

28. Ia. A. Chistovich, *Ocherki iz istorii russkikh meditsinskikh uchrezhdenii XVIII stoletiia* (St Petersburg, 1870), pp. 298–325.

29. *Polnoe sobranie zakonov Rossiiskoi imperii*, 1st series, 45 vols (St Petersburg, 1830), XLIV, pt. 2, *Kniga shtatov*, p. 131 – hereafter PSZ.

30. Ibid., pp. 136, 197; V. B. Frederiks, *200-letie Kabineta Ego Imperatorskogo Velichestva, 1704–1904* (St Petersburg, 1911), p. 398.

31. Anon., 'Puteshestvie tsesarevicha Pavla Petrovicha za granitsu: zapiski unchastnika', *Russkii arkhiv*, no. 12 (1902), p. 451.

32. Tooke, *View*, I, pp. 561–4.

33. SIRIO, VII, pp. 116, 144.

34. Medical college correspondence about practitioners' salaries, 1772, Tsentral'nyi gosudarstvennyi arkhiv drevnikh aktov (Moscow), *fond* 16, *delo* 322, pt. I, pp. 352–352v., 359.

35. Ministerstvo imperatorskogo dvora, *Kamer-fur'erskii tseremonial'nyi zhurnal*, annual vols for 1762–96 (St Petersburg, 1853–96), vol. for 1785, app., pp. 15–16 – hereafter *Kfzh* with year.

36. Frederiks, *200-letie Kabineta*, p. 383.

37. Alexander Brueckner, *Die Aertze in Russland bis zum Jahre 1800* (St Petersburg, 1887), pp. 39–43, 68–9.

38. RBS, IX, p. 454; John H. Appleby, 'A survey of some Anglo-Russian medical and natural history material in British archives from the seventeenth century to the beginning of the nineteenth century', in Janet M. Hartley (ed.), *The Study of Russian History from British Archival Sources* (London, 1986), p. 114; idem, 'John Grieve's correspondence with Joseph Black and some contemporaneous Russo-Scottish medical intercommunication', *Medical History*, XXIX (1985), p. 403.

39. E. G. Baldinger, *Russisch physisch-medicinische Litteratur dieses Jahrhunderts*, pt. I (Marburg, 1792), pp. 43, 46, 60–1.

40. Anon, 'Bek, Ivan Filippov', RBS, II, p. 676; *Kfzh*, 1784, app., pp. 59–60.

41. Anon, 'Kel'khen, Ivan Zakharovich', RBS, VIII, p. 611.

42. *Memoirs of the Princess Dashkov*, edited and trans. by K. Fitzlyon (London, 1958), pp. 110–11, 194, 225, 236, 304–5.

43. Nicholas Hans, 'Russian students at Leyden in the eighteenth century', *Slavonic and East European Review*, XXXV (1957), pp. 557–8.

44. *Kfzh*, 1784, app., p. 75.
45. 'Iz zapisok doktora Veikarta', *Russkii arkhiv*, no. 3 (1886), pp. 230, 236.
46. *Kfzh*, 1784, pp. 31–2.
47. 'Iz zapisok Veikarta', p. 236.
48. Ibid., pp. 230, 236.
49. William Coxe, *Travels in Poland, Russia, Sweden, and Denmark*, 5th edn, 5 vols (London, 1802), II, p. 134.
50. 'Iz zapisok Veikarta', pp. 236–7, 256.
51. Ibid., p. 233.
52. Ibid., pp. 242–50.
53. Anthony Cross, 'John Rogerson: physician to Catherine the Great', *Canadian Slavic Studies*, IV (1970), pp. 594–601; Appleby, 'A survey', pp. 117–18.
54. A. El'nitskii, 'Rodzherson (Rozherson), Ivan Samoilovich', RBS, XVI, p. 290.
55. *Daily Advertiser* (London), 20 March 1776.
56. SIRIO, XLII, pp. 279, 411.
57. 'Dnevnik grafa Bobrinskago vedennyi v kadetskom korpuse i vo vremia puteshestviia po Rossii i za granitseiu', *Russkii arkhiv*, no. 3 (1877), pp. 127–8, 134.
58. Dimsdale diary excerpt in Anthony Cross (ed.), *Russia Under Western Eyes 1517–1825* (London, 1971), pp. 219–27. See also A. G. Cross (ed.), *An English Lady at the Court of Catherine the Great* (Cambridge, 1989).
59. SIRIO, XXVI, pp. 280–1.
60. Cross, 'John Rogerson', pp. 597–8.
61. Appleby, 'A survey', pp. 117–18.
62. George K. Epp, *The Educational Policies of Catherine II* (New York, 1984), p. 91.
63. *Kfzh*, 1784; 1785, pp. 263, 274, 478, 513, 527.
64. John Parkinson, *A Tour of Russia, Siberia, and the Crimea, 1792–1794*, ed. W. Collier (London, 1971), p. 32.
65. Appleby, 'A survey', pp. 119–21; and Anthony Cross, 'British residents and visitors in Russia during the reign of Catherine the Great: tapped and untapped sources from British archives', in Hartley, ed., *The Study of Russian History*, p. 90; Anthony Cross, 'A Royal blue-stocking: Catherine the Great's early reputation in England as an authoress', in R. Auty, L. R. Lewitter, and A. P. Vlasto (eds), Note 66, *Gorski Vijenatas: A Garland of Essays Offered to Professor Elizabeth Mary Hill* (Cambridge, 1970), pp. 91, 96–7.
66. Anthony Cross, 'The British in Catherine's Russia: a preliminary survey', in J. G. Garrard (ed.), *The Eighteenth Century in Russia* (Oxford, 1973), p. 252.
67. El'nitskii, 'Rodzherson', pp. 290–1.
68. SIRIO, I, p. 289.
69. SIRIO, X, p. 249.
70. *Moskovskie vedomosti* (Moscow), supplement, 19 November 1762; 6 June 1780; Hermann Schelenz, *Geschichte der Pharmazie* (Hildesheim, 1962), p. 598. (Cf. also, Appleby, 'John Grieve's

correspondence', pp. 408–9.

71. N. Barsukov (ed.), *Dnevnik A. V. Khrapovitskago 1782–1793* (St Petersburg, 1874), p. 8.

72. M. Semevskii (ed.), 'Imperatritsa Ekaterina II v eia neizdannykh ili izdannykh ne vpolne pis'makh k I. G. Tsimmermannu', *Russkaia starina*, LV (1887), pp. 240, 243, 246, 248, 254, 279.

73. *Kfzh*, 1784, pp. 31–2.

74. *Daily Advertiser*, 20 August, 6 September, 21 September 1784.

75. PSZ, XVII, No. 12,505, 8 November 1765.

76. *Despatches and Correspondence of John, Second Earl of Buckinghamshire, Ambassador to the Court of Catherine II of Russia, 1762–1765*, 2 vols (London, 1900–2), II, pp. 177, 230.

77. George Macartney, 'The court of Russia, 1767', Macartney papers, Osborne collection, Yale University, p. 16.

78. Donald R. Hopkins, *Princes and Peasants: Smallpox in History* (Chicago, 1983), pp. 63–5.

79. *London Magazine*, February 1768, p. 95.

80. Thomas Dimsdale, *Tracts on Inoculation* (London, 1781), p. 17.

81. Public Record Office, State Papers Russia, 91/79, p. 211 – hereafter PROSP.

82. Tooke, *View*, I, p. 589; Ia. A. Chistovich, *Istoriia pervykh meditsinskikh shkol v Rossii* (St Petersburg, 1883), app., p. cccxl.

83. Dimsdale, *Tracts*, pp. 99 –112; S. M. Grombakh, *Russkaia meditsinskaia literatura XVIII veka* (Moscow, 1953), p. 274.

84. PROSP, 91/79, pp. 198v–199.

85. V. O. Gubert, *Ospa i ospoprivivanie*, I (St Petersburg, 1896), p. 248.

86. Frederiks, *200-letie Kabineta*, pp. 373–4.

87. *Kfzh*, 1787, app., p. 23; PSZ, XX, no. 16,533, 20 April 1787. Apparently the physician mentioned in this decree was Dr Otto Huhn (1764–1822).

88. Roderick E. McGrew, with the collaboration of Margaret P. McGrew, *Encyclopedia of Medical History* (New York, 1985), p. 155.

89. John T. Alexander, *Bubonic Plague in Early Modern Russia* (Baltimore and London, 1980), pp. 107–8, 112, 161.

90. Ibid., p. 145.

91. Ibid., pp. 245–51.

92. J. T. Alexander, 'Ivan Vien and the first comprehensive plague tractate in Russian', *Medical History*, XXIV (1980), pp. 419–31.

93. N. K. Borodii, 'Deiatel'nost' D. S. Samoilovicha na Ukraine', *Mikrobiologicheskii zhurnal*, XLII (1980), pp. 531–4.

8

The *Médecins du Roi* at the End of the *Ancien Régime* and in the French Revolution

Colin Jones

A Bourbon king of France woke up to his *premier médecin*.[1] The latter was an unfailing participant in the *première entrée* to the bedside of the king – long preceding the admission of the high officers of state – and checked the monarch's pulse, complexion, and chamberpot before allowing the day's rituals to begin. The day closed too with the *premier médecin du roi* among the last to leave the royal bedside. At all times he attended to the infirmities of the royal person, but also – in the name of preventive medicine – closely supervised the king's diet, had his wine tasted, and watched over his general regimen.

This was a position of considerable symbolic and potential power. No other subject of the absolute kings of France told his or her ruler what to do. That might only be, it is true, to bare his arm (or his arse), but even this was replete with symbolic meanings in *ancien régime* France, where political authority was conventionally focused on the corporeal being of the ruler. Even if we (rightly) dismiss as apocryphal the old 'l'État, c'est moi' tag, the personalized propaganda, coronation ceremonial, portraiture and coinage of Bourbon monarchs, and the thaumaturgic powers ascribed to the king's touch all in their different ways demonstrated that successive monarchs constituted, in some sense, the anthropomorphic expression of 'national' sovereignty.[2]

The *premier médecin*'s propinquity to the person of the monarch was much envied, for by the unwritten rules of court politics, propinquity spelt power. As far as one can judge, this strategic position never led the *premiers médecins* of the last Bourbons at least to generate court intrigue, and though, as we shall see, they were occasionally used as instruments or accessories of court faction, politics of state seem to have passed them by. This seeming failure to exploit their position may partly be explained by another characteristic feature of *premiers médecins*: their social hybridism. The *premier médecin* was of the court all right, but he was not a courtier. His birth was usually respectable, but was emphatically not aristocratic. He was a man of talent, not of birth; a representative of learned culture, not the repository of court lore; and though he might blench at the thought, his status was probably viewed by his superiors at court as contiguous to the world of domesticity. This did, however, give him a certain freedom. He could observe the intricacies of court etiquette; but he would never be expected to master them. In cricketing terms, he was a player among gentlemen. As such, he might even be excused behaviour which in those greater than he would involve ostracism or disgrace. Fagon, Louis XIV's last personal physician, for example, was dirty and repulsive, while Lieutaud, one of Louis XVI's *premiers médecins*, was a kind of bumpkin. In this respect, the king's physicians inhabited the realm of licensed folly which fools and jesters had occupied in the courts of Renaissance princes. A study of such figures will not tell us much, then, about the vagaries of court politics in the last years of the *ancien régime* monarchy. Yet if the *premier médecin*, and others who were entitled to call themselves *médecin du roi*, cut little ice at court, being part of the court meant a lot in the smaller and more parochial world of medical institutions. Indeed, the royal medical household which the king's *premier médecin* headed constituted one of the most important and prestigious parts of the medical establishment of *ancien régime* France – albeit one which has been almost wholly neglected by historians.[3]

It is, of course, eminently unsurprising that the French Revolutionaries – who, fully sensitive to the corporeal transcendance of royal power, cut off the head of Louis XVI – should spare few kind thoughts for officials so deeply encysted within the nexus of privilege, corporatism, parasitism, and treachery which they came to locate in the royal court. The very oath of fealty which the *premier médecin* took between the hands of the king on assuming office – it was stated

Vous jurez et promettez à Dieu de bien fidellement servir le Roi ... ; d'apporter pour la conservation de sa personne et pour l'entretenement de sa santé tous les soins et toute l'in-

dustrie que l'art et la connaissance que vous avez de son tempérament vous feront juger nécessaires; de ne recevoir pension ni gratification d'autre prince que Sa Majesté; ... et
génerallement faire en ce qui la concerne tout ce qu'un fidèle
sujet doit et est tenu de faire, ainsi que vous le jurez et promettez.[4]

– embodied precisely the kind of 'feudal' dependence which the
revolutionaries excoriated as incompatible with the exercise of
political rights. It was at the antipodes too of the kind of relationship between physicians and the wider society which had
emerged as an ideal during the Enlightenment and which the
revolutionaries were to endorse.[5] The last decades of the *ancien
régime* witnessed the emergence of a strain of medical ideology
which prized service and utility to society, largely through commitment to state involvement in public health, and which radi-
ated scientifically based and humanitarian values. A number of
historians in recent years have emphasized the extent to which
this new medical ideology was promoted by the Royal Society
of Medicine, founded in 1776, initially to supervise epidemics
and public health.[6] The disinterested and universalist facets of
the new medical ideology seemed in clear conflict with the archaic, personalized character of service in the royal medical
household. Yet paradoxically, court physicians – and most notably Lassonne, the penultimate *premier médecin* of Louis XVI –
played an important part in the emergence and success of the
Royal Society of Medicine. Clearly, French court medicine
deserves to be better known. As I hope to show, an understanding of the institutional being, the personnel, and the influence of the royal medical household throws unexpected
shafts of light upon the character of the medical profession in
late-eighteenth-century France, and some of the problems
which physicians seeking fame and fortune faced in late Enlightenment and Revolutionary Paris.

The automatic bestowal of transmissible nobility and the title
of *Conseiller d'état* on the *premier médecin du roi* (or *archiâtre*, as
he was sometimes called) demonstrated the esteem which the
post commanded. He had a kind of moral authority over all individuals practising medicine in France, an authority which successive holders of the post in the last generations of the *ancien*

régime sought to expand. More meaningfully for his everyday activities, he was at the apex of the royal medical household, a sprawling corporate entity which at the end of the *ancien régime* had swollen to nearly 200 posts.[7] The *archiâtre* had formal authority over the score or so of physicians attached to the person of the king, who took their oaths between his hands. He had powers of supervision over surgeons – from the *premier chirurgien* down[8] – and apothecaries attached to the royal household. He also had precedence over all physicians and other medical personnel attached to the main personages of the royal family. Table 8.1 shows the size and composition of the royal medical household in 1789, and compares it with the surgical household which was in theory subordinate to it. There is clearly a rough parallelism between the two sides. If the surgeons slightly outnumbered the physicians, it was by nothing like the margin by which they did so in French society at large. In no other community or institution (village, town, hospital, army regiment, and so on) was the ratio of doctors to surgeons as favourably weighted towards the former. In the city of Paris, surgeons outnumbered physicians nearly two to one, and elsewhere in France by as much as ten to one.[9]

Of the numerous individuals whose posts are here listed, all of whom could in social parlance or legal documents call themselves *médecins du roi*, only a very few would in fact have prolonged contact with the monarch, and many might never encounter him at all. Over half the physicians were attached to the main personages of the royal family, each of whom had their own *premier médecin*, and in most cases a considerable medical entourage to boot. Most of these would not expect to come into contact with Louis XVI. Those attached to household regiments attended to the health of officers and men, while those attached to royal châteaux, to royal officials and perhaps servants within them. Even some of the personal physicians of the monarch – the two *médecins oculistes*, for example, and some of the *médecins consultants* – would not have more than fitful intercourse with the monarch.

The seemingly corporative character of the royal medical household was thus in practice something of a sham. The bulk of the work of surveillance of the king's health in the eighteenth century fell on a small number – probably less than 20 per cent – of the *médecins du roi*, working under the direction of the *premier médecin* (Table 8.2). The key role the latter played in the

Table 8.1: Structure of the royal medical and surgical households of Louis XVI in 1789[10]

	Physicians	Surgeons	
A. LOUIS XVI: PERSONAL			
Premier médecin	*(1)*	2	*Premier chirurgien*
Premier médecin ordinaire	1	1	*Premier chirurgien ordinaire*
Médecins servant par quartier	8	11	*Chirurgiens servant par quartier*
Médecin n'ayant pas de quartier		1	—
Médecins honoraires	2	—	
Médecins consultants	8	—	
Médecins oculistes	2	2	*Chirurgiens oculistes*
Médecin pour les analyses	1	—	
	—	2	*Chirurgiens-renoueurs*
	—	2	*Chirurgiens dentistes*
	—	2	*Opérateurs pour la taille*
	—	1	*Chirurgien pédicure*
Total	(24)	(23)	
B. LOUIS XVI: INSTITUTIONAL AND MILITARY			
Royal Châteaux:			
Tuileries & Louvre	1	2	Tuileries & Louvre
Marly	2	—	
Fontainebleau	1	—	
Meudon	2	—	
Bellevue	1	—	
Bâtiments du roi	1	2	Bâtiments du roi
Ecuries du roi	2	—	
	—	1	Venerie
Maison du roi	2	—	
Infanterie	1	—	
Cavalerie	1	2	Cavalerie
Hussards	1	1	Hussards
Gardes Françaises	1	2	Gardes Françaises
Saint-Cyr	1	—	
Cent-Suisses	2	2	Cent-Suisses
	—	4	Gardes Suisses
	—	4	Garde du corps du roi
	—	1	Chargé de la visite des recrues
	—	1	Chargé de la visite des déserteurs, etc.
Total	(19)	(22)	

Continued ...

king's everyday life has already been evoked. He came into his own, of course, when the king fell ill. He called in other physicians for major consultations – always the *premier médecin ordinaire* (Pierre de La Servolle in 1789), who like him was permanently stationed in Versailles, and who deputized for him in his absence – together with any number or combination of

Table 8.1: Continued

	Physicians	Surgeons	
. ROYAL FAMILY			
(a)The Queen			
Premiers médecins	2	2	Premiers chirurgiens
	—	1	Accoucheur
	—	3	Chirurgiens du commun
(b) Dauphin & Enfants de France			
Médecin	1	2	Chirurgiens
(c) Monsieur (=the comte de Provence)			
Premier médecin	1	4	Chirurgiens
Médecin ordinaire	1	—	
Médecins servant par quartier	5	4	Chirurgiens servant par quartier
Médecins consultants	7	5	(miscellaneous)
(d) Mme la Soeur du Roi			
Médecins	6	5	Chirurgiens
(e) Comte d'Artois			
Premier médecin	1	3	Premiers chirurgiens
Médecin ordinaire	1	—	
Médecins servant par quartier	4	4	Chirurgiens servant par quartier
Médecins consultants	10	5	(miscellaneous)
(f) Comtesse d'Artois & les princes ses enfants			
Médecins	3	6	Chirurgiens
(g) Mme Adelaïde (Louis XVI's aunt)			
Médecin	1	2	Chirurgiens
(h) Mme Victoire (Louis XVI's aunt)			
Médecins	2	3	Chirurgiens
(i) Mme Elizabeth			
	—	2	Chirurgiens
Total	(45)	(51)	

RECAPITULATION:	(%)	No.	No.	(%)
Louis XVI: personal	27·3	24	23	24·0
Louis XVI: institutional & military	21·6	19	22	22·9
Royal Family	51.1	45	51	53.1
	100.0			100.0
Total	Physicians	88	96	Surgeons

médecins consultants, depending on their specialisms, plus any surgeons or apothecaries he felt necessary. If the king had to be bled, for example, the premier médecin held the candle and directed operations whilst the premier chirurgien wielded the knife and the principal apothecary the palette.[11] The premier médecin

Table 8.2: Premiers médecins du roi *in the eighteenth century*

Fagon (Guy-Crescent)	1693–1715
Dodart (Claude-Jean-Baptiste)	1715–30
Chirac (Pierre)	1730–32
Chicoyneau (François)	1732–52
Sénac (Jean-Baptiste)	1752–70
Lieutaud (Joseph-François)	1774–80
Lassonne (Joseph–Marie-François de)	1780–88
Le Monnier (Louis-Guillaume)	1788–92

was responsible for issuing medical bulletins on the monarch's health, and for supervising autopsies of the royal corpse – a fate the last two Bourbons in fact avoided, Louis XVI because of the attentions of the public executioner, and Louis XV on account of the contagious and evidently repulsive character of his small-pox(?)-ridden cadaver.[12]

Also assiduous in the personal service of the monarch, in theory at least, were the *médecins du roi servant par quartier* – four groups of two physicians who were permanently stationed in Versailles on a quarterly basis and attended the principal rituals of the king's day (Table 8.3). In practice, it may well be that at the end of the *ancien régime* these officials were not expected to be at Versailles unless specifically convoked.[13] An additional duty incumbent upon them was the holding of free consultations for the Paris population at large between 3 and 5 o'clock every Tuesday afternoon in the Louvre.[14] They also, under the general supervision of the *premier médecin*, vetted potential candidates for the king's cleansing the feet of thirteen paupers on Ash Wednesday, and for the royal ritual of touching for the King's Evil.[15]

The duties of the *médecins honoraires* and *médecins consultants*

Table 8.3: Médecins du roi servant par quartier *in 1789*

January	Michel (Jean-François), DMM Daignan (Guillaume), DMM
April	MacSheehy, DM Reims Magnan (Victor-Amédée), DMM
July	Daniel des Varennes (Léonard), DM Reims La Coudraye de Basseville (Antoine-Thadée)
September	Raulin (Joseph), DMM Retz (Gérard-Hubert), DM Douai

Table 8.4: *Other personal physicians of Louis XVI in 1789*

Médecin n'ayant pas de quartier	Séguy, DM Rome
Médecins honoraires	Poissonnier-Desperrières (Antoine)
	Deslon des Lassaigne (Gérard-Louis), DMM
Médecins consultants	Poissonnier (Pierre), DMP
	Richard d'Uberherrn (François-Marie-Claude)
	Gatti (Angelo)
	Ninnin (Henri), DM Reims
	Thierry, DMP
	Pomme (Pierre), DMM
	Carbury (Jean-Baptiste, comte de), DM Bologna
	Barthez (Paul-Joseph), DMM
Médecins oculistes	Demours (Pierre), DM Avignon
	Demours (Antoine-Pierre), DMP
Médecin pour les analyses	Piot, DM Reims

Note: see list of abbreviations preceding notes.

du roi (Table 8.4) appear to have been no more onerous than attending consultations on the king's health when convoked by the *premier médecin*. In Louis XV's terminal illness, for example, acting *premier médecin* Le Monnier brought in from Paris the eminent practitioners Théophile de Bordeu and Lorry, who were soon supplemented by Lieutaud, Lassonne, and Deslon de Lassaigne.[16] The consultants constituted a kind of pool of varied medical talent: the Tuscan Gatti, for example, was a celebrated practitioner of inoculation for smallpox, while Pierre Pomme was the renowned expert on the vapours. The Poissonnier brothers were experts on naval hygiene and colonial medicine (though Versailles did not have a problem with yellow fever).

This, then, was the official hierarchy of the royal medical household. In fact, as was often the case with other court hierarchies, formal power relations were often undermined by opposing or contrapuntal forces.[17] Théophile Bordeu, the great Gascon proto-vitalist, for example, was probably the most influential court physician in the late 1760s and early 1770s because he was favoured by the king's last mistress, Madame du Barry.[18] Similarly, in the late 1770s, the effective power of *premier médecin* Lieutaud was consistently checked by other powerful court figures such as Joseph Raulin *père* and Lassonne, at that stage only the physician of Marie-Antoinette. It was Lassonne rather than Lieutaud, for example, on whom the young Louis XVI appears to have called to treat the phimosis which was nullifying his marriage.[19] His apparent success seems to have won him the gratitude of the young king – and presumably of his queen – for he succeeded to the post of *premier médecin* on Lieutaud's death.

What were the factors influencing the monarch's choice of his medical officials (if choice there was)? It would appear that the post of *premier médecin* implied neither scientific standing nor even prowess as a practitioner. True, some brilliant luminaries did hold down court appointments: for example, the Montpellier vitalist Paul-Joseph Barthez was *médecin consultant du roi*, Antoine Portal was *médecin consultant de monsieur*, and Félix Vicq d'Azyr was, from 1788, physician to Queen Marie-Antoinette (who coyly called him 'her' *philosophe*).[20] Such men were, however, only on the periphery of the court establishment. Of the men who occupied the post of *premier médecin* in the eighteenth century, only Sénac and Lieutaud cast much of a shadow in the scientific world: Sénac for his work on cardiology, Lieutaud for his commitment to 'practical medicine'.[21]

Nor was the post of *premier médecin* much of a platform for scientific achievement. The domestic round of court ritual for all physicians stationed at Versailles was wearyingly time-consuming. The royal medical household only met together in the pages of the *Almanach Royal*, and had no existence as an organizational, pedagogical, or scientific entity. Indeed, claims on the time of top court physicians were such that little sustained or thorough-going scientific research was possible. It was noticeable that, for example, Sénac's best work was done before he received a court appointment, while a great deal of the scientific output of Lieutaud, Lassonne, and Le Monnier took the form of articles, often written in collaboration with junior colleagues. The career of Claude-Melchior Cornette illustrates the difficulties of pursuing research at court.[22] While still a young apothecary, Cornette had been selected by Lassonne to run his laboratory at Marly for him, and the young man worked hard, producing, both under his own name and in collaboration with Lassonne, a stream of interesting pieces on the applications of chemistry to medical preparations which were read before the *Académie des Sciences* and elsewhere. Doubtless as a reward for his services, Lassonne pushed Cornette through the medical course at Montpellier and, as soon as he was qualified – and after a spell on a commission cleaning up court latrines – he was appointed physician to the queen's aunts. The scientific work dried up almost at once, as Cornette became caught up in the court round and in making his fortune as a practitioner.

Proven scientific ability or practical ability counted far less than the familiarity of a face that fitted or a network of good contacts. Chicoyneau's scientific claims were virtually nil, for example, and even his ability as a practitioner was widely disparaged; Lieutaud was able but preoccupied with dissecting cadavers; while Le Monnier was first and foremost a botanist. It seems clear that private friendships and court clientage systems helped some – and disadvantaged others. Pierre Chirac, for example, was the personal physician of the powerful duc d'Orléans before the latter, as Regent, bestowed him on Louis XV.[23] Chicoyneau, for his part, seems to have been a compromise candidate whose name was acceptable to a number of groups united in their desire to exclude from the post the ambitious *arriviste* Adrien Helvetius, the personal physician of Louis XV's queen.[24] Lieutaud, too, in 1774, seems to have benefited from a similar conjunction of circumstances. Théophile de Bordeu was the front runner for the post in terms of court experience and practical ability, but his fatal association with Madame du Barry ruled him out as personal physician to the puritanical young Louis XVI. 'Ainsi s'est évanoui comme la fumée', he recorded with the poignant dignity of one whose whole career had, Julien Sorel-like, been manipulated towards achieving success, 'je ne sais quel espoir d'avancement et de fortune que j'avais en perspective'.[25]

The patronage of the great was an essential factor for those reaching the highest offices. Lassonne, for example, chosen as *premier médecin* in 1780, had been a court physician since 1757 when queen Marie Leczinska, who would have known his father, also a court physician, had attached him to her retinue. Fortune had smiled in a rather different way on Le Monnier: Louis XVI's last *premier médecin* had been appointed doctor in the hospital at Saint-Germain-en-Laye in the 1730s, and it was seemingly quite by chance that his leisure-time botanizing had won him friendships with the marshal de Noailles and, through him, with Louis XV, a keen gardener. The call to court soon followed.[26] Pierre-Edouard Brunyer, for his part, *médecin des Enfants de France*, buttered up the Polignac clan at court, and probably owed to them his advancement in the favour of Marie-Antoinette.[27]

Family connection could be a key factor in achieving appointment to and advancement within the royal household. Pierre Poissonnier, for example, *médecin consultant* since 1761, helped the career of his younger brother Antoine Poissonnier-Desperrières.[28] Jacques Audirac, physician at Saint-Cyr from 1753, seems to have given a leg up to his younger brother, Félix Audirac de Scieurat, and the two men enjoyed a long court career, specializing in the cumulation of minor household appointments.[29] The father–son relationship was another axis of advancement. Pierre Demours, for example, *médecin oculiste* from the 1760s, brought in his son Antoine-Pierre as his *adjoint* in the 1780s.[30] Joseph Raulin, *médecin servant par quartier* from the 1760s, promoted his son within the royal household, as well as securing him posts in the *Collège Royal* and as a royal censor.[31] The most flagrant example of nepotism concerned the Lassonnes. Himself the son of a *médecin ordinaire* of Louis XV, François de Lassonne groomed his son Xavier for high medical office from an early age. He rushed him through his doctorate at Montpellier in the early 1780s, had him elected as associate member of the Royal Society of Medicine, and made him a royal censor. By the mid 1780s, young Lassonne was doctor in the Versailles infirmary, one of Marie-Antoinette's *médecins ordinaires* and a member of the *conseil de santé* established to oversee military hospitals. It was only the rather unexpected death of Lassonne *père* in 1788 which caused the young man's star to wane.[32]

The importance of patronage and connection in appointments did not rule out the possibility of worthy practitioners achieving court office. Moreover, if one back-door appointee like Raulin *fils* proved to be of little worth, another, Antoine-Pierre Demours, who was to serve as the personal optician of Louis XVIII and Charles X, proved an excellent choice. And one can take it that the king, who did have some choice in the matter, would not wish to be surrounded entirely by medical incompetents. Moreover, the tendency of the king to reward past services brought into the court establishment people of proven worth. Pierre Poissonnier, for example, owed much to the success of a delicate diplomatic mission in the court – only the malicious said in the bed – of the Russian empress Elizabeth in 1759.[33] Medical experience in the king's armies was the more conventional form of prior service. Of eighteenth-century *premiers médecins*, Chirac, Sénac, and Le Monnier had all been military men. Richard d'Uberherrn – originally known as

Richard de Hautesierck – had begun his long career in military medicine in the 1730s. First physician of the French armies in Germany in the Seven Years War, Richard had been picked out in the 1760s by the influential War Minister, Choiseul, and he was soon promoted to the post of principal inspector of military hospitals in France, as well as of *médecin consultant du roi*, and was charged with running an ambitious journal on military medicine.[34] He helped the early careers of a number of young physicians who went on to court appointment, including Jacques de Horne and Menuret de Chambaud. Barthez, Brunyer, Crémoux, Daignan, Jauberthon, Maloët, and Ninnin were other examples of court physicians who had come up through this channel, while Retz and Poissonnier-Desperrières had naval service behind them.

Men with a military background brought tough practical experience, consequent on campaigns pursued in regimental infirmaries or military hospitals – as well as a thorough acquaintance with treatment of venereal disease which could come in handy at court where, according to the plodding analyst of court illnesses, Langhans, more time in bed was devoted to Venus than to Morpheus.[35] A group which was collectively well versed in practical medicine, the court medical establishment had a less top-heavy age profile than, for example, the Paris Faculty (Table 8.5). While the stream of Paris graduates dwindled to a trickle in the 1780s, causing an inevitable ageing in the corpus of the faculty as a whole, the court physicians tended to enter the royal household in their thirties or forties, old enough to have amassed a degree of practical experience, but still young enough to represent a different generation from the increasingly crusty faculty. Moreover, though some court physicians stayed decades at their jobs, there was also a fairly high turnover in some posts (notably for the *médecins servant par quartier*).

Table 8.5: Age of court physicians

	At entry into court	In 1789
30–9	8	3
40–9	15	9
50–9	6	8
60–9	2	6
70–9	—	6
80–9	—	1

Money and connection, then, rather than merit as judged by scientific credentials or the number of one's patients, seem to have been the major determinants of the composition of the royal medical household. The whole edifice was in fact riddled with the system of venal office. The post of *premier médecin*, experts in medical jurisprudence concurred, was not venal and lay entirely within the gift of the monarch.[36] But the same was not true of other positions. The places of *médecin consultant*, for example, were venal in the technical sense of the term: four such posts had been created by the Regency government in 1718, and this number had swollen to eight by mid-century. [37] The other medical posts were outside the formal embrace of state venality, but the government accepted that money exchanged hands over new appointments, and gave its formal endorsement to the practice. In 1755, for example, Lassonne, the future *premier médecin*, sold his place as *médecin ordinaire* to queen Marie Leczinska to Maloin; while in 1764, Chomel sold his place as *médecin servant par quartier* to Daniel des Varennes for 26,000 livres; (hereafter, l.)[38] Although formal governmental monitoring of these posts seems to have been negligible, the State in fact underwrote the whole system by issuing *brevets d'assurance* (or *brevets de retenue*) to those holding medical posts. The *brevet d'assurance* was in essence a state requirement that, on the exchange of an office, the new incumbent should pay the old an agreed sum. The *brevets* that I have been able to uncover show a clear rise over the century (Table 8.6). This may, or may not, have been in line with the trend in other venal offices, for it seems likely that the purchase price of a post was likely to be higher than the sum fixed by *brevet* – Raulin *fils* had purchased his post as *médecin servant par quartier* in 1784 for 32,000 l., yet the *brevet d'assurance* was set at 18,000 l.[39] Even so, the price levels are not strikingly high when set against the formal levels of venal offices: the 60,000 l., attached to the post of *premier médecin* and *premier chirurgien*, for example, would have purchased a place as councillor in a provincial *Cour des Aides*, but represented only about half the going rate for a post of *secrétaire du roi*, the conventional way to purchase noble status; while the level of 15–20,000 l., for a *médecin servant par quartier* at the end of the *ancien régime* was only on a par with a minor judicial official.[40] The issuing of *brevets d'assurance* added a welcome element of financial security for medical officials, since, both inheritable and saleable, they could also be used for securing

Table 8.6: Some brevets d'assurance *issued by the king to members of the royal medical household in the eighteenth century*[41]

1729 *Médecin servant par quartier*	Lassonne *père*	10,000 l.
1753 *Médecin servant par quartier*	Deslon de Lassaigne	12,000 l.
	(increased to 15,000 in 1758)	
1755 *Médecin servant par quartier*	Faure de Beaufort	10,000 l.
	(increased to 15,000 in 1759)	
1755 *Médecin servant par quartier*	Garnier	12,000 l.
	(increased to 15,000 in 1760)	
1757 *Médecin servant par quartier*	Poissonnier-Desperrières	12,000 l.
	(increased to 15,000 in 1761)	
1761 *Médecin ordinaire du roi*	Le Monnier	40,000 l.
1769 *Premier médecin du roi*	Sénac	60,000 l.
1771 *Médecin servant par quartier*	Daniel des Varennes	20,000 l.
1781 *Médecin des écuries du roi*	Erhart	6,000 l.
1782 *Médecin servant par quartier*	Magnan	12,000 l.
1784 *Médecin servant par quartier*	Daignan	15,000 l.
1784 *Médecin servant par quartier*	Retz	20,000 l.
1786 *Médecin servant par quartier*	La Coudraye de Basseville	15,000 l.
1786 *Médecin des écuries*	Ménuret de Chambaud	6,000 l.

loans. In some cases, documents stated categorically that an individual who had lent the capital sum necessary to purchase the office should have first claim on the proceeds of any further sale. In the *brevet d'assurance* issued to Retz in 1783, it is stipulated that the heirs of Bosc d'Antic, Retz's predecessor in the post, should have first claim on the sum of 20,000 l. should Retz die.[42] Similar though less formalized arrangements were probably common. Pierre de La Servolle, whom in early 1790 Louis XVI accepted as *premier médecin ordinaire* and as *survivancier* to the post of *premier médecin* occupied by Le Monnier, was a case in point. La Servolle, born in 1747 in the Périgueux and educated at Montpellier, had come to Paris as a young man to make his fortune. In the late 1760s he served as secretary to Lieutaud, and helped him revise the second edition of his work on the heart. With Lieutaud's blessing – and perhaps his capital – La Servolle took a second medical degree from the Paris Faculty, and showed himself a useful polemical and journalistic aide. In the late 1770s, he served as close adviser to Lieutaud, who by that time was *premier médecin*, in particular serving as his replacement in the free medical consultations offered at the Louvre. The death of Lieutaud in 1780 almost left him bereft, but he managed to wangle a pension out of the government in the light of his services to Lieutaud. He now seems to have switched horses, inveigling himself into Le Monnier's circle. In

Table 8.7: Stipends attached to posts in the royal medical household towards the end of the ancien régime [47]

Premier médecin du roi	34,000 l.
Médecin ordinaire du roi	16,700 l.
Médecin consultant	9,000 l.
Médecin servant par quartier	1,473 l.
Médecin pour les analyses	1,200 l.
Médecin des écuries	200 l.
Premier médecin de la reine	600 l.
Médecin ordinaire de la reine	300 l.
Médecin des enfants de France	15,000 l.
Médecin de Mme Adelaïde	6,000 l.

1790, he made Le Monnier an offer which could only with difficulty be refused. In return for the right to survivance, La Servolle agreed to pay Le Monnier a life annuity of 2,000 l. each year, calculated as 5 per cent of the value of the post according to the *brevet d'assurance* issued for it (though in fact the real price was probably higher).[43]

The purchase of court position was clearly, then, some kind of career investment. Table 8.7, which shows the stipends of a number of court offices towards the end of the *ancien régime*, reveals great inequalities in revenue, which suggest that the formal returns could be nugatory. At the top of the tree, it is true, the emoluments of the *premier médecin* were, in general terms, extremely good. A sum of 34,000 l. represented an income which far outdistanced that of most generals, judicial officials and high household officials.[44] (Moreover, on top of this not inconsiderable sum was income accruing from the *premier médecin's* surveillance of secret remedies and mineral waters.) In contrast, the formal income of many of the lower posts was small – ridiculously small, in the light of the size of the sums necessary for acquiring them – and seemed not to have kept up with secular inflation.[45] The *médecins servant par quartier*, to take another example, each received on top of their regular salaries the princely sum of 17 l. 9s. 4d. for attendance at the ceremony of touching for the King's Evil, an amount which was supposed to cover the expense of a dozen loaves of bread, two *quartes* of table wine and six pieces of game.[46] If this was a career investment, then it was a risk investment, in which elements besides formal remuneration played a part.

To offset the lowness of the formal wages of their posts, some medical officials tried hard to cumulate posts. Non-court posts could be added to a physician's portfolio: Richard d'Uberherrn was chief inspector of military hospitals, a post which Bordeu in the 1770s reckoned was worth 20,000 l.[48] A similar pension was alleged to be attached to the post which Poissonnier held, as superintendent of health and hygiene in the navy and the colonies.[49] De Horne, for his part, picked up a useful pension after 1785 worth 4,400 l. per annum as physician with responsibility for the hygiene of Paris.[50] Court posts too could be cumulated. Deslon de Lassaigne, for example, was in 1789 *médecin honoraire du roi, médecin ordinaire de monsieur*, and *médecin du palais des Tuileries et du Louvre*. The market for pluralism was dominated by the haves rather than the have- littles. Both the last two *premiers médecins* of Louis XVI, Lassonne and Le Monnier, had accumulated posts within the royal household with alacrity. On his death in 1788, for example, Lassonne had also been the queen's *premier médecin* – indeed, Lassonne was said to be the first physician to serve as first physician to a reigning king and queen since Fernel – and also physician to Madame Adelaïde, one of the king's aunts. On succeeding Lassonne, Le Monnier was also *premier médecin* of the numerous medical retinue attached to the person of monsieur (the king's brother, the future Louis XVIII) and in addition the physician of the king's sister.

Pluralism may in any case partly be explained by the fact that there were few physicians willing to attach themselves permanently to the court and reside in Versailles. Only about a dozen of the royal medical household actually lived in Versailles (Table 8.8).[51] That appointment of hospital physician in the town of Versailles was often a way into court service – this was how Le Monnier and Brunyer got started, for example – suggests there was often a hesitancy on the part of court physicians to move from Paris to Versailles. It was, the story ran, only when his clients in Paris began to desert him, that Sénac allowed his name to be put forward for the post of *premier médecin*.[52] There was, it is true, a good, wealthy captive audience at the court in the form of the high aristocracy. The high aristocracy were, however, notoriously bad payers. Nor were there really enough of them to provide good livings for all Versailles-based physicians. The young Claude-Melchior Cornette, for example, after being set up by Lassonne as physician to the king's aunts in 1784, treated dukes and duchesses and their ilk; but the econ-

Table 8.8: Royal physicians resident at Versailles in 1789

Le Monnier (*premier médecin du roi, premier médecin de Monsieur, premier médecin de Mme la Soeur du roi*)

La Servolle (*médecin ordinaire du roi, médecin consultant du comte d'Artois*)

Brunyer, Pierre-Edouard (*médecin du dauphin et des enfants de France, médecin consultant de Monsieur*)

Crémoux, Pierre-Bertrand (*médecin consultant de Monsieur, premier médecin de la comtesse d'Artois*)

Audirac, Jacques (*médecin ordinaire de Mme la Soeur du roi, premier médecin de la comtesse d'Artois, médecin des écuries du roi*)

Audirac de Scieurat, Félix (*médecin ordinaire de Mme la Soeur du roi, médecin adjoint des écuries du roi, médecin de la maison royale de Saint-Cyr*)

De la Bordère (*médecin du comte d'Artois*)

Aubry (Jean-François), (*médecin consultant du comte d'Artois, médecin ordinaire de la comtesse d'Artois*)

Cornette, Claude-Melchior (*médecin de Mme Adelaïde, médecin de Mme Victoire*)

Forestier (*médecin en survivance du comte d'Artois, médecin de la maison du roi et du grand commun*)

Lassonne fils, François-Xavier de (*médecin ordinaire de la reine et du commun*)

Lamairan, Paul (*médecin du château de Bellevue, médecin consultant du comte d'Artois*)

---

omics of his situation also dictated that he spend a great deal of his time attending to the world of domesticity and the trades and professions which serviced the court.[53] Moreover, though income might be good for the popular practitioners, the expense of keeping up appearances at court was great. Even a modish physician like Bordeu, with his embroidered waistcoats and pleasing ways, who had risked everything to secure the jackpot of appointment to the post of *premier médecin*, died a not very rich man, and by 1792 his favourite nephew on whom he had bequeathed much of his estate was writing begging letters to Marie-Antoinette pleading impoverished gentility and invoking his uncle's sterling services at court.[54]

The scale of the pickings to be derived from the town of Versailles and from the denizens of the court was not much of an incentive for establishment at Versailles. Yet the size of the royal medical household grew dramatically in the last decades of the *ancien régime* (Table 8.9). Adventitious factors like the demography of the royal family partly explain such a fluctuation, it is true: the coming of age of the brothers and sisters of Louis XVI in the 1770s and 1780s led to a new rash of jobs, and this expansionist phase was only slightly attenuated by the death of the duc d'Orléans in 1785 and the dissolution of his

Table 8.9: Size of the royal medical household, 1720–89 [56]

1720	17
1730	29
1740	30
1750	35
1760	35
1770	46
1780	89
1789	88

medical household.[55] Nor should we underestimate the importance of possession of the title *médecin du roi* in a very status-conscious society, in leading individuals to seek offices. The possibility of court physicians securing posts in the armed forces or as medical functionaries also probably stimulated demand for places within the royal medical household. Yet it seems likely that it was the access which *médecins du roi* had to the large fashionable and professional clientele to be found in Paris which was perhaps the crucial factor in explaining the growing market for court appointments.

One of the most attractive privileges accruing to household physicians was the right to practise anywhere in France without having a degree from the Paris Faculty. All seem to have chosen the capital.[57] The Paris Medical Faculty had struggled hard over the centuries to keep Paris a virtual closed shop for its own graduates, but its grip was clearly slipping by the late eighteenth century. By the end of the *ancien régime*, high fees – it was said that one would have to pay 10,000 l. for the privilege of a Paris degree, and the course dragged on for anything between five and eight years – were deterring all but a handful: in fact, there was not a single doctorate awarded from 1786 up to the Revolution.[58] This, moreover, at a time when everything we know about Parisian society in the late eighteenth century – the State's increasing utilization of the medical profession, the decline of mortality crises and the growing longevity of the comfortably off, a developing sensitivity to health matters by a population less willing to see in the onset of illness God's immutable judgement – suggests a rapidly rising demand for medical services.[59] A *brevet d'assurance*, as its name suggests, was a useful stand-by if things went badly; the stipend too was a useful fall-back; and court connections might be useful for securing clients and in career terms. In Paris, however, there was big money to be made.

Though the faculty endeavoured valiantly to keep its finger in the dyke, the last decades of the *ancien régime* witnessed a new tide of practitioners in Paris who used royal court appointments as a means of circumventing the traditional faculty monopoly, and setting themselves up in the capital. A number of trials of strength between court and faculty in the last half-century of the *ancien régime* shifted the balance of forces emphatically in the court's favour. In 1743, the faculty had taken legal proceedings against the king's *premier chirurgien* La Peyronie, who had taken a degree at Reims – hardly an exacting qualification: it was said one went to sleep in Reims and woke up a doctor – and had himself appointed *médecin consultant du roi*. However, La Peyronie was able to get a royal *arrêt du conseil* to rule in his favour.[60] Quesnay, scourge of the Paris Faculty in the 1740s, was a surgeon by training who secured a paper medical degree at Pont-à-Mousson as a means of entry into the royal medical household, and this avenue of advancement remained open down to 1789 despite the faculty's protestations.[61] The faculty may have had more success in 1770 when it tried to resist the right to practise in Paris claimed by Ernon and Mahoney, two recent court appointments, and it protested loudly to the king against the build-up in the court's medical establishment following the coming of age of the counts of Provence and Artois.[62] The build-up continued, however. In 1778, it failed to stop the administration of the Paris Hôpital Général from appointing as its physician Gaulard, a non-Parisian graduate who was *médecin des écuries du roi*, even though it argued that hospital appointments in the capital had always been within the sole purview of the faculty.[63] Unofficial directories of medical practitioners working in Paris in 1776 and 1777 reveal a veritable jungle of medical practice – in which physicians were cheek by jowl with surgeons, apothecaries, herbalists, charlatans, wisewomen, and the purveyors of staple remedies – whose spread the faculty was evidently powerless to prevent.[64]

The faculty may have been rendered even more indignant by the fact that many of the court physicians practising in Paris competed with its members in the best neighbourhoods for middle- and upper-class custom. The poorer neighbourhoods of the city had to rely on surgeons, apothecaries, and unlicensed practitioners for the bulk of their medical services; but the court physicians – besides the appeal to snobbery in their very titles

Table 8.10: Known educational backgrounds of royal-household physicians in 1789

	Montpellier	26
	Paris	7
	Reims	6
	Aix	1
	Avignon	1
	Bordeaux	1
	Douai	1
	Nancy	1
	Strasbourg	1
	Italy	3[a]
	Germany	1[b]

Notes: a. One each: Pisa, Rome, Bologna.
b. Giessen (Hesse).

– had many of the most fashionable addresses.[65]

This stage in the age-old battle between the medical faculty and the court had swung emphatically, then, in the latter's favour. Was a new breed of physician threatening the old? The evidence on this point seems equivocal. The geographical origins of household physicians and members of the faculty were not dissimilar.[66] Faculty doctors were almost as likely as household physicians to be provincials. There was probably some kind of gap in age between the two bodies, as we have noted. There was, however, a striking difference in their educational backgrounds: very few household physicians were doctors of the Paris Faculty. Most of the outsiders whose educational background is known were southerners, and a very high proportion of these comprised doctors of the Medical Faculty at Montpellier (Table 8.10).[67]

The struggle between the faculty and the court could be seen, to a certain degree, as merely an epiphenomenon of a more generalized rivalry between Paris and Montpellier. The celebrated imbroglio in the mid-seventeenth century between the Paris Faculty and the Montpellier journalist and medical entrepreneur Théophraste Renaudot had permanently soured relations between the two schools.[68] The Parisians resented the dictum that the kings of France viewed Montpellier – as Louis XIV is claimed to have said – as 'une pépinière d'archiâtres', [69] and tended to choose their *premiers médecins* from the ranks of Montpellier graduates. The zenith of the influence of the great southern medical city was probably between the 1720s and 1740s when, with the aged but sprightly Lodévois Cardinal

Fleury as principal minister, Montpellier luminaries Pierre Chirac and François Chicoyneau served successively as *premier médecin*, aided by their underrated fellow-countryman Eustache Marcot, *médecin des enfants de France*, while the Montpellier surgeon La Peyronie, as *premier chirurgien*, ruled the surgeons of France (and, it was whispered, the *premier médecin*)[70] with an iron fist. From 1752, it is true, no Montpellier graduate was *premier médecin*: Sénac (1752–70) had studied for some time at Montpellier but was a Paris graduate; Lieutaud (1774–80) had passed through the tiny faculty at Aix-en-Provence; while both Lassonne (1780–8) and Le Monnier (1788–92) were Paris graduates. The Montpellier mafia, however, had ways of making its presence felt. Sénac's son-in-law, Jean-François Imbert, was Chancellor of the Montpellier Faculty and, stationed permanently in the capital as military hospitals inspector and then as physician attached to the household of the comtesse d'Artois, he served as Sénac's closest adviser.[71] Perhaps the most influential court physician in the 1760s and early 1770s, moreoever, was the great proto-vitalist Bordeu, who never forgot that he was 'enfant de Montpellier'.[72] Lieutaud had good Montpellier connections, too, for he had studied in the city following his graduation from Aix.[73] Lassonne also cultivated the southern city. His father had been a Montpellier graduate; he pushed his protégé, Claude-Melchior Cornette, through the faculty in the late 1770s; and he did the same for his own son. Although Le Monnier had no evident Montpellier links, his *survivancier* from 1790, La Servolle, was a Montpellier graduate.

Diversity in the educational origins of court physicians signified an ideological variety which often emerged in internecine disputes even within the royal medical household: Pomme was at daggers drawn with Vicq d'Azyr, for example, while Retz was highly critical of the Royal Society of Medicine, which counted many court physicians amongst its membership.[74] Such educational diversity also brought into Paris a doctrinal heterodoxy that the capital might otherwise have lacked, for the Paris Faculty was a stern watch-dog against many forms of innovation. Doctors who had qualified at one of the famous degree mills on the university circuit of eighteenth-century France – 'des boutiques où l'on vend des lettres de docteurs à qui veut en acheter'[75] – would not have much, it is true, to contribute from their Alma Mater. International influences did, however, make themselves felt through those trained in Italy like Carbury, Gatti, and Séguy, or those susceptible to German influences like Will, a graduate of Strasbourg, or Buchoz of Nancy. The numerous royal physicians who had qualified at Montpellier also brought with them a peculiarly strong element of diversity, for the southern faculty had long been renowned for its openness to new approaches. While relations in the eighteenth century between the Paris Faculty and the surgeons degenerated, the Montpellier Faculty managed an interesting *rapprochement* with surgery, and had since the 1720s pioneered a doctorate of surgery which was well ahead of its time, and prefigured the unified medical degrees introduced in 1794 by the Convention.[76] Inoculation against smallpox, too, found more enthusiastic champions among the royal medical household than within the faculty: the practice was popularized in the 1760s by the Tuscan *médecin consultant* Gatti, who had to put up with endless provocation from Paris doctors;[77] Montpellier-educated Bordeu gave it his wholehearted endorsement;[78] and the famous inoculation of the royal family in 1774 did much to popularize the practice among 'enlightened' familes.[79] In 1785, Jauberthon, a qualified surgeon who had taken a medical degree and become *médecin consultant du comte d'Artois*, was charged by the Crown to undertake the inoculation of every foundling and orphan within the walls of the nation's hospitals.[80]

However, doctrinal heterodoxy also signified ideas and practices which found less acclaim with posterity than inoculation. Witness, for example, the career of Pierre Pomme, whose bestselling *Traité des affections vapoureuses* was published in 1763 and who was able to utilize his appointment as *médecin consultant du roi* from 1768 in a calculated campaign of self-promotion which made him an avowed millionaire. If the faculty tended to take the vapours lightly, it gave no credence either to the somewhat quizzical theories on medical electricity preached by a certain *médecin des écuries du comte d'Artois* (from 1778 to 1785) called Jean-Paul Marat (whose medical writings found their way into the library of Marie-Antoinette). Doubtless it took more than faculty disapproval to turn him into the ardent revolutionary, regicide, and *ami du peuple* of the 1790s.[81] Banau, Seiffert, and Faure de Beaufort (the latter a zealous enthusiast for baths in all shapes and sizes)[82] were other court physicians around whom there was an aura of charlatanism.

The work of men like Pomme and Marat made the faculty

frown; that of Mesmer turned it apoplectic. It was noticeable that ardent enthusiasts of the Mesmerist creed were to be found among the ranks of court physicians. The most prominent French Mesmerist, for example, whom the faculty expelled from its midst in 1784, was Charles-Nicolas Deslon, *médecin ordinaire du comte d'Artois* from 1776 to 1785.[83] Another court physician associated with the Mesmerists was Delaporte, who in the early 1780s declared himself the 'partisan outré de M. Mesmer'[84] and whom the faculty censured in 1784.[85] In 1787, when the Mesmerist bubble had almost burst, Mesmer's practice on the Rue Coq Heron was transferred to the Rue neuve Sainte-Eustache where its direction was entrusted to de la Motte, *médecin du duc d'Orléans*.[86]

The Bourbon court seems to have acquired a reputation in the final years of the *ancien régime* as a kind of open house for medical con men. Every passing medical fad or fancy seemed to provoke ripples among the denizens of Versailles. In 1781, even as France's medical and scientific establishment was heaping opprobrium on Mesmer, Marie-Antoinette offered to found a clinic for the Viennese charlatan and to award him a fat pension for carrying out experiments in France.[87] Earlier, in 1771, the ducs de Chaulnes and de Chartres (the future Philippe-Egalité) had become involved in a sensational episode involving the physician Guilbert de Préval, who claimed to have invented a prophylactic against venereal disease, and who, to prove its worth, displayed himself to the voyeuristic young princes having intercourse with a syphilitic prostitute.[88] A number of court figures had been involved, too, with the entertainingly entrepreneurial Lefebvre de Saint-Ildephont, *médecin de la Prévôte de l'Hôtel du Roi* in 1776, whose idea of anti-venereal chocolate drops – one could even medicate one's wife against infection by offering her regular boxes of chocolates – scandalized the faculty.[89] Geille de Saint-Léger, *médecin de la cavalerie* in 1789, was another slightly disreputable venereologist, 'très renommé', it was said, 'parmi les filles'.[90] It seemed symptomatic of the court's approach to medical exoticism that even at the deathbed of Louis XV – as indeed earlier at that of Louis XIV – a charlatan was admitted to the royal bedside to offer help where the royal physicians had failed.[91]

The faculty retained its most caustic criticisms of the medical charlatanism at the court of Louis XVI for the Royal Society of Medicine, which was founded in 1776.[92] The Society, presided over by the *premier médecin du roi*, and with the ambitious Norman physician Vicq d'Azyr, who in 1788 would be made Marie-Antoinette's personal physician, as its permanent secretary, constituted an information network and research institute for epidemic disease and medical topography, as well as a licensing body for mineral waters and proprietary remedies.

The faculty's attack on the Royal Society of Medicine over charlatanism may well seem – in the light of the Society's own crusade to outlaw medical charlatanism – somewhat surprising to recent historians, who have tended to view the Society as the scourge rather than the refuge of medical charlatanism, as the bearer of professional modernization and societal medicalization, and as situated at the confluence of knowledge and power. In none of the recent accounts of the Society does the court figure except episodically and peripherally. It would, of course, be silly to suggest that the scientific and utilitarian creed preached by the Society was somehow artificial or hypocritical (though it must be admitted that historians of the Society have tended to study the words of the Society's main eulogist and ideological mouthpiece, Vicq d'Azyr, rather than to scrutinize his pockets). Nevertheless, it does seem worth considering motivations behind the foundation and functioning of the Society which go beyond the evocation of scientific curiosity and state power, and which reflect values of the court milieu which sponsored the Society. While it is certainly helpful to visualize the activities of the Society as a kind of medical crusade against ignorance and error, it is revealing, too, to see them as an enterprise, and perhaps even as a racket. Certainly, a great many contemporaries of good faith – Joseph Lieutaud, *premier médecin* for one – had their suspicions.[93]

Such has been historians' identification of the Society of Medicine with its apologist, Vicq d'Azyr, that it needs to be underlined that the main progenitor of the whole operation was in fact Lassonne, a court physician based at Versailles since the 1750s, and from 1780 *premier médecin*.[94] While the Society's origins may be traced back to the mission on which Contrôleur-Général Turgot sent the young Vicq d'Azyr in 1774 to review and to combat the progress of a serious epizootic raging in south-west France, the promotion of this enterprise into the kind of league the Society achieved from 1778 was unthinkable without powerful friends at court. *Premier médecin* Pierre Chirac's attempts in the 1720s and early 1730s to establish a 'medical academy' had died with him before anything effective could be achieved.[95] Similarly, Richard d'Uberherrn had in the 1760s attempted to create a body for the collection and diffusion of medical information with the backing of the powerful duc de Choiseul; but when Choiseul fell from favour, the whole enterprise had aborted.[96] The Society would never have achieved the position it enjoyed without Lassonne's help at court. Lassonne secured the correct authorizations for the Society; he had himself placed as life president of the Society; and he constantly worked for favours at court for the new body. He was a canny operator: his decision to create a category of members of the Society, the so-called *membres associés*, who were patrons rather than practitioners of medicine, was particularly astute.[97] One of the first such members was Le Noir, the powerful Lieutenant-général de police for Paris. When in 1781, the Society became embroiled in a pamphlet war against the faculty, Lassonne was able to call on Le Noir to suppress the publication in Paris of any polemics aimed at the Society.[98]

Lassonne was also adept in using cash and prestige benefits as a means of winning the Society supporters within the wider medical profession. The prestige attached to being a member of the Society helped account for the enthusiastic adhesion of many country practitioners throughout France, who would also have been sensitive to the possibility of the Society acting as a pressure group to limit the influence of the activities of the *Académie de chirurgie* and the *premier chirurgien du roi*. There was also the possibility that the Society could act as a ladder for meritocratic promotion – an 'openness to talent' which could only enthuse the neglected provincial practitioner. For the more hard-boiled, prestige was backed up by cash inducements. The Society was able to commandeer funds from the central government at which the cash-starved Paris Faculty could only look askance.[99] Pensions were paid to all associate members – in 1786, for example, over a score of physicians drew them – while expenses were also paid to all members who attended the Society's meetings and to those who engaged in its works (missions to report on epidemics, reviews of secret remedies, and so on).[100] It is noticeable that, while members of the court medical household were numbered within the Society – Cornette, Lassonne *fils*, Michel, de Horne, the Poissonnier brothers, Barthez, Brunyer, La Servolle, Menuret de Chambaud, Delaporte, Coquereau, and Read were all connected with it – Lassonne was able to divide the ranks of the Paris Faculty by inveigling a number of its members into key positions (not least Vicq d'Azyr, but also Poissonnier, Coquereau, Delaporte, ...) and this inevitably undermined the cohesion of the faculty's opposition to the Society.

Arrangements relating to pensions and other inducements underline the importance of the purely commercial side of the operations of the Society of Medicine. The most striking example of a commercial mentality related to the Society's policing of medical charlatanism, namely the controls which it exercised over staple remedies and mineral waters.[101] In both cases, the Society's control represented a repossession of rights which had formerly belonged to the *premier médecin* but whose commercial exploitation had been lost. The *premier médecin's* authority over mineral waters went back to the sixteenth century, and it had been merged with control over proprietary remedies in government legislation early in the eighteenth century.[102] Of *premiers médecins* at mid-century, it was Sénac above all who was most zealous in his exploitation of these rights: he activated the mineral waters trade by appointing a number of inspectors to investigate their supply; he appointed superintendents of different spas to attend to distribution; while his wife (who was said to earn 100,000 l. a year from 'le département des charlatans') oversaw the granting of licences for remedies. It was widely claimed that the *premier médecin's* control over such remedies was little more than a tax from which he and his wife alone benefited.[103]

This lucrative source of additional income to the post of *premier médecin* had, however, been lost in the early 1770s, much to the disenchantment of Lieutaud, who was forever grumbling about his lost prerogatives.[104] While the post of *premier médecin* was temporarily vacant, from 1770, a clique of court physicians, seemingly headed by Joseph Raulin *père*, managed to get the government to approve the establishment of a special standing committee – which became known as the *Commission du Louvre* – which was to be composed of a number of physicians from the court and faculty, together with a group of surgeons and apothecaries, and which was to have sole purview over the licensing of remedies. The commission continued to operate even after the appointment, in 1774, of Lieutaud as *premier médecin*.

Lassonne's role in creating the Royal Society of Medicine should be partly viewed at least as a counter-coup against

Raulin and the *Commission du Louvre*. True, control of remedies did not pass back simply within the control of the *premier médecin*, nor of Lassonne himself, as *médecin ordinaire*. The diversion of control to the Society was, however, an astute move. It satisfied the penchant of Enlightenment medicine – and doubtless Lassonne's own convictions – in favour of committee structures which combined scientific enquiry with authority. It also disguised the extent to which the Society could be manipulated from the top. Although proceeds from the granting of licences in theory passed through the books of the Society, auditing was primitive in the extreme – even that white knight of scientific altruism, Vicq d'Azyr, was a poor accountant.[105] There was a penumbra of uncertainty over the granting of licences, and of appointments as superintendents of mineral spas, which could bring dividends.[106] Despite its neutral and 'enlightened' form, the Society could constitute a powerful lever of potential patronage and self-enrichment.

Did Lassonne use the lever in this way? It is impossible to say with any certainty. However, it is clear that this kind of entrepreneurial stratagem was very much in Lassonne's character; and that his enemies were sure that the Society was a vehicle for personal ambition. Since 1762, Lassonne had been in charge of making up the so-called *boîtes de remèdes*, or *boîtes d'Helvétius*, which since the late seventeenth century the government had sent out to provincial areas devoid of trained medical care as a preservative of the health of the people. Lassonne's assumption of this task was accompanied by moves to rationalize production and distribution, to increase the volume of business – the number of medical chests was increased eightfold in 1769, and augmented yet again in 1776 – and to sponsor research into the product. The research seems to have been lucrative, and Lassonne was able to revise the list of medicines in the chests, introducing products which had been vetted in laboratory research under Cornette at Marly. It was also said that this kind of research was aimed at bringing down cost price: while the government paid Lassonne 55,000 l. each year for superintending this service, it was rumoured that Lassonne spent only 18,000 l. on production.[107] A similar spirit of enterprise was displayed in the Society's monitoring of the mineral waters trades: the number of distribution centres for mineral waters grew from twenty in 1778 to forty-nine by the eve of the Revolution.[108]

While the French economy slumbered, therefore, business boomed for medical entrepreneurs. The fact that Vicq d'Azyr and Lassonne seemed to be operating from behind the protective skirts of the State scandalized the opposition all the more. While stout representatives of traditional medicine like Joseph Lieutaud had their doubts, less principled opponents of the manœuvres of the Society went on to the attack. Lassonne and Vicq d'Azyr were pitilessly lampooned in a string of scurrilous pamphlets.[109] The *premier médecin* should stick to looking after the health of the monarch, it was said. Lassonne was known to have expressed admiration for the Austrian system of medicine, in which the emperor's first physician was 'the head of medicine'.[110] (Contrast the Paris Faculty, where the *premier médecin* was not allowed to jump the queue of precedence.)[111] The motivating forces behind the establishment of the Royal Society of Medicine had been ambition, self-interest, calumny, and intrigue.[112] Where the adjectives of opprobrium heaped on the head of Lassonne dried up, the attack was directed against Vicq d'Azyr, 'un Bas-Normand des plus rusés', a Cromwell.[113] The two men shared all the profits gained by the Society between them. Lassonne was grooming his son as his successor. The Lassonne clique was using for its fell designs men who were not even proper doctors, such as Cornette and most of the *associés libres*, or who, through the Society's system of pensions and rewards or through investment in mineral waters and proprietary medicines, were financially obliged to them.[114] Worst of all, the basis of the Society was 'the cupidity of charlatans', for it was confidently believed that the system of vetting of proprietary medicines was tantamount to getting their owners to pay for the privilege of peddling them.[115] After all, this was how Sénac had operated, and the faculty's hacks did not let Lassonne forget that the Society had approved Laffecteur's notorious *rob anti-syphilitique* in 1780, which made its maker's fortune despite condemnation by the faculty.[116] Through the Society, doctors had become the *confrères* of crooks and charlatans of every hue:

> ... tout Jongleur, Bateleur, Charlatan,
> Homme à Secret, Vendeur d'Orviétan,
> Coupeur de Cors, Prévôt d'Anatomie,
> Faiseur de Baume, Opérateur, Châtreur,
> Baigneur, Major, Renoueur, Herboriste,
> Tondeur de Chiens, Maréchal, Ecorcheur,

Italien, Guérisseur de Vérole,
(Et) ... tous Forbans de la salubre Ecole.... [117]

The picture is of course grossly overdrawn; but there were elements of truth in it. There clearly was a *rapprochement* of a sort between 'establishment medicine' and more 'popular' forms of medicine implicit in the involvement of the *premier médecin* and the Royal Society of Medicine with the 'charlatanism' which was one of the bugbears of Enlightenment medicine. The faculty and its acolytes saw, ranged alongside the Society, the Mesmers, the Guilberts de Préval and the Lefebvres de Saint-Ildephont. The point of the old adage, *hors la Faculté, point de salut,* had not merely been that medical theories without the imprimatur of the faculty were dangerous, but that the faculty promoted an ethic of medical service which contrasted with the brazen commercialism of the open market. Yet in point of fact, these secular certainties were being eroded in the late eighteenth century. The opponents of the faculty could point out that a number of the leading medical charlatans of the period were Paris graduates. The core of Parisian doctors espousing Mesmerist theories were *docteurs en médecine de Paris* – Deslon, Delaporte, and de la Motte to take only three of the best known. Faculty members had uncomfortably close links with the world of modish and even demotic charlatanism too. Guilbert de Préval was a member of the faculty, which had a torrid time in the late 1770s trying to expunge his name from its ranks. [118] The faculty maintained its age-old condemnation of the popular wonder-drug *orviétan*: but the person who had the franchise on its manufacture throughout the kingdom was Dionis, a member of the faculty. [119] There were hosts of other examples which could show that the ideological purity which the faculty claimed for itself was a sham. Medical commercialism – which we may judge a less value-ridden term than 'charlatanism' in describing the social and economic processes at work – transcended politicking and polemic.

Much of the faculty's bleatings about charlatans and about the Royal Society may well have been caused by a shrinkage of its pockets. There was a clear element of anxiety in its complaints caused by the fact that the services of practitioners out of its control – the growing numbers of court physicians practising in Paris, 'charlatans', surgeons, apothecaries, and so on – were being preferred to their own by the public at large. The faculty's closed shop in Paris was breaking down. The changing shape of demand for medical services was, in turn, promoting a more commercially aware medicine. Reputation and publicity were keys to success, as medical satirists pointed out (though they failed to appreciate that science and self-promotion were not necessarily mutually exclusive). What is striking, from the point of view of court medicine, was the way in which a number of court physicians, led by the *premier médecin*, were in the vanguard of this movement. The royal medical household was not collectively involved in the Society's affairs: as one would expect, the movement was individualistic rather than collective. Nevertheless, on the eve of the French Revolution, a group of court physicians was displaying an actively entrepreneurial spirit which was only partly obscured by the rhetoric of and belief in the neutrality of science. In this, they were reflecting changes detectable in the practice of medicine in late-eighteenth-century France.

To scan the pages of the *Almanach Royal* devoted to the royal medical household in the years from 1789 to 1792 is to savour the *ancien régime* apparently uncontested: not even set in aspic, for there was a certain amount of the normal comings and goings in the personnel of the medical household. Le Monnier appears in the 1790 edition for the first time as *premier médecin*, Adam is named as *médecin consultant du comte d'Artois*, Bunel as *médecin ordinaire des bâtiments du roi*, Jacquemin as *médecin des Tuileries et du Louvre*; while in 1791, d'Angerville appears for the first time as *médecin des écuries*, Delaporte as *médecin ordinaire du roi*. Parisian addresses are given for all practitioners (the court having been forcibly shifted from Versailles to Paris in the *journées* of 5 and 6 October 1789). In fact, even at that time, the first trickle of the emigration had started – Artois left Paris the day after the storming of the Bastille, for example – and was already dispersing the personnel of the court, and the royal medical household with it, in a way which made the entries in the *Almanach* little more than a polite fiction.

A considerable literature has raged over the relationship between science and politics in the French Revolution.[120] The most recent scholarship – distinguished by the quality and the perception of its writing – has tended, however, to concentrate on the institutions of 'high science'. To consider the impact of the Revolution on the royal medical household is thus to bring down discussion to a less elevated intellectual level, one less studded with big names and as much grounded in general practice as in research. The trajectory of the institution's fortunes over the 1790s was moreover more uniformly depressing than that of many *ancien régime* scientific institutions: the Académie des Sciences, for example, was eventually transmuted into the Institut, the Jardin du Roi into the Muséum, the Collège Royal into the Collège de France, and so on. The royal medical household, in contrast, lacks this element of continuity, for although there would be court physicians in the nineteenth century, there would never again be an institution with the powers and structure of the *ancien régime* court establishment. The Revolution, for reasons I will outline, made the royal medical household an anachronism and an irrelevance. It also had a major impact, for better and for worse, on the lives of the men who had in 1789 prided themselves on being *médecins du roi*.

Court physicians, and indeed all state pensioners, had found their sources of income increasingly questioned even before the outbreak of the Revolution. The Parisian doctor (and future mayor of Paris under the Terror) Chambon de Montaux, for example, had castigated the 'soi-disans médecins qui achètent des charges illégales qu'on perpétue par un abus dangereux à la société'.[121] Such criticisms may well have been fuelled by the faculty's noisy polemics against Lassonne, and against the burgeoning size of the royal medical household. The growth in prestige of the surgical profession over the eighteenth century, too, left many medical post-holders rather vulnerable to flanking attack.[122] Criticisms swelled in number in the final years of the *ancien régime*, as successive governments, and most notably that of Loménie de Brienne (1787–8), attempted to resolve the State's acute financial problems by massive cuts in household positions and sinecures.[123] The Revolution was to witness the accentuation of this trend. With the financial crisis still looming large, all state pensionaries found their positions subject to close public scrutiny for the first time. Publication in 1790 of the notorious *Livre rouge* – the register of all state pensions – brought into the open forum of revolutionary politics financial affairs which had hitherto enjoyed secrecy and discretion.[124] The establishment of a much-reduced royal Civil List on the English model in 1791 meant the wholesale liquidation of numerous court posts.[125] 'Moins on a de médecins', smugly remarked one polemicist, as if in consolation, 'plus on se porte bien'.[126] The royal medical household crumbled fast.

An additional feature of the Revolution's effect on the royal medical household sprang from the politicization of court service after 1789. The court under the *ancien régime* had been the locus of intrigue and dispute among physicians, but the royal medical household had not represented a political grouping with a clear ideological orientation. Acceptance of a post at court had been a social distinction, not a political statement. Now, with the king and the royal family increasingly entangled in party politics, *ancien-régime*-style apolitical partnership between State and scientist yielded to polarization and partisanship.[127] Whereas many court physicians had viewed their positions at court as a means of serving the State, the revolutionaries now detested them as so many ties of dependence and clientage, undesirable in themselves and probably motivated by reactionary opinions.[128] Even before the famous Law of Suspects of September 1793, which placed a question mark against anyone with court links, the position of a *médecin du roi* was dangerously exposed. The increasingly Manichean discourse on the court thus squashed into one easily labelled bloc which under the *ancien régime* had been a varied and competing spectrum of political and scientific opinion.

Debates on the exercise of medicine and on medical education had a similar effect. In this respect, Vicq d'Azyr was willing to play turncoat. In the elaborate project on medical training which he submitted to the Constituent Assembly in 1790 in the name of the Royal Society of Medicine (*Nouveau Plan de constitution pour la médecine en France*), he launched a surprisingly bitter attack on the royal medical household:

> Si tous les médecins dont les noms sont inscrits sur les listes des cours avaient été seulement une fois appelés à remplir leurs fonctions ensemble, cette réunion d'hommes qui ne se connaissent pas entre eux et qui sont également inconnus aux princes, aurait paru si bizarre que la réforme s'en serait opérée d'elle-même. La plupart de ces médecins n'ont acheté les privilèges dont ils jouissent que pour se soustraire aux examens qu'il faut subir avant d'être admis à pratiquer dans les grandes villes.[129]

Médecins servant par quartier Retz and Daniel des Varennes tried to combat these assertions in a piece which they had inserted in the *Moniteur*. Elsewhere, Retz even proposed the establishment of free medical services throughout France funded out of taxation – a suggestion which fitted in with the (ultimately unsuccessful) endeavours of the national assemblies to erect a kind of 'welfare state'.[130] However, their contention that Vicq was merely exhibiting that 'esprit de corporation' which the Paris Faculty had always exhibited towards court physicians had some truth in it.[131] The Royal Society's pretensions to academic neutrality did not stand very well either against some of the more murky episodes of its history, while it too was a *corps privilégié*. The pot had called the kettle black: what was new in medical polemics?

The vagaries of the medical profession generally in the 1790s were to exact a heavy toll on court physicians.[132] The widespread desire, displayed from the earliest months of the Revolution, to recast the training and the exercise of medicine in France combined in the period following the overthrow of the king with a socially levelling aspiration to cut down to size 'docteurs à perruque payés chèrement pour tenir des séancees académiques', [133] especially after the overthrow of the king in August 1792 and the dismantling of the court establishment. 'Academic' became a dirty word[134] as, in the autumn of 1793, faculties of medicine and even the Royal Society of Medicine (which had unwisely renamed itself the 'Academy of Medicine') were abolished.[135] The exigencies of war – the need for trained medical personnel to care for the wounds and fevers of the *citoyens-patriotes* at the front – brought a rebirth of medical education.[136] In December 1794, three new *Ecoles de Santé* were established, at Paris, Montpellier, and Strasbourg, which were to offer for the first time a unified degree in medicine and surgery, thus destroying the 'medical *ancien régime*', with its archaic division between surgery and medicine.[137] The late 1790s were to witness the restructuring of the forms of medical training throughout France. New links had been forged between the faculties and the State which would place any court establishment in the future firmly on the sidelines.

These changes in the training and practice of medicine were wrought with surprisingly little help from the medical profession in general, and from the former members of the royal medical household in particular. No court physician was to be appointed to the staff of any of the three *Ecoles de Santé* in 1794–5,

Colin Jones

and indeed there were more ex-surgeons on the staff of the Paris school than there were physicians.[138] The only former court physicians to be appointed to the Institut in 1794–5 were Le Monnier and Portal. Nor was the contribution of physicians to the deliberations of the revolutionary assemblies very great. Only twelve of the 600 or so members of the Third Estate were doctors. There were seventeen doctors in the Constituent Assembly, twenty-six in the Legislative Assembly, and thirty-nine in the Convention (none of whom spoke out in favour of the old faculties).[139] At all stages they were quite massively outnumbered by lawyers. Indeed, there was something remarkably anaemic – in all senses of the word! – about the performance of the doctors in the Revolutionary upheavals of the 1790s: only 112 doctors and surgeons were executed during the Terror; no court physician suffered this fate, as far as I can ascertain.[140] Only 294 doctors (together with 293 surgeons) emigrated.[141] The humdrum life of general practice seemed to insulate them from Revolutionary passions: it was as if clients came before commitment.

The core of the royal medical household – the individuals Louis XVI probably would have had most to do with even without a revolution – continued to display the now outmoded virtue of *fidélité*. Le Monnier, La Servolle, and Vicq d'Azyr attended to the minor indispositions of the monarch, issuing medical bulletins read out to the National Assembly amid pious murmurs of concern.[142] Things changed fast in 1792, however. The post of *premier médecin* meant little after the overthrow of the monarch on 10 August 1792, and indeed dark suspicion attended the doctors who were allowed to see the wretched monarch and his family in prison in late 1792 and early 1793. Brunyer, erstwhile *médecin des enfants de France*, whom Marie-Antoinette on the eve of the Revolution had found 'familier, humoriste et clabaudeur', [143] did, at his own peril, come to the Temple prison to care for the infirmities of the king's children (he would suffer a bout of imprisonment for his pains at the height of the Terror).[144] Le Monnier too showed loyalty. He had been at the king's side during the attack on the Tuileries on 10 August, and his life had only been spared, so the story went, because he was recognized as a charitable benefactor of the poor; a stout *sans-culotte* had cleared a path for him through the mêlée and the piles of corpses with the condescending cry, 'Laissez passer le citoyen, c'est le médecin du roi, mais il n'a pas

242

peur, c'est un bon bougre.'[145] Le Monnier visited the king in the Temple, too, though his *protocolaire* insistence on standing bare-headed before the monarch while Louis's *sans-culotte* gaolers lounged around in their *bonnets rouges* can have done him little good.[146] Court manners seemed as antiquated as they were out of place for a monarch soon to have his ultimate, vicarious encounter with the good doctor Guillotin....

Few other members of the royal medical household demonstrated, in the throes of ideological polarization, attachment to their masters. Indeed, as far as it is possible to judge, the overwhelming majority, deprived of the oxygen of pension and place, simply disappeared from view. Several were, it is true, already well advanced in years by 1789, so it comes as no surprise that they had little impact on events. The optician Demours was 87 in 1789, and he died peacefully in 1795. Pierre Poissonnier, Jean-François Aubry, and Claude Coquereau were other court physicians to die unremarked in the 1790s. The military specialist Richard d'Uberherrn had died in 1789. It is simply impossible to say what happened to most of the others. Directories of practising physicians in the Napoleonic period – probably incomplete, it should be noted – reveal a clutch of former court figures still practising: in Paris, there were Portal, Maloët, La Servolle, Antoine-Pierre Demours, and Delaporte; in the environs, Séguy, Michel, and Marescheau; in the Versailles hospital, though Lassonne *fils* had long since been dismissed ('puisqu'il ne fait rien' had been the lapidary comment of the hospital administration), Brunyer and Lamairan continued at their posts until their deaths in 1811 and 1812 respectively;[147] while elsewhere in France one notes Barthez in Montpellier and Magnan on the eastern frontier.[148] It is thus regrettably possible to reconstruct the impact of the Revolution on only a minority of court physicians.

If the performance of the royal medical household over the 1790s seems to have been very low-key, it was also highly diverse, and underlined how little the corporate organization of the household was a factor in their fortunes. Many more court physicians than those suggested by statistics derived from directories of general practice probably chose the path of internal exile at some stage in the 1790s. This was, after all, a stratagem adopted by large numbers of the *ci-devant* privileged classes.[149] Lying low in Paris was not always successful: Brunyer, Séguy, and Poissonnier were imprisoned under the Terror.[150] Le Monnier had sought refuge in the village of Montreuil, just outside the capital and spent his last years – he was to die in 1799 – working as a small-time herbalist, consoled by the warm embraces of his young second wife.[151] The provinces were not always so thoroughly policed. The vapourist Pomme packed his bags for his native Arles and died there peacefully in his bed in 1812. Barthez too chose the path of internal exile. In 1789 he had made a foolish speech urging the nobility to stay aloof from the Third Estate, and had had his windows broken and had been attacked in the streets for his pains. He now moved prudently south, stopping off in Montpellier – he was still Chancellor of the Medical Faculty – then moving on to quieter towns such as Narbonne and Carcassonne. It would only be in December 1800, as Revolutionary passions were subsiding, that he would be recalled to his chair at Montpellier by another Montpelliérain survivor, Jean-Antoine Chaptal, then Napoleon's Minister of the Interior.[152] The fame of the great vitalist was such that, even while still resident in Montpellier, he was appointed physician to the Consular government, and soon to Napoleon's person, as the Emperor strove to recreate the ambience of court life.

Another of Napoleon's personal physicians under the empire was to be Pierre-Louis-Marie Maloët, physician to the king's aunt, Madame Victoire in 1789, and who had had the distinction of nursing the dying Diderot.[153] He – and certain other court physicians – chose external rather than internal exile. When Madame Victoire and her sister Adelaïde resolved on emigration in February 1791, they took to Turin with them their physicians, Maloët and Cornette. The two were an ill-assorted pair: Maloët was committed to the Revolution, and was willing to countenance a republican régime – he petitioned the Convention in 1793 for permission to return to France without being arrested as an *émigré*.[154] Lassonne's former protégé, Cornette, on the other hand, regretted his appointment at Versailles, which had elevated him from a humble background to a life of ease and comfort.[155] Both men had their goods and property in Paris confiscated as *émigrés*. Cornette, who lost thereby a well-stocked laboratory and natural history collection, became increasingly morose, and sickened and died of a fever in Rome in 1794. Maloët, however, while continuing to serve the increasingly impecunious ranks of the *émigrés* in Italy, established links with the Republic's diplomats, and negotiated a safe return to France for himself, probably towards the end of the 1790s. Back in Paris, he re-established contacts with the re-emergent scientific establishment, built up his practice, and was serving as one of the emperor's personal physicians when he died in 1810.

Northern Italy was the destination of other medical *émigrés*. Pierre-Bertrand Crémoux had accompanied the comtesse d'Artois thither as early as the autumn of 1789, and the comte de Carbury returned to Padua a little later, to become professor of physiology at the university.[156] Carbury doubtless felt at home, but Crémoux fretted and pined away from Paris. His views were evidently mixed, for he had made a handsome voluntary donation of 4,000 l. in the *Contribution patriotique* of November 1789. This was not enough, however, to prevent the confiscation of all his property under anti-*émigré* legislation. He tried to hold on to his national identity in these trying circumstances – 'en pays ennemi, le citoyen Crémoux n'a jamais cessé d'être français', his widow claimed in the late 1790s, as she struggled to extract a state pension from the Directorial régime. *Veuve* Crémoux can have done her case little good, however, when she pointed out that her husband had given free medical care to French prisoners-of-war when he had served with the *émigré* forces: the republican government regarded such men as traitors.[157]

Two other former court physicians, Desvergnes and Forestier, also served in the *émigré* armies. Desvergnes, a Montpellier graduate who had been *premier médecin en survivance* to the king's sister in 1789, was by the mid-1790s formally listed as an *émigré*. He served in the medical corps attached to the army of the prince de Condé at Koblenz, and died in uncertain circumstances in 1798. His second-in-command at Koblenz was Forestier, who had served under Rochambeau in the American War of Independence. Though Forestier must have shown at least the trappings of patriotism in 1789, for he was elected a member of the Versailles municipality, he had evidently emigrated shortly afterwards.[158]

It was only to be expected that the onset of war in 1792 should allow the prior military experience of court physicians to reassert itself, and former court physicians served on the republican as well as the *émigré* side. Guillaume Daignan, *médecin servant par quartier* in 1789, who had served in the Seven Years

War, welcomed the Revolution and under the Terror served on the important *Comité de santé aux armées* established by the Committee of Public Safety with a responsibility for all health provisions in the Republic's armies and military hospitals. He would go on to work as a doctor attached to a number of hospitals in northern France, before retiring in 1807. Raulin *fils* was another example of a court physician with military experience putting it at the disposal of the Republic. In the late 1760s and 1770s, Raulin had worked in military hospitals at the Ile de Ré, Valenciennes, and Philippeville before settling down in Paris. Perhaps financially embarrassed by the running down of the court medical household, Raulin still paid 1,700 l. as his *contribution patriotique* in 1789, and was by April 1793 regarded as politically trustworthy enough to be appointed *premier médecin* to the Armée des Côtes du Nord, which was waging war against the Vendéan rebels in western France. Here he established good relations with the fierce *représentant en mission*, Jean-Baptiste Carrier, was assiduous in ensuring good order and sound health measures in military hospitals, and even began short courses of medical instructions for young *officiers de santé*. Carrier's recall and subsequent disgrace left Raulin dangerously exposed, but he died peacefully in the late 1793 leaving a widow, three children, big debts, but a well-stocked wine-cellar and library.[159]

It is conceivable that other minor court physicians filtered into the medical services of the Revolutionary armies. Though most were too old to participate in the general call-up of medical personnel by the law of 1 August 1793, it was well known that 'the reassuring anonymity of military bureaucracy'[160] was a convenient way of losing police tabs and re-establishing political credibility. Vicq d'Azyr's remark to young Des Genettes – who would go on to a distinguished career in military medicine, including outstanding service during Napoleon's Egyptian campaign – as Des Genettes prepared to depart to the army of the Alps – was revealing: 'j'envie votre sort; allez sortir de la tourmente où nous sommes'.[161]

For physicians who had chosen the royal road to fame and fortune in *ancien régime* medicine, the Revolution, with its oscillating fortunes and political uncertainties, posed a frightening range of possibilities. Though it had at first seemed like a great opportunity for the ambitious, the Revolution's ambiguities soon spilled over into the lives of court physicians. At the be-

ginning of the Revolution, Daignan and Retz had made osten-
tatious gifts to the nation,[162] Enthusiasm or patriotism? The
gesture was, of course, one whose sincerity was not easily
judged, and all the more so under the Terror. Faure de Beaufort sent 4,000 bottles of his notorious *eau anti-putride* to the
Convention in Year II, for dispatch to military hospitals at the
front (a gift which one would have imagined was open to mis-
interpretation in that, before the Revolution, members of the
Royal Society of Medicine had adjudged the remedy a dangerous fraud).[163] Piot offered to put on a free medical course for
medical officers destined for the armies, as did the great practitioner Antoine Portal, who in the socially deflationary language of Year II styled himself a mere 'officier de santé'.[164]
(The brilliant Montpellier-trained anatomist would refurbish
his career under Napoleon before going on to found the Academy of Medicine in 1820). However we judge the sincerity of
such gestures, it is hard not to see in them the small chance of
survival for figures whom court connections all too easily condemned.

The ambiguities implicit in the commitment of a former
court physician to the Revolutionary cause came out well in the
careers of Chanvot de Beauchesne, Menuret de Chambaud,
and Chévetel. Beauchesne, *médecin consultant de Monsieur*, had
professed open support for the patriotic party in 1789, and
served on the Paris Commune. Yet when the comte de
Provence emigrated in the summer of 1791, Faure rode post-
haste to Koblenz to assure him of his unswerving devotion, before returning to France.[165] He found this difficult to live down,
and returned to his native Sens on the overthrow of Louis XVI.
He attended meetings of his local *société populaire*, but his failure
to add his name to a petition congratulating the Convention on
voting the king's death led to his imprisonment. He did survive,
however, returning to Paris after Thermidor to rebuild his
practice, and he was to have a distinguished career under the
empire, though in 1815 he rallied to the Bourbons, and was rewarded by appointment as physician to Louis XVIII. Menuret
de Chambaud, too, had welcomed the Revolution, and moved
close to the centre of political action as the physician of Dumouriez, who took him to the front as *premier médecin* of the Armée
du Nord. When in 1793 Dumouriez rebelled against the authority of the Convention, however, and escaped punishment by
fleeing to the Austrians, Menuret, feeling himself utterly com-

promised, fled too. He slipped back into France towards the turn of the decade, and resumed a medical career now increasingly linked to philanthropy.[166] The ambiguities of prior attachment to the Crown come out clearly too in the Revolutionary career of Chévetel, who up to 1788 had been *médecin consultant de monsieur*. Somehow, he became a government spy. He had offered protection to (Doctor) Marat when the latter was on the run from the police in 1790, but this does not seem to have inhibited his penetration of a counter-revolutionary conspiracy concocted by his fellow Breton, the marquis de la Rouërie. He blew the Rouërie conspiracy plot in 1793 to the Revolutionary authorities, going on to marry de la Rouërie's mistress. Further spying assignments, in London and Liège, followed before, under the empire, he settled down to become mayor of Orly. He none the less rallied to the Bourbon cause in 1815.[167]

The experiences of Jean-Geoffroy Seiffert – *ci-devant médecin consultant du comte d'Artois* – offer a further illustration. Just before Robespierre's fall, we find him sending in to the Convention three patriotic songs which he had penned in his native German.[168] The Saxon doctor was either being shrewd or naïvely sincere, for he had only just been released from goal.[169] Seiffert was well naturalized in 1789, having already spent about a decade and a half in Paris. His reputation was evidently good enough for the young new duc d'Orléans to woo him as his physician in 1784 and 1785 (in 1790 he would visit the duke in temporary exile in England, where he had contracted venereal disease). Seiffert's stock rocketed after 1787, when he successfully treated the vapour-prone princesse de Lamballe, the close confidante of Marie-Antoinette. Indeed, Seiffert – whom the Paris Faculty regarded as a charlatan – was even consulted by the queen. Court appointment did not, however, mean court politics, and it was said that the princesse de Lamballe 'traitait (Seiffert) de Republiquain et de Démocrate' [170] – a tendency which can only have been increased by his growing interest in the activities of the Cordelier Club. In the winter of 1793–4, he was arrested as a suspect and closely interrogated by the section de la Montagne. His defence was eloquent: he had always neglected his great clients to serve generously the poor and needy; he was currently sheltering in his home a homeless old man; he had written patriotic odes, polemics, and even plays in German and had offered to have them disseminated as propaganda in

German occupied-territories. A search of his effects revealed piles of papers, written mainly in German but which, it was alleged, 'ne respirent que le plus pur patriotisme'. His release followed soon after. We lose sight of him soon after, though it would appear that his last days were spent preaching the virtues of crackpot philological theories.

There must be no more poignant a parable on the destructive influence of prior court attachment on even the most patriotic revolutionary in 1789 than the final stages of the career of Vicq d'Azyr, the *dauphin* of the French medical establishment on the eve of the Revolution, who, court gossip had it, had only been prevented from acceding to the post of *premier médecin* on the death of Lassonne by his close connections with Condorcet and philosophic salons, and who was still trailing clouds of glory following his succession to Buffon in the *Académie française* in 1788. Vicq d'Azyr's attack on court physicians in his well-publicized plans for the reform of medical education in France in 1790 suggests that he saw a good chance of an outstanding medical and/or political career outside the confines of the royal household. However, the anti-hierarchical, even occasionally anti-intellectual, trend of the Revolutionary years left him increasingly bereft. By 1793, he was writing to Lavoisier (not a wise choice: the great chemist would soon be guillotined for his pre-Revolutionary activities as a *fermier-général*) for help in rescuing the Royal Society of Medicine from the blanket dissolution of academic and university institutions.[171] The progress of the Terror made him consider internal exile, but he felt as compromised in his native Valognes as at Paris and soon returned to the capital. He attempted to maintain political credibility, accepting a number of humble patriotic chores. He presided over the collection of *salpetre* in the *section du Muséum*. David got him nominated to the *Jury national des arts*, and he served on the Commission which inventoried *objects d'art* throughout the Republic.[172] His reports on the teaching of natural history and the education of orphans were competent if unexciting. Still only in his early forties, terminal illness stalked him. It is arguable whether we should believe the Thermidorian propaganda, which had it that he fell fatally ill on witnessing the Fête de l'Etre Suprême (an understandable reaction, by all accounts), and that he died shuddering uncontrollably with the words 'Le Tribunal révolutionnaire' on his lips. One story about his last days, even if apocryphal, does however have a powerful symbolic appeal. 'On disait autrefois à la cour que j'étais complice des philosophes', he remarked self-pityingly in 1793 to Des Genettes 'on dit maintenant que j'étais un valet'.[173]

The royal medical household was perhaps, as Vicq's words suggest, too deeply entangled in the *ancien régime* court to avoid destruction in the Revolutionary maelstrom. To Revolutionary assemblies committed to liberal, constitutional politics and the 'career open to talents', the royal medical household court signified the faction-fighting, intrigue, corporate values, and nepotism which were thought to be the common currency of court life. The importance of courts in political life would never be the same again, since the locus of power had shifted to the ballot-box and the chamber of deputies. Sovereignty was now firmly embedded in the nation, no longer in the body of the dynast. Even before 1792, moreover, the public, utilitarian flavour of the new medical ideology contrasted with the personalized, private, and 'feudal' nature of the link between the *médecins du roi* and the monarch. The logic of change in the 1790s was far too intractable for an institution like the royal medical household – whose capacity for corporative defence was in any case limited – to continue to exercise an important role in medical organization.

The Revolutionary decade cannot thus be said to have had the kind of positive long-term impact on the collective membership of the royal medical household which some historians have detected in other component parts of the medical and scientific establishment. Court physicians were not, in the main, academic high-flyers. But whereas, for example, the history of the *Académie des Sciences* in the 1790s may help to illuminate the future development of science and medicine, the diverse fates of members of the royal medical household provide a more representative cross-section of the medical profession as a whole. The Revolutionary decade constituted a kind of obstacle course in which the fittest to survive proved precisely those who could adapt – and who were lucky. *Mutatis mutandis*, this was probably not so very different from the qualities required for success prior to 1789, among physicians and indeed among a good part of the *ancien régime* bourgeoisie. Historians have been much exercised of late about the composition and the nature of the social elite in late-eighteenth-century France. To the gallery of species now in place in the historiographical menagerie – alongside the proto-capitalistic bourgeoisie of the Jacobino-

Marxist vulgate, the sedate rentiers of G. V. Taylor, Michel Foucault's sinister technocrats and the (well ... *boring*) *notables* of Restoration France – let us now add the Janus-faced court physician, with one foot firmly entrenched in the world of patronage and privilege, the other in the burgeoning field of enterprise and commercialism. Further research on the professions and on other trades associated with the State under the *ancien régime* will be necessary to show how widespread this type really was.

A court medical establishment would be re-established under Napoleon, then Louis XVIII. Its size never approached pre-1789 levels. Despite a few flutters of excitement in the Restoration period, moreover,[174] court physicians would never again have a major role in medical politics. Court medical appointments were now highly politicized: the physicians of Charles X, for example, still had to go along with the ceremony of touching for the King's Evil, with all that that implied about divine-right kingship, and were hardened royalists representing sectional interests rather than the common aspirations of the medical community.[175]

The post-1789 demise of the court as a major influence in France's medical establishment had two other aspects which deserve mention. It represented, first of all, the perpetual subordination of the Montpellier Faculty to the Paris Faculty – a switch in fortunes which has never been adequately explained (though clearly the removal of the easy pathway into Paris-based general practice after 1794 was a major feature reducing the attractiveness of a Montpellier degree and a court appointment). Second, the revitalized and reorganized Paris Faculty had triumphed over the court as well as over its southern rival in a way which had been wholly unpredictable in 1789. The medical ideology which would prevail in the nineteenth century, championed most vividly by the great Paris Medical School – that medicine was a key contributory factor in human perfectibility and happiness; that science was at the disposal of public health; and the medical man was a kind of lay saint – had in the years prior to 1789 been championed by the key court physicians ensconced in the Royal Society of Medicine. By 1800, the Society had been abolished, court physicians were in eclipse, and the Paris Faculty was rising like a phoenix from the ashes of the royal medical household.

Colin Jones

Abbreviations used

AAM	Archives de l'Académie de Médecine
ADH	Archives départmentales de l'Hérault
AFMM	Archives de la Faculté de Médecine de Montpellier
AFMP	Archives de la Faculté de Médecine de Paris
AN	Archives Nationales
BMM	Bibliothèque Municipale de Montpellier
BN	Bibliothèque Nationale
DMM	Docteur en médecine de Montpellier
DMP	Docteur en médecine de Paris
MC	Minutier Central
SRM	Archives de la Société Royale de Médecine

Place of publication, London (for English works), or Paris (for French works) unless otherwise stated.

Acknowledgements

Part of the research for this chapter was funded by the British Academy. It was much improved as a result of discussions at the Wolffenbüttel conference and when I presented a shorter version to a Society for the Social History of Medicine seminar in London in December 1986. Thanks to all contributors there and also to Nigel Aston, Jonathan Barry, Bill Doyle, and Michael Sonenscher for reading and commenting on earlier drafts.

Notes

1. [J]. Verdier, *La Jurisprudence de la médecine en France*, 2 vols (Alençon, 1762–3), II, 58ff.; N. F. J. Eloy, *Dictionnaire historique de la médecine ancienne et moderne* ... , 4 vols (Mons, 1778), III, pp. 249–53; P. J. J. G. Guyot, *Traité des droits, fonctions, franchises, exemptions, privilèges annexés en France à chaque dignité*, 4 vols 1786–8, I, pp. 537–48. These three works are of vital importance in assessing the juridical position of the *premier médecin* and the royal medical household, though they are of less value on the underlying social realities. Useful too are the manuscript notes of Des Essarts, *doyen* of the Paris Faculty, in AAM ms. 3.

2. The *Annales* have been showing renewed interest in the court of late. See in particular M. Valensise, 'Le sacre du roi: stratégie symbolique et doctrine politique de la monarchie française', *Annales. Economies. Sociétés. Civilisations (ESC)*, 1986; and in the same issue, R. E. Giesey, 'Modèles de pouvoir dans les rites royaux en France'; plus E. Le Roy Ladurie, 'Auprès du roi, la cour', ibid., 1984. Cf. too L. Marin, 'Le corps pathétique du Roi. Sur le *Journal de la santé de Louis XIV*', *Revue des sciences humaines*, 1985.

3. There is only a glancing reference to court employment, for example in R. Hahn, 'Scientific careers in eighteenth-century France', in M. P. Crosland (ed.), *The Emergence of Science in Western Europe* (1975), p. 133.

4. Verdier, *Jurisprudence*, II, pp. 249–50; Eloy, *Dictionnaire*, III, pp. 57–8.

5. For medical ideology in the late eighteenth century, see T. Gelfand, *Professionalizing Modern Medicine. Paris Surgeons and Medical Science and Institutions in the Eighteenth Century* (Westport, Connecticut, 1980); M. Staum, *Cabanis. Enlightenment and Medical Philosophy in the French Revolution* (Princeton, New Jersey, 1980); H. Mitchell, 'Politics in the service of knowledge: the debate over the administration of medicine and welfare in late eighteenth-century France', *Social History*, 1981; M. Foucault, *The Birth of the Clinic*, English translation, 1974; J. P. Goubert (ed.), *La Médicalisation de la société française, 1770–1830* (Waterloo, Ontario, 1983); F. Lebrun, *Se soigner autrefois. Médecins, saints et sorciers aux XVIIe et XVIIIe siècles* (1983); and D. Roche, 'Talents, raison et sacrifice: l'image du médecin des lumières d'après les Eloges de la Société Royale de Médecine (1776–89)', *Annales. ESC*, 1977. Cf. also the works cited in note 6.

6. C. Hannaway, 'Medicine, Public Welfare and the State of Eighteenth-century France: The 'Société Royale de Médecine' (1776–93)', University Microfilms (Johns Hopkins University Ph.D. thesis, 1974), 1975. See too her 'The Société Royale de Médecine and epidemics in the *Ancien Régime*', *Bulletin of the History of Medicine*, 46 (1972); *Médecins, climat et épidémies à la fin du XVIIIe siècle* (1972) (esp. the articles by J. P. Peter and J. Meyer); and the excellent C. C. Gillispie, *Science and Polity in France at the End of the Old Régime* (Princeton, New Jersey, 1980), esp. pp. 194–244. Valuable material too in *Histoire et Mémoires de la Société Royale de Médecine. 1776–89*, 9 vols (1779–90).

7. Listings of the royal medical household are given in the annual *Almanach royal*. Biographical materials on individuals holding office in 1789 were found in a very wide variety of sources, many of which are listed below. Particularly useful among printed sources were: L. G. Michaud (ed.), *Biographie universelle, etc.*, 2nd edn, 45 vols (1842–65); Didot *frères*, *Nouvelle Biographie générale*, 46 vols (1852–70); J. Balteau *et al.*, *Dictionnaire de biographie française*, 16 vols (to 'G') (1933–); C. C. Gillispie (ed.), *Dictionary of Scientific Biography*, 16 vols in 8 tomes (New York, 1970); J. E. Dezeimeris, *Dictionnaire historique de la médecine ancienne et moderne*, 4 vols (1828–39); A. J. L. Jourdan, *Dictionnaire des sciences médicales: biographie médicale*, 7 vols (1820–5); L. Dulieu, *La Médecine à Montpellier. iv. L'Age classique (2e. partie)* (1986). Highly useful material was also found in G. Stenheil (ed.), *Commentaires de la Faculté de Médecine de Paris. 1777–86*, 2 vols (1903); and P. Delaunay, *Le Monde médical parisien au XVIIIe siècle* (1905). The catalogues of the BN and the British Library also provided useful details. Of non-published sources, especially helpful were the

archives of the royal household (AN, series 0/1); the compendious *fichiers* of the *Section moderne* of the AN relating to political police under the Terror (series F 7) and to *émigrés*; and the *fichier* concerning the Revolutionary period and the First Empire in the MC. Blanks were often drawn in investigations in these sources; but they were important blanks to make. Pressure of space will necessitate omission of many references from these sources in the footnotes below.

8. In the present chapter, I have chosen not to consider the royal surgical household, a subject which deserves fuller treatment. An excellent overview of the role of the *premier chirurgien* outside the court is provided by Gelfand, *Professionalizing Modern Medicine*. I have also omitted analysis of the rather less important group of royal apothecaries.

9. Surgeons were between four and ten times more numerous than doctors in the different regions of France: J. P. Goubert, 'La médicalisation de la société française', *Francia*, 1980, p. 249.

10. In the 1789 edition of the *Almanach Royal*, on which this table is based, the place of *premier médecin* was left vacant because of the death of the incumbent Lassonne; but in fact Le Monnier had already acceded to the post by January 1789.

11. Verdier, *Jurisprudence*, II, p. 92; Eloy, *Dictionnaire*, I, p. 652.

12. A. Corlieu, *La mort des rois de France depuis François I jusqu'à la Revolution* (1873).

13. This is the view propounded in Eloy, *Dictionnaire*, III, p. 252, and Guyot, *Traité*, I, pp. 545–6 (though not in the earlier Verdier, *Jurisprudence*).

14. The *Almanach royal* gives these details. For the medical household generally, cf. Verdier, *Jurisprudence*, II, p. 71ff.; and Eloy, *Dictionnaire*, III, pp. 251–3.

15. Verdier, *Jurisprudence*, II, p. 73; Eloy, *Dictionnaire*, III, p. 252. See too the classic work of Marc Bloch, *The Royal Touch: Sacred Monarchy and Scrofula in England and France*, English translation (1973).

16. Théophile de Bordeu, *Correspondance*, ed. M. Fletcher, 4 vols (Pau, 1973), III, p. 118 (a wonderfully entertaining source); A. Cabanès, *Le Cabinet secret (1e série)* (1895), pp. 321–31; Delaunay, *Le Monde médical*, p. 137.

17. Cf. N. Elias, *The Court Society*, English translation (Oxford, 1983), pp. 91, 269–71; and Le Roy Ladurie, 'Auprès du roi'.

18. Bordeu, *Correspondance*, III, p. 23, and *passim*.

19. Cabanès, *Cabinet secret, (2e série)* (1897), 17ff.; P. Girault de Coursac, 'La vie conjugale de Louis XVI et Marie-Antoinette', *Découverte*, 1983.

20. Delaunay, *Le Monde médical*, p. 157.

21. Out of all eighteenth-century *premier médecins*, the *Dictionary of Scientific Biography*, for example, has entries for Le Monnier (mainly devoted to botany), Lieutaud and Sénac. Chirac and Lassonne also conducted notable research.

22. A. Desormonts, *Contribution à l'étude du XVIIIe siècle médical:*

Claude-Melchior Cornette (1933), esp. p. 120. Good background to the Versailles medical scene in P. Brassart, 'Contribution à l'étude du monde médical versaillais sous le règne de Louis XVI et pendant la Révolution', unpublished thesis, University of Rennes, 1965.

23. L. Dulieu, 'Pierre Chirac, sa vie, ses écrits, ses idées', *Montpellier médical*, 51 (1957).

24. L. Lafond, *La Dynastie des Helvétius. Les remèdes du roi* (1926), p. 113.

25. Bordeu, *Correspondance*, III, p. 281. Cf. ibid., pp. 95–6. See also G. Cuvier, 'Eloge historique de Louis-Guillaume Lemonnier', *Recueil des éloges historiques lus dans les séances publiques de l'Institut*, 3 vols (1819–27), I, pp. 99–100.

26. Cuvier, 'Eloge de Lemonnier', pp. 88–90.

27. Marquis de Bombelles, *Journal. 1. 1780–4* (Geneva, 1978), p. 289: *II. 1784–9* (1982), p. 84.

28. AN 0/1 685; P. Sue, *Eloge de Pierre-Isaac Poissonnier*, an VII.

29. AN 0/1 606.

30. 'Notice sur M. Demours, père de l'auteur', preface to the first volume of A. P. Demours, *Traité des maladies des yeux*, 2 vols (1818).

31. AN MC XVII 1081 (9 nivôse III) for Raulin *fils*; and for his father, AN 0/1 686.

32. Cf. AN 0/1 679.

33. Sue, *Eloge*.

34. Richard [de Hautesierck], *Recueil d'observations de médecine des hôpitaux militaires* (1767–72); AN 0/1 686.

35. [D.] Langhans, *Essai sur les maladies auxquelles sont sujettes les personnes qui vivent à la cour et dans le grand monde*, new edn (1772), pp. 46–7.

36. Verdier, *Jurisprudence*, II, p. 17; Eloy, *Dictionnaire*, iii. Cf. M. Fay, 'La charge du premier médecin, était-elle vénale?' *Bulletin de la Société française d'histoire de la médecine*, 1903.

37. Verdier, *Jurisprudence*, II, p. 73.

38. Delaunay, *Le Monde médical*, p. 98.

39. AN MC XVII 1081 (19 nivôse III).

40. W. Doyle, 'The price of office in pre-Revolutionary France', *Historical Journal*, 1984, p. 839 and *passim*. Doyle's article subverts the old contention that the value of venal offices fell in the eighteenth century.

41. Details from the 0/1 series in the AN, as follows: 73; 97 & 102; 99 & 103; 99 & 104; 101; 99 & 104; 101 & 105; 114; 117; 125; 126; 127; 127; 128; and 128.

42. AN 0/1 127.

43. AN MC III 1199 (contract 14 March 1789). Some biographical details in 0/1 679; and in La Servolle, *Eloge de Lieutaud* (1781).

44. Verdier, *Jurisprudence*, II, pp. 59 and 71ff.; Eloy, *Dictionnaire*, III, pp. 250–3. Cf. G. Chaussinand-Nogaret, 'Nobles médecins et médecins de cour au XVIIIe siècle', *Annales. ESC*, 1977, p. 854.

45. The rather higher figures given by Chaussinand-Nogaret

('Nobles médecins', pp. 854–5: no source reference given) are likely to be from the very final years of the *ancien régime*, or even from the Revolution.

46. Verdier, *Jurisprudence*, II, pp. 59 and 71ff.; Eloy, *Dictionnaire*, III, pp. 250–3.

47. Sources as at note 46; plus AN 0/1 3799 (Médecin des Enfants de France) and AN 0/1 3765 (Médecin de Madame Adelaïde).

48. Bordeu, *Correspondance*, III, p. 27, Cf. AN 0/1 686.

49. AN 0/1 685.

50. Delaunay, *Le Monde médical*, p. 68.

51. Details of addresses are given in the *Almanach*. Cf. Brassart, 'Contribution', p. 92ff.

52. *Journal et Mémoires du Marquis d'Argenson*, 9 vols (1859–67), vii, p. 204.

53. Desormonts, *Cornette*, pp. 124–5.

54. AN 0/1 3791.

55. His successor – the future Philippe-Egalité – was not a close enough relation to the king to be included in the *Almanach*'s listings, but he did have a medical household, which included Seiffert.

56. *Almanach royal* for the relevant years.

57. Verdier, *Jurisprudence*, II, p. 82; Eloy, *Dictionnaire*, III, p. 253; *Almanach royal*.

58. Delaunay, *Le Monde médical*, p. 22; Stenheil (ed.), *Commentaires*, II, p. 256; Gillispie, *Science and Polity*, p. 216. Cf. (J. Offray de la Mettrie), *Ouvrage de Penelope, ou Machiavel en médecine*, 3 vols (Berlin, 1748–50).

59. Some of these issues are handled, brilliantly, in J. McManners, *Death and the Enlightenment: Changing Attitudes to Death among Christians and Unbelievers in Eighteenth-century France* (Oxford, 1981). Cf. C. Jones, 'Montpellier medical students and the medicalisation of eighteenth-century France', in R. Porter and A. Wear (eds), *Problems and Methods in the History of Medicine* (1987).

60. Verdier, *Jurisprudence*, II, p. 82; Guyot, *Traité*, I, p. 547.

61. Of members of the royal medical household in 1789, both Crémoux and Jauberthon (and possibly others) had surgical training.

62. Stenheil, (ed.) *Commentaires*, II, pp. 15, 72, and so on; Delaunay, *Le Monde médical*, p. 103; Brassart, 'Contribution', p. 78.

63. Stenheil (ed.), *Commentaires*, II, pp. 77–8.

64. [Lefebvre de Saint-Ildephont, Cézan], *Etat de la médecine, chirurgie et pharmacie en Europe pour l'année 1776* (1776); and [de Horne, La Servolle], *Etat de la médecine, chirurgie et pharmacie en Europe et principalement en France pour l'année 1777* (1777). Cf. C. Maillé-Virole, 'La naissance d'un personnage. Le médecin parisien à la fin de l'Ancien Régime', in Goubert, *La Médicalisation*, esp. p. 155ff.

65. Addresses listed in the *Almanach*. Cf. Maillé-Virole, 'La naissance', p. 156.

66. Cf. Maillé-Virole, 'La naissance', p. 166.

67. Figures for Paris are absolute maxima, as they have been checked against lists of Paris graduates in the *Almanach*. La Servolle was a graduate of Montpellier before becoming a DMP, Le Monnier of the faculty at Aix-en-Provence.

68. G. Gilles de la Tourette, *La vie et les oeuvres de Théophraste Renaudot* (1892); H. M. Solomon, *Public welfare, Science and Propaganda in Seventeenth-century France: The Innovations of Théophraste Renaudot* (Princeton, New Jersey, 1972), esp. pp. 162–200.

69. BMM, ms. 142.

70. The correspondence of H. Haguenot, professor at Montpellier, with, *inter alia*, Chirac, Chicoyneau, La Peyronie, and Marcot, is especially instructive on this era of court medicine: ADH Archives de l'Hôtel-Dieu de Montpellier (antérieures à 1790), B 84–93. Cf. also Gelfand, *Professionalizing Modern Medicine*, p. 61.

71. A great deal of detailed information on this partnership may be found in the AFMM. See especially C 71, C 88, F 51, F 52. Cf. ADH C 555.

72. Bordeu, *Correspondance*, II, p. 71.

73. La Servolle, *Eloge de Lieutaud*, p. 5.

74. Delaunay, *Le Monde médical*, p. 148; [Retz], *Nouvelles, ou Annales de l'art de guérir*, t. vi (1790), p. 272.

75. AFMM F46.

76. Gelfand, *Professionalizing Modern Medicine*, p. 153; Dulieu, 'Pierre Chirac'.

77. Delaunay, *Le Monde médical*, esp pp. 291–2.

78. Bordeu, *Correspondance*, III, p. 9.

79. Cabanès, *L'Enfer de l'histoire* (1925), p. 273ff.

80. SRM 168. For a regional example (Languedoc) of the effect of this measure, see ADH C 525, C 4834, 8 F 99 and Archives de l'Hôpital Général de Montpellier G 4.

81. Gillispie, *Science and Polity*, pp. 290–330, for a valuable discussion of Marat's medical ideas.

82. SRM 201.

83. Good discussions of the social phenomenon of Mesmerism in Gillispie, *Science and Polity*, pp. 261–89 (and p. 272ff. for Deslon); and in R. Darnton, *Mesmerism and the End of the Enlightenment in France* (Cambridge, Massachusetts, 1968).

84. SRM 190.

85. Stenheil (ed.), *Commentaires*, II, p. 1170.

86. Delaunay, *Le Monde médical*, p. 355; Stenheil (ed.), *Commentaires*, II, 1557–8.

87. Delaunay, *Le Monde médical*, pp. 296–7; Gillispie, *Science and Polity*, p. 275.

88. Gillispie, *Science and Polity*, p. 259.

89. Delaunay, *Le Monde médical*, p. 100.

90. L. P. de Bachaumont, *Mémoires secrets pour servir à l'histoire de la république des lettres en France*, 26 vols (London, 1780–9), vi, p. 164.

91. Corlieu, *La mort des rois de France*.

92. See above, note 6.

93. Lieutaud was at first designated co-president (with Lassonne) of the Society, but withdrew almost at once and came close to siding openly with the Paris Faculty.

94. The SRM archive was compiled by Vicq d'Azyr; but the role of Lassonne as catalyst and fixer is shown quite clearly.

95. Stenheil (ed.), *Commentaires*, II, pp. x–xi, 52–3; AFMP ms. 578.

96. The best guide to the enterprise, which in many respects resembled the objectives of the Royal Society of Medicine, is the *Journal d'observations*.

97. Lists of members in SRM 114; and in the *Almanach* from 1778.

98. Hannaway, 'Medicine, Public Welfare and the State', pp. 512–13; Delaunay, *Le Monde médical*, p. 326; Bachaumont, *Mémoires secrets*, XVII, p. 62.

99. Gelfand, *Professionalizing Modern Medicine*, pp. 95–7; Bachaumont, *Mémoires secrets*, XI, p. 82.

100. SRM 114. Cf. Gillispie, *Science and Polity*, p. 224, n. 132.

101. For the legal position, cf. Verdier, *Jurisprudence*, pp. 71 and 157; and Eloy, *Dictionnaire*, III, p. 251.

102. Hannaway, 'Medicine, Public Welfare and the State', gives the most complete account of this phenomenon. See also M. Ramsey, 'Traditional medicine and medical enlightenment: the regulation of secret remedies in the Ancien Régime', in Goubert, *La Médicalisation*.

103. Delaunay, *Le Monde médical*, p. 300; Bordeu, *Correspondance*, III, 94. Cf. SRM 114; and M. Tourneux (ed.), *Correspondance littéraire, philosophique et critique par Grimm, Diderot, Raynal, Meister, etc.*, 16 vols (1877–82), IX, pp. 228–9.

104. La Servolle, *Eloge*, p. 11; SRM 114; SRM 33.

105. Gillispie, *Science and Polity*, p. 224 and n. 132.

106. P. Muller, 'Les eaux minérales en France à la fin du XVIIIe siècle', Mémoire de maîtrise, Paris–I, 1975; and *idem* (as P. Cosma-Muller), 'Entre science et commerce: les eaux minérales à la fin de l'Ancien Régime', in Goubert, *La Médicalisation*.

107. Lafond, *La Dynastie des Helvétius*, p. 127ff., 163ff., 195–9; Bordeu, *Correspondance*, III, p. 27; and the polemical piece *Lettre du Signor Miracoloso Fiorentini*.

108. Muller, 'Les eaux minérales', p. 153.

109. A great deal of the polemical literature attacking the Royal Society of Medicine (cited in the notes below) is conveniently grouped in a volume (shelf-mark: 38 435) in the library of the Académie de Médecine. Matthew Ramsey ('Traditional medicine') argues powerfully for the scientific neutrality and disinterestedness of the society over remedies in general and the Rob Laffecteur in particular. However, the economic underpinnings of the trade in proprietary medicines are not examined in his article, which is based largely on the opinions of participants in the trade and in the vetting of medicines, who were in a position to profit from both.

110. *Dialogue entre un citoyen et un docteur-régent de la Faculté de Médecine de Paris, sur la Société Royale de Médecine*, s.l.n.d., pp. 17–18.

111. *Très Humbles et Très Respectueuses Représentations de la Faculté de Médecine en l'Université de Paris au Roi*, s.l.n.d., p. 16.

112. *Lettre de M. Andry à M. Le Vacher de la Feutrie, doyen de la Faculté*, s.l.n.d., p. 7.

113. *Nouvelle Chanson historique sur un air vieux*, s.l.n.d., no page.

114. *Lettre à M. de Lassonne*, s.l.n.d., pp. 1–2.

115. *Dialogue*, p. 11.

116. Delaunay, *Le Monde médical*, pp. 242–3.

117. *Mr. T .... D'O .... à M. le Doyen et à ses respectables confrères*, s.l.n.d., pp. 2–3.

118. Stenheil (ed.), *Commentaires*, II, pp. 62ff. See also Bachaumont, *Mémoires secrets*, X, esp. months April to August, 1777, for the running saga.

119. Verdier, *Jurisprudence*, II, p. 157.

120. See esp. C. C. Gillispie, 'The *Encyclopédie* and the Jacobin philosophy of science: a study of ideas and consequences', D. P. Williams, 'The politics of science in the French Revolution', and comments on these papers by H. B. Hill and H. Guerlac, in M. Clagett, (ed.), *Critical Problems in the History of Science* (Madison, Wisconsin, 1959); R. Hahn, *The anatomy of a scientific institution: the Paris Académie des Sciences, 1666–1803* (Berkeley, Los Angeles, 1971); and *idem*, 'The problems of the French scientific community, 1793–5', *Actes du XIIe. Congrès international d'histoire des sciences* (1968); and D. Outram, 'The ordeal of vocation: the Paris Academy of Sciences and the Terror, 1793–5', *History of Science*, 1983, pp. 251–73.

121. Cited in [Retz], *Nouvelles*, t.v. (1789), p. 264.

122. Gelfand, *Professionalizing Modern Medicine*, esp. pp. 145–8.

123. J. Egret, *The French Pre-Revolution, 1787–8* (Chicago and London, 1977), pp. 43, 45–6.

124. Volumes XIII to XV of the *Archives parlementaires* contain the *Livre rouge* in its entirety.

125. *Procès-verbaux de l'Assemblée nationale*, IV, pp. 11–12.

126. *De la future Maison du Roi* (Saint Cloud, 1790), p. 32. For the *Liste civile*, see J. F. Bosher, *French finances, 1770–95: from business to bureaucracy* (Cambridge, 1970), p. 246.

127. Cf. Gillispie, *Science and Polity*, p. 550.

128. For the Revolutionary critique of domesticity and dependence as incompatible with political freedom, see C. Petitfrère, *L'Oeil du maître. Maîtres et serviteurs de l'époque classique au romantisme* (1986), esp. pp. 190–9.

129. Cited in the *Moniteur*, 31 December 1789 (réimpression, vol. VI, p. 765–6).

130. [Retz], *Nouvelles*, t. iv (1790), pp. 397ff. (This piece was also published separately as a pamphlet.) For the general picture, see C. Jones, *Charity and 'Bienfaisance': The Treatment of the Poor in the Montpellier Region, 1740–1815* (Cambridge, 1982), esp. Chapter 8.

131. *Moniteur*, p. 766.

Colin Jones

132. The history of the medical profession in the 1790s can be followed in D. M. Vess, *Medical Revolution in France, 1789–96* (Gainesville, Florida, 1974); and Foucault, *The Birth of the Clinic*.

133. J. B. Bo. *Rapport et project de décret sur les bases de l'organisation générale des secours publics*, an II, p. 8.

134. Cf. David's swingeing attack in the Assembly on academies as the 'restes trop longtemps subsistants du régime royal et ministériel'. *Moniteur*, XVII, p. 346.

135. The academies were suppressed on 8 August 1793, the Faculties of Medicine on 15 September 1793.

136. Vess, *Medical Revolution*, pp. 137ff.; C. Jones, 'The welfare of the French foot-soldier', *History*, 1980, pp. 206–9.

137. Gelfand, *Professionalizing Modern Medicine*, pp. 175–6.

138. Ibid., p. 176 and n. 10 on p. 252.

139. G. Saucerotte, *Les Médecins pendant la Révolution* (1887), pp. 7, 10, 26, 39.

140. D. Greer, *The Incidence of the Terror during the French Revolution: A Statistical Interpretation* (Cambridge, Massachusetts, 1900), p. 133. In comparison, 433 lawyers and magistrates and 277 high public functionaries were executed over the same period.

141. *Idem, The Incidence of the Emigration during the French Revolution* (Cambridge, Massachusetts, 1951), p. 187.

142. *Procès-verbaux de l'Assemblée nationale*, XXVI; A. Cabanès, *Légendes et curiosités de l'histoire (5e série)* (1922), p. 312. Cf. also the curious (*Lettre de MM Monnier* (sic), *Vicq d'Azir* (sic) *et la Servolle à M. l'abbé Chabrol*, s.l.n.d. (=1791?).

143. F. S. Feuillet de Conches, *Louis XVI, Marie-Antoinette et Madame Elisabeth. Lettres et documents inédits*, 6 vols (1864–73), II, pp. 243–4.

144. Marquis de Beaucourt, *Captivité et derniers moments de Louis XVI*, 2 vols (1892), I, pp. 73n, 138; II, p. 245. See also AN F 7 4620.

145. Saucerotte, *Les Médecins*, p. 104.

146. Beaucourt, *Captivité*, II, p. 137.

147. See esp. the *Dictionnaire des médecins, chirurgiens et pharmaciens de l'Empire française*, an X.

148. Brassart, 'Contribution', p. 33.

149. For example, Greer *(Incidence of the Emigration*, p. iii) reckons that about 10,000 nobles emigrated in the 1790s. As the size of the noble estate was anything between 120,000 and 400,000 individuals, clearly the majority must have lain low during this decade.

150. AN F 7 4620; F 7 4775 (16); F 7 4774 (78).

151. Cuvier, 'Eloge de Lemonnier', pp.106–7.

152. Cf. [R. D. Dufriche Des Genettes], *Souvenirs de la fin du XVIIIe siècle et du commencement du XIXe siècle*, 2 vols (1835–6), gives entertaining details of Barthez's stay in Montpellier.

153. Cabanès, *Légendes*, IV, p. 285.

154. *Procès -verbaux de la Convention nationale*, I, pp. 52, 512.

155. Desormonts, *Cornette*, pp. 161–4, 172–3.

156. *Dizionario biografico degli Italiani*, s. v. Carburi.

157. AN F 7 5036; Saucerotte, *Les Médecins*, p. 109ff.

158. For Desvergnes and Forestier, AN 0/3 2565; for the former, see also AN F 7 4336; and for the latter, Brassart, 'Contribution', *passim*.

159. AN MC XVII 1081 (19 nivôse III); R. Mercier, *Le Monde médical*, pp. 59–61.

160. R. Cobb, *The Police and the People. French Popular Protest, 1789–1820* (Oxford, 1974), p. 161.

161. Delaunay, *Le Monde médical*, p. 158. Cf. B. Pariset, *Histoire des membres de l'Académie royale de Médecine*, 2 vols, 1850, II, p. 201.

162. *Procès-verbaux de l'Assemblée nationale*, V, p. 11; Cf. for Retz, ibid. (23 January 1790); and for Daignan, AN MC II (25 frimaire II).

163. J. Guillaume (ed.), *Procès-verbaux du Comité d'Instruction publique de la Convention Nationale*, 6 vols (1891–1907), iv, p. 271.

164. Ibid., II, p. 600; III, p. 139; AN MC XVI (2 floréal II = 'officier de santé'); and eulogy in Pariset, *Histoire*, II, pp. 1–9.

165. 'Eloge de M. Beauchesne', in Pariset, *Histoire des membres de l'Académie royale de Médecine*, I, pp. 265–6.

166. Including AN F 7 5646; and L. Tuetey (ed.) *Procès-verbaux de la Commission des Arts*, 2 vols (1912–14), II, p. 74.

167. R. Mercier, *Le Monde médical dans la guerre de Vendée* (Tours, 1959), pp. 168–9; and A. Goodwin, 'Counter-Revolution in Brittany: the royalist conspiracy of the marquis de la Rouërie, 1791–3', *Bulletin of John Rylands Library*, 1956–7, esp. pp. 344–7.

168. Guillaume (ed.), *Procès-verbaux*, IV, p. 934.

169. A. Cabanès, *La Princesse de Lamballe intime*, s. d., gives a great deal of biographical material on Seiffert. Much of it is based on the documents concerning him in AN F 7 4775(9) and W 369 which I have consulted.

170. AN W 369.

171. Guillaume (ed.), *Procès-verbaux*, II, pp. 344, 514. Cf. AN F 17 1094.

172. Guillaume (ed.), *Procès-verbaux*, II, pp. 572–5, 829–32; Tuetey (ed.), *Procès-verbaux*; and *SRM* 199.

173. Delaunay, *Le Monde médical*, pp. 158–9. More recently, P. Thillaud ('Vicq d'Azyr: anatomie d'une election', *Histoire des Sciences médicales*, 1986) has diagnosed suicide, albeit on the strength of virtually nothing but a couple of scraps of circumstantial evidence.

174. G. Weisz, 'Constructing the medical elite in France: the creation of the Royal Academy of Medicine, 1814–20', *Medical History*, 1986. For post-1815 circumstances generally, cf. *idem*, 'The medical elite in the early 19th century', *Minerva*, 1987; and J. Léonard, 'La Restauration et la profession médicale', in Goubert, *La Médicalisation*.

175. Bloch, *The Royal Touch*, pp. 226–7 (where it is pointed out that everyone was rather embarrassed by Charles's commitment to the royal touch).

9

Medicine at the English Court, 1688–1837

W. F. Bynum

For God's sake, let us sit upon the ground
And tell sad stories of the death of kings

W. Shakespeare, *Richard the Second*, Act III, Scene ii, 155–6

Introduction

The famous and powerful, doctors sometimes tell themselves, do not always receive the best medical care. Uncomfortable or embarrassing diagnostic procedures may be omitted, with therapy tending towards the conservative as fame and power shield those who possess it from the full panoply of medical knowledge and capacity. Better, this line of reasoning has it, to be an ordinary patient on an active teaching ward, surrounded by young, energetic, newly trained resident staff, than a guest in a five-star hospital, built like a hotel, dishing up good food and cheerful nurses, but more concerned with privacy and comfort than top-flight medical care. Another way of putting this sentiment is that patient domination – often stated to have characterized medical relationships before the rise of modern medicine – may not be in the best interests of the patient him- or herself.[1]

These issues are even starker if the subject is a member of the royal family, or even the monarch himself. How does a mere medical commoner treat that half of the king's two bodies, without which he could neither reign nor rule? In this chapter I will survey briefly some of these ramifications during the long eighteenth century, between the William of William and Mary and the William whose own queen has been described as more Victorian than the monarch who succeeded and bestowed her name on the age itself. In the first main section I will look at the variety of medical problems which confronted the last of the Stuarts and their Hanoverian successors. I will then examine some of the personal relationships between royals and their doctors during the period. Finally, I will attempt to assess the kind of men who were given the responsibility (and reward) of looking after the royal bodies and at the way in which court appointments fit into the changing career patterns of the time. Records of Georgian court life are plentiful, of which those of Lord Hervey, Horace Walpole, and Fanny Burney represent merely the best known. And not simply sovereigns but also their spouses, offspring, and lovers have been subjected to detailed historical scrutiny. Accordingly, this short chapter can do no more than scratch the surface of a topic for which a good deal of useful digging still remains to be done.

Royal patients

It was a widely held eighteenth-century belief that madness could protect from ordinary bodily disease, and seemingly in confirmation of this, the mad King George III lived the longest of the monarchs of our period. To be sure, his longevity was at best a mixed blessing, since the old king spent the last decade of his life at Windsor, in a padded room, blind and demented, hardly aware of the Regency which had first been mooted more than twenty years previously.[2] Only the mad king's grandfather, George II, had also reached the biblical 'three score years and ten', dying as a relatively vigorous old man of 77 years. George I, George IV, and William IV all made it to their later 60s, the more usual Hanoverian norm. George I was five years older than Queen Anne whom he succeeded, and William III and his queen died in their fifty-second and thirty-second years respectively. Anne herself had just missed a half-century.

These may seem respectable achievements in the circumstances – no reigning British monarch since Victoria has yet lived as long as George II, much less George III – but it should be remembered that medical problems and premature deaths did bear significantly on the succession to the throne during the long eighteenth century. Neither Queen Mary nor Queen Anne was able to produce a child to follow them.[3] Frederick, Prince of Wales ('Poor Fred, who was alive and is dead / There's no more to be said') would have become king had he survived his father George II, and William IV spent most of his life out of the line of immediate succession, having to outlive two elder brothers and a niece and her stillborn child to become monarch.[4] His own marriage had produced pregnancies but no live children, which in turn paved the way for another niece, Victoria. Despite these hiccups in the orderly chain of succession, the Hanoverians were a vigorous and highly sexed dynasty and seemed to have had little trouble with fertility *per se*: George III produced fifteen children by his plain wife Sophia Charlotte, and the other Georges and William all had plentiful offspring (sometimes too plentiful for the royal purses) by acknowledged mistresses or common-law wives. In fact, the begetting of royal children could be one of the chores rather than joys of royal life. George IV (as Prince of Wales) had had years of domestic felicity with a commoner (and a Roman Catholic to boot), Mrs Fitzherbert, before being forced to lie back and think of England (he married Caroline only under pressure, insisting that he would prefer to die unmarried, leaving it to one of his brothers to beget heirs to the throne).[5] George consummated his marriage on his wedding night (or rather, next morning, having collapsed dead drunk that evening in front of the fireplace) and apparently never slept with Caroline again.[6] George I had already put his wife away before he came over from Hanover to ascend the English throne, but the marriages of William and Mary, and of Anne, George II, and William IV were compatible, even if William preferred the company of men to that of his wife, and his later namesake was distressed when he had to give up his happy, long-established liaison with an actress, Mrs Jordan, in order to take his royal (and financial) responsibilities more seriously.[7] The chosen lady – Princess Adelaide of Saxe-Meiningen – was to prove a popular queen and an ideal wife who mothered his illegitimate children and grandchildren.

Reproduction was thus a major royal priority and seeing potential heirs safely into the world a key medical task. The eighteenth century witnessed the rise to fashion of the man-midwife, and there is ample evidence that royal pregnancies (not necessarily births, however) were managed by men, as well as several instances in which medical men with large obstetrical practices secured more general court appointments.[8] William

Hunter, for instance, was appointed Physician-in-Ordinary to Queen Charlotte, George III's wife.[9] Earlier, Sir David Hamilton had become not just the physician to, but the trusted friend and adviser of, Queen Anne.[10] Sir Richard Croft, the man-midwife who had managed the disastrous pregnancy of the Princess Charlotte, committed suicide after the doubly fatal birth.[11] By then – the early nineteenth century – it seems to have been routine for physician-accoucheurs to have handled the actual births. Midwives were in charge earlier, despite the fact that formal appointments (as opposed to specific engagement for an expected confinement) of female midwives were unusual, throughout the period.

Royal births were generally quasi-public events witnessed by many ladies of the court and (at a respectful distance) by members of the Privy Council and other branches of government and agents of authority. There were several eye-witness accounts of the birth of the future Old Pretender. Unfortunately, most of those present were Roman Catholics, pious Protestants being in church on the Sunday morning when it happened. The rumour that his mother had never been pregnant and that the child had been smuggled in in a warming pan was quickly begun, and while one doctor later stated that he believed that James II's wife, Mary, had indeed been with child, he could not be absolutely certain since as a male he had not been permitted to examine her properly. The birth itself was presided over by a midwife, Mrs Judith Wilkes, 'whose hand was to bring the child out of the body'. She left a deposition stating that the infant was indeed Mary's, but she seems to have disappeared soon after its birth in 1688. Naturally, she was also a Roman Catholic and had been rewarded on the spot with 500 guineas ('for your breakfast') by the delighted king. The queen's physician, Dr William Waldegrave, was also knighted at the time, but he was not noted for his obstetrical knowledge and apparently took no part in the delivery. Dr Hugh Chamberlen had been engaged in case of difficulty, but in the event, he was out of town.[12]

The most complicated royal obstetrical history was, of course, that of Mary's stepdaughter, Queen Anne. She had seventeen pregnancies, including one double conception, but managed to produce only one child who survived infancy, the sickly and backward Duke of Gloucester, who did not learn to talk until he was three years old or to walk properly until he was five.[13] He died when he was 11. In addition to her numerous pregnancies, miscarriages, and labours, she also had a false pregnancy beginning sometime in 1694, and accompanied by swelling of the breasts and abdomen. It may well have been her descriptions rather than actual examinations that led her doctors to confirm this as a genuine pregnancy, but by April 1695, Dr John Radcliffe was prepared to swear that 'Her Highness' Distemper was nothing but the Vapours, and that she was in as good a state of Health as any woman breathing, could she but give into the Belief of it.'[14] She was furious with his presumption and thereafter harboured an aversion to him, replacing him with William Gibbons. By June it was apparent that Radcliffe had been correct although the unfortunate queen had something of a (brief) last laugh, since she was genuinely pregnant by the end of the year, only to miscarry in February 1696.[15]

Despite Radcliffe's disfavour, his reputation was such that Anne used him again in the terminal illnesses of her young son (1700) and husband (1708). She also used his prescriptions herself, although he was not permitted to attend her. He is said to have refused to come when summoned to Anne's deathbed.[16]

Anne's sister Queen Mary had her own obstetrical history, which was briefer but no happier than Anne's: a couple of pregnancies, supervised by a Dutch physician (while she was still in Holland) which ended in miscarriages.[17] George I already had grown children when he arrived in England: his daughter-in-law bore her children on both sides of the Channel (her first child was also rumoured to be a changeling, since no official witnesses were present at the birth), and produced a stillborn son and four further children after she arrived in England. Midwives seem to have delivered all of Princess Caroline's children. Her first English-born child was delivered by a German midwife after a labour of five days and despite pleas from the ladies of the court 'to have the Princess laid by Sir David' [Hamilton].[18] Her husband refused on grounds of propriety. The child died, but, remarkably, Caroline produced another child within the year. She had, however, given up the breeding business when her first grandchild was born – a daughter to her detested son Frederick. This was probably the most bizarre of the royal births. Frederick was determined that his wife should not deliver in the presence of his parents. Her mother-in-law was equally determined:

At her labour I positively will be, let her lie-in where she will; for she cannot be brought to bed as quick as one can blow one's nose, and I will be sure it is her child. For my part, I do not see she is big; you all say you see it, and therefore I suppose it is so, and that I am blind.[19]

Augusta went into labour rather unexpectedly when the family all happened to be together at Hampton Court. So vague were the arrangements and so hasty was the midnight flight from Hampton Court to St James's that the pretensions of Frederick's valet to midwifery were the extent of the professional skills initially available for Frederick's wife. A midwife was hastily summoned and successfully delivered the girl, who grew up to become the despised wife of George IV. Caroline so hated her son that she had believed him incapable of exercising his conjugal rights, but Augusta bore her husband eight further children, including one after the unhappy father's death.[20]

The most successfully fertile of English monarchs was George III, whose own wife Charlotte produced a veritable regiment of potential heirs. Finding a legitimate grandchild was to prove somewhat more difficult, but Charlotte's obstetrical history was regular and remarkably uncomplicated. From the beginning her pregnancies were supervised by her surgeon Caesar Hawkins, her accoucheur William Hunter, and her midwife, Mrs Draper. During the first three pregnancies, the two men had to content themselves with the ante- and post-natal care, Mrs Draper overseeing the deliveries with Hunter being forced merely to wait in the wings. A more tractable midwife, Mrs Johnson, then replaced Mrs Draper and, quietly at first, Hunter took charge: 'Mrs Chetwynd told me [wrote Lady Mary Coke in 1766] that the Queen was to be brought to bed by Dr Hunter, instead of the old woman, but that it was kept as quiet a secret as if the fate of the country depended on the change.'[21] Henceforth, males were in charge of the royal delivery room, although Hunter himself did not live to see Charlotte to the end of her child-bearing. He was replaced for the last child by Dr James Ford, whose son's mistress (Mrs Jordan) ultimately bore Charlotte's third son, the Duke of Clarence (afterwards William IV), a bevy of children.[22] Michael Underwood delivered Caroline (George IV's wife) of the tragic Charlotte (1796–1817), who in turn was ministered to by Sir Richard Croft.[23] The use of forceps was, of course, a male prerogative, but both

Hunter and Croft were part of a generation of medical men who reacted against what they saw as the over-hasty employment of forceps in the early eighteenth century.[24] Ironically, modern opinion holds that their use might have saved the lives of both the later Charlotte and her infant. Letters between Charlotte and Croft bespeak a lively and open relationship between royal patient and doctor.[25]

The obstetrical history of the later Stuarts and Hanoverians is thus a mixed one, with the ousting of midwives by medical men rather following than setting fashion. However, life at court consisted of more than simply the begetting and delivery of heirs and potential heirs. In other ways, the medical histories of the royals mirror the medical history of their times.

Smallpox, for instance, dogged royal lives in the late seventeenth and early eighteenth centuries, but not nearly so much later.[26] Anne, for instance, could not attend the wedding of her sister Mary to William of Orange because she was laid low with smallpox.[27] William himself had been orphaned by the disease but had survived an attack himself. The immunity which this conferred meant that he could safely nurse his wife when she at last (aged 32) was stricken by a disorder which one of her doctors at first attributed to measles but which finally manifested the tell-tale signs of smallpox. Regular medical bulletins during a time of serious royal illness were as common then as now, and the uncertainty surrounding those which had attended Mary's fatal illness of nine days, led to a published first-hand account of her final days by one of the physicians who had attended her:

> The symptoms of illness on the first day did not prevent the queen from going abroad; but as she was still out of sorts at bedtime, she took a large dose of Venice treacle, a powerful diaphoretic which her former physician, the famous physiologist Dr Lower, had recommended her to take as often as she found herself inclined to a fever. Finding no sweat to appear as usual, she took next morning a double quantity of it, but again without inducing the usual effect of perspiration. Up to that time she had not asked advice of the physicians. To this severe dosing with one of the most powerful alexipharmac or heating medicines, the malignant type of the ensuing smallpox was mainly ascribed by Harris, who was a follower of Sydenham and a partizan of the cooling regimen. On the third day from the initial symptoms the eruption ap-

peared, with a very troublesome cough; the eruption came out in such a manner that the physicians were very doubtful whether it would prove to be smallpox or measles. On the fourth day the smallpox showed itself in the face and the rest of the body 'under its proper and distinct form'. But on the sixth day, in the morning, the variolous pustules were changed all over her breast into the large red spots 'of the measles'; and the erysipelas, or rose, swelled her whole face, the former pustules giving place to it. That evening many livid round petechiae appeared on the forehead above the eyebrows, and on the temples, which Harris says he had foretold in the morning. One physician said these were not petechiae, but sphacelated spots; but next morning a surgeon proved by his lancet that they contained blood. During the night following the sixth day, Dr Harris sat up with the patient, and observed that she had great difficulty of breathing, followed soon after by a copious spitting of blood. On the seventh day the spitting of blood was succeeded by blood in the urine. On the eighth day the pustules on the limbs, which had kept the normal variolous character longest, lost their fulness, and changed into round spots of deep red or scarlet colour, smooth and level with the skin, like the stigmata of the plague. Harris observed about the region of the heart one large pustule filled with matter, having a broad scarlet circle round it like a burning coal, under which a great deal of extravasated blood was found when the body was examined after death. Towards the end, the queen slumbered sometimes, but said she was not refreshed thereby. At last she lay silent for some hours; and some words that came from her shewed, says Burnet, that her thoughts had begun to break. She died on the 28th of December, at one in the morning, in the ninth day of her illness.[28]

As Walter Harris's clinical history makes clear, there was room for medical debate over the treatment of smallpox, but there could be relatively little doubt that few would escape having the disease at some point in their lives. It is often stated that Queen Anne's son died of it.[29] One of the future George II's daughters (Anne) caught smallpox in April 1720; perhaps the episode made George and Caroline (who with her husband had smallpox after their marriage) more receptive to the news of inoculation, circulating from 1718 through the efforts, among

others, of Lady Mary Wortley Montagu, herself a member of
the court circle. Her own daughter was inoculated in 1721, in
the first variolation to be performed in England. [30] In 1723, following inoculation trials at Newgate Prison and on pauper
children, two daughters of George and Caroline were inoculated. The procedure was successful, each girl coming down
with a mild case of the disease, although the potential danger
of variolation was underscored by the death, from smallpox, of
a footman inoculated at the same time.[31]

It is not yet possible to say whether inoculation became routine for the royal children of the next two generations. Certainly Frederick's wife Augusta, whose face was pitted as a result
of her own encounter with smallpox, would have known first
hand what the sequelae could be.[32] After the initial wave of enthusiasm of the 1720s – stimulated of course by royal patronage
– the procedure fell into a certain amount of disrepute before
being revived and popularized by the safer, cheaper, and more
sensible modifications introduced by the Suttons and their followers from the 1750s.[33] Thomas Dimsdale achieved fame and
fortune by taking these newer methods to the Russian court and
systematic research may well show that Frederick's children
were inoculated (though his eldest son – later George III –
caught smallpox in 1745), as at least some of George III's
were.[34] The future George IV was inoculated when he was four,
the same age as his younger brother Octavius, who was inoculated in 1783 along with the Princess Sophia. Octavius died a
few days later, probably from smallpox.[35] The young Duke of
Clarence (William IV) had also been inoculated in 1769, along
with the future Mrs Papendiek (who caught the disease itself six
years later) and Prince Ernest, of Mecklenburg-Strelitz.[36]
These instances suggest that variolation continued to find royal
favour, and certainly the later Georges and their families did
not suffer from smallpox to the extent that the late Stuarts and
early Hanoverians had. Princess Victoria was vaccinated three
times, when she was 10 weeks old (in 1819), and again in 1827
and 1835.[37]

Other childhood diseases and exanthema could threaten the
health and even the life of the royal offspring. George and
Charlotte had lost another child in 1782, the year before Octavius's unfortunate inoculation, and there were princes and
princesses of the period who did not grow to maturity. However, there can be no doubt about the basic sturdiness of the

Hanoverians, or of the fact that it was the more typical eighteenth-century diseases of adulthood which took their toll in terms of morbidity and mortality. Two particularly common ones were gout and asthma.

'Gout' was of course a standard and usefully elastic eighteenth-century diagnostic category. Dr Johnson defined it as 'the arthritis; a periodical disease attended with great pain', relying on the royal physician John Arbuthnot for a further elaboration:

> the *gout* is a disease which may affect any membranous part, but commonly those which are at the greatest distance from the heart or brain, where the motion of the fluids is the slowest, the resistance, friction, and stricture of the solid parts the greatest, and the sensation of pain, by the dilaceration of the nervous fibres, extreme.[38]

Virtually any inflammatory process, generally but not necessarily involving the joints or lower limbs, and virtually any internal affliction, especially if accompanied by acute pain, might warrant the label, 'gout'. It was a disease of high living, ampleness, and plethora, consequently a disorder much in evidence in court circles. And though males might suffer from it more commonly than females, the latter could also suffer its slings and arrows.

Queen Anne, for instance, when finally beyond her melancholy task of trying to produce a viable heir, began to experience a chronic process which left her so weak in the lower extremities that walking became impossible without the aid of a stick. For the last few years of her life, she was virtually immobile, a situation compounded by her bulky frame. For the eighteenth century, this was 'gout' although her clinical history does not fit easily into any single modern diagnostic category.[39] In addition to her chronic difficulties in walking, she was often laid low by episodes of acute distress which sometimes seemed incongruent with the majesty that should attend royalty. As the Scotsman Sir John Clerk observed in 1706, in a description which makes rather poignant reading in view of the fact that Anne was the last British monarch to touch for the 'King's evil':

> I had occasion to observe the Calamities which attend humane nature even to the greatest dignities of Life. Her Ma-

271

jesty was labouring under a fit of the Gout, and in extream
pain and agony, and on this occasion everything about her
was much in the same disorder as about the meanest of her
subjects. Her face, which was red and spotted, was rendered
something frightful by her negligent dress, and the foot affected was tied up with a pultis and some nasty bandages. I
was much affected by this sight, and the more when she had
occasion to mention her people of Scotland, which she did
frequently to the Duke [of Queensberry]. What are you, poor
mean-like Mortal, thought I, who talks in the style of a Sovereign? Nature seems to be inverted when a poor infirm
Woman becomes one of the Rulers of the World.[40]

This was eight years before her terminal acute illness, which
may have been erysipelas, but which contemporaries attributed
to the same general process, in this case the gout being 'suppressed', the ulcer (called 'scorbutic' in her autopsy report) on
her inner thigh being symptomatic of the body's inability to discharge the gouty humours.[41]

'Suppressed gout' was also invoked early in George III's episode of 'mania' in 1788, his stomach pains being attributed to
a collection of morbific matter in his hypochondrium.[42] The
irony is that George was assumed to have gout not because of
his luxury but as a result of the sparseness of his diet and lean-
ness of his habit. As Sir Nathaniel Wraxall commented, his
symptoms were

> ... gouty. Probably the humour might have exhausted its
> force in the extremities, in the shape of gout, if his majesty
> had eat and drunk like almost any other gentleman. But
> natural disposition to temperance ... impelled him to adopt
> the habits of an ascetic.[43]

Gout – 'suppressed', 'wandering', or 'flying' – continued to be
bandied about as an explanation of George's strange complex
of symptoms, but the king himself knew better: 'They would
make me believe I have the gout, but if it was gout, how could
I kick [my heel against my foot] without any pain?'[44] The further deterioration of the king's mental faculties left gout on the
periphery of serious diagnoses.

George IV possessed, of course, a more 'typical' gouty habi-
tus, and, not surprisingly, a good deal of the incapacitation of

his later life was attributed to it. He himself described what was called an 'assession of gout', in a letter of 1827 to his physician, friend, and keeper of his privy purse, Sir William Knighton:

> Royal Lodge,
> June 18th, 1827.
>
> ... As to myself, I am pretty well bodily, but I have little or no use of my poor limbs, for I can neither walk up nor down stairs, and am obliged to be carried, and in general to be wheeled about everywhere; for my powers of walking, and even of crawling about with crutches, or with the aid of a strong stick are not in the smallest respect improved since you last saw me, – at the same time that my knees, legs, ankles and feet swell more formidably and terribly than ever. This, I am sure you will agree with me, ought now to be seriously attended to without delay by some plan devised and steadily acted upon, in order to stop the further progress, and to remedy it effectually and finally; for there is no question it is an increasing and progressive evil (at least so I fear) unless steps are found, and that speedily too, of averting it.[45]

It was difficult for an eighteenth-century aristocrat to make it to middle age or beyond without someone diagnosing 'gout', but, in fact, many of the Hanoverians displayed symptoms which seem more consistent with the modern experience of cardiovascular disorders. William III was a life-long asthmatic (although a vigorous horseman in his youth for all that), and William IV had an annual attack of asthma in late May or June.[46] His brother, the Duke of York, however, was described towards the end of his life as 'gouty' and dropsical, with difficulty in breathing (called 'asthmatic' in the period), and George IV had trouble sleeping flat during his last months - suggestive of cardiac failure.[47] Apoplexy, which killed George I, George III's uncle the Duke of Cumberland, and possibly grandfather George II, also points to the tendency of cardiovascular disorders in the royal family.

This brief discussion does not begin to exhaust the medical problems of the Stuarts and Hanoverians. George I had an anal fistula, a daughter of George III died from what was probably tuberculosis, several royals (including George I and William IV) were alleged to have had venereal disease, and a number of unmarried daughters coped with their lonely, boring, and isolated existences through lives of valetudinarianism. George III's mental incapacitation (whether due to porphyria or to some more conventional 'psychiatric' disorder is not relevant here) was the most public – and constitutionally sensitive – illness during the period, and few deathbed scenes have ever been so vividly and ruthlessly described as that of Queen Caroline, by Lord Hervey.[48] Much, too, could be said about the psychopathology of the Hanoverians. Not so much porphyria as violent hatred seems to have been the 'genetic' disorder which ran through the family. George I despised his eldest son, who set up a rival court in opposition. With a repetition so chilling as to appear almost biological, George II rejected his own eldest son with a vengeance in excess of anything his own father had thrown at him. Since 'Poor Fred' died when his own heir was a mere boy, the pattern skipped a generation, but the relations between the Georges III and IV rekindled the passion and rivalry of the early dynasty. 'Family life' was never dull in the eighteenth-century court, but since the age has not medicalized such things, no one suggested a court psychiatrist (except for George III's 'mania'), and the evidence for these psychodynamics has been left to us by witnesses, diarists, letter-writers, caricaturists, and satirists who, on balance, were probably more reliable, and certainly more entertaining, than doctors would have been.[49]

Patients and doctors

As we shall see below, the number of medical men involved in caring for members of the royal family during our period ran into the hundreds. The royal household was divided into four departments – the Lord Chamberlain's department, the bedchamber, the household below stairs, and the stables. The Lord Chamberlain's was the largest of these and contained the medical staff, who eventually were organized into a separate 'Medical Department' (but still under the Lord Chamberlain's jurisdiction). In George I's reign, total household staff ran to about 950, including two or three 'physicians to the person', two 'apothecaries to the person', two 'surgeons to the person', and a surgeon and an apothecary 'to the household'.[50] Later courts contained larger medical departments, as the queen often had her own medical men, and when offspring received their own allowances and set up their own households, these created additional opportunities for ambitious men desiring royal appointments. Queen Charlotte apparently kept two doctors on call in case any of her and George III's numerous children should need medical attention.[51] Although the monarch could dismiss, appointments were normally made by the Lord Chamberlain, which thus put him in a strategic position of patronage.

Treating the monarch was of course a delicate business, although if the illness was at all serious, multiple medical men were generally in attendance. There are occasional instances of professional disagreement about diagnosis or therapy of choice. John Radcliffe, for instance, continued to be a somewhat irrascible colleague. His difficulties with Anne and her family had not prevented his appointment as physician to William and Mary, although his relationships with them were not much happier. He was rude about the diagnosis of smallpox which Mary's other doctors had given her during her final illness, believing it a case of measles but also declaring that she was 'a dead woman, for it was impossible to do any good in her case, where remedies had already been given that were so contrary to the nature of the distemper'.[52] Most historians believe that Radcliffe had been wrong on the diagnosis, even if he was correct to predict Mary's imminent death. He later told William that, were he to give up hard drinking, he would 'engage to make you live three or four years longer; but beyond that time no physic can protect your Majesty's existence'. William, in fact, lived for five more years, although he finally dismissed Radcliffe when, two years later, the physician quipped of William's oedematous legs, 'Why, truly, I would not have your Majesty's two legs for your three Kingdoms.'[53]

The presence of foreign medical staff could also be a source of professional conflict and jostling for royal favour. This could be particularly aggravated by the linguistic problems of the non-English-speaking royals of the early period. William III, for instance, brought Govert Bidloo over from Holland in 1701, when his legs had become particularly troublesome. Unlike Radcliffe, Bidloo was prepared to countenance the king's alcoholic consumption. This pleased William even if he was less than happy with Bidloo's recommendation of hot poultices on his legs, which he complained kept him awake at night. Bidloo and a surgeon (a Frenchman named Ronjat) also differed about the nature of William's injury after the fatal fall from his horse Sorrel. It was Bidloo (rather than an English physician) who primarily ministered to the king during the last hours.[54]

George I also brought with him a German physician, J. G. Steigerdahl (or Steighertahl) who stayed with him even after most of his German attendants had been sent back to Hanover for a combination of financial and diplomatic reasons. Steigerdahl was travelling with the royal party on its way to Hanover when the king had his fatal stroke in 1727. It cannot have been with a great deal of enthusiasm that this man, with an MD from Utrecht, had been elected a Fellow of the Royal Society and an Honorary Fellow of the College of Physicians.[55] Nationalism also reared its head when the Danish husband of Princess Charlotte criticized Sir Richard Croft's handling of her confinement, and it has already been noted that the German midwife ran afoul of British medical men during Caroline of Ansbach's lengthy labour.[56]

The relations between the royals and most of their medical attendants were formal, of course, and what has been called positional.[57] Illness, however, creates situations of particular intimacy and stress, and not surprisingly, perhaps, several medical men managed to acquire close personal relationships with their sovereigns. I shall look briefly at three examples, and then consider a few ramifications of the most complicated medical interaction with royalty, George III's 'madness'.

Queen Anne's reign was of course marked by the heightened political consciousness surrounding the succession issue. Her physicians, however, with several of whom she had quite close relationships, included both Tories, such as John Arbuthnot (whose brother was a Jacobite agent in France) and Whigs such as Radcliffe and, towards the end, Richard Mead. No one achieved more intimacy with her than the Whig physician and man-midwife, David Hamilton, whom she knighted in 1703, the year he was appointed one of her physicians-in-ordinary.[58] Although his medical training was from Leiden, and he was at the time only a licentiate of the college, his election to a fellowship swiftly followed. The appointment naturally did wonders for his private practice, although he did not actively attend the queen for more than five years after his elevation. She no longer had need of his obstetrical skill, although his experience in dealing with women probably held him in good stead. His later frustration, after Anne's death, arose during Caroline's labours. He did practise his obstetrical skills on various ladies associated with the court, including delivering Lady Hervey's tenth son.[59]

Hamilton's *Diary*, which has recently been published, shows just how close his relationship with Anne was. While her 'gout' was the object of much of his medical attention, and while Hamilton was in attendance during episodes of acute illness, their conversations ranged across many topics, some political, some personal (including Hamilton's unhappy marriage and his wife's adultery). Hamilton acted as the primary go-between when Anne and Sarah, Duchess of Marlborough, were undergoing their final breach of friendship. He was as trusted an adviser as she had during the last five years of her life. That trust was also reflected in their joint understanding of her health and of the measures to be taken to preserve it as well as possible. Hamilton's *Diary* shows him as a committed psychosomatist (he attributed her death to 'Disquiet of Mind') who tried his best to protect her from unpleasant matters ('A new Illness returning, my Mouth was stop'd, probably about Family of Hanover coming to Britain'). [60]

Hamilton's position had of course aroused jealousies among some courtiers and politicians, who resented the ease with which he could command an audience with the Queen. He also had his friends, however, who supported his petition – to George I – to continue his place at court after Anne's death. Although successful in this attempt, his subsequent appointment proved much of a sinecure, both with George and his daughter-in-law. Hamilton died without a will, so there is no evidence of the extent of his estate, but he must have done well by his service at court. He was said to have lost £80,000 in the South Sea Bubble.[66]

Another royal physician who secured the utter confidence of the royal family, and who also combined medical with diplomatic service, was Sir William Knighton (1776–1836) associated with George IV as both Regent and king. Like Hamilton, Knighton had to work his way up from provincial obscurity and overcome the lack of an Oxbridge education. His medical training was somewhat haphazard, including an apprenticeship with a surgeon-apothecary uncle, a few months at Guy's, and a year as assistant surgeon at the Naval Hospital at Plymouth. Determining on a career in London, he found that his training was inadequate for the certificate of the College, and so went to

Edinburgh for a couple of years, taking an Aberdeen MD in 1806. Like Hamilton, too, midwifery stood him in good stead, his appointment as domestic physician to the Marquis of Wellesley resulting from the successful handling of a noblewoman's confinement.[62] Knighton's medical skills do not appear to have been in any way outstanding, but his capacity to impress the great and powerful came out during his stay with Wellesley during the latter's political mission in Spain. He returned with an influential patron who convinced the Prince of Wales that Knighton was the material that royal physicians are made of. An appointment and a baronetcy swiftly followed, as well as a personal relationship which was cemented when Knighton managed to secure the return of some potentially embarrassing private letters to the Prince of Wales[63] Once in a position of confidence, Knighton was able in turn to work on behalf of his friends, securing for Robert Gooch (who had taken over Knighton's private practice) the post of Librarian to the king.[64] Once he became George's private secretary and keeper of the privy purse ('I write no more prescriptions for money', he described the necessary abandonment of his practice), the press for patronage became even more intense. One letter from James Northcote contained six specific requests for favours with the added comment, 'other inferior petitions I shall not trouble you with at present'.[65]

Lady Knighton's memoir of her husband was a pious, laundered affair, but there is sufficient correspondence published there, along with that of George IV published since, to show the ease with which Knighton moved in royal circles, corresponding on terms of familiarity not just with the king but with two of the king's brothers as well. ('I cannot sit down to talk with common minds', he wrote to his daughter.) Letters from the king ('Dearest friend', he generally addressed Knighton) have occasional references to his health, or directives to come and attend him, but they are also filled with familiar domestic gossip and, as George made increasingly diplomatic use of his friend, with the stuff of international politics. Although he continued to give medical advice to the king, his role was more nearly that of confidant, and his presence at George's final illness was not really in a medical capacity.

By then, in fact, the medical man of the hour was Sir Henry Halford (1766–1844), perhaps the most successful royal physician of the period. He served four monarchs and presided over the deathbeds of no fewer than seven members of the royal family. Halford was born Henry Vaughan, son of a successful Leicester medical practitioner who devoted much of his substance to educating his several sons. He changed his name to Halford after inheriting the estate of his mother's cousin, Sir Charles Halford. Educated at Oxford, Halford was a quintessential example of the cultured, classically minded, conservative physician, who kept a volume of Horace by his bedside and drafted into Latin a speech his friend the Duke of Wellington had to deliver as the Chancellor of the University of Oxford. His rise in the world was aided by a marriage into the aristocracy and the friendship and patronage of Dr Richard Warren (1731–97), then at the head of the London profession, and physician to George III. The year after Halford had settled in London he was the youngest man ever appointed physician to a monarch (George III). He served George IV during George III's lifetime (in itself no mean feat), and William IV and Victoria, although by the latter's reign, his appointment was almost *pro forma*.[66]

By all accounts, Halford was a shrewd man, polished and tactful with his patients, and lavish in his entertainments, even if some of his younger colleagues (perhaps out of envy) felt that his diagnoses were rather superficial, and that his failure to adopt the newer pathological approach or the diagnostic methods (such as the stethoscope) of the French betrayed a lack of interest in 'modern' medicine. His patients probably did not mind, and those patients included not just the extended list of royalty, but a long string of the aristocracy, politicians (Wilberforce and several prime ministers), and churchmen (three archbishops and seven bishops). What he believed in was the capacity of the physician, if the patient had sufficient faith in him, to help the patient recover, through the healing power of nature and a variety of prescriptions which were supposed to keep the patient comfortable while the body was doing its work. Like many of his colleagues, he also possessed the ability to stop active treatment when the end was near, and to prepare the patient and his family for the last moments. Until he himself had decided that hope was no longer appropriate, he vigorously strove to keep all depressing thoughts from his patient, orchestrating deathbed scenes with a sense of drama and a good deal of experience.

The royals loved him, although he was probably fortunate

not to have been old enough to have been involved in George III's 1788 episode, where tensions ran high and there was much parliamentary scrutiny of the king's physicians. Instead, he entered the scene during the ageing king's lucid Indian summer, and eventually gained such confidence of his royal charge that the king made him promise that, should he (the king) lose his reason again, Halford would not abandon him – and that he would call on William Heberden and Matthew Baillie (in that order) to assist him if necessary.[67] He seems to have been off-stage during the king's brief illness in 1801, but from the final lapse into dementia, from 1810, he was there to direct operations. He had already impressed everyone with his handling of Princess Amelia's fatal consumption.

In the early days, it was assumed that George's illness in 1810 was just another episode, which, like the others, would end in recovery. Efforts were accordingly made to treat the king vigorously. Halford apparently spent much of his time for six months ministering to the old monarch. Hope was eventually abandoned, the Regency formalized, and the doctors increasingly left things to the king's five attendants (supplied, incidentally, by Thomas Warburton, whose private madhouses came under such unfavourable scrutiny during the parliamentary hearings of 1815–16).[68] Although the care became routine, Halford and his four medical colleagues (Baillie, Heberden, and John and Robert Willis) called at Windsor on most days and hence were eligible for their daily consulting fee of 30 guineas. The royal surgeon, Sir David Dundas, received half that amount, while the ordinary attendants each got 12/6d. per day. Warburton received a pound a day, simply for supplying the nurses. During most of George's final years, medical and nursing fees alone cost the nation almost £35,000 per annum. Total medical cost of caring for the king in his room at Windsor from 5 January 1812 until his death just over eight years later was £271,691/18s.[69]

> They murmured, as they took their fees,
> There is no cure for this disease.

The king's final illness eventually lapsed into the routine, if expensive, pattern of chronic care. In its early days, however, some of the tensions surfaced which had characterized the doctor–patient relationships of the previous breakdowns of 1788–9 and 1801. In the first place, George never liked doctors very much, even in the best of circumstances, and given the nature of his symptoms, caring for him was particularly difficult. His wife, too, although genuinely concerned, found it hard to cope with the unpredictability of the king's behaviour, and early in the first illness, found it necessary to sleep in another bedroom.[70]

The strain of what can only be called a 'psychiatric' illness (regardless of its aetiology) told on the family, the family's doctors, and on their relationships. Sir George Baker, who was initially in charge of the case during the 1788–9 episode, gave him the usual round of purgatives – castor oil and senna – and laudanum, but he was clearly puzzled at the complex of symptoms and the occasional bouts of 'delirium' – agitation, rapid speech, and even foaming at the mouth. William Heberden (the elder) was called in but could not offer much more, in diagnosis, therapy, or assurance to the politicians, particularly those sympathetic to the Prince of Wales. Richard Warren was then brought in (at Baker's request), but he was also physician to the Prince of Wales, which complicated the delicate constitutional dilemma: 'You may come here as an acquaintance but not as my physician, you cannot be mine', the king told Warren. 'No man can serve two masters. You are the Prince of Wales's physician – you cannot be mine.'[71] Warren's pessimism about the king's chances of recovery did not endear him to those loyal to the monarch, but neither Warren nor any other of the eminent physicians, including Sir Lucas Pepys and Dr Thomas Gisborne, seemed able to arrest the deterioration of the king's mental condition. The consequence was the employment of the physician-clergyman Rev. Dr Francis Willis and his son Dr John Willis, keepers of a private madhouse in Lincoln. 'The poor Queen had most painfully concurred in a measure which seemed to fix the nature of the King's attack in the face of the world.' Nor was the king any happier: 'He told one of his Pages, that as Dr Willis was now come He could never more shew his face again in this Country that He would leave it for Ever, & retire to Hanover.'[72]

The engagement of the Willises eloquently symbolizes the emerging strength of the medical profession – and of its weakness – against the backdrop of the eighteenth-century horror of madness. The Willises were neither society doctors nor London elite. They were summoned in desperation, because they were believed to be experts, and whatever modern opinion might say

about the humanity (or lack of it) of their methods, they perse-
vered, ultimately winning the confidence of the queen and if
not the love, at least the awe of the king.

The Willises were *sui generis* during our period, however, and
though the sons returned to tend the king in his later bouts,
they were hardly the sort of people who would be kept around
the English court longer than necessary. Although there was
some haggling over the amount they should receive, in the end
Francis Willis (already 73 years old) received a pension of
£1,000 for 21 years, while his son John got £650 a year for life.
Sir George Baker had received £1,380, but, then, he also stayed
on as physician to the king.[73] It was men like him who provided
the continuity of royal care. In the final section, I shall make
some preliminary observations about the considerable group of
men who held medical appointments at the English court.

Royal doctors

Through the efforts of Ben Barkow and with the help of S. D.
Clippindale's two manuscript volumes, 'Medical Court-Roll',
held by the Royal College of Surgeons of England, it has been
possible to construct a list of about 480 individuals who held
some sort of a medical appointment to royalty during our period.[74] Most of these are physicians, surgeons, or apothecaries,
but there were smaller numbers of cuppers, dentists, and midwives, and the curious post of Anatomist to the king. Of course,
the group contains the elite and the obscure and I am not yet
in a position to say much about the wider patterns which pros-
opographical analysis should display. Accordingly, this final section merely details three broad themes which I hope to examine
more extensively at some future date.

First, the sheer number of individuals involved testifies to the
importance of the court for the Georgian medical world. Royal
appointments were not the sole prerogative of the few born
with silver spoons in their mouths. Successful careers in medicine could be achieved by those from humble backgrounds.
Eighteenth-century medical practitioners saw themselves
above all as engaged in the business of medicine, and court medicine was obviously good business.[75] Leslie Matthews has demonstrated that the royal apothecaries were, as a group,
prosperous men.[76] Furthermore, since the court spread its ten-

tacles to include not simply the nuclear royal family, but as-
sorted relatives and favourites, we must see court medicine as
part of a larger network of aristocratic practice. Eighteenth-
century obituarists were often interested in the size of the deceased's fortune, and royal or at least aristocratic clients were
virtually a *sine qua non* for a medical man to accumulate a large
fortune. The retainer fees of between £200 and £500 per
annum for formal royal appointments provided a comfortable
base, but additional consultation fees could be paid for actual
services rendered, and this royal and aristocratic largess was an
important source of medical income for those lucky enough to
secure it.[77] There were a few, of course, like John Hunter, who
hated having to chase the 'damned guinea', but even Hunter
spent much time and energy chasing it, and for the overwhelming majority of practitioners during the period, making money
was what medicine was about.[78] Most of the best medical fortunes of the century, from physicians like Radcliffe, Mead, William Hunter, Warren, Baillie, and Halford, to surgeons like
Caesar Hawkins, Astley Cooper, and John Hunter, and apothecaries like Daniel Malthus or the Brande family dynasty, were
got by men with court connections. These are of course some
of the most visible among the royal doctors, and undoubtedly
others lived and died in more modest circumstances. Nevertheless, the concentration of wealth and power in the court could
not fail to attract ambitious practitioners.

A second theme is that of patronage, which oiled the wheels
of Georgian Britain.[79] Once in positions of prestige and wealth,
doctors quite naturally attempted to ensure that their sons or
nephews, pupils or friends, succeeded them. By and large, they
seem to have had a good deal of say in the matter, despite the
fact that the ultimate power to hire and fire lay with the Chamberlain or the member of royalty to whose person or household
the appointment was attached. There was no quasi-apostolic
succession, of course; no gold-headed cane that automatically
passed from one person to another. However, the analogy of
succession is significant. *The Gold-headed Cane* was written by
one royal physician (William Macmichael), dedicated to the
widow of another (Sir Henry Halford), and in passing from
Radcliffe to Mead to Askew to Pitcairn to Baillie, more often
than not the cane itself would have been carried to court on official business. Only Askew had no court appointment of any
kind.[80] Richard Warren secured Henry Halford and Michael

Underwood their positions. William Heberden, Jr came after Heberden, Sr (though the latter had remained somewhat aloof from the most ardent demands of court).

The father–son pattern is even more striking in the case of surgeons and apothecaries – unsurprisingly, perhaps, given the nature of the apprenticeship.[81] No fewer than five Brandes served as royal apothecaries, there were three Grahams, and the partnership begun in the mid-eighteenth century by John Truesdale and Joseph Partridge continued to supply appointments until the early twentieth century.[82] Among surgeons, royal service extended across the generations for quite a few, including the Hawkins family; Astley Cooper got his nephew and protégé Bransby Cooper a position and there were other families, like the Thompsons or the Davises where more than one member did well at court. These are simply instances, and a careful study of marriages would undoubtedly reveal additional networks to those already familiar, like the Hunter–Baillie–Home one. In the nineteenth century, Thomas Wakley was to use the journal he founded in 1823, the *Lancet*, to campaign against nepotism in medicine more generally and it is unexceptional that something akin to it should have permeated the Georgian medical court scene.[83]

The final theme which would repay more systematic exploration is no less exceptional: the connections between court and military service. Until George II, the association of the monarch with the army was direct and throughout the period, males in the extended royal family tried their hands at commanding battles and laying sieges. One of the formal tasks of the 'Sergeant Surgeon' was to attend the monarch in battle, and a large number of royal surgeons and physicians seem to have come to royal attention through their military service. I have not attempted to compile a systematic list, but several of the leading names in military medicine of the period – including Sir John Pringle and Sir Gilbert Blane – as well as other familiar names with less familiar military attachments (for example, John Hunter, Robert Keate) pursued their careers on multiple fronts.[84]

Each of these themes would warrant a good deal more investigation. In the end, medicine at the English court was not a world apart, but one of a continuum of practice and precept, and in that sense, its study opens a window into that wider medical world.

Notes

1. A standard analysis of patient domination is N. Jewson, 'Medical knowledge and the patronage system in eighteenth-century England', *Sociology*, vol. 13. (1974), pp. 369–85; cf. Roy Porter (ed.), *Patients and Practitioners* (Cambridge University Press, Cambridge, 1985); and Roy Porter and Dorothy Porter, *In Sickness and in Health: The British Experience 1650–1850* (Fourth Estate, London, 1988).

2. A lively introduction is J. H. Plumb, *The First Four Georges* (Batsford, London, 1956); a good, old-fashioned survey of medicine during the latter part of my period is Arnold Chaplin, *Medicine in England during the Reign of George III* (Henry Kimpton, London, 1919); an introduction to the general medical literature of the period is W. F. Bynum, 'Health, disease, and medical care', in G. S. Rousseau and Roy Porter (eds), *The Ferment of Knowledge* (Cambridge University Press, Cambridge, 1980), pp. 211–53.

3. Henri and Barbara van der Zee, *William and Mary* (Macmillan, London, 1973); Edward Gregg, *Queen Anne* (Routledge & Kegan Paul, London, 1980); Jack Dewhurst, *Royal Confinements* (Weidenfeld & Nicolson, London, 1980).

4. Averyl Edwards, *Frederick Lewis, Prince of Wales* (Staples Press, London, 1947); Philip Ziegler, *King William IV* (Collins, London, 1971).

5. W. H. Wilkins, *Mrs. Fitzherbert and George IV*, 2 vols (Longmans, Green & Co., London, 1906).

6. Plumb, *The First Four Georges*, p. 171.

7. Ziegler, *King William IV*.

8. On man-midwifery and obstetrics during the period, cf. Edward Shorter, *A History of Women's Bodies* (Penguin, Harmondsworth, 1984); Judith Schneid Lewis, *In the Family Way, Childbearing in the British Aristocracy, 1760–1860* (Rutgers University Press, New Brunswick, New Jersey, 1986); Jean E. Donnison, *Midwives and Medical Men* (Schocken Books, New York, 1977).

9. W. F. Bynum and Roy Porter (eds), *William Hunter and the Eighteenth-century Medical World* (Cambridge University Press, Cambridge, 1985), especially the essays by Porter, Helen Brock, Angus McLaren, Adrian Wilson, and Edward Shorter.

10. Philip Roberts (ed.), *The Diary of Sir David Hamilton, 1709–1711* (Clarendon Press, Oxford, 1975).

11. Dewhurst, *Royal Confinements*; Franco Crainz, *An Obstetric Tragedy* (Heinemann, London, 1973); Lewis, *In the Family Way*; Henry Vincent Corbett, *A Royal Catastrophe* (n. p., for the Author, 1985).

12. Dewhurst, *Royal Confinements*, pp. 17–22; van der Zee, *William and Mary*, pp. 232–3.

13. Jenkin Lewis, *Queen Anne's Son: Memoirs of William Henry, Duke of Gloucester* (Stanford, London, 1881 [originally published in 1789]); Gregg, *Queen Anne*.

14. Gregg, *Queen Anne*, p. 106; Campbell R. Hone, *The Life of Dr*

John Radcliffe (Faber & Faber, London, 1950), p. 51.

15. Dewhurst, *Royal Confinements*, pp. 30–47; David Green, *Queen Anne* (Collins, London, 1970).

16. William Macmichael, *The Gold-headed Cane* (Facsimile of the author's interleaved copy of 1827 edition, Royal College of Physicians, London, 1968), p. 39, states that Radcliffe did not come simply because he was indisposed himself. In fact, Radcliffe himself was dead three months after the incident (Macmichael, p. 55).

17. van der Zee, *William and Mary*, pp. 134–6; Dewhurst, *Royal Confinements*, pp. 27–30.

18. W. H. Wilkins, *Caroline the Illustrious* (Longmans, Green & Co., London, 1904), pp. 225–7; Dewhurst, *Royal Confinements*, pp. 55–6.

19. Romney Sedgwick (ed.), *Some Materials towards Memoirs of the Reign of King George II, by John, Lord Hervey*, 3 vols (n. p., London, 1931), III, p. 757.

20. Ibid., III, pp. 614–18, 749ff.

21. J. N. Stark, 'An obstetric diary of William Hunter, 1762–1765', *Glasgow Medical Journal*, vol. 70, (1908), pp. 167–76, 241–56, 338–49; J. A. Horne (ed.), *The Letters and Journals of Lady Mary Coke*, 4 vols (David Douglas, Edinburgh, 1889–96).

22. Ziegler, *King William IV*, pp. 76–85.

23. W. J. Maloney, 'Michael Underwood: a surgeon practising midwifery from 1764–1784', *Journal of the History of Medicine*, vol. 5 (1950), pp. 289–314; Crainz, *Obstetric Tragedy*; Lewis, *In the Family Way*; Corbett, *Royal Catastrophe*.

24. Edward Shorter, 'The management of normal deliveries and the generation of William Hunter', in Bynum and Porter (eds), *William Hunter*.

25. Letters from Charlotte to Croft reproduced by Crainz, *Obstetric Tragedy*, p. 4ff, freely discuss sickness, dysuria, vaginal bleeding, and breast discomfort.

26. Donald R. Hopkins, *Princes and Peasants. Smallpox in History* (University of Chicago Press, Chicago, 1983), especially Chapter 2.

27. Gregg, *Queen Anne*, pp. 16–17.

28. Quoted by Charles Creighton, *A History of Epidemics in Britain*, 2 vols (reprinted from 1894 edition, Frank Cass, London, 1965), II, p. 459; William III's smallpox is described in van der Zee, *William and Mary*, pp. 100–1.

29. Gregg, *Queen Anne*, p. 120.

30. Hopkins, *Princes and Peasants*; Genevieve Miller, *The Adoption of Inoculation for Smallpox in England and France* (University of Pennsylvania Press, Philadelphia, 1957); R. Halsband, *The Life of Lady Mary Wortley Montagu* (Clarendon Press, Oxford, 1956).

31. Miller, *Adoption of Inoculation*.

32. Charles Chenevix Trench, *George II* (Allen Lane, London, 1973), p. 179.

33. Peter Razzell, *The Conquest of Smallpox* (Caliban Books, Firle, Sussex, 1977); David van Zwanenberg, 'The Suttons and the business of inoculation', *Medical History*, vol. 22 (1978), pp. 71–82.

34. John Brooke, *King George III* (Constable, London, 1972); Hopkins, *Princes and Peasants*, p. 61.

35. Derrick Baxby, 'A death from inoculated smallpox in the English royal family', *Medical History*, vol. 28 (1984), pp. 303–7.

36. Mrs Vernon Delves Broughton (ed.), *Court and Private Life in the Time of Queen Charlotte: Being the Journals of Mrs Papendiek, Assistant Keeper of the Wardrobe and Reader to Her Majesty*, 2 vols (Richard Bentley, London, 1887), I, pp. 41–2.

37. Cecil Woodham-Smith, *Queen Victoria. Her Life and Times*, 2 vols (Hamish Hamilton, London, 1972), I, p. 38.

38. Samuel Johnson, *A Dictionary of the English Language* (facsimile reprint of first (1755) edition, Times Books, London, 1983), entry 'Gout'; W. S. C. Copeman, *A Short History of the Gout and the Rheumatic Diseases* (University of California Press, Berkeley, California, 1964); J. P. W. Rogers, 'Samuel Johnson's Gout', *Medical History*, vol. 30 (1986), pp. 133–44.

39. In addition to Gregg, *Queen Anne*, and Green, *Queen Anne*, Queen Anne's medical history is discussed by Dewhurst, *Royal Confinements*, and Roberts, *Diary of Sir David Hamilton*.

40. Quoted in Gregg, *Queen Anne*, p. 231; for touching for scrofula, cf. Marc Bloch, *The Royal Touch*, trans. J. E. Anderson (Routledge & Kegan Paul, London, 1973).

41. There is a transcription of the autopsy in *Guy's Hospital Gazette*, n. s. vol. 24 (1910), pp. 397–8.

42. The fullest study of George III's illness is Ida Macalpine and Richard Hunter, *George III and the Mad-business* (Allen Lane, London, 1969); but Charles Chenevix Trench's earlier study is still useful: *The Royal Malady* (Longmans, London, 1964).

43. Macalpine and Hunter, *George III*.

44. Ibid., p. 21.

45. Lady Knighton, *Memoirs of Sir William Knighton*, 2 vols (Richard Bentley, London, 1838), I, pp. 375–6.

46. van der Zee, *William and Mary*, p. 300; Ziegler, *King William IV*, p. 131.

47. Roger Fulford, *George the Fourth* (Duckworth, London, 1949), p. 290ff; Knighton, *Memoirs*, I, pp. 340–2; II, pp. 24–5, 51, 139–44.

48. Sedgwick (ed.), *Materials towards Memoirs*, III, pp. 877–917.

49. For George I and his son, cf. Ragnhild Hatton, *George I, Elector and King* (Thames & Hudson, London, 1979); for George II, cf. Sedgwick (ed.) *Materials towards Memoirs*; Trench *George II*. In addition to Hervey (see note 19), and Mrs Papendiek (see note 36), especially valuable first-hand accounts of life at the English court include those of Fanny Burney (Madame D'Arblay), Charlotte Barnett (ed.) *Diary and Letters of Madame D'Arblay*, 4 vols (Dickers & Son, London, 1876); Horace Walpole: A. F. Steuart (ed.), *The Last Journals of Horace Walpole during the Reign of George III from 1771–1783*, 2 vols (John Lane, London, 1909); and Charles Greville: Henry Reeve (ed.), *The Greville Memoirs*, 8 vols (Longmans, Green & Co., London, 1896).

50. John M. Beattie, *The English Court in the Reign of George I*

W.F. Bynum

(Cambridge University Press, Cambridge, 1967), p. 279.

51. Brooke, *King George III*, pp. 264–6.

52. van der Zee, *William and Mary*, p. 385; Hone, *Life of Dr John Radcliffe*, p. 57.

53. Hone, *Life of Dr John Radcliffe*, p. 58; Macmichael, *Gold-headed Cane*, p. 23; van der Zee, *William and Mary*, pp. 458–9.

54. van der Zee, *William and Mary*, pp. 474–5; G. A. Lindeboom, *Dutch Medical Biography* (Rodopi, Amsterdam, 1984), pp. 135–7.

55. Hatton, *George I*, pp. 280–7; William Munk, *The Roll of the Royal College of Physicians of London*, 3 vols (The College, London, 1878), II, pp. 38–9.

56. Crainz, *Obstetric Tragedy*, pp. 27–8, 70–1; Wilkins, *Caroline*, p. 218; Dewhurst, *Royal Confinements*, pp. 55–7.

57. Mary Douglas, *Natural Symbols* (Penguin, Harmondsworth, 1973) discusses the differences between 'positional' and 'personal' relationships.

58. Roberts (ed.), *Diary of Sir David Hamilton*; Gregg, *Queen Anne*; Green, *Queen Anne*.

59. Roberts (ed.), *Diary of Sir David Hamilton*, pp. xxviii, xxx.

60. Ibid., p. 48ff.

61. Ibid., p. xxii.

62. Knighton, *Memoirs*; Lewis, *In the Family Way*, 94–5, 115–18.

63. Fulford, *George the Fourth* pp. 222–4; Lady Anne Hamilton, *Secret History of the Court of England* (Reynold's, London, n. d.), p. 364.

64. Knighton, *Memoirs*, p. 137.

65. Ibid., pp. 198, 355–6.

66. William Munk, *The Life of Sir Henry Halford* (Longmans, Green & Co., London, 1895).

67. Ibid., p. 143; Macalpine and Hunter, *George III*, p. 143ff.

68. William Ll., Parry-Jones, *The Trade in Lunacy* (Routledge & Kegan Paul, London, 1972; Macalpine and Hunter, *George III*, pp. 114–15; A. D. Morris, *The Hoxton Madhouses* (Goodwin Brothers, March, Cambridgeshire, 1958); 'Warrants for payments to Physicians', Mss. vol. (2593), Wellcome Institute Library.

69. Brooke, *King George III*, pp. 385–6.

70. Macalpine and Hunter, *George III*, p. 25.

71. Quoted by Trench, *Royal Malady*, p. 60.

72. Macalpine and Hunter, *George III*, p. 52.

73. Trench, *Royal Malady*.

74. In addition to Clippindale's two volumes, available for consultation at the library of the Royal College of Surgeons of England, use was made of various editions of Edward Chamberlayne or John Chamberlayne, *Magnae Britanniae Notitia, or, the Present State of Great-Britain*, published periodically between 1669 and 1755, and the annual volume, published under various names, for example *Court and City Kalendar*, and *The Royal Kalendar*, from the mid-1750s.

75. This theme has been most forcefully put by Irvine Loudon, *Medical Care and the General Practitioner, 1750–1850* (Clarendon

288

Press, Oxford, 1987).

76. Leslie G. Matthews, *The Royal Apothecaries*, (Wellcome Historical Medical Library, London 1967).

77. Basic retainers are listed in the various editions of Chamberlayne, *Magna Britannia Notitia*. Aspects of the economics of medical practice in the period are discussed, *inter alia*, in Loudon, *Medical Care*; Geoffrey Holmes, *Augustan England: Professions, State and Society, 1680–1730* (George Allen & Unwin, London, 1982); and W. F. Bynum, 'Physicians, hospitals and career structures in eighteenth-century London', in Bynum and Porter (eds), *William Hunter*. Payments over and above the retainer fees would repay further study. Mrs Papendiek (see note 36), I, p. 59, comments that both those holding court appointments and their families had the benefit of free medical advice. Details of a royal career in Victoria's household may be found in the recent biography of Sir James Reid, Michaela Reid, *Ask Sir James* (Hodder & Stoughton, London, 1987).

78. Although much has been written about Hunter, there is still much to recommend George Peachey, *A Memoir of William and John Hunter* (The Author, Plymouth, 1924).

79. Roy Porter, *English Society in the Eighteenth Century* (Penguin, Harmondsworth, 1982), pp. 73–87, 125–30.

80. Macmichael, *Gold-headed Cane*.

81. Joan Lane, 'The role of apprenticeship in eighteenth-century medical education in England', in Bynum and Porter (eds), *William Hunter*.

82. Matthews, *Royal Apothecaries*, p. 149ff.

83. S. Squire Sprigge, *The Life and Times of Thomas Wakley* (Longmans, Green & Co., London, 1899).

84. The military connections are presently being investigated by Mr Charles Gordon, at the Wellcome Institute, who is working on a Ph.D. thesis on Sir John Pringle, and who made a number of helpful suggestions on an earlier version of this chapter.

Index

Cousinot, J. 127
Coxe, W. 194
Craig, T. 91
Crato von Crafftheim, J. 9–11
Crémoux, P.-B. 220, 225, 245
criticism: of court doctors 118–20, 122, 127, 133, 138, 236, 238, 240–1, 249; of court life 18
Croft, Sir Richard 265, 267–8, 276
Croll, O. 89–93
cultural interests 59
Cumberland, Duke of 272
Cureau de la Chambre, M. 126

da Brescia, J. 69–70
da Macerata, G. 54
da Monte, G. B. 9
da Vigo, G. 59
D'Aguesseau, H. F. 135–6
Daignan, G. 215, 220, 222, 245–7
Dalechamps, J. 11
D'Angerville 238
Daniel des Varennes, L. 215, 221–2, 240–1
Danzig 83
D'Aquin, A. 130–1, 133–4, 144
D'Aquin, L.-H.-T. 127–8
Dashkova, Princess 192, 195
Davis family 284
de Commynes, P. 24
de Grassis, P. 69
De Horne, J. 220, 224, 233
de la Bordère 225
de la Brosse, G. 127
de la Motte 231, 238
de la Rivière, J. 86, 93, 123
de la Rouerie, Marquis 248
de Lamballe, Princesse 249
de l'Estoile, P. 122–6, 140, 142
de l'Orme, C. 127
de Tournefort, J. P. 166
Dee, J. 88
Delaporte 231, 233, 238, 244
Democedes of Croton 4
Demours, A.-P. 216, 219–20, 244
Demours, P. 216, 219
Denmark 84, 91

dentistry 6–7, 192
Des Genettes 246, 250
Deslon, C.-N. 231, 238
Deslon de Lassaigne, G.-L. 216, 224
d'Estrées, Gabrielle 124
Desvergnes 245
Dimsdale, N. 200
Dimsdale, T. 200–2, 269
Dioscorides 9
diplomacy 1–2, 61–2, 90, 92, 95, 103, 111, 123, 196, 199, 220, 277–8
Dippel, J. C. 8, 175
diseases 15–41, 129, 183–5, 197, 199, 202–3, 216–17, 220, 262–80
Dodart, C.-J.-B. 136, 140, 215
Dodoens, R. 11
Drake, Sir Francis 90
Draper, Mrs 266
Dreier, M. 191
du Barry, Madame 217–18
Du Laurens, A. 122–4, 144
Du Moulin, J. 141
Duchesne, J. B. 136
Duchesne, Joseph (Quercetanus) 86, 89–90, 92–3, 101, 103–6
Duden, Barbara 171–2
Dudith, A. 11
Dumoulin, M. 143
Dundas, Sir David 279

Eberhard, of Württemberg 34
Edinburgh, university 186, 195–6, 200, 278
Egidio, P. 56
Egypt 2
Eiler, K. 191
Eisenach 171
Elena Pavlovna, Grand Duchess, of Russia 193
Elias Artista 87, 107
Elias, N. 2
Elijah 87, 107
Elizabeth, of Russia 183, 199, 204, 219
Elizabeth I, of England 4, 82, 88, 117–18

Index

231, 249; Philippe, Duc d'
136–9, 218; university 86
Orlov, G. 185, 195, 199
Ottheinrich, Elector Palatine
82–3
Oxford 6; university of 279

Padua, university 9–11, 15, 56–
8, 60, 108, 245
Palelli, T. 60–1
Panin, N. 197, 199–201
Paracelsianism 5–6, 11, 79–94,
97, 99, 101, 107, 109, 125
Paracelsus 18, 79–94, 102, 106
Pare, A. 85
Paris 85, 87, 90, 93, 104, 108,
130, 138, 216, 230, 238–9,
244–5, 249–50; Academy of
Sciences 251; Faculty of
Medicine 85–6, 128, 220–1,
223, 226–34, 236–7, 240–2,
249, 252; Royal Society of
Medicine 219, 231–8, 241–2,
247, 250, 252
Parkinson, J. 196
Partridge, J. 284
Pasqua, S. 72
Patin, G. 86, 124–30, 143, 145
Paul, Grand Duke, of Russia
185, 190–2, 195, 199–201,
203
Paul III, Pope 51, 56–60, 63–4,
67–8, 70, 72
Paul IV, Pope 53–5, 62–5, 68, 71
Paulsohn, C. 191
Pavia, university 64
Peacham, H. 96–7
peasantry 27–33, 36
Pecquet, J. 144
Pepys, Sir Lucas 280
Persia 4
Peter III, of Russia 183, 185
Petit, J.-L. 123–4
Petraeus, H. 100
Petronio, A. 52, 54, 56, 62–3, 66
pharmacology 4, 8, 56, 97, 99–
107, 198, 236, 237–8
Philip V, of Spain 136–7, 144
physical exercise 22–3
Piccolomini, A. 59

Piot 216
Pitcairn 289
Pius II, Pope 61
Pius III, Pope 52, 55, 69–70
Pius IV, Pope 52, 62–4, 71–2
Pius V, Pope 52, 60, 64–5, 68,
70–1
plays 109–10, 117–18, 120
Pliny the Elder 8
Plutarch 17
poetry 109–10, 118–20
Poirier, L. 138
poison 59, 68, 81, 118, 124–5,
128, 136–9
Poissonnier, P. 216–17, 219–20,
233–4, 243
Poissonnier-Desperrières, A.
216, 219, 222, 233
Poland 8, 10, 83, 89, 93
Pole, Cardinal 5
politics 125–7, 130, 134–5, 139,
141, 144, 155, 184, 242, 244–
5, 247–51, 275
Pomme, P. 216–17, 230–1, 244
Poppius, J. 101
Portal, A. 217, 242–3, 247
post-mortems 24, 68
Prague 9–11, 39, 89, 109
Priestley, J. 197
prince-practitioners 82, 95–116
Pringle, Sir John 284
privileges 55–6, 69–72
Protestantism 79, 82, 84–94
Protomedicato of Spain 7
Prussia 7, 37–8, 155–81, 185
pulse-diagnosis 3
Puzos, N. 142

quackery 12, 68, 81, 86, 118,
128, 130–2, 134, 137, 145,
156, 160–2, 198, 227, 231–2,
234, 237–8, 247, 249
Quedlinburg 163
Quesnay, F. 227

Rabelais, F. 88
Radcliffe, J. 266, 275, 276, 283
Ramazzini, B. 15–16, 20, 27–
30, 32–3, 35–6, 40–1
Rameses II, of Egypt 1–2

298

Index